D1065088

Capital Flows and the
Emerging Economies

A National Bureau
of Economic Research
Conference Report

Capital Flows and the Emerging Economies
Theory, Evidence, and Controversies

Edited by **Sebastian Edwards**

The University of Chicago Press

Chicago and London

SEBASTIAN EDWARDS is the Henry Ford II Professor of International
Economics at the Anderson Graduate School of Management,
University of California, Los Angeles, and a research associate of the
National Bureau of Economic Research.

The University of Chicago Press, Chicago 60637
The University of Chicago Press, Ltd., London
© 2000 by the National Bureau of Economic Research
All rights reserved. Published 2000
Printed in the United States of America
09 08 07 06 05 04 03 02 01 00   1 2 3 4 5
ISBN: 0-226-18470-6 (cloth)

Library of Congress Cataloging-in-Publication Data

Capital flows and the emerging economies : theory, evidence, and
controversies / edited by Sebastian Edwards.
    p.   cm. — (A National Bureau of Economic Research
conference report)
Includes bibliographical references and index.
ISBN 0-226-18470-6 (cloth : alk. paper)
1. Capital movements—Developing countries—Congresses.
I. Edwards, Sebastian, 1953– II. Conference report (National
Bureau of Economic Research)

HG5993.C37 2000
332′.042—dc21

                                                       99-086529

Contents

III. CAPITAL FLOWS TO LATIN AMERICA, ASIA, AND EASTERN EUROPE

Acknowledgments

The papers and commentary collected in this volume were presented at a conference held in Cambridge, Massachusetts, on 20–21 February 1998. We are grateful to the Starr Foundation, the Ford Foundation, and the Center for International Political Economy for supporting the National Bureau of Economic Research's project on capital flows. We are also indebted to Kirsten Foss Davis, Rob Shannon, and the staff of the NBER's Conference Department for efficient support.

Introduction

Sebastian Edwards

Introduction

The 1990s were characterized by a number of spectacular currency crises in the emerging countries. When the Mexican peso collapsed in December 1994 most analysts believed it to be an isolated event. At most, it was thought, the crisis would spread to the weaker Latin American nations. The reasoning was similar in July 1997 when the Thai baht was devalued and, shortly thereafter, went into a free fall. Reality differed from expectations, however, and in a short period of time Malaysia, Indonesia, South Korea, and the Philippines were subject to severe speculative attacks that caused major devaluations, deep recessions, and costly adjustment processes. By then it had become increasingly apparent that emerging countries were subject to "contagion," and that currency crises could rapidly move from country to country.

By early 1998 market participants were asking themselves where the next crisis would erupt. Russia and Brazil, with large fiscal deficits and overvalued exchange rates, were obvious candidates and eventually joined the ranks of nations in crisis. The Russian default was particularly traumatic, sending investors throughout the world scrambling for cover and inflicting heavy losses on a number of large financial institutions. As a result of this crisis, interest rate spreads widened significantly, seriously straining the financial markets in the United States and other industrialized countries.

The Russian and Brazilian crises represented a severe blow to the credi-

Sebastian Edwards is the Henry Ford II Professor of International Economics at the Anderson Graduate School of Management, University of California, Los Angeles, and a research associate of the National Bureau of Economic Research.

bility of the International Monetary Fund (IMF). In both cases the IMF publicly defended policies—overvalued exchange rates in the light of large fiscal imbalances—that were deemed clearly inappropriate by the vast majority of private sector and academic analysts, and that eventually proved to be flawed. In both cases the IMF put together, a few weeks before the final collapse, large rescue packages that turned out to be vastly insufficient. While in the case of Brazil the postcrisis period turned out to be less traumatic than many analysts had anticipated, crisis management continues to be one of the most pressing issues in modern macroeconomic analysis.

Large capital flows have been at the heart of each one of these crisis episodes. The stories are, in fact, remarkably similar: Attracted by high domestic interest rates and rosy prospects, large volumes of foreign funds—mostly in the form of portfolio capital—moved into these economies, propelling stock market booms and helping finance large current account deficits. At some point, and for a variety of reasons, these funds slowed down or were reversed. This change in conditions required significant corrections in macroeconomic policies. Invariably, however, the adjustment was delayed or was insufficient, increasing the level of uncertainty and the degree of country risk. As a result, increasingly large volumes of capital left the country and international reserves dropped to dangerously low levels. Eventually the pegged exchange rate had to be abandoned and the country was forced to float the currency. In some cases, such as those of Brazil and Russia, a runaway fiscal deficit made the situation even more explosive.

For many years, "official capital" dominated capital inflows into the developing countries. During the 1960s, 1970s, and most of the 1980s, private capital was restricted to foreign direct investment. Moreover, the conditions under which foreign direct investment was allowed into these countries were severely regulated by the authorities. This situation changed dramatically in the early 1990s when, as a result of the broad implementation of market-oriented reforms, an increasingly large number of countries opened up their economies to international competition. The sense that these countries had a bright economic future resulted in massive private portfolio inflows. Innovation in financial markets in the United States and Europe—including the proliferation of mutual funds—also contributed to the increase of capital flows into the emerging economies. After the fall of the Berlin Wall in 1989 the countries in the former Soviet Union joined the world economy and demanded large volumes of capital to restructure their productive sectors. The industrial countries responded promptly, and large flows of capital moved into a region of the world that for decades had been isolated from global financial markets.

Almost a decade after private flows became the dominant source of foreign funds in the emerging economies, experts continue to debate the effects of increased capital mobility. For example, in the aftermath of the East Asian, Russian, and Brazilian crises a number of observers have argued that the free mobility of capital had increased the degree of vulnerability of the emerging economies, making them more prone to externally triggered crises. Some have argued that the imposition of controls on (short-term) capital inflows could help avoid major crises—or, at least, reduce their magnitude. Advocates of this approach have invoked Chile's experience with capital controls since 1991 to support their views. For example, Joseph Stiglitz, the World Bank's chief economist, had been quoted by the *New York Times* (1 February 1998) as saying, "You want to look for policies that discourage hot money but facilitate the flow of long-term loans, and there is evidence that the Chilean approach or some version of it, does this." Michel Camdessus, the IMF's managing director, has recently endorsed the view that capital controls should only be lifted toward the end of a market-oriented reform effort. In an interview in the *Financial Times* (9 February 1998) he said, "We need to be audacious but sensitive. We need to push ahead with capital flow liberalisation but in an orderly manner" (1). He added, "The last thing you must liberalise is the very short term capital movements" (13).

A number of authors have pointed out that in the face of increased private capital mobility, banking supervision and regulation become crucially important. Poorly regulated banks will intermediate the inflows of capital in an inefficient or even corrupt way, increasing the probability of a systemic financial crisis (Calvo 1998).

It has long been recognized that legal impediments to capital mobility are not always translated into actual restrictions on these movements. This distinction between *actual* and *legal* capital mobility has affected economists' ability to measure the "true" degree of financial integration in specific countries and has been at the center of recent debates on the effectiveness of capital controls. Some authors have followed Feldstein and Horioka (1980) and have relied on the correlation (or lack thereof) between savings and investment as a measurement of the degree to which capital markets in different countries are integrated. Other authors have concentrated on interest rate differentials in trying to determine whether a particular country is actually integrated into world financial markets (Dooley, Mathieson, and Rojas-Suarez 1997).

More recently, some authors have used information contained in the IMF's *Exchange Rate and Monetary Arrangements* to construct indexes on capital controls for a panel of countries. Alesina, Grilli, and Milesi-Ferretti (1994), for example, constructed a dummy variable index of capital controls. This indicator—which takes a value of one when capital controls are in place and zero otherwise—was then used to analyze some of the political forces behind the imposition of capital restrictions in a score of countries. Rodrik (1998) used a similar index to investigate the effects of capital controls on growth, inflation, and investment between 1979 and 1989. Rodrik's (1998) work is based on the empirical growth literature and suggests that, after controlling for other variables, capital restrictions have no significant effects on macroeconomic performance.

A serious limitation of these IMF-based indexes, however, is that they are extremely general and do not distinguish between different intensities of capital restrictions, nor do they distinguish between the type of flow that is being restricted. For example, according to this IMF-based indicator, Chile, Mexico, and Brazil were subject to the same degree of capital controls in 1992–94. In reality, however, the three cases were extremely different. Whereas Chile had restrictions on short-term inflows, Mexico (for all practical purposes) had free capital mobility and Brazil had in place an arcane array of restrictions. These measurement difficulties are not unique to the capital flows literature, however. In fact, as Edwards (1993, 1998) and Rodrik (1995) have argued, the literature on trade openness and growth has long been affected by serious measurement problems. Constructing comprehensive and high-quality comparative measures of openness has indeed proved to be extremely elusive. A major challenge in empirically oriented work on capital flows, international trade, and economic performance is to generate results that are robust to alternative measures of capital mobility and trade restrictions. Future work along these lines should recognize, at the outset, that these indexes are likely to be subject to measurement error, and that there is a need to strive for robustness in the empirical analysis.

The increase in capital flows into the emerging markets during the first half of the 1990s helped generate significant stock market booms and allowed these countries to increase aggregate expenditure substantially. This, in turn, generated pressure on domestic prices and large real exchange rate appreciations (Calvo, Leiderman, and Reinhart 1993). A number of analysts have argued that these real exchange rate appreciations induced by capital inflows have tended to reduce the country's degree of international competitiveness, and that they may eventually result in an external crises and in a reversal of market-oriented reforms. As a result, some authors have argued that capital controls should be lifted only at the end of a reform effort (McKinnon 1991).[1]

The recent experiences on the part of emerging markets of large private inflows have generated a series of important questions:

What is the appropriate exchange rate regime for a developing or transitional country in a world with massive capital mobility?

Does free capital mobility increase a small country's degree of financial vulnerability?

---

1. This, of course, is the "sequencing of reform" debate.

How do countries respond once capital flows reverse and a crisis erupts? What is the nature of "contagion"?

Following a crisis, does foreign direct investment welfare improve matters or does "fire-sale FDI" have a detrimental effect on poor countries?

What has been the behavior of financial market indicators in periods following a financial liberalization?

What has been the role of Japan in the unfolding of the East Asian crisis?

What have been the causes behind the massive capital flows to Eastern Europe and the former Soviet Union?

To what extent are risk considerations reflected in the bond spreads of emerging markets?

How do capital flows behave in the aftermath of the opening of the capital account?

How effective are controls on capital inflows?

The papers collected in this volume were presented at a National Bureau of Economic Research conference entitled Capital Inflows to Developing Countries held in Cambridge, Massachusetts, on 20–21 February 1998; the conference papers addressed many of the questions posed above. In preparing this volume I have divided the papers into three groups. The first part deals with different theoretical aspects of capital inflows into emerging economies and includes papers by Guillermo A. Calvo and Enrique G. Mendoza, Paul Krugman, and Philippe Bacchetta and Eric van Wincoop. The second part deals with broad cross-country empirical aspects of capital mobility and includes papers by Barry Eichengreen and Ashoka Mody, Swati Ghosh and Holger Wolf, and Geert Bekaert and Campbell R. Harvey. The third part deals with capital inflows to Latin America, Asia, and Eastern Europe and includes papers by me, Takatoshi Ito, and Stijn Claessens, Daniel Oks, and Rossana Polastri. In addition, I have included discussants' comments. In the rest of this introduction I provide a reader's guide to the volume.

Capital Flows to Developing Countries: Theoretical Aspects

The first paper in this section, "Contagion, Globalization, and the Volatility of Capital Flows" by Guillermo Calvo and Enrique Mendoza, deals with contagion, investors' herd behavior, and the costs of gathering information in a globalized financial market. The authors argue that in a world with increased capital mobility, optimal portfolio diversification results in a higher degree of financial volatility. According to them, as the global capital market grows, so does the probability of "contagion." The authors develop a model of an integrated global financial market with a large number of countries and a (very) large number of identical investors. The model assumes that there are costs of gathering and processing information regarding specific country's performance, and that investors—or, more specifically, asset managers—incur a cost if their portfolio underperforms the market portfolio. The authors show that, within the context of their model, the benefits of acquiring country-specific information declines as the number of countries in the global portfolio increases. This means that, with a portfolio with a large enough number of countries, it may not pay to verify "rumors"; as a consequence, it is possible for the world financial markets to experience rumor-initiated contagion. According to the Calvo-Mendoza model, if asset managers face variable performance incentives and the number of countries in the world portfolio is large, it is possible to observe herd behavior. More specifically, it is possible that all investors simultaneously reallocate their portfolios, generating massive capital flows in and out of the emerging markets. In the last section of their paper Calvo and Mendoza calibrate their model and present a number of simulation exercises. The most interesting ones relate to the case of Mexico. According to their model, if the costs of gathering Mexico-specific information is 6.5 percent, a rumor that reduces the expected return on Mexico's equities to that of the member countries of the Organization for Economic Cooperation and Development (OECD) could result in a reduction in foreigners' holdings of Mexican equities of 40 percent of the total. In terms of 1997 levels this would have exceeded US$20 billion, a figure similar to Mexico's holdings of international reserves. Their simulations also suggest that even if the number of countries in the global portfolio is as low as twenty, herding panics can generate very large outflows. Their calculation is that in 1997 these flows could have exceeded US$25 billion.

In "Fire-Sale FDI" Paul Krugman develops a model to investigate the nature of capital flows in the aftermath of a currency crisis in a developing country. The point of departure is the observation that a crisis is usually followed by two-way capital flows. On the one hand, short-term portfolio ("hot") capital flows out; on the other, foreign direct investment (FDI) flows in, as foreigners try to take advantage of new opportunities to buy local firms. The aim of this paper is twofold: first to provide some theoretical explanation for the currency crises of the 1990s, and second to evaluate the welfare implications of what Krugman terms "fire-sale FDI." Krugman argues that from a conceptual point of view there are two possible explanations of the recent East Asian currency crises. One is based on the moral hazard–overborrowing argument, while the other is based on the classical liquidity crisis theory. According to Krugman the exact nature of postcrisis FDI depends on the causes of the currency collapse. If, on the other hand, the crisis is caused by moral-hazard-induced overborrowing, the decline in the price of domestic assets would allow foreigners to take control over them. In this case foreigners represent the most "efficient" possible operator of the asset in question, and the crisis would imply that control over the asset is reallocated to the most efficient party. If the crisis is the result of a liquidity-generated panic, the foreign party—which is not liquidity constrained—has the opportunity of taking over domestic assets. According to Krugman, in this case fire sales will usually transfer control over to firms that are less efficient than the domestic firm. An important feature of fire sales that arises independently of the nature of the crisis is that, by limiting the fall in asset prices, they have a stabilizing effect in the crisis country.

The third paper in this section of the volume, "Capital Flows to Emerging Markets: Liberalization, Overshooting, and Volatility," is by Philippe Bacchetta and Eric van Wincoop and deals with the impact of financial liberalization on the dynamic of capital flows. The starting point of this paper is the observation that in most developing countries capital flows appear to overshoot in the period following the opening of the capital account. This has been the case even if the capital account is opened up only partially. According to the authors, the analysis of capital flows dynamics will provide a better understanding of the issue of capital account sustainability. They argue that optimal policy responses would be very different if lending surges are short-term booms rather than long-term sustainable trends. In order to address this issue Bacchetta and van Wincoop develop a portfolio model with a large number of developed and developing countries. Individuals in emerging countries invest locally, while individuals in advanced countries can diversify internationally. It is further assumed that initially the developing countries impose a tax on foreign investors, and that there is an installation cost of capital. The authors solve the portfolio allocation problem and analyze the way in which a reduction in the tax on foreign investors affects the dynamics of capital flows into the developing countries. According to their model, following a once-and-for-all financial liberalization capital inflows will immediately jump, overshooting their (new) long-term level. The magnitude of the overshooting will depend on the importance of the installation cost. The larger this cost, the smaller the overshooting. Bacchetta and van Wincoop calibrate their model and perform a number of simulation exercises. In their first exercise they assume that the initial tax on foreign investors is equal to 5 percent and that it is reduced exponentially through time. In order to gain additional insights into the effects of liberalization, they analyze the case when only one country liberalizes as well as the case in which all developing countries liberalize simultaneously. They find that in both cases capital inflows will be characterized by an overshooting. Next, Bacchetta and van Wincoop extend their model to the case where there is imperfect information and learning. They show that in this instance liberalization processes will be characterized by high volatility and, under some circumstances, by contagion.

Capital Flows to the Emerging Markets:
Evidence from Cross-Country Analyses

The three papers included in this second part of the volume use vast volumes of cross-country data to investigate a number of important issues related to capital flows into the emerging countries. In "What Explains Changing Spreads on Emerging Market Debt?" Barry Eichengreen and Ashoka Mody use data on more than thirteen hundred bond issues in developing countries to analyze the factors behind bond spreads. Their analysis differs from previous work in several respects. First, they cover a period (1991–97) when bond financing had become very important in many emerging countries. Second, their sample covers every region in the world, whereas most of the previous literature did not incorporate data from Africa. And third, the data set includes bonds issued by both the private and the public sector. In this paper, Eichengreen and Mody analyze both the country's decision to issue a bond as well as the determinants of bonds' spreads. By looking at both aspects of the problem, potential selectivity biases are avoided. The results obtained suggest that the decision to issue a bond is affected by both demand and supply considerations. Some of the most interesting results are that issues tend to increase when interest rates on U.S. treasury bonds decline, that more creditworthy countries tend to issue more frequently, and that countries with higher debt have a lower probability of issuing bonds. The spreads analysis suggests that there are differences across regions, in particular between Latin America and the rest of the sample. For Latin America the results suggest that larger issues command smaller spreads and that private issues on average have higher spreads when controlling for other factors. Eichengreen and Mody use their vast data set to analyze whether changes in spreads on emerging nations' bonds have been the result of changing fundamentals or whether they have responded to changing "sentiments." They found, somewhat to their surprise, that changes in spreads during the first half of 1997 had been related to changes in "sentiments" that were largely unrelated to fundamentals.

In their paper "Is There a Curse of Location? Spatial Determinants of Capital Flows to Emerging Markets," Swati Ghosh and Holger Wolf use a cross-country data set to investigate the geographical distribution of capital flows to developing countries. The authors point out that capital flows have largely been concentrated in a small group of countries in East Asia and Latin America, and they ask whether this phenomenon is a reflection of the recipient countries' fundamentals or whether geography plays a role in the allocation of capital flows across countries. In order to investigate this issue the authors estimate a series of equations taken from the international trade "gravity models" literature. According to gravity models (bilateral) trade is largely explained by the proximity—or lack thereof—

of a pair of countries: countries that are closer to each other have a larger volume of trade than do countries that are farther apart. Ghosh and Wolf begin their analysis by discussing possible reasons why the gravity models applicable to trade would also apply to capital mobility. In the actual estimation they distinguish between three types of capital flows: bank lending, short-term finance, and what they call "capital market," which includes syndicated loans and bond issues. Their findings indicate that location is related to the ability of emerging markets to have access to these three different forms of foreign financing. They also find that gross domestic product (GDP) per capita is the only variable other than distance that helps explain capital flows. According to the authors, these results help explain why Africa has traditionally had limited access to capital markets.

In their paper "Capital Flows and the Behavior of Emerging Market Equity Returns," Geert Bekaert and Campbell Harvey analyze in great detail the relation between U.S. equity flows to emerging markets and both the behavior of these countries' capital markets, equity returns, and exchange rates, and the structural characteristics of the economies. They use data on seventeen emerging countries for the period 1977–96 to investigate break points in net equity flows from the United States to each of these countries. These break points are estimated endogenously using the actual time series for capital flows. The authors argue that these estimated break points correspond to the time when foreign investor's attitudes to the emerging countries experienced a significant change and, thus, can be labeled as the dates when the financial liberalization actually occurred. The next step of the analysis consists of investigating the behavior of four groups of financial indicators during the periods preceding and following each of the break points. These indicators are related to (1) the cost of capital, (2) market structure, (3) characteristics of the economy, and (4) country risk. An important point made by this paper is that, in principle, using changes in legislation to date capital market liberalization may result in misleading results. Bekaert and Harvey's analysis suggests that in sixteen out of the seventeen countries in their sample, foreign ownership of stocks increased significantly after the break point. Some of the paper's most important results include the following: (1) On average, the dividend yield declined from approximately 4.3 percent to 2.5 percent in the period following the break point; (2) average ex post returns declined from 20 percent to 13.4 percent in the postliberalization period; (3) individual countries' βs increased significantly after the liberalization period but remained, on average, below 0.5; (4) there are small declines on average volatility (both conditional and ex post) in the period after the liberalization; (5) the number of listed stocks increases after the liberalization, as does market capitalization; (6) average GDP growth increases very slightly after the break points; and (7) after the break points, there is a significant increase in the degree of openness of these economies.

Capital Flows to Latin America, Asia, and Eastern Europe

The last three chapters in the volume investigate in great detail the regional experiences with capital inflows in Latin America, Asia, and Eastern Europe.

In "Capital Flows, Real Exchange Rates, and Capital Controls: Some Latin American Experiences," I analyze capital flows to Latin America. The paper concentrates on five broad areas: (1) a historical analysis of capital flows trends; (2) the relationship between capital flows and real exchange rates in the Latin American countries; (3) capital flows and the ability to engage in independent monetary policy; (4) the role of the banking sector in recent Latin American currency crises; and (5) the role of capital controls in Latin America. The historical analysis highlights the cyclical nature of capital flows to the region during the last twenty five years. During this period Latin America has gone through a number of borrowing booms followed by major crises. An interesting aspect of this history, however, is that in the more recent period international investors appear to be more willing to distinguish between different Latin American countries. While the debt crisis of 1982 affected every country, the Mexican crisis of 1994 basically spared some of the countries with stronger fundamentals. Although it is too early to pass definitive judgment, it would seem that the Brazilian crisis of 1999 will also have limited impact on the region. In discussing the historical record, I deal with a number of analytical and policy controversies, including the measurement of capital mobility and the adequate sequencing of liberalization in the emerging economies. I analyze in detail the effect of capital inflows on real exchange rate behavior in a group of Latin American countries and find that capital flows have Granger-caused real exchange rate appreciations in most of these countries. My results also suggest that almost every one of the Latin nations has tried to sterilize large capital inflows in an effort to maintain greater control over monetary policy. These efforts, however, have been rather unsuccessful. My analysis of capital controls concentrates on restrictions to capital inflows and pays particular attention to the Chilean system, which consists of taxing short-term capital. I point out that this approach has been significantly less effective than most casual analysts have argued. In particular, the Chilean system has not succeeded in reducing the extent of real exchange rate appreciation, nor has it given the central bank a greater degree of control over monetary policy.

In "Capital Flows in Asia," Takatoshi Ito presents a detailed analysis of the behavior of capital flows in that region and gives an interpretation of the events that led to the East Asian crisis of 1997. A fascinating aspect of this paper is that it provides a clear and persuasive interpretation of Japan's role in this episode. According to Ito, until 1996 the emerging East Asian countries were subject to a virtuous cycle that was sustained by a great sense of optimism about the future of the region and financed with very large capital flows, mostly coming from Japan. In late 1996, the virtuous cycle was interrupted, as exports from East Asia declined sharply. Both Japan's recession and the depreciation of the yen played an important role in the unfolding of these events. The East Asian currency crises in mid-1997 made things worse, as they were followed by substantial cuts in capital flows into the region. Ito investigates in detail the way in which Japanese FDI and the behavior of the yen affected growth in the emerging East Asian countries. His results indicate that changes in FDI from Japan have an important effect on the region's rate of growth, with a one-year lag. More specifically, according to Ito's estimates, the effect of changes in Japanese FDI on growth is twice that of FDI from the United States.

The final chapter in the volume is "Capital Flows to Central and Eastern Europe and the Former Soviet Union" and is co-authored by Stijn Claessens, Daniel Oks, and Rossana Polastri. They concentrate on the period 1991–97 and investigate the way in which different forms of capital flows evolved during that period. While in the early years (1991–93) FDI was almost the only type of flow into the region, starting in 1993 portfolio flows became increasingly important. According to the authors the increase in flows to the region has been the result of a series of interconnected factors, including a reduction in perceived country risk in most of these countries and the expectations that some of them would join the European Union. The authors argue that official flows—mostly from the multilateral institutions—have played an important role in helping pave the way for the structural reforms undertaken by the East European nations. The authors provide detailed analyses of the way in which the Czech Republic, Poland, Estonia, Hungary, and Russia responded to the large capital inflows of the mid-1990s. The paper ends with cautionary note regarding the potential dangers of fiscal imbalances and of low-quality financial intermediation. In retrospect, and in light of the Russian debacle of August 1998, these remarks appear to have had an element of premonition.

Concluding Remarks

The papers collected in this volume deal with a wide array of issues related to capital inflows to developing countries. They provide historical and empirical analyses of some of the most important issues. The theoretical models presented here throw new light on important questions, and some of the regional studies point toward unresolved issues. These papers also suggest areas for future research. Among the most important of these is optimal exchange rate regimes in a world with capital mobility. This issue has acquired particular interest in the aftermath of the Brazilian crisis of 1999 and the debate on Argentina's potential dollarization. A second important topic concerns controls on capital mobility—in particular on capital inflows—and their effects on the emerging economies. More specifically, it is important to investigate whether this type of restriction helps countries reduce their degree of financial vulnerability. Issues related to contagion and the channels through which it manifests itself are also important, as are questions dealing with the sequencing and speed of liberalization. Finally, it appears that in spite of tremendous progress during the last few years, the economic profession still does not understand fully the anatomy of currency crises. Additional research in that area will certainly be welcomed.

References

Alesina, Alberto, Vittorio Grilli, and Gian Maria Milesi-Ferretti.1994. The political economy of capital controls. In *Capital mobility: The impact on consumption, investment and growth,* ed. L. Leiderman and A. Razin, 289–321. Cambridge: Cambridge University Press.

Calvo, Guillermo. 1998. Capital flows and capital-market crises: The simple economics of sudden stops. *Journal of Applied Economics* 1, no. 1 (November): 35–54.

Calvo, Guillermo, Leonardo Leiderman, and Carmen Reinhart. 1993. Capital inflows and real exchange rate appreciation in Latin America: The role of external factors. *IMF Staff Papers* 40 (March): 108–51.

Dooley, M., D. Mathieson, and L. Rojas-Suarez. 1997. Capital mobility and exchange market intervention in developing countries. NBER Working Paper no. 6247. Cambridge, Mass.: National Bureau of Economic Research.

Edwards, Sebastian. 1993. Openness, trade liberalization and growth in developing countries. *Journal of Economic Literature* 31:1358–93.

———. 1998. Openness, productivity and growth: What do we really know? *Economic Journal* 108 (March): 383–98.

Feldstein, Martin, and Charles Horioka. 1980. Domestic saving and international capital flows. *Economic Journal* 90 (June): 314–29.

McKinnon, Ronald. 1991. *The order of economic liberalization: Financial control in the transition to a market economy.* Baltimore, Md.: Johns Hopkins University Press.

Rodrik, Dani. 1995. Trade policy and industrial policy reform. In *Handbook of development economics,* vol. 3B, ed. Jere Behrman and T. N. Srinivasan. Amsterdam: North-Holland.

———. 1998. Who needs capital-account convertibility? In *Should the IMF pursue capital-account convertibility?* Essays in International Finance, no. 207, 55–65. Princeton, N.J.: Department of Economics, Princeton University.

I

Capital Flows to Developing Countries
Theoretical Aspects

1

Contagion, Globalization, and the Volatility of Capital Flows

Guillermo A. Calvo and Enrique G. Mendoza

The "contagion effect" . . . was thought to be a very common occurrence by almost all the market participants interviewed. It was attributed by many either to demonstration effects arising from the reassessment of the value of the totality of emerging market paper in light of the information highlighted by the particular characteristics of the crisis in one country, or to technicalities of the portfolio management methods used by many investors or fund managers.
—Group of Ten (1996, 33)

1.1 Introduction

One of the most puzzling features of the recent balance-of-payments crises has been the simultaneous collapse of securities markets at regional and global levels. In the case of Mexico's 1994 crash this phenomenon was named the *tequila effect:* As the crisis in Mexico surged, investors reduced their exposure both in markets of vulnerable countries like Argentina and Brazil, and in countries widely believed to be more stable, like Chile or Singapore. All of these countries had few, if any, economic linkages with Mexico. Similarly, the Russian default and the collapse of the ruble in October 1988 had major ramifications for equity markets worldwide, including a major "run for quality" in the U.S. stock market, despite the small share of world output that Russia accounts for and its very limited economic linkages with the United States. This behavior seems indicative of contagion by global investors: Equity positions and prices displayed major shifts that were not related to market "fundamentals."[1]

The recent crises have led observers and some policy makers to conclude that along with the efficiency gains resulting from the unprecedented globalization that securities markets have attained also came a high degree

Guillermo A. Calvo is distinguished university professor and director of the Center for International Economics at the University of Maryland, College Park. Enrique G. Mendoza is associate professor of economics at Duke University.

The authors thank V. V. Chari, David Bowman, Rudi Dornbusch, Jon Faust, David Howard, Sebastian Edwards, and Matt Pritsker for helpful comments and suggestions.

1. Calvo and Mendoza (1996) review factual evidence of herding by holders of Mexican securities. Calvo and Reinhart (1995) provide statistical evidence of contagion effects in emerging markets.

of volatility of private capital flows. In light of this increased volatility, countries have resorted in some instances to the introduction of controversial capital controls, taxes, and other barriers to asset trading (see, e.g., Chile's taxes and timing restrictions on short-term capital flows, and the more drastic controls introduced in Malaysia in 1997). All these barriers were judged traditionally as major policy flaws, but they are gaining increasing popularity in the wake of the recent crises. This need to respond quickly to a critical situation, however, contrasts sharply with our very limited understanding of the mechanisms that may drive contagion, of the quantitative significance of this phenomenon, and of the kind of policies that can be effective to prevent it.

The urgent question at hand is this: Is there a tendency for larger, or globalized, securities markets to become more volatile, or more susceptible to contagion, as globalization progresses? More precisely, are there mechanisms that lead investors to be influenced by contagion that grow stronger with globalization? This paper aims to answer these questions by showing that contagion is an outcome of optimal portfolio diversification that can become more pervasive as securities markets grow. We define contagion as a situation in which investors optimally choose to react to a rumor regarding a country's asset return characteristics, or to mimic the perceived optimal portfolio share assigned to a particular country by an arbitrary "market" portfolio.

Our analysis illustrates how two characteristics of imperfect information produce equilibria in which mean-variance portfolio optimizers are more likely to exhibit contagion as capital markets grow.[2] First, if there is a fixed cost of gathering and processing country-specific information, the expected utility gain made by paying this cost generally falls as the number of countries where wealth can be invested grows. Portfolios also become more sensitive to changes in perceived asset returns as markets grow, and thus contagion is more likely to prevail and to produce larger capital flows in globalized markets. Second, if investors (or fund managers) bear variable costs that depend on the performance of their portfolios—in particular, if the marginal cost of producing a mean return lower than the market exceeds the marginal gain of beating the market—there is a "contagion range" within which investors rationally choose to mimic arbitrary "market" portfolios. Globalization works to widen this contagion range.

Information frictions have been widely used in the extensive literature

---

2. The model does not differentiate global markets from domestic markets. We believe, however, that information frictions are more pervasive in global markets. This assumption is supported by some empirical regularities documented later in the paper and is also in line with the elaborate warnings that mutual funds give investors to highlight the special risks of global investing (see, e.g., Franklin Partners Funds, *Prospectus,* 1 May 1996, p. 13), particularly, sudden currency collapses, differing legal and accounting practices, and unanticipated large policy changes.

on contagion and herding in financial markets. To date, however, the interaction between the distortions generated by information frictions and the size of financial markets has remain largely unexplored. Thus, we begin by exploring analytically what conditions are required for the growth of securities markets to have the perverse effect of enlarging the information frictions that induce contagion. In addition, since the magnitude of the actual shifts in portfolio allocations that contagion may induce is also largely unknown, we examine the model's quantitative implications by conducting some basic numerical simulations.

Our quantitative analysis is based on a version of the model calibrated to capture key stylized facts of historical data from equity markets and country credit ratings (CCRs). Equity-market measures of the mean and variance of country asset returns are viewed as free information, while the information embodied in CCRs is assumed to be costly. These CCRs are very stable for industrialized and least-developed countries, while the ratings of emerging economies are very volatile, suggesting that historical equity-market data are significantly less useful for predicting future asset returns in emerging economies than in industrialized countries.

The numerical exploration suggests that the model can generate large capital flows driven by contagion. If the block of emerging economies is viewed as a segmented market, we found that investors will not assess the veracity of country-specific rumors if fixed information costs exceed one-sixth of the mean portfolio return prior to the emergence of a rumor. The full adverse effect of globalization on information gains is transmitted with about a dozen countries. The contagion range predicted by a rough parameterization of variable costs that depend on portfolio performance measures about 2.5 percentage points, even for small total costs. Simulations applied to Mexican data suggest that the model can rationalize capital outflows in excess of $15 billion triggered by contagion.

Keynes's (1936) classic analysis of speculation, which he defined as "the activity of forecasting the psychology of the market," anticipated our work in predicting that speculation can be more pervasive in larger or better organized markets. He also proposed other mechanisms that could drive speculation—sudden changes of opinion driven by mass psychology, perverse incentives of professional investors induced by information or reputational costs,[3] and changes in the confidence of lenders that finance speculators. These mechanisms have been the focus of the modern literature on herd behavior, which has made notable progress in providing the microfoundations of contagion and in justifying the information and reputational costs that we take for granted in this paper (see, e.g., Scharfstein

---

3. Keynes (1936, 157) wrote: "Investment based on genuine long-term expectation is so difficult to-day as to be scarcely practicable. He who attempts it must surely lead much more laborious days and run greater risks than he who tries to guess better than the crowd how the crowd will behave. . . ."

and Stein 1990; Bikhchandani, Hirshleifer, and Welch 1992; Banerjee 1992; and Morris and Shing 1995).

The rest of the paper is organized as follows. Section 1.2 analyzes the relationship between herd behavior and the globalization of securities markets. Section 1.3 examines the quantitative implications of the analysis. Section 1.4 concludes with a discussion of normative issues.

1.2 Optimal Global Portfolio Diversification with Contagion

The presentation that follows is a less technical version of that found in Calvo and Mendoza (2000a). We have omitted proofs and focused instead on developing the intuition. Consider a globalized securities market consisting of J countries, for $2 \le J \le \infty$, and a large number of identical investors. Wealth is normalized to 1 for simplicity. The representative investor must choose a portfolio to be divided between a "world fund" of $J - 1$ identical countries and a single country (country i). Each of the $J - 1$ countries in the world fund pays an independent and identical normally distributed stochastic return with mean ρ and variance σ_j^2. The return of country i also follows a normal distribution, but with mean r^* and variance σ_i^2, that will generally differ from those of the world fund, and with a correlation with the world fund determined by the correlation coefficient η. Since all $J - 1$ countries in the world fund are identical, in equilibrium the share of the portfolio invested in each of these countries is identical. Hence, the relevant choice is between the fraction of the investor's wealth allocated to the world fund, defined as θ, and the fraction allocated to country i, $1 - \theta$.

The investor sets θ so as to maximize the following indirect expected utility function:

$$(1) \quad EU(\theta) = \mu(\theta) - \frac{\gamma}{2}\sigma(\theta)^2 - \kappa - \lambda[\mu(\Theta) - \mu(\theta)], \qquad \gamma, \kappa > 0,$$

where γ is the coefficient of absolute risk aversion; μ and σ are the mean and standard deviation of the return for a particular portfolio θ. The model's information frictions are introduced by the costs reflected in κ and λ: κ is a fixed cost of acquiring country-specific information and λ is a variable cost (benefit) resulting from obtaining a mean return lower (higher) than that of an arbitrary "market" portfolio Θ. This variable cost can be interpreted as a reputational cost or as an incentive scheme for fund managers. We show below that these information frictions strengthen incentives for contagion as the global market grows (i.e., as J rises).

1.2.1 Contagion with Fixed Information Costs

The investor can acquire and process country-specific information at the fixed cost κ to update the estimates of the mean and variance of country i's returns he obtained using free information. If the investor chooses not to pay the information cost, the portfolio choice involves the world fund, with asset return moments ρ and σ^2, and country i, with mean return r^*, variance σ_i^2, and correlation with the world fund η. On the other hand, if he pays the information cost, the characteristics of asset returns in the $J - 1$ countries are unchanged, but the mean and variance of country i returns are updated.

We simplify significantly the model so as to characterize the nature of costly information in a manner that enables us to derive clear analytical results, leaving to section 1.3 the numerical analysis of the more general setting. In particular, costly information lets investors learn the "true" return of country i with full certainty. Thus, investors who pay κ learn a rate of return r^I with zero variance. Before paying κ, however, the potential update of the return is a random variable drawn from a known probability distribution function (pdf). Clearly, the investor will pay the information cost only if the expected utility obtained by gathering information, EU^I, exceeds that of remaining uninformed, EU^U (i.e., the gain from information searching $S \equiv EU^I - EU^U$ must be positive).

Consider an initial equilibrium in which country i is identical to the rest (i.e., $r^* = \rho$ and $\sigma_i = \sigma_J = \sigma$) and asset returns are uncorrelated ($\eta = 0$). It is trivial to show that in this initial equilibrium the share of the portfolio invested in each country is $1/J$ and the mean and variance of the portfolio return are ρ and σ^2/J, respectively. We offer two motivations for investors to have incentives to acquire costly information. First, investors may be willing to pay for eliminating the uncertainty of investing in country i. Second, investors may use information to assess the veracity of an exogenous and "reliable" rumor that country i's mean return is r, $r \leq \rho$, while the variance is still σ^2.[4]

Let θ^U and θ^I be the portfolio shares chosen by the investor if he decides to be uninformed or informed respectively. Ignoring variable costs, θ^U is set so as to maximize expected utility:

$$(2) \qquad EU^U = \theta^U \rho + (1 - \theta^U)r - \frac{\gamma}{2}\left[\frac{(\theta^U)^2}{J - 1} + (1 - \theta^U)^2\right]\sigma^2.$$

The solution for the optimal portfolio is

$$(3) \qquad \theta^U = \left(\frac{J - 1}{J}\right)\left(1 + \frac{\rho - r}{\gamma\sigma^2}\right).$$

4. Note that in the first case we must impose the consistency condition $E(r^I|\kappa) = r^*$, since r^* is an expectation based on free information and the distribution of r^I is also known at no cost, while in the second case this condition is not required because investors are trying to assess the veracity of an exogenous rumor that they regard as credible.

Short positions are ruled out by assumption. Thus, $\theta^U = 1$ for $r \leq r^{\min}$, where $r^{\min} = \rho - [\gamma\sigma^2/(J - 1)]$, and $\theta^U = 0$ for $r \geq r^{\max}$, where $r^{\max} = \rho + \gamma\sigma^2$. Notice that as J goes to ∞, the interval of returns that supports internal solutions shrinks to $r^{\max} - r^{\min} = \gamma\sigma^2$.

For rumors within the interval $r^{\min} < r < r^{\max}$, expected utility valued at the maximum is

$$(4) \qquad EU^U = \left\{ r - \frac{\gamma\,\sigma^2}{2\,J} + \frac{(\rho - r)}{2}\frac{J - 1}{J}\left[2 + \frac{(\rho - r)}{\gamma\sigma^2}\right]\right\}.$$

Alternatively, if $r \leq r^{\min}$, $EU^U = \rho - [\gamma\sigma^2/2(J - 1)]$, and if $r \geq r^{\max}$, $EU^U = r - \gamma\sigma^2/2$.

Next we study the portfolio problem if the investor pays for country i information. An investor that paid κ and learned r^I will maximize the following state-contingent utility function:

$$(5) \qquad U^I(r^I) = \theta^I\rho + (1 - \theta^I)r^I - \frac{\gamma}{2}\left[\frac{(\theta^I)^2}{J - 1}\right]\sigma^2 - \kappa.$$

The optimal, state-contingent portfolio is

$$(6) \qquad \theta^I(r^I) = (J - 1)\left(\frac{\rho - r^I}{\gamma\sigma^2}\right).$$

Short positions are again ruled out, so $\theta^I(r^I) = 0$ if $r^I \geq \rho$, and $\theta^I(r^I) = 1$ if $r^I \leq r^I_{\min}$ where $r^I_{\min}$ is

$$(7) \qquad r^I_{\min} = \rho - \frac{\gamma\sigma^2}{J - 1}.$$

Note that $r^I_{\min}$ rises with J, and converges to ρ as J grows without bound. Thus, the interval that allows the portfolio of an informed agent not to be specialized shrinks to almost zero as the market grows infinitely large.

The solution in equation (6) is only for the realization r^I. Expected utility in the scenario in which the investor chooses to acquire information is determined by

$$(8) \quad EU^I = \int_{-\infty}^{\infty}\left(\theta^I(r^I)\rho + [1 - \theta^I(r^I)]r^I - \frac{\gamma}{2}\left\{\frac{[\theta^I(r^I)]^2}{J - 1}\right\}\sigma^2\right)f(r^I)dr^I - \kappa,$$

where $f(r^I)$ is the pdf of r^I, and the corresponding cumulative distribution function (cdf) is defined as $F(r^I)$.

Obviously, the fixed cost can be set large enough so that S is negative, and hence agents would choose not to be informed. Less obvious is the fact that, under fairly general conditions, S is a decreasing function of J for any given κ, as the following proposition argues.

PROPOSITION 1. *For any "pessimistic" rumor such that $r^{min} < r < r^{max}$ and $r \leq \rho$, and assuming that both F and f are continuously differentiable, the gain of acquiring country-specific information S is a decreasing function of J (i.e., dS/dJ < 0) if the number of countries in the market is at least $J < 1/[1 - F(\rho)^{1/2}]$.*

The proof of this proposition is provided in Calvo and Mendoza (2000a). Here we simplify the exposition by adopting that result for dS/dJ in the case in which short positions are ruled out:

$$(9) \qquad \frac{dS}{dJ} = \frac{\gamma}{2} \frac{\sigma^2}{(J-1)^2} F(r_{min}^I) + \int_{r_{min}^I}^{\rho} \frac{1}{2} \frac{(\rho - r^I)^2}{\gamma \sigma^2} dF(r^I)$$

$$- \frac{\gamma}{2} \frac{\sigma^2}{J^2} - \frac{(\rho - r)}{2J^2} \left[2 + \frac{(\rho - r)}{\gamma \sigma^2} \right].$$

Setting $r^I = r_{min}^I$ in equation (9), we obtain

$$(10) \qquad \frac{dS}{dJ} \leq \frac{\gamma}{2} \frac{\sigma^2}{(J-1)^2} \left[F(\rho) - \left(\frac{J-1}{J} \right)^2 \right] - \frac{(\rho - r)}{2J^2} \left(2 + \frac{(\rho - r)}{\gamma \sigma^2} \right).$$

Since $r^{min} < r \leq \rho$, it follows that $J > 1/[1 - F(\rho)^{1/2}]$ is sufficient for $dS/dJ < 0$.

A simple interpretation of this result is the following. Consider a case in which there is no rumor (i.e., $r = \rho$), so that costly information eliminates the variance of country i returns (i.e., the last terms in equations [9] and [10] vanish). It follows from equation (10) that as J increases, both the expected utility of being informed and of being uninformed increase to the extent that a higher J makes the world fund a less risky asset. Proposition 1 establishes a sufficiency condition for the utility gain of being uninformed to be larger than that for being informed, so S falls as J rises. What lies behind this condition is the fact that in those "bad" states of nature in which costly information reveals that agents should short country i, the "second best" choice *if these positions are ruled out* is to allocate the entire portfolio to the world fund. State-contingent utility for those states of nature increases as J rises but at a rate that (1) declines as J rises and (2) declines faster than the rate at which the utility gain of being uninformed falls as J rises. As a result, eventually the utility of being uninformed increases by more than that of being informed as J rises, and S falls.

The above scenario (in which there is no rumor and costly information eliminates the variance of one asset in the investor's portfolio) is comparable to the standard analysis of the value of information to individual investors in the finance literature (see Pritsker 1994). However, our findings are strikingly different because of the assumption ruling out short positions. If there were no restrictions on short positions, as in the standard case in the value-of-information literature, dS/dJ eventually becomes *increasing* in J as J rises, instead of decreasing. This is because with unlimited short positions the utility of being informed rises as J rises at a rate that does not depend on J, while that of being uninformed still increases at a rate that is declining in J.

While absolutely ruling out short positions seems unrealistic, some form of short-selling constraints can be easily justified in the conventional way, by arguing that they will emerge naturally because of the risk of bankruptcy. Consider a case in which J has grown so large as to make the world fund virtually risk free. There could be states of nature in which the earnings of the riskless asset are not sufficient to cover the losses of the risky asset. In our framework with information frictions, one can argue in addition that short-selling constraints make sense because otherwise as J rises informed agents would take infinitely large positions in the world fund—as predicted by equation (6). It is difficult to argue that information would remain costly to gather in an environment like this. Moreover, in exploring the implications of allowing limited short selling in the model presented above, we found that the key results described here are robust to this modification (Calvo and Mendoza 2000a).

Equations (9) and (10) show that there are two key determinants of the critical market size after which S becomes a negative function of J: The first is the position of the mean return of the world portfolio (i.e., ρ) in the distribution of country i returns that agents learn if they pay the fixed cost. For example, if f is symmetric and $E(r') = \rho$, $F(\rho) = 0.5$ and dS/dJ is negative with as few as four countries. If $F(\rho)$ is smaller (larger) than one-half, which implies that $E(r')$ is larger (smaller) than ρ, the critical value of J falls (rises). The intuition is that, if investors are "bullish" on country i in the sense that $E(r') > \rho$, the incentives to gather information begin to decrease with J for a smaller market than when investors are "bearish" on country i. When costly information is *expected* to produce good news, incentives for acquiring it are weak. The second determinant is the size of the rumor. If the rumor is very optimistic, in the sense that $r \geq r^{\max}$, one can show that dS/dJ is always positive. At the other extreme, for very pessimistic rumors $r \leq r^{\min}$, one can show that dS/dJ is always nonpositive. Pessimistic rumors inside the interval relevant for proposition 1 play a similar role. Consider again the case in which f is symmetric. A pessimistic rumor such that $r^{\min} < r < \rho$ implies that dS/dJ may be negative even if $F(\rho)$ is somewhat larger than one-half (i.e., with $r < \rho$, the critical value of J falls for any given $F(\rho)$). Thus, a bad rumor reduces the benefits of gathering information on country i as the market expands even if investors are bearish about country i (i.e., $E(r') < \rho$).

Two final remarks. First, as the market grows infinitely large the gain of gathering country-specific information becomes independent of the size of the global market. This is because in the limit, as $J \to \infty$, both $r^{\min}$ and

r^l_{min} converge to ρ, as a very large global market offers a risk-free asset at the rate of return ρ.[5] Second, as J rises, not only are the incentives to gather information diminishing as J goes to infinity, but the impact of rumors on the allocation of investment funds to a single country by uninformed investors, relative to the initial allocations $1/J$, grows without bound. This is because $-d\theta^U/dr$ converges to $1/\gamma\sigma^2$ in the limit as $J \to \infty$.

1.2.2   Variable Performance Costs

Consider now the effects of variable costs linked to the performance of portfolio managers, and set $\kappa = 0$. Variable costs allow the model to produce contagion as a result of multiple equilibria in optimal portfolio shares, and this has the advantage of making the response to rumors identified above more persistent. This is useful because otherwise contagion could be ruled out by arguing that whenever investors react to a rumor there is a sell-off in the affected country's stock market, and the ensuing "price correction" drives expected returns high enough to undo the effect of the rumor. The persistence of contagion could also be justified by self-fulfilling crises related to policy imbalances (as in Calvo 1998).

We consider identical mutual fund managers that pay a variable cost, or collect a benefit, when the mean return of the portfolio they manage deviates from the mean return of an arbitrary market portfolio. These costs and gains are given by the function $\lambda(\mu(\Theta) - \mu(\theta))$, which satisfies the following properties:[6]

(11) $\lambda > 0$ if $\mu(\theta) < \mu(\Theta)$, $\lambda \le 0$ if $\mu(\theta) > \mu(\Theta)$, $\lambda(0) = 0$,

$$\lambda' \ge 0 \text{ with } \lambda'(x) > \lambda'(-x) \text{ for all } x = \mu(\Theta) - \mu(\theta) > 0,$$

$$\lambda'' \le 0.$$

Hence, there is a cost (benefit) when the mean return of the investor's portfolio is smaller (larger) than that of the market portfolio and the marginal cost exceeds the marginal gain.

Fund managers choose θ, given some Θ, so as to maximize

(12) $EU(\theta) = \theta\rho + (1 - \theta)r - \lambda(\mu(\Theta) - \mu(\theta))$

$$- \frac{\gamma}{2}\left\{\frac{(\theta\sigma_J)^2}{J - 1} + [(1 - \theta)\sigma_i]^2 + 2\sigma_J\sigma_i\theta(1 - \theta)\eta\right\}.$$

The variances of investing in country i (σ_i^2) and in all J countries except i (σ_J^2) differ, and asset returns are correlated according to the correlation

5. Note that this also implies that the result that S declines as J rises cannot be obtained if the portfolio included a riskless asset even for small J. However, the focus of our study is on the composition of portfolios of country-specific risky assets, not on the choice between risky and riskless assets.

6. It is also assumed that $\lambda'(0)$ does not exist to capture the notion of fixed costs.

coefficient η. This portfolio optimization problem displays contagion in the sense that, for rumors within a certain *contagion range* of values of Θ, choosing θ = Θ is optimal for all investors in the global market. Within this range, a rumor calling for a different Θ results in a panic that induces all investors to reoptimize their portfolios and choose that new Θ.

The above result is not all that surprising since the assumption that poor performance is punished relatively more than good performance is rewarded provides an incentive to mimic market portfolios. We are more interested in a second result showing that in the presence of performance-related costs or benefits it is again the case that globalization strengthens incentives for contagion (i.e., the contagion range widens as the global market grows for a given cost function). These results are established in propositions 2 and 3.

> PROPOSITION 2. *If in the neighborhood of the optimal portfolio θ* corresponding to an investor free of information frictions, the marginal performance cost (gain) of deviating from the mean return of the market portfolio μ(Θ) is sufficiently large (small), there exists a contagion range of individual portfolio allocations θ, such that investors optimally choose θ = Θ.*

The proof is provided in Calvo and Mendoza (2000a). Here we provide a graphical example showing that, as long as near θ* the marginal performance cost exceeds the marginal gain, there is a range of values of Θ for which setting θ = Θ is optimal.

Consider the first-order condition for maximization of equation (12) with respect to θ:

(13) $E\hat{U}'(\theta) - \lambda'(\cdot)(r - \rho) = 0,$

where

$$E\hat{U}'(\theta) \equiv \rho - r - \gamma\{\theta\sigma_J^2/(J-1) - (1-\theta)\sigma_i^2 + \eta\sigma_J\sigma_i[(1-\theta) - \theta]\}$$

is the marginal utility of θ for an investor that does not face information frictions, so $E\hat{U}'(\theta^*) = 0$ at the optimum θ*. Note that the second-order condition $E\hat{U}''(\theta) < 0$ requires $\sigma_J^2/(J-1) + \sigma_i^2 > 2\eta\sigma_J\sigma_i$. Clearly, it follows from equation (13) that if r = ρ the solution θ* is the unique solution of the model, and there is no contagion. Thus, contagion in this model requires that r and ρ differ.

A particular case of equation (13) is illustrated in figure 1.1, which assumes that r > ρ, that the marginal gain for beating the market is zero, and that there is a constant marginal cost paid for producing below-market returns (i.e., a linear function for the performance incentives). Any value of Θ within the indicated contagion range implies that it is optimal to set θ = Θ. To see why, first consider what would happen if the investor

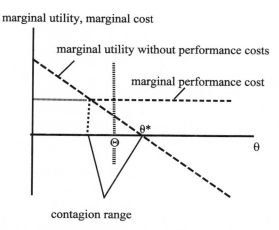

marginal utility, marginal cost

Fig. 1.1   Multiple optimal portfolios in the presence of performance costs

tried $\theta < \Theta$. He would be beating the market—this can be easily confirmed because the difference between individual and market returns can be expressed as $(\Theta - \theta)(\rho - r)$. Given a zero marginal gain for beating the market and the fact that $E\hat{U}'(\theta)$ is positive for $\theta < \Theta \leq \theta^*$, the marginal utility of portfolio reoptimization is positive. If, on the other hand, the investor tried $\theta > \Theta$, he would now produce a mean return lower than the market and pay the constant marginal cost. Within the contagion range this marginal cost exceeds the marginal utility of an investor not subject to information frictions, as shown in figure 1.1, and hence the net marginal utility of setting a portfolio $\theta > \Theta$ is negative. Thus, $\theta = \Theta$ is the optimal choice. Moreover, it is easy to see that contagion equilibria cannot exist in figure 1.1 for any $\Theta \geq \theta^*$. A similar argument can be constructed to show that, for $r < \rho$, there is a contagion range for some values of Θ in the region $\Theta \geq \theta^*$, and that in this case there are no contagion equilibria for $\Theta \leq \theta^*$.

PROPOSITION 3. *The contagion range, defined by the values of Θ in the interval $\theta^{low} < \Theta < \theta^{up}$ for which proposition 2 holds, widens as the global market grows (i.e., $\theta^{up} - \theta^{low}$ is increasing in J).*

The proof is again in Calvo and Mendoza (2000a), where we show that, for a linear marginal cost function as the one in figure 1.1, the total differential of equation (13) and the second-order condition stated earlier imply that $d\theta/dJ$ is positive and *increasing* in θ. Thus, as J rises both θ^{up} and θ^{low} rise but, since $\theta^{up} > \theta^{low}$, θ^{up} rises more than θ^{low} and hence the contagion range widens. In graphical terms, the downward sloping line that represents $E\hat{U}'(\theta)$ in figure 1.1 shifts counterclockwise around its vertical intercept as J rises.

The intuition for this result is simple. Given a marginal reputational cost invariant to J or θ, the growth of the global market can only affect the expected marginal utility of optimal portfolios in two ways. First, as J rises, the effective variance of the world fund ($\sigma_J^2/(J-1)^2$) falls, and thus the marginal utility of θ rises. This effect is proportional to the portfolio share invested in the world fund. Second, the reduced variance of the world fund makes this asset more attractive relative to country i, providing an incentive to increase θ, which in turn reduces marginal utility. The magnitude of this second effect is independent of θ because the rate at which marginal utility falls as θ rises is invariant to portfolio shares with a linear marginal utility (as in fig. 1.1). Hence, the portfolio shift induced by market growth is larger the larger the initial θ. We also prove (Calvo and Mendoza 2000a), however, that $d\theta/dJ$ is decreasing in J and converges to 0 as J goes to infinity because in a large market the world fund becomes riskless.

Since the portfolio θ^* of the investor free of information frictions is Pareto-efficient, all portfolios within the contagion range are suboptimal. This is because θ^* maximizes $E\hat{U}(\theta)$, and $EU(\theta) = E\hat{U}(\theta)$ whenever $\theta = \Theta$ since $\lambda(0) = 0$. Moreover, the existence of multiple optimal portfolios for a given pair of mean returns r and ρ implies that there can be capital outflows from country i even in the absence of rumors about country asset returns. This also implies that a price correction following a rumor about r may not prevent persistent contagion.

1.2.3 A Comparison with Models of Costly Information, Contagion, and Herd Behavior

The fixed cost of acquiring information featured in our model is reminiscent of the information costs driving the models of informational efficiency in the tradition of Grossman and Stiglitz (1976, 1980). Our focus, however, is on the implications of market size for the profitability of gathering costly information in a partial equilibrium setting where asset prices are exogenous. In contrast, the classic finding of Grossman and Stiglitz that incentives to gather costly information are reduced by the fact that prices can partially or totally reveal that information emphasizes the general equilibrium determination of prices. The Grossman-Stiglitz argument suggests that if our model is examined in general equilibrium it may yield even smaller expected utility gains of gathering costly country-specific information, for any given J, because endogenous changes in asset returns would reveal some or all of the information at no cost. Through this channel, therefore, we would expect a general equilibrium analysis to strengthen our results rather than weaken them.

Our framework also considers a global market consisting of a large number of identical investors formulating simultaneous decisions. This differs from the sequential decisionmaking setup typical of game-theoretic models of herd behavior.[7] These models show that when information is incomplete and the signals that transmit it are noisy, agents *waiting in line* to make a decision may imitate agents ahead of them rather than use their own information (a situation referred to as an "informational cascade").

Our framework can easily be incorporated into a sequential decision-making setting. Consider the case with variable performance incentives, viewed as the "sharing-the-blame" reputational effects that induce herding externalities in Scharfstein and Stein (1990). Assume N investors waiting in line to choose their portfolios observe the portfolios chosen by investors ahead of them, with the first one facing an arbitrary Θ. Each investor draws a piece of news at random that acts as a shift parameter in λ', so marginal costs are indexed by h for $h = 1, \ldots, N$. The λ_h's are like the signals introduced in Banerjee (1992) or Bikhchandani, Hirshleifer, and Welch (1992), with the distribution of λ' defined to have positive (negative) support for $\theta > \Theta$ ($\theta < \Theta$). Under these conditions, there can be informational cascades in which the agents first in line may draw λ_h's such that they choose Θ, thereby increasing the incentives for followers to also choose Θ. In some of these cascades everybody chooses Θ, and herd behavior dominates. Since for any λ_h the contagion range widens as J rises, a set of signals that supported an equilibrium without herding in a small market can produce an informational cascade with herding in a large market.

The contagion models examined by Shiller (1995) also have an interesting connection with our model. Contagion by word of mouth provides microfoundations for the determination of Θ or r, and for the process leading from one value of Θ to another within the range of herding equilibria. Survey data collected by Shiller and Pound (1986, 1987) provide further evidence of word-of-mouth contagion among institutional investors in the United States.

1.3   Quantitative Implications of the Model

We proceed next to explore the model's quantitative implications. In order to conduct numerical simulations, we calibrate a benchmark version of the model to reflect basic statistical properties of international asset returns and portfolio holdings. We do not test the model's ability to explain actual investment behavior, since it is well known that the mean-variance

---

7. Our analysis adopts some assumptions similar to those used in game-theoretic models. In Banerjee (1992) payoffs are discontinuous at the "true value" of asset returns, resembling the discontinuity of λ' at $\theta = \Theta$. Banerjee (1992) and Bikhchandani, Hirshleifer, and Welch (1992) require two sources of uncertainty (about outcomes and about signals), while in our model investors considering whether to pay the fixed information cost face uncertainty about asset return "fundamentals" and about potential updates of mean and variances of assets returns.

model cannot explain actual portfolio allocations, particularly the "home" bias of international portfolios (see Tesar and Werner 1995a). Our intent is simply to quantify how large contagion effects can be because of the information frictions we proposed.

1.3.1 Calibration

The benchmark calibration requires a value for the preference parameter γ, estimates of the mean and variance of country asset returns, and a framework for characterizing the nature of costly information and for how this information maps into updates of the mean and variance of country asset returns. The value of the coefficient of absolute risk aversion, γ, is set to make the model consistent with existing estimates of the mean and variance-covariance structure of asset returns, and data on net holdings of foreign equity by global investors, assuming a conventional mean-variance setup without information or reputational costs. The equation that relates γ to θ and the statistical moments of asset returns is derived by solving equation (13) for γ setting $\lambda'(\cdot) = 0$. Using various data sets that exist in the home bias literature (see, e.g., Bohn and Tesar 1994; Lewis 1995; and Tesar and Werner 1995b), we found that plausible values of γ range between near 0 and $1/2$. We chose the middle point $1/4$ for the benchmark calibration. Note, however, that there are also several data combinations that produce negative values of γ, highlighting the weaknesses of the mean-variance model.

The best available measure of costly country-specific information is embodied in the CCRs constructed by investment banks, and compiled and published every six months, in March and September, by *Institutional Investor*. Figure 1.2 plots the time-series average of each country's CCR against the corresponding standard deviation, using all available data, which in most cases covers the period September 1979–March 1996. Figure 1.3 is a similar plot that includes only member countries of the Organization for Economic Cooperation and Development (OECD) and Latin American countries.

Figures 1.2 and 1.3 show that credit ratings are significantly more variable in emerging markets than they are in either industrialized or least-developed economies. Emerging markets are defined here as those with credit ratings between 20 and 80—high-risk countries have ratings lower than 20 and industrialized countries have ratings higher than 80. This evidence suggests that when asset trading restrictions among industrial countries were lifted in the 1980s, the newly created global market consisted of countries of roughly similar risk quality. The globalization of the 1990s expanded to emerging markets where asset returns are intrinsically more risky, and where information gathered on economic, social, and political issues results in much larger innovations to credit ratings than in OECD countries. Under these conditions, it may in principle be valuable to ac-

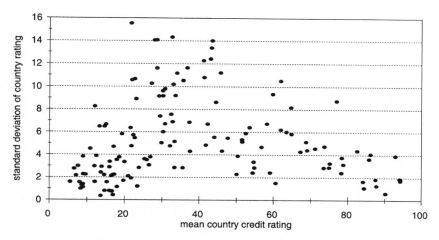

Fig. 1.2   Variability of country credit ratings

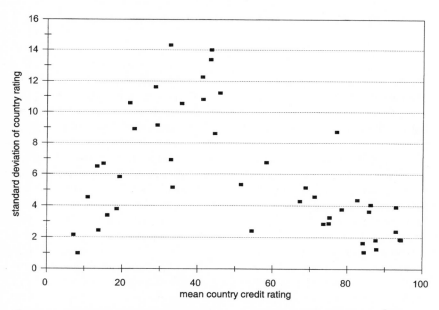

Fig. 1.3   Variability of country credit ratings in Latin America and the OECD

quire costly country-specific information. We must still determine, however, whether a globalized market provides enough incentives for investors to pay for this information.

The calibration is completed by specifying a framework for mapping the costly information of the CCRs into probability distributions from which updates of means and variances of asset returns are drawn.[8] We adopt a framework created by Erb, Harvey, and Viskanta (1996) to forecast the mean and variance of asset returns in eighty countries for which CCRs exist but equity markets do not. These authors estimated log-linear panel regressions of the mean and variance of returns on the information innovations measured by CCRs for countries with equity markets, and used them to forecast means and variances of returns in countries *without* equity markets. In particular, they estimated panel regressions of the form $x_{ht+1} = \alpha^x + \beta^x \ln(CCR_{ht}) + u_{ht}^x + 1$, where x = the mean (μ) or standard deviation (sd) of asset returns in country h. This exercise assumes normal distributions for the one-step-ahead mean and variance of returns, which are defined by

$$E[r^I] = \alpha^\mu + \beta^\mu E[\ln(CCR_h)],$$

$$E[\sigma_h^I] = \alpha^{sd} + \beta^{sd} E[\ln(CCR_h)],$$

$$\sigma_r^I = (\beta^\mu)^2 \text{VAR}[\ln(CCR_h)] + (\sigma_u^\mu)^2,$$

and

$$\sigma_\sigma^I = (\beta^{sd})^2 \text{VAR}[\ln(CCR_h)] + (\sigma_u^{sd})^2.$$

Assuming that the regressions are homogenous across countries, the regression coefficients and the data on CCRs can be combined to compute these four moments for the 144 countries with credit ratings data. A table listing these moments for each country is available from the authors on request.

For countries with equity markets, the predicted moments based on the regressions created by Erb, Harvey, and Viskanta can be compared to the estimates of the mean and standard deviation of returns produced using historical equity-market data, as shown in figure 1.4. This chart plots updates of the mean and standard deviations of returns based on the September 1996 CCRs against each country's CCR. Updates are measured as a difference relative to the corresponding statistical moment based on historical equity-market data. Figure 1.4 shows that costly information generally results in positive updates of mean returns and reduced estimates of the variability of asset returns. Moreover, emerging markets yield relatively large upward adjustments in expected returns and large downward revisions in standard deviations of returns, while updates of the mean and variance of returns for OECD countries are generally small.

---

8. Note that although *Institutional Investor* provides CCRs at a trivial cost, the published ratings are not free information at the relevant moment in which investment banks design portfolios.

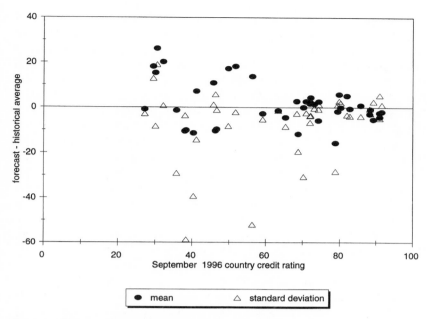

Fig. 1.4   Updates of the mean and variance of asset returns

1.3.2   Contagion Due to Fixed Information Costs

The simulations use the following expected utility function for informed agents:

$$(14)\quad EU^I - \kappa = \int_{-\infty}^{\infty} \int_{-\infty}^{\infty} \theta^I(r^I,\sigma_i^I)\rho + (1 - \theta^I(r^I,\sigma_i^I))r^I$$

$$- \frac{\gamma}{2}\left[\frac{(\theta^I(r^I,\sigma_i^I)\sigma_J)^2}{J-1} + ((1 - \theta^I(r^I,\sigma_i^I))\sigma_i^I)^2 \right.$$

$$\left. + 2\sigma_J\sigma_i^I\eta\theta^I(r^I,\sigma_i^I)(1 - \theta^I(r^I,\sigma_i^I)) \right] f(r^I)g(\sigma_i^I)dr,$$

where f and g are normal, independent probability distribution functions and $\theta^I(r^I,\sigma_i^I)$ is the optimal portfolio of an informed investor contingent on updates (r^I,σ_i^I). The simulations consider an evenly spaced grid of rumors about the country i return, with 120 elements spanning the interval $[r^{min},r^{max}]$, and allow J to vary from two to forty-two countries. The double integral in equation (14) is computed by Gauss-Legendre quadrature, setting integration limits so that the integral captures 98 percent of the joint cumulative distribution function of r^I and σ_i^I.

Consider first a case simplified to illustrate the theoretical results of section 1.2 within the context of the relatively stable equity markets of OECD countries. This requires the restrictive assumptions that (1) asset returns are uncorrelated ($\eta = 0$), (2) ex ante the mean and variance of asset returns are the same in all countries ($r^* = \rho$ and $\sigma_i = \sigma_J$), (3) the information acquired at a fixed cost reveals the true country i asset return (i.e., $E[\sigma_i^I] = \sigma_\sigma^I = 0$), and (4) the expected update of country i's return equals the world return, $E(r^I) = \rho$. The values of ρ, σ_J, and σ_i^I are set to $\rho = 15.31$ percent, $\sigma_J = 22.44$ percent, and $\sigma_i^I = 6.46$ percent. The first two moments are arithmetic averages of the annualized mean and standard deviation of monthly stock returns in U.S. dollars over the period 1979–95 for OECD countries with "stable markets," and the third moment is an average of the estimates of σ_i^I computed using the forecasting framework of Erb, Harvey, and Viskanta (1996). The OECD countries with "stable markets" include OECD members during the entire 1979–95 period for which the standard deviation of returns did not exceed 30 percent. This excludes Greece, New Zealand, Portugal, and Turkey.

Figure 1.5 plots S, ignoring κ, as a function of J for values of the rumor equal to r^{min}, r^{max}, and the neutral rumor $r = r^* = \rho$. The chart confirms proposition 1 and its implications for very pessimistic and very optimistic rumors. S is generally decreasing in J for all moderate-to-pessimistic rumors and increasing in J for a very optimistic rumor. S is decreasing in J even for $J < 4$ in the neutral-rumor case because proposition 1 establishes only a sufficiency condition. In this example, however, investors facing pessimistic rumors ($r \leq \rho$) are willing to pay hefty fixed information costs exceeding 30 percent (in terms of mean portfolio return) if $J = 2$. As J grows to include about a dozen countries, S falls sharply but still converges to a relatively large amount of nearly 4 percent. At 4 percent, the fixed cost would have to be about one-third of the expected portfolio return before the rumor emerged (15.3 percent) in order to induce contagion. Still, this experiment shows that only twelve countries are required for the adverse effect of globalization on information gains to be in full force, and that this effect cuts information gains sharply.

Next we strengthen the effects of the informational frictions by considering the more realistic case in which information cannot reveal true asset returns. Hence, agents only learn updates of the mean and variance of returns drawn from known probability distributions. The moments that fully describe these normal, independent distributions are again determined using the forecasting model of Erb, Harvey, and Viskanta (1996) applied to "stable" OECD markets. This implies setting $E(r^I) = 15.18$, $E[\sigma_i^I] = 21.81$, $\sigma_r^I = 6.46$, and $\sigma_\sigma^I = 1.84$. We maintain for now the assumptions that ex ante all countries are perceived to be identical ($r^* = \rho$ and $\sigma_i = \sigma_J$) and that asset returns are uncorrelated. The resulting S function is plotted in figure 1.6.

A comparison of figures 1.5 and 1.6 shows that, when information

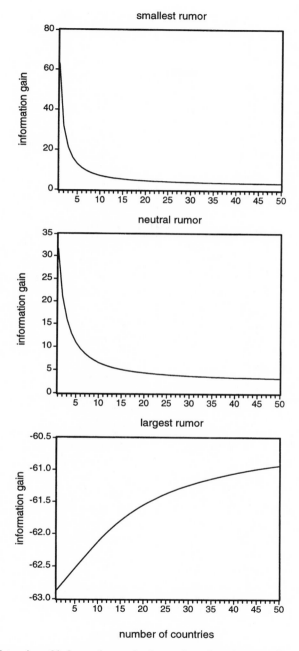

Fig. 1.5   Net gains of information gathering and market size: case I

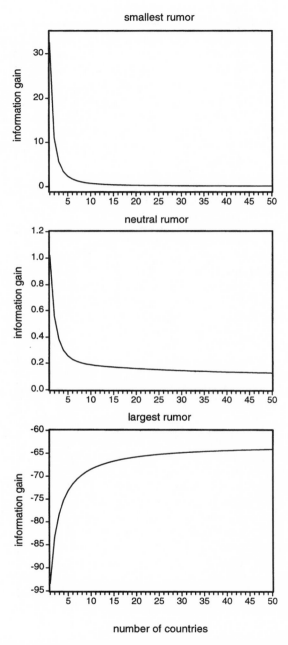

Fig. 1.6　Net gains of information gathering and market size: case II

cannot reveal true asset returns, the gains of information gathering can fall very sharply. In the case of the neutral rumor $r = r*$ (the middle panels of figs. 1.5 and 1.6), the gains of acquiring information decline from 31 to 1 percent for a market with two countries, and from about 4.0 to 0.1 percent in markets with more than twelve countries. A cost of 0.1 percent is only 0.6 percent of the ex ante mean return of the total portfolio ($r* = \rho = 15.31$), so in this circumstances investors are very reluctant to pay information costs. S is small even for mildly pessimistic rumors (a rumor that country i's return is 11 percent yields $S = 3.1$ percent for $J = 2$ and $S = 0.4$ percent for $J = 12$). Moreover, in a large market with at least twelve countries, S converges to less than 0.45 percent for any rumor $r^{min} \leq r \leq r*$.

The above exercise can be easily modified to consider the fact that the correlation of asset returns in the OECD ranges from 0.3 to 0.6 (see Bohn and Tesar 1994; Lewis 1995; and Erb, Harvey, and Viskanta 1996). This is done by setting $\eta = 0.35$.[9] This positive correlation of returns yields even smaller gains of information gathering, with the value of S for r^{min} and $J = 2$ falling from 32 to 22 percent. Note, however, that positive correlation between country i and the world fund can bias the results against gathering information on country i because of the implicit assumption that the asset returns of the $J - 1$ countries in the world fund are uncorrelated and hence provide better diversification opportunities. Still, modifying the experiment to introduce correlation of asset returns across countries in the world fund at 0.35 does not alter the results significantly.

We are also interested in exploring how the model behaves when we consider that the global capital market includes a larger number of emerging markets than stable OECD markets. In fact, the growing set of emerging markets is often viewed as a group segmented from OECD markets. Thus, the relevant question might not be whether it is worthwhile to gather information about a single emerging economy in a market with $J - 1$ OECD countries, but whether it is rational to acquire information in a market where most of the $J - 1$ countries are also volatile emerging markets. To simulate this scenario, consider a case in which all countries are identical emerging markets ex ante, with probabilistic parameters set to the averages for the Latin American countries that result from applying the model of Erb, Harvey, and Viskanta (1996) as in the previous cases. The resulting parameterization is as follows: $E(r^I) = 33.12$, $E[\sigma_i^I] = 34.57$, $\sigma_r^I = 49.31$, $\sigma_\sigma^I = 14.04$, $r* = \rho = 31.21$, and $\sigma_i = \sigma_J = 50.03$. In this case rumors will prevail in a market with at least ten countries if information costs exceed 5 percent, or one-sixth of the ex ante expected portfolio return (which is now 31.2 percent). Information gains still fall very sharply

---

9. Given the means and variances of asset returns, and the value of γ, higher correlation coefficients would violate the second-order conditions of the optimization problems of informed and uninformed investors.

as the market grows, and the full effect of market growth on S is transmitted with as few as ten countries.

This last case assumed that information gathering yields average updates of the mean and standard deviations of returns equivalent to 1.06 and 0.69 of the corresponding moments computed with historical equity market data. However, figure 1.4 showed that the moments that describe the distributions of updates can vary widely across countries. For instance, in the cases of Argentina, Colombia, the Philippines, Taiwan, and South Africa, information yields sharply lower expected returns than historical equity market statistics, while updates of the standard deviation vary from sharp reductions to moderate increases. In Colombia's case, for example, the average update of the mean return is 0.77 of the equity market forecast, while the standard deviation of returns is virtually the same with or without gathering information. In this case the information gain for a neutral rumor $r = r^*$ is 7 percent if $J = 2$. As J grows to include twenty countries, information gains fall to about 0.5 percent for any rumor $r^{min} \leq r \leq r^*$. With the ex ante expected portfolio return at 31.2 percent, this implies that investors in a large global market will not pay information costs exceeding 1.6 percent of the ex ante portfolio return. Indonesia's case is quite different, at least over the sample period under study. Information gathered on Indonesia results in sharp upward updates of the mean return, while revisions to the standard deviation remain negligible as in Colombia's case. Since information yields much higher returns than the history of Indonesia's stock market, with about the same standard deviation, S reaches about 18 percent for any rumor $r^{min} \leq r \leq r^*$ with $J \geq 20$. Thus, investors are willing to pay up more than one-half of the ex ante portfolio return to learn about rumors affecting Indonesia.

It is also important to quantify the international capital flows that may take place in situations in which there is contagion among global investors. To gain an insight on this issue, we simulated the model setting parameters so that the $J - 1$ countries represent stable OECD markets and country i is calibrated to Mexican data using the framework of Erb, Harvey, and Viskanta (1996). The probabilistic parameters are now set as follows: $E(r^I) = 33.12$, $E[\sigma_i^I] = 34.57$, $\sigma_r^I = 49.31$, $\sigma_\sigma^I = 14.04$, $r^* = 22.4$, $\rho = 15.31$, $\sigma_i = 50.03$, and $\sigma_J = 22.44$. In this scenario, the simulations show that if the fixed information cost exceeds 6.5 percent (or about two-fifths of the ex ante mean portfolio return of 15.4 percent), pessimistic rumors about Mexico would prevail. A rumor that reduces the expected return on Mexican equity from the equity market forecast of 22.4 percent to the level of the OECD mean return of 15.3 percent leads to a reduction in the share of the world portfolio invested in Mexico from 1.7 percent to 0.7 percent—a reduction of 40 percent. According to the *Bolsa de Valores de Mexico* (the Mexican stock exchange), direct foreign holdings of Mexican equity exceeded $50 billion by the end of 1997, and hence a 40 percent cut amounts to $20 billion,[10] which is a very large amount for a country where foreign reserves rarely exceed that same figure. For rumors that set r below 10 percent, the short-sale restrictions become binding and Mexican equity is eliminated from the portfolio, with a resulting outflow of the full $50 billion.

1.3.3   Variable Costs and the Contagion Region

The simulation exercises conclude with an analysis of the contagion region created by performance-related variable costs. We maintain the settings of the last example involving Mexico and the OECD. The variable cost function takes the following form: $\lambda = \varphi(\mu(\Theta) - \mu(\theta))$ with $\varphi = 15$ for all $\mu(\Theta) > \mu(\theta)$ and $\varphi = 0$ otherwise.[11] The contagion range shows that, when $J = 2$, the share of portfolio invested in Mexico can fluctuate between 20.2 and 22.5 percent, or about 2.3 percentage points, on account of contagion. With ten OECD countries the range widens by about one-half of a percentage point, with the portfolio share invested in Mexico varying between 3.8 and 6.6 percent.

The total reputational costs avoided by displaying herding behavior or contagion are small. When $J = 20$, and assuming $\Theta = \theta^*$, the maximum reputational cost paid for choosing the largest θ within the contagion range is one-tenth of the mean portfolio return. Thus, contagion can potentially induce large capital flows into and out of emerging markets even in the presence of small total performance-linked costs. The marginal cost, however, is large in the sense that it represents a punishment for poor performance fifteen times the difference between the mean return paid by the market and that paid by the investor's portfolio. Note also that, as shown in section 1.2, the contagion range is increasing in J but does not grow without bound as J rises. The size of the range converges to about 2.8 percentage points as J approaches ∞.

Next we measure the capital flows triggered by reputational effects. Assume that the investors' total wealth corresponds to the holdings of foreign equity by U.S. investors. The latest *Benchmark Survey of U.S. Holdings of Foreign Securities* conducted by the treasury department reports that by end-March 1994 the holdings of foreign equity by U.S. investors amounted to $566 billion. The model predicts that with $J = 20$ the fraction of U.S. foreign equity invested in Mexico fluctuates between 2.53 and 5.31 percent.[12] Thus, herding panics triggered by reputational effects can

---

10. The figure on the value of foreign holdings in Mexico's market was quoted in the Mexican newspaper *Reforma*, 15 January 1998, p. 1A, citing as source the Mexican stock exchange.

11. Calvo and Mendoza (2000a) examine the sensitivity of the results to changes in the value of φ and in the other exogenous parameters of the model (η, γ, σ_J, and σ_j). The results show that our findings are generally robust to parameter variations.

12. Interestingly, the treasury's *Survey* estimates the U.S. holdings of Mexican equity at 6.2 percent of the total holdings of foreign equity by U.S. investors.

account for sudden capital flows into and out of Mexico as large as \$15.7 billion. If we add foreign investment in bonds, the total foreign security holdings of U.S. investors reach about \$870 billion, and thus herding could account for Mexican capital flows of up to \$24.2 billion. As noted earlier, in a country where foreign reserves normally amount to less than \$20 billion, of which \$10 billion are widely regarded as the desirable minimum (see Calvo and Mendoza 1996), these flows can be an important determinant of vulnerability to balance-of-payments crises.

Despite the large capital flows that contagion can produce, it does not appear to embody significant welfare costs. We computed the percentage change in consumption needed for a portfolio within the contagion range to yield the same utility of a portfolio chosen in the conventional mean-variance model without information frictions (i.e., θ^*). These calculations make use of the model's direct utility function: $E - \exp(-\gamma C)$. The welfare costs never exceed 2.5 percent, and for portfolio share variations of 100 basis points around the first-best optimum the costs are actually smaller than one-fourth of a percentage point. Moreover, since $E\hat{U}(\theta)$ and θ^* are invariant to λ, it follows that variations in the marginal reputational cost do not alter this result—although of course lowering the marginal cost narrows the contagion range.

1.4   Concluding Remarks

We used a basic model of international portfolio diversification with incomplete information to show that the globalization of securities markets can reduce incentives for information gathering, and hence produce high volatility in capital flows as a result of contagion. In our model this occurs because globalization generally reduces the gains derived from paying fixed costs for country-specific information or because, in the presence of variable performance-linked or reputational costs, globalization widens the contagion range of portfolios within which investors find it optimal to mimic arbitrary market portfolios.

The notion that a fixed information cost may be of practical relevance, given the large amount of investment resources in the hands of securities firms, seems controversial. While it is quite reasonable to argue that fixed costs are less relevant for these firms, it is important to note two related issues that are particularly complex in an international context. First, the cost of learning about the macroeconomic features of a country is not very different regardless of the size of the country and the amount of the investment involved. Hence, information gathering in an international setting is relatively costly. Second, the possibility that fixed costs can be easily overcome by clusters of investors setting up securities firms in which other investors could invest can be a source for further complications, rather than a solution. For instance, as Calvo and Mendoza (2000b) show, market volatility can be exacerbated by the interaction of a cluster of "sophisticated" (i.e., informed) traders with a group of uninformed investors in the face of systemic shocks forcing sophisticated traders to sell their assets, assuming that traders face binding borrowing constraints.

Contagion resulting from variable performance costs, or reputational considerations, can be challenged on the premise that securities firms would not be maximizing the payoff to their investors if they implemented incentive schemes like the one we studied, which yield inefficient, contagion-driven outcomes. While we lack specific evidence on incentive structures to determine if they resemble the one we assumed, the survey evidence documented by Shiller and Pound (1986, 1987) indicates that reputational concerns, the "fear of being different," and contagion by word of mouth seem to play an important role. Moreover, in some instances the perverse incentive structure may be the result of government regulation. In Chile, for example, individual private pension funds are required by government regulation to produce returns within a certain range of the average return for all pension funds. Thus, the regulation sets a cost for producing below-market returns and no gain for producing above-market returns, which is the main feature of the incentive structure leading to contagion in the model we studied.

In light of our findings, it is natural to raise the question of whether globalization is necessarily welfare improving, and to suggest that the pros and cons of abolishing capital controls may deserve further consideration. Our results do not challenge classic notions related to the efficiency gains derived from global market integration in a frictionless environment, although evidence indicates that these gains, at least from the perspective of risk sharing and consumption smoothing, could be small (see Mendoza 1991 and Tesar 1995). However, this paper does suggest that in the presence of severe information frictions, capital flows can be extremely volatile and optimal portfolios are generally Pareto-inefficient.

The inefficiencies seemed small when we computed the corresponding welfare costs in a basic model in which all agents are global investors; but it is easy to imagine situations in which these costs can be substantial, as the recent experiences of Mexico, Argentina, Russia, and several East Asian countries indicate. One example is the case of a typical developing country that depends on capital inflows to finance imports of consumer and capital goods, and uses the latter as inputs to produce tradable and nontradable goods. There could be two types of agents in this economy: "workers," who derive income only from labor services and cannot access global capital markets to insure themselves against income fluctuations induced by capital flows; and "global investors," with their wealth and income globally diversified. Contagion in this environment could be devastating for "workers," particularly those that produce nontraded goods, and to the extent that "investors" enjoy nontradables consumption, their welfare could also suffer. Heterogeneity in this setting would play a key role, since it is well known that welfare costs of country-specific risk implied by limited world asset trading in pure consumption-smoothing models are trivial (see Mendoza 1991), unless there is a channel linking volatility and growth (as in Obstfeld 1994 and Mendoza 1997).

Increased global market volatility can also induce large social costs if it serves as a vehicle that enhances distortions leading to self-fulfilling crises. For example, if, as in Calvo (1998), there are situations in which the ability of a government to roll over its debt is compromised by a sudden run on its securities in global markets, agents may expect that current fiscal adjustment may need to be so large in order to pay for maturing debt that it will cripple the economy and affect adversely future government revenues. The latter could justify the expectation that the government will default, making the beliefs about default self-fulfilling.

References

Banerjee, Abhijit V. 1992. A simple model of herd behavior. *Quarterly Journal of Economics* 107:797–817.

Bikhchandani, Sushil, David Hirshleifer, and Ivo Welch. 1992. A theory of fads, fashion, custom, and cultural change as informational cascades. *Journal of Political Economy* 100:992–1026.

Bohn, Henning, and Linda L. Tesar. 1994. Can standard portfolio theory explain international portfolio investment? Department of Economics, University of California, Santa Barbara. Mimeo.

Calvo, Guillermo A. 1998. Varieties of capital market crises. In *The debt burden and its consequences for monetary policy,* ed. G. A. Calvo and M. King. London: Macmillan.

Calvo, Guillermo A., and Enrique G. Mendoza. 1996. Mexico's balance-of-payments crisis: A chronicle of a death foretold. *Journal of International Economics* 41 (November): 235–64.

———. 2000a. Rational contagion and the globalization of securities markets. *Journal of International Economics,* forthcoming.

———. 2000b. Capital-markets crises and economic collapse in emerging markets: An informational frictions approach. *American Economic Review,* forthcoming.

Calvo, Sara, and Carmen M. Reinhart. 1995. Capital flows to Latin America: Is there evidence of contagion effects? Washington, D.C.: World Bank. Mimeo.

Erb, Claude B., Campbell R. Harvey, and Tadas E. Viskanta. 1996. Expected returns and volatility in 135 countries. *Journal of Portfolio Management* 22 (3): 46–58.

Grossman, Sanford J., and Joseph E. Stiglitz. 1976. Information and competitive price systems. *American Economic Review* 66:246–53.

———. 1980. On the impossibility of informationally efficient markets. *American Economic Review* 70:477–98.

Group of Ten. 1996. *The resolution of sovereign liquidity crises.* Washington, D.C.: International Monetary Fund.

Keynes, John Maynard. 1936. *The general theory of employment, interest, and money.* New York: Harcourt, Brace.

Lewis, Karen K. 1995. Stocks, consumption, and the gains from international risk-sharing. Wharton School of Business, University of Pennsylvania. Mimeo.

Mendoza, Enrique G. 1991. Capital controls and the dynamic gains from trade in a business cycle model of a small open economy. *IMF Staff Papers* 38:480–505.

———. 1997. Terms-of-trade uncertainty and economic growth: Are risk indicators significant in growth regressions? *Journal of Development Economics* 52 (December): 322–56.

Morris, Stephen, and Hyun Song Shing. 1995. Informational events that trigger currency attacks. Working Paper no. 95-24. Philadelphia, Pa.: Economic Research Division, Federal Reserve Bank of Philadelphia.

Obstfeld, Maurice. 1994. Risk-taking, global diversification, and growth. *American Economic Review* 84:1310–30.

Pritsker, Matt G. 1994. The value of information to an individual agent. Washington, D.C.: Board of Governors of the Federal Reserve System. Mimeo.

Scharfstein, David S., and Jeremy C. Stein. 1990. Herd behavior and investment. *American Economic Review* 80:465–79.

Shiller, Robert J. 1995. Conversation, information, and herd behavior. *American Economic Review Papers and Proceedings* 85, no. 2 (May): 181–85.

Shiller, Robert J., and John Pound. 1986. Survey evidence on diffusion of interest among institutional investors. NBER Working Paper no. 1851. Cambridge, Mass.: National Bureau of Economic Research.

———. 1987. Are institutional investors speculators? *Journal of Portfolio Management* (spring): 46–52.

Tesar, Linda L. 1995. Evaluating the gains from international risksharing. *Carnegie-Rochester Conference Series on Public Policy* 42:95–143.

Tesar, Linda L., and Ingrid M. Werner. 1995a. Home bias and high turnover. *Journal of International Money and Finance* 14 (4): 467–92.

———. 1995b. U.S. equity investment in emerging stock markets. *World Bank Economic Review* 9:109–29.

Comment   Rudiger Dornbusch

Calvo and Mendoza's paper is an enviable piece of research in being both topical and thoroughly elegant. The theory is state of the art, the execution is flawless. Here is a theory of speculative attacks caused by masses of investors who find it far more profitable to run away than to ascertain whether the rumors are true: "Don't ask questions, run" is the bottom line and this follows rigorously from the model. It is an uncomfortable conclusion but not altogether an implausible one, since the world does appear to warmly welcome emerging market assets one day and then, on sheer rumor, desert those assets at the drop of a hat.

Fortunately for world capital markets, Calvo and Mendoza's conclusions are far less threatening than they might appear at first sight. While the conclusions do follow rigorously from their assumptions, the authors omit a key aspect of this world—financial intermediaries. Calvo and Mendoza envisage a continuum of "unit-size" investors who face fixed costs of

Rudiger Dornbusch is the Ford Professor of Economics and International Management at the Massachusetts Institute of Technology.

ascertaining the facts; this is the way to make information really costly, and all the rest follows. Of course, their model is a parade piece in explaining how in the real world we would quickly see the emergence of financial intermediaries.

Financial intermediaries would pool resources from all the unit-size investors and, using scale to reduce the costs of information gathering, they avoid or sharply reduce the prevalence of Calvo-Mendoza runs. True, in their world people should run rather than assume the risk of throwing good money after bad to find out whether the bad news is *really* bad. But once we include financial institutions that specialize in establishing information in a cost-effective way, all this simply goes away.

There is a second flaw in the paper. In an attempt to catch the theme of the day, "contagion," the paper tries to categorize the simultaneous flight of all unit-size investors on learning the rumor as contagion. There is no contagion here: Just because everybody does the same thing—correlation—does not mean that some Lotka-style infection is spreading. The authors state, "When a rumor suddenly favors another 'market portfolio' . . . contagion prevails and 'all investors follow the herd.'" But this is not necessarily so; the investors may simply all be doing the same thing—no leader, no follower, nobody egging others on or infecting.

A third concern regards the finding that globalization is bad. This is a surprising result in a microeconomic perspective. Why would market segmentation dominate, in rigorous welfare assessment, an open world capital market? Anyone finding such a result ought to be suspicious unless market failure is patent and remedy is left out of consideration. Globalization in the Calvo-Mendoza model means that investors have available low-risk, diversified portfolios not including any one particular country—that is why a policy of running without further questions is not costly—as they note "the full adverse effect of globalization on information gains is transmitted with about a dozen countries."

Somewhere along the line the benefits of diversification disappear and the focus is put sharply on the country that can be dropped from the portfolio without much loss. In this paper, one reason not to desert a rumor-struck country is poor diversification once it is dropped from the portfolio. But if there are many countries in the world, any single country becomes dispensable. This is the key ingredient for the Calvo-Mendoza conclusion that globalization is a problem. Having already concluded that financial intermediaries are there to develop the useful information on any one country, we can safely dismiss the globalization alarm that comes from this paper. Diversified portfolios are wonderful for investors and financial intermediaries are wonderful in developing useful information essential to sound investment; when the two meet we have the best of all worlds. This paper does nothing to dismiss the case and, unfortunately, does nothing to add to our understanding of financial crises on the periphery.

2

Fire-Sale FDI

Paul Krugman

Picture Mom, Dad, and the kids in an upper-middle-class Asian family in 10 years' time: After loading up with cash at the corner Citibank, they drive off to Walmart and fill the trunk of their Ford with the likes of Fritos and Snickers. On the way home, they stop at the American-owned Cineplex to catch the latest Disney movie, paying with their Visa card. In the evening, after putting the kids to bed, Mom and Dad argue furiously about whether to invest in a Fidelity mutual fund or in a life insurance policy issued by American International Group. (*New York Times,* 1 February 1998)

OK, it's a bit silly, and was meant to be. When the *New York Times* painted this portrait in early 1998, it was a deliberate caricature. Nonetheless, it drew attention to a real phenomenon: The Asian financial crisis, although marked by massive flight of short-term capital and large-scale sell-offs of foreign equity holdings, has at the same time been accompanied by a wave of *inward* direct investment. This inward investment to some extent reflects policy changes, as Asian governments, under pressure from the International Monetary Fund (IMF) and in any case desperate for cash, have dropped old policies unfavorable to foreign ownership. But it also reflects the perception of many multinational firms that they can now buy Asian companies and assets at fire-sale prices.

A similar, though probably less marked, boom in inward direct investment took place in Latin America, especially Mexico, during 1995; so we can, at least preliminarily, regard the nexus of crises, fire sales, and surging

Paul Krugman is the Ford International Professor of Economics at the Massachusetts Institute of Technology and a research associate of the National Bureau of Economic Research.

foreign direct investment (FDI) as an empirical regularity. As such, it raises several interesting questions:

1. Why should direct investment surge at a time when foreign capital in general is fleeing a country? What does this tell us about the nature of such crises?

2. Is the transfer of control that is associated with foreign ownership appropriate under these circumstances? That is, loosely speaking, are foreign corporations taking over control of domestic enterprises because they have special competence, and can therefore run them better, or simply because they have cash and the locals do not?

3. Does the fire sale of domestic firms and their assets represent a burden to the afflicted countries, over and above the cost of the crisis itself? (This question is likely to be raised with considerable force if the nationalistic backlash in Asia, which is clearly present although so far still surprisingly muted, becomes a more important aspect of the situation. "We must realize the great danger facing our country," Malaysia's Prime Minister Mahathir has already warned. "If we are not careful we will be recolonized.") Or is the ability to sell firms to foreigners, on the contrary, a mitigating factor in the crisis?

These are all, I believe, relatively novel questions. As already noted, the phenomenon of "fire-sale FDI" was indeed present in earlier crises; but it has become far more prominent this time because of the scale of the Asian crisis, the extraordinary collapse of asset values, and—perhaps most important—the abruptness of our reevaluation of an economic and corporate system that before the crisis was widely regarded as superior to that of the West. Moreover, the Asian crisis—to a far greater extent than the Latin crisis of 1995—has led to the creation of a set of "new wave" crisis models that seem better suited to the discussion of direct investment than the traditional currency crisis literature.

This paper, then, has three purposes. The first is simply to draw attention to the phenomenon of fire-sale FDI and to stimulate discussion of what is likely to become a major economic and political issue in the coming years. The second is to indicate, in a preliminary way, how this phenomenon might emerge in the context of alternative crisis models. The third is to examine the welfare implications of crisis-induced sales of domestic assets to foreign firms, and in particular to ask how those implications depend on our diagnosis of the crisis itself.

2.1 The Fire Sale: What Is the Evidence?

At the time of this writing, hard statistical evidence of a surge in FDI into Asia was not yet available. However, even a quick search of news databases turns up a plethora of anecdotes about foreign purchases of

Asian firms—actual, impending, or potential—especially in South Korea. Titles of recent articles in the financial press include "Korean Companies Are Looking Ripe to Foreign Buyers" (*New York Times,* 27 December 1997), "Some U.S. Companies See Fire Sale in South Korean Crisis" (*Los Angeles Times,* 25 January 1998), "Some Companies Jump into Asia's Fire Sale with Both Feet" (ouch!) (*Chicago Tribune,* 18 January 1998), and "While Some Count Their Losses in Asia, Coca-Cola's Chairman Sees Opportunity" (*Wall Street Journal,* 6 February 1998). The latter article described Coke's buyout of its Korean bottling partner, as well as its increased stake in its Thai operations. Other reported deals in prospect or under negotiation included the following:

General Motors was reported in January 1998 to be considering buying stakes in South Korean manufacturers of both automobiles and parts, while Ford was reported to be planning to increase its stake in Kia Motors.

Seoul Bank and Korea First Bank were supposedly likely to be auctioned off to foreign bidders.

Procter & Gamble purchased a majority share of Ssanyong Paper Co., a producer of sanitary napkins, diapers, and kitchen towels.

Royal Dutch Shell was negotiating to buy Hanwha Group's oil refining company; the group had already sold its half of a joint venture in chemicals to the German company BASF.

My favorite: "Michael Jackson is getting into the action, negotiating to acquire a ski resort from its owner, a bankrupt Korean underwear maker."

In addition to being entertaining, lists like this one serve to demonstrate an important point about the new surge of acquisitions: It is very widely spread across industries. It is one thing for U.S. financial service companies to be buying up Asian counterparts; this is an area in which the United States has long been perceived to hold a substantial technological and managerial advantage, and has indeed been a focus of U.S. demands for liberalized trade and investment for precisely that reason. Until recently, however, few would have argued that U.S. firms held a comparable advantage across the board, in areas as diverse as auto manufacturing and paper products. This indicates clearly that the source of the investment surge must lie in a change in conditions that affect all industries, namely the financial situation.

In a proximate sense there is, of course, no mystery about that change in conditions. In 1997 South Korea's currency lost half its value against the dollar, and its stock market lost 40 percent of its value in domestic currency. Thus the price of South Korean corporations to foreign buyers in effect fell by 70 percent, in some cases producing what appeared to be spectacular bargains (Korean Air, with a fleet of more than one hundred jets, had a market capitalization at the end of 1997 of $240 million, roughly the price of two Boeing 747s—although any buyer would also have acquired its $5 billion debt). Moreover, heavily indebted corporations, facing a credit crunch, were desperate to sell off factories and subsidiaries to raise cash.

The more difficult question, however, is to explain why the prices of assets should have fallen so much, so suddenly—which comes down to the question of how to explain the crisis itself. As we will see, our assessment of the apparent surge in FDI depends in some ways on our model of the crisis.

The next step is therefore to set out two alternative (though not necessarily mutually exclusive) models of the Asian financial crisis; once we have these models under our belt we can try to see what they say about FDI.

2.2   Modeling the Crisis I: Moral Hazard and Asset Deflation

One thing that quickly became apparent in the Asian crisis was that the depth and scope of the calamity put it outside the range of what could be explained by traditional speculative-attack models—whether of the "first-generation" type developed in the late 1970s and early 1980s (Krugman 1979; Flood and Garber 1984) or the "second-generation" type that became popular after the European currency attacks of 1992 (Obstfeld 1994). A heavy majority of the theoretical efforts to make sense of the crisis focus on the role of financial intermediaries; indeed, many of us believe that as a first cut it may actually be useful to ignore exchange rates and monetary aspects entirely, focusing on the demand for and pricing of real assets.

Within this agreed-on focus on the financial system, much of the recent discussion of the Asian crisis has clustered around an approach that stresses the role of implicit guarantees in producing moral hazard, of moral hazard in producing overborrowing, and then of the implosion of the unsound financial system thus created, producing a self-reinforcing collapse of asset values. The moral hazard–overborrowing view was emphasized in a series of initially underappreciated papers by McKinnon and Pill (especially McKinnon and Pill 1996). My own simplified exposition of how moral hazard can create overpricing of assets, and how an endogenous policy regime—in which implicit guarantees are maintained only as long as they do not prove too expensive—can cause self-fulfilling crisis (Krugman 1998a, 1998b), seems for the moment at least to have provided the seed around which opinion has crystallized. As we will see, there are other possible models that are by no means out of the running. However, it seems appropriate to begin with this canonical-model-of-the-minute, since it does offer one way to make sense of fire-sale FDI.

Here is how the story goes: The problem began with financial intermediaries—institutions whose liabilities were perceived as having an implicit government guarantee, but which were essentially unregulated and therefore subject to severe moral hazard problems. The excessive risky lending of these institutions created inflation—not of goods but of asset prices. The overpricing of assets was sustained in part by a sort of circular process, in which the proliferation of risky lending drove up the prices of risky assets, making the financial condition of the intermediaries seem sounder than it was.

And then the bubble burst. The mechanism of crisis, I suggest, involved that same circular process in reverse: Falling asset prices made the insolvency of intermediaries visible, forcing them to cease operations, leading to further asset deflation. This circularity can explain both the remarkable severity of the crisis and the apparent vulnerability of the Asian economies to self-fulfilling crisis, which in turn helps us understand the phenomenon of contagion between economies with few visible economic links.

The story can be illustrated using a highly simplified example, in which there exists a class of owners of financial intermediaries ("ministers' nephews") who are able to borrow money at the safe interest rate—because lenders perceive them as being backed by an implicit government guarantee—and invest that money in risky assets. For the sake of simplicity, the moral hazard involved in this situation is pushed to an extreme by assuming that (1) the owners of intermediaries are not obliged to put any of their own capital at risk, and (2) there are many ministers' nephews competing to buy risky assets.

In such a worst-case scenario for moral hazard, the owner of an intermediary will view investing in an asset as profitable if there is *any* state of nature in which that asset yields a return greater than the safe interest rate. At the same time, competition among intermediaries will eliminate any economic profits. The result must therefore be that the prices of assets are driven to their "Pangloss values": what they would be worth based not on the expected outcome but on what would happen if we lived in the best of all possible worlds.

To see the implications of this setup, consider first a one-stage game in which intermediaries initially compete to buy an asset with uncertain future payoff—call it land—and then learn what that payoff is. In particular, consider land that may yield a present value of future rent of either 100 (with probability 1/3) or 25 (with probability 2/3). In the absence of moral hazard, risk-neutral investors would be willing to pay a price of 50, the expected value of the land. In the extreme moral hazard regime we have described, however, each minister's nephew will realize a profit in the favorable state of nature as long as the price is less than 100, and will simply walk away from the intermediary if the state of nature is unfavorable. So competition among the nephews will drive the price to its Pangloss value of 100.

Next consider a two-stage game. In period 1 land is bought. In period

2 initial rents are revealed and land may be resold. Finally, in period 3, a second round of rents are revealed. It simplifies matters, without changing the substance, if we suppose both that rents are identically independently distributed (iid) (specifically 25 with probability 2/3, 100 with probability 1/3) and that the safe interest rate is zero.

In an undistorted economy we can solve backward for the price. The expected rent in period 3, and therefore the price of land purchased at the end of period 2, is 50. The expected return on land purchased in period 1 is therefore the expected rent in period 2 (50) plus the expected price at which it can be sold (also 50), for a first-period price of 100. This is also, of course, the total expected rent over the two periods. (In this example, the price of land declines over time, from 100 to 50, even in the undistorted case. This is merely an artifact of the finite horizon and should simply be regarded as a baseline.)

Now suppose that intermediaries are in a position to borrow with guarantees. Again working backward, at the end of period 2 they will be willing to pay the Pangloss value of third-period rent, 100. In period 1 they will be willing to pay the most they could hope to realize from a piece of land: the Pangloss rent in period 2 plus the Pangloss price of land at the end of that period. So the price of land with intermediation will be 200 in period 1—again, twice the undistorted price.

Our next step is to allow for the possibility of changes in the financial regime. Let us continue to focus on our three-period economy, with random rents on land in periods 2 and 3. And let us also continue to assume that in the first period competition among intermediaries with guaranteed liabilities causes asset prices to be determined by Pangloss rather than expected returns. However, let us now introduce the possibility that this regime may not last—that liabilities carried over from period 2 to period 3 might *not* be guaranteed.

As a first step, let us simply posit that the regime change is exogenous, that from the point of view of investors there is simply some probability p that the government will credibly announce during period two that henceforth creditors of intermediaries are on their own. (Perhaps this reflects the election of a reformist government that is no longer prepared to tolerate "crony capitalism"; or perhaps the end of moral hazard is imposed by the IMF.)

Again, we work backward, and consider the price of land in the second period. If liabilities of intermediaries are not guaranteed, then nobody will lend to them (the moral hazard will remain, but its burden would now fall on investors rather than on the government). So intermediation will collapse and the price of land will reflect only its expected return of 50. On the other hand, if intermediaries are guaranteed, the price will still be 100.

What about the price of land in the first period? Investors now face two sources of uncertainty: They do not know whether the rent in the second period will be high or low, and they do not know whether the price of land in the second period will reflect expected values or Pangloss values. As long as there is competition among intermediaries in the first period, however, the price of land will once again be driven to a level that reflects the most favorable possible outcome: rents of 100 and a price of 100. So even though this is now a multiperiod world in which everyone knows that disintermediation and a decline in asset prices is possible, current asset prices are still set as if that possibility does not exist.

Finally, let us ask what happens when the change in regime is endogenous. In reality, of course, throughout Asia's arc of crisis there has indeed been a major change in financial regime. Finance companies have been closed; banks have been forced to curtail risky lending at best and close their doors at worst. Even if the IMF were not insisting on financial house-cleaning as a condition for aid, the days of cheerful implicit guarantees and easy lending for risky investment are clearly over for some time to come. But what provoked this change of regime? Not an exogenous change in economic philosophy. Rather, financial intermediaries have been curtailed *precisely because they were seen to have lost a lot of money.*

This suggests that a more or less realistic way to model the determination of implicit guarantees is to suppose that they are available only until they have had to be honored (or more generally until honoring them has turned out to be sufficiently expensive—the criterion used in Krugman 1998b). In the context of our three-period example, this criterion can be stated alternatively as the proposition that creditors of financial intermediaries will be bailed out precisely once.

To see what this means, first suppose that rents in period 2 are disappointing—25, not 100. Given the structure of our model, in the absence of intermediaries this should have no effect on the price of land at the end of the second period, since it does not change the probability distribution of future rents. But a less-than-panglossian rent in period 2 means that creditors of intermediaries need to be bailed out in that period, and therefore that future creditors can no longer expect the same. So the intermediaries collapse, and the price of land drops from 100 to the expected rent of 50.

Notice that this means that there is a magnification effect on the losses of the intermediaries established in the first period. The "real" news about the economy is that rents in period 2 were 25, not the hoped-for 100. But land bought for 200 will now yield only 25 in rents plus 50 in resale value, a loss of 125 rather than merely 75. The magnification effect is caused, of course, by the circular logic of disintermediation: The prospective end to intermediation, driven by the losses of the existing institutions, reduces asset prices and therefore magnifies those losses.

And now we come to the possibility of multiple equilibria. Suppose that in fact intermediaries have been lucky and that second-period rents do turn out to be 100. Now if everyone then expects that the government will continue to guarantee intermediaries in the future, the land price at the end of the second period will also be 100. In that case no bailout will be needed; and so the government guarantee for intermediation will in fact continue.

But suppose, on the other hand, that despite the high rents in the second period potential creditors become convinced that there will be no guarantee on newly incurred liabilities of intermediaries. Then they will not be able to attract funds, and the price of land in the second period will be only 50. That means, however, that intermediaries that borrowed money in the first period based on Pangloss values, including the Pangloss value of 100 for land sales, will require a bailout—and since the government's willingness to provide for bailouts is now exhausted, investors' pessimism is justified.

In short, our stylized little model appears to generate a story about self-fulfilling financial crises, in which plunging asset prices undermine banks, and the collapse of the banks in turn ratifies the drop in asset prices. But it is not the only such story.

2.3   Modeling the Crisis II: Disintermediation and Liquidation

Even as the conventional wisdom has appeared to crystallize around the view that moral hazard and the resulting asset price inflation created the preconditions for the Asian crisis, some observers have disagreed. Recently Radelet and Sachs (2000, 149) have argued that "the East Asian crisis resulted from vulnerability to financial panic . . . , combined with a series of policy missteps and accidents that triggered the panic. Since we view the crisis as a case of multiple equilibria, our hypothesis is that the worst of the crisis could have been largely avoided with relatively moderate adjustments. . . ." In effect, they argue that the precrisis asset values were more or less reasonable, and that it is the current deflated values that are an aberration—obviously an important point for assessing fire-sale FDI.

What kind of model could make sense of this view? The main contender is a "bank run" model along the lines of the classic paper by Diamond and Dybvig (1983). Such models, like the moral hazard model, attribute crisis to the collapse of financial intermediaries. However, financial intermediaries are now seen as essentially benign institutions, which reconcile the need for long-term commitment of capital to projects without short-term payoffs with the desire of individual investors to be able to withdraw funds on demand. The problem with such intermediaries, according to the model, is that they are vulnerable to self-fulfilling investor panics: If investors believe that sufficiently many other investors will try to cash in early, they will follow suit—and in so doing force destructive early liquidation of real investments.

In this section I offer a simplified exposition of a Diamond-Dybvig model. It is a highly abstract example, substantially harder to map into real-world developments than the simple Pangloss-collapse model of the previous section, but it does give us at least a first pass at the alternative view.

As in the crisis model above, we consider a three-period world. (Three periods is the minimum for financial crises, which must involve an initial investment and then something going wrong with expectations rather than or as well as actual earnings. While three-period models may seem artificial—why not an infinite horizon?—my own experience, in which the infinite-horizon Krugman 1998b actually preceded the finite-horizon Krugman 1998a, suggests that for exploratory theorizing simplicity wins out over the marginal gain in realism.) In this case, however, there are real investment opportunities of two kinds. Investors can put their wealth into a short-term asset—say, dollar treasury bills—that yields a known rate of return r. Or they can back investment projects that yield a higher rate of return, say π, but that take two periods to mature. That is, one of these projects takes one unit of initial capital and transforms it into $(1 + \pi)^2$ units of output in period 3, where $\pi > r$.

Crucially, we assume that for some reason it is *not* possible to sell a halfway-completed project to some other investor who will finish it. One can imagine a variety of reasons for this—perhaps some kind of lemons problem—but for the purposes of this model we simply take the nonmarketability as a given. Thus an investor who decides to liquidate a long-term asset in period 2 must actually scrap the real investment, realizing only a liquidation value v that we assume less than $1 + r$.

The need for financial intermediaries is created, following Diamond and Dybvig, by the need of individuals for liquidity. Each individual starts with one unit of capital but does not know when he will want to consume: Only after investing does he discover whether he wants to consume in period 2 or in period 3. This creates a dilemma: An individual who invests in a long-term project, then discovers a need for short-term consumption, is stuck with only the liquidation value. On the other hand, an individual who invests in the safe asset, then discovers that his consumption will take place in period 3, has forgone an opportunity to achieve a higher standard of living.

Figure 2.1 illustrates the dilemma of an individual investor in state space, with consumption in period 2 (if he turns out to be a period-2 consumer) on the horizontal axis, consumption in period 3 (if he turns out to be a period-3 consumer) on the vertical. If he invests only in the short-term asset, he will have consumption of $1 + r$ if he turns out to be a period-2 consumer, $(1 + r)^2$ (because he must then reinvest his capital in the short term) if he turns out to be a period-3 consumer. On the other hand, if he invests only in the long-term asset, he will receive only v if he

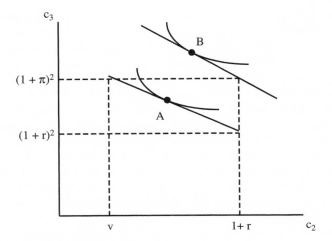

Fig. 2.1   The Diamond-Dybvig story

must consume in period 2, but $(1 + \pi)^2$ if he consumes in period 3. And he can, of course, choose any convex combination of the two.

But now suppose that there is a financial intermediary that pools the capital of a large number of individuals, investing some in the short-term and some in the long-term asset. Ignoring for a moment the possibility of a bank run, such an intermediary can in effect exploit the law of large numbers to allow each investor to withdraw money at will, while still having a predictable aggregate withdrawal in period 2. To see the advantage of this, suppose that the intermediary were to allow each contributor of capital to withdraw $1 + r$ in period 2, and suppose that the intermediary knows that a fraction p of the population will turn out to be period-2 consumers. Then all the intermediary needs to do is put a fraction p of the funds it receives into the short-term asset, $1 - p$ into the long-term asset; then each investor will expect to receive $1 + r$ if he consumes in period 2, $(1 + \pi)^2$ if he consumes in period 3—dominating the range of possibilities available without the intermediary. In general, of course, investors will choose some other point on the budget constraint passing through that point, so that they will do even better.

So far so good. But such an intermediary is, as Diamond and Dybvig pointed out, potentially subject to a bank run. In our case this possibility arises because the liquidation value v is less than the promised payout to early withdrawers. The point is straightforward. Suppose that for some reason—it does not matter what that reason is—investors who would ordinarily not have withdrawn their funds become convinced that many other such investors will attempt to withdraw *their* funds. Should investors who plan to consume in period 3 nonetheless withdraw funds in period 2, the intermediary will not have enough of the safe asset and will therefore have to liquidate projects in midstream; and since the liquidation value is less than the promised payout, not all investors will in fact be able to withdraw their funds. The rumor of such a run will therefore lead to a rush to withdraw funds by investors anxious not to be last in line. (Of course, in principle the possibility of a run should be taken into account in the initial investments and offers by the intermediary; one can justify the approach here by supposing that such a run is perceived as a very unlikely event.)

As in the previous model, this gives us a story about a crisis that can be sparked merely by self-fulfilling expectations. In the moral hazard model, however, the precrisis state of affairs is fundamentally unsustainable; in effect, the asset market is in a "metastable" state, like a sandpile with a "supercritical" slope, and any small shock causes an avalanche—a slump in asset values *toward* their appropriate level. In the bank-run model, the precrisis state is reasonable and capable of being sustained, but is undermined by an unnecessary panic—which produces real costs due to the premature interruption of productive activities.

Both views can be given some support from anecdotal evidence, as argued below. But let us turn next to the implications of the two views for FDI.

2.4   The Role of FDI

As Kindleberger (1969) pointed out long ago, FDI is essentially about transfer of control rather than movement of capital per se. Indeed, a quick look even at balance-of-payments measures of FDI for emerging market economies reveals that there is very little relationship between overall capital flows and FDI. Figures 2.2 and 2.3 show overall capital inflows and inward FDI for Mexico and Argentina from 1990 to 1996; even though such balance-of-payments numbers tend to confuse internal capital transfers within firms (which behave like portfolio capital) with true changes in

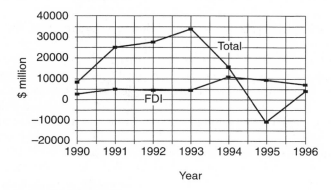

Fig. 2.2   Mexican capital inflows

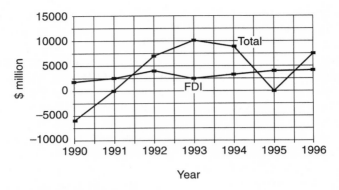

Fig. 2.3   **Argentine capital inflows**

control, there is still a striking lack of correlation—or perhaps even an inverse correlation—between overall capital inflow and FDI.

Kindleberger's discussion suggested that in order to think about FDI we must therefore not ask why capital might flow into a country, but rather why some particular asset would be worth more under foreign than under domestic control. This in turn could reflect either higher expected earnings under foreign control, or a lower foreign cost of capital and hence a higher valuation on given earnings. The interesting point is that this dichotomy between two possible reasons for foreign ownership neatly matches our two different stories about financial crisis.

Consider first the moral hazard view. The only reason for foreign ownership, in a pure model of that sort, would be that foreign firms could manage the assets better than domestic rivals, and therefore extract higher rents. Suppose, for example, that under foreign owners a given piece of land would yield 20 percent more than under domestic management. Then land would yield 120 in the good state, 30 in the bad, for an expected value of 60. Absent moral hazard, foreigners would outbid domestic investors for the physical assets.

But if domestic firms can borrow with implicit guarantees, they will be willing to pay higher prices than foreign owners despite their lower expected returns. As a result, foreign firms will be crowded out of the domestic market. (In terms of the balance of payments, this might well mean that domestic firms raise capital directly or indirectly by borrowing abroad.)

The fire-sale FDI story is now clear. Suppose that in period 2 there is a collapse of the Pangloss regime, either because of actual bad news or because of self-fulfilling expectations. Then the prices that domestic firms are willing to pay for assets will drop—in our case from 100 to 50—while foreign firms will still be willing to pay 60. So the result will be a transfer of ownership to the more efficient foreign firms. In a pure moral hazard version of the crisis, then, the drop in asset values is basically appropriate, and the transfer of ownership is an efficient move from the world's point of view: Assets are being placed under the control of those who can use them best.

If we take a financial panic point of view, matters look quite different. Suppose that foreign firms, unlike domestic investors during a panic, are not liquidity constrained; they can borrow and lend at the safe rate r throughout. But they are less efficient at running domestic investment projects than domestic firms (which must be the case here, otherwise they would have made the investments in the first place). In the absence of a crisis the foreign firms will not get involved. But once there is a crisis, any foreign firm that can take over a project in midstream and do sufficiently well to earn a final return greater than $v(1 + r)$—that is, any firm that is not liquidity constrained and can earn more than the liquidation value by keeping the project in existence—will be in a position to buy the project from the crisis-stricken domestic intermediary. In this case there will truly be a fire sale. And such fire sales will typically transfer ownership to a foreign firm that is *less* efficient than the domestic firm but that is now able to outbid domestic residents because of its superior cash position.

Thus our two alternative crisis stories seem to have opposite implications for the efficiency consequences of fire-sale FDI. If the drop in asset values really reflects the collapse of a moral-hazard-driven bubble, the reallocation of control is putting assets into the "right" hands; if it reflects an essentially arbitrary run on domestic intermediaries, it puts assets into the "wrong" hands.

Before we make too much of this distinction, however, we should notice that in either case the presence of foreign buyers will limit the actual fall in asset prices. In the moral hazard case, land falls from 100 to 60, not 50, which means that the losses to domestic investors (and taxpayers) are less than they would have been if foreign acquisitions had been blocked. In the financial panic case, the willingness of foreign investors to buy half-completed projects means that the costs of liquidation are avoided, which is necessarily a gain that more than offsets the loss from the transfer into less efficient hands.

Finally, we should note a final point: The availability of potential foreign buyers may in itself be a stabilizing factor. Suppose that we take the pure financial panic model, but add a large number of potential foreign buyers who could complete a project with a return of at least $d(1 + r)$—that is, who would be willing to pay a price high enough to pay off all investors, even if everyone decided to withdraw funds early. In that case investors, knowing that they had nothing to lose by failing to join in a run on the intermediary, would not in fact withdraw their funds unless they needed to consume in period 2, which means that the possibility of a bank run would be eliminated. Or to put it a bit differently, the presence of potential foreign buyers would provide sufficient liquidity to make a liquidity crisis impossible. This suggests an unconventional additional payoff to opening one's economy to foreign direct investment: Quite aside from any transfers of technology, managerial skills and so on, the mere potential for FDI may act as a stabilizer against the risk of domestic financial panics.

In any case, our analysis of both models seems to indicate that whether or not foreign investors are getting bargains—whether asset prices have fallen because they were initially overpriced or because they are now underpriced—given that a crisis *has* occurred, the "fire sale" of domestic companies is currently in the interest of the afflicted countries. It remains interesting, however, to ask which of these stories we believe to be closer to the truth.

2.5   What Kind of Fire Sale?

As long as we view the Asian crisis as a matter of collapsing financial intermediaries, it is easy to explain why that crisis should be accompanied by the sale of domestic assets to foreign firms. However, we have also seen that the efficiency implications of those sales—whether assets are being sold into or out of the "right" hands—depends on whether asset values are slumping toward or away from their appropriate levels.

What evidence do we have on the nature of the crisis? It seems hard to deny that there was a very significant moral hazard issue on the eve of the crisis. The role of "finance companies" in Thailand fits the "minister's nephew" story almost perfectly; in Indonesia many dubious investments (including the ambitious plans of a taxi company, which caused the spectacular failure of Hong Kong's Peregrine) involved members of the president's family. In South Korea, all accounts suggest that the *chaebol* were engaged in reckless, ill-conceived expansion plans—with the industrial groups moving into businesses far from their core competencies, and in many cases overseas ventures that seemed foolhardy even at the time— that would surely have come to grief even without the speculative attack. Indeed, a series of *chaebol* bankruptcies took place even before the onset of speculation against the currency.

To some extent the "overborrowing syndrome" (as McKinnon and Pill [1996] call it) shows up in balance of payments statistics. Figure 2.4 shows total capital flows into South Korea, inward direct investment, and *outward* direct investment. The striking points are both the very low level of inward investment given the size of overall inflow and the remarkable position of Korea as a net direct investor abroad. Whatever the strengths of Korean management, this seems a peculiar position for a middle-income country; a parsimonious explanation of the pattern is that moral-hazard-driven lending allowed Korean firms both to crowd out potential inward investors and to pursue grandiose schemes abroad.

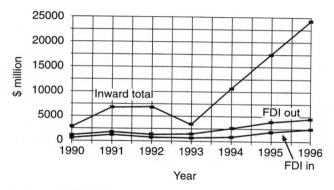

Fig. 2.4   Korean capital flows

And yet while asset prices were surely overheated on the eve of the crisis, it is also easy to make the case that the crisis itself has overshot. The market values of Asian firms do seem extraordinarily low, even given their debt burdens. Moreover, while much of the real slump in Asia may be due to demand-side effects of plunging asset values and to the effects of the high interest rates being used to defend currencies against hyperdevaluation, there is also considerable anecdotal evidence of a supply-side disruption of activity due to a breakdown of the credit system; this may be viewed as a version of the liquidation costs in our financial panic model.

So, does the foreign purchase of Asian assets represent the transfer of control to efficient owners who were previously unable to buy at a reasonable price? Or does it represent sales to inefficient owners who happen to have cash? Alas, probably some of both. What we need—surprise—is more research. Luckily, the issue of fire-sale FDI is not likely to go away anytime soon; even if the Asian crisis eases, its legacy of foreign ownership will be contentious for years to come.

References

Diamond, D., and P. Dybvig. 1983. Bank runs, deposit insurance, and liquidity. *Journal of Political Economy* 91:401–19.

Flood, R., and P. Garber. 1984. Collapsing exchange rate regimes: Some linear examples. *Journal of International Economics* 17:1–13.

Kindleberger, C. 1969. *American business abroad.* New Haven, Conn.: Yale University Press.

Krugman, P. 1979. A model of balance of payments crises. *Journal of Money, Credit, and Banking* 11:311–25.

————. 1998a. Bubble, boom, crash: Theoretical notes on Asia's crisis. Department of Economics, Massachusetts Institute of Technology. Mimeo.

————. 1998b. What happened to Asia? Department of Economics, Massachusetts Institute of Technology. Mimeo.

McKinnon, R., and H. Pill. 1996. Credible liberalizations and international capital flows: The overborrowing syndrome. In *Financial deregulation and integration in East Asia,* ed. T. Ito and A. O. Krueger. Chicago: University of Chicago Press.

Obstfeld, M. 1994. The logic of currency crises. *Cahiers Economiques et Monetaires* 43:189–213.

Radelet, S., and Sachs, J. 2000. The onset of the East Asian financial crisis. In *Currency crises,* ed. P. Krugman. Chicago: University of Chicago Press.

Comment   Aaron Tornell

Krugman's paper concerns the sale of domestic assets in the aftermath of the Asian crisis. He states that there has been a wave of such sales to foreigners and at much lower prices than in preceding months. Does this constitute a fire sale of productive assets to foreigners that will use them less efficiently? Or does it actually constitute a productivity-enhancing transaction?

The answer depends on one's view regarding the lending mechanism underlying the Asian crisis. If domestic entrepreneurs are more efficient at running such projects, and the crisis simply reflected a run against the country, then the obvious conclusion is that the forced sale of assets to foreigners is inefficient. On the other hand, if domestic agents had access to cheap credit, the creditors did not monitor the quality of the investment projects, and the domestic agents invested in socially inefficient projects, then the sale of assets to foreigners is a good thing.

Krugman connects these two views to alternative crises models. In one model, there are implicit government bailout guarantees and a group of privileged agents that can borrow at the riskless interest rate and invest in very risky projects with low expected returns. As a result, a lending boom accompanied by asset price inflation develops. Once the future arrives and the country defaults on its debt, asset prices collapse and foreigners are able to acquire the assets at fair prices and (maybe) use them more efficiently.

The second view is connected with the celebrated Diamond-Dybvig model of bank runs. In this model the crisis is caused by liquidity problems, not by insolvency. As a result, domestic residents are forced to liquidate their assets at an unfairly low price.

The question then becomes which view is empirically correct? Was the

Aaron Tornell is associate professor of economics at Harvard University.

crisis a result of a significant amount of inefficient projects that made the economies unable to repay, or was it simply the result of a run? More work would be helpful in this area.

Finally, I would like to note that the fact that asset prices collapsed is consistent with a lending boom explanation in a world where collateral is an important determinant of lending, and where future asset prices are themselves determinants of the value of collateral. Thus a more detailed analysis of the ex ante characteristics of the investment projects in the precrisis years would be very useful in identifying the true causes of the crisis.

Capital Flows to Emerging Markets
Liberalization, Overshooting, and Volatility

Philippe Bacchetta and Eric van Wincoop

3.1 Introduction

3.1.1 Capital Flows in the 1990s

The surge in capital flows toward a group of developing countries in the 1990s is remarkable more because of the nature of these flows than their quantities. Total lending to developing countries has indeed increased compared to the mid-1980s, but is not higher than in the early 1980s. Figure 3.1 shows the current account and net capital flows as a fraction of gross domestic product (GDP) for seventeen emerging market countries.[1] Net errors and omissions have been included in the capital account. This figure describes the broad trend seen over the last two decades: large current account deficits during the late seventies and early eighties, followed by a sharp decline in net capital flows to approximately zero in the mid-1980s, and subsequently another net foreign lending boom.

Philippe Bacchetta is director of Study Center Gerzensee (a foundation of Swiss National Bank) and professor of economics at the University of Lausanne. Eric van Wincoop is senior economist at the Federal Reserve Bank of New York.

Part of this paper was written while the first author was visiting the NBER in Cambridge. The authors thank Sebastian Edwards, Stijn Claessens, Holger Wolf, and John Clark for discussions at an early stage, and Laura Brookins for research assistance. The views expressed in the paper are those of the authors and do not necessarily reflect the position of the Federal Reserve Bank of New York or the Federal Reserve System.

1. This group of countries is determined by data availability and is used throughout the paper. They include most major recipients of recent capital flows, except for China. The seventeen countries are Argentina, Brazil, Chile, Colombia, India, Jordan, Korea, Malaysia, Mexico, Pakistan, Peru, the Philippines, South Africa, Sri Lanka, Thailand, Turkey, and Venezuela. The data for this and the other illustrative figures in the paper involving capital flows are from the IMF Balance of Payments Statistics.

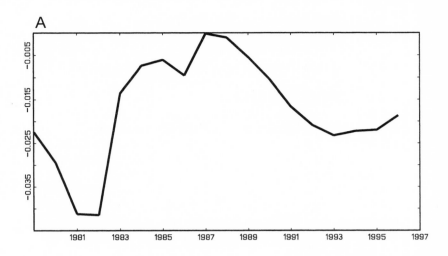

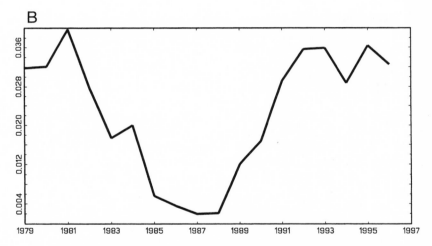

Fig. 3.1   Net current account/GDP (*A*) and net capital account/GDP (*B*) for sum of seventeen emerging markets

During the previous foreign lending boom of the late 1970s, commercial bank lending to developing country governments, firms, and banks was most important. The recent lending boom of the 1990s was quite different in nature. Instead of direct lending to developing countries, portfolio flows and foreign direct investment (FDI) became the dominant source of capital inflows. The governments of developing countries have also come to rely more on issuing debt securities than on foreign commercial bank loans. Most commercial bank lending to developing countries now goes directly to the private sector, often channeled through banks and other financial institutions. Moreover, syndicated bank loans have become far less important (see Chadha and Folkerts-Landau 1999).

These stylized facts are illustrated in figure 3.2. The figure breaks down capital flows into four components. The first is FDI, which has been by far the smoothest of all components. It rose from about 0.5 percent of GDP in the early 1980s to almost 1 percent of GDP in 1996. The second, portfolio flows, is associated with trade in equity and debt securities. Net portfolio flows rose from practically zero in the mid-1980s to almost 4 percent of GDP in 1993. These flows have been very volatile as well, dropping to less than 1 percent of GDP in 1995 as a result of the Mexican crisis, and rising again to 3 percent of GDP in 1996.

The remaining components are classified under "other investment" by the International Monetary Fund (IMF): loans, currency and deposits, and trade credits. For illustrative purposes we have broken "other investment" up into two components. The first, "nonportfolio net private flows," are net flows to the private sector other than portfolio and FDI flows. The debt crisis of the early 1980s was marked by a sharp drop in net "nonportfolio net private flows" from 3 percent of GDP in 1981 to -2 percent of GDP in 1983. Since the mid-1980s these flows have slowly increased again as confidence was restored and the old debt restructured. The second component, "nonportfolio net government flows," are net flows to the government sector other than portfolio flows, including official loans. These have clearly declined since the early 1980s. During the 1990s total net nonportfolio flows, while volatile, have been close to zero on average.

The remainder of the paper will focus on capital inflows rather than net flows. As illustrated by figure 3.3, almost all the action is associated with inflows. Outflows have been relatively steady at a level fluctuating between zero and 1 percent. Their recent increase may even be overestimated since capital flight seems to have declined (see Schineller 1997). The story of net capital flows is therefore almost entirely a story of capital inflows.

3.1.2 Liberalization, Overshooting, and Volatility

What are the factors behind the increase in lending to emerging economies? This question is crucial as its answer will determine whether the flows pouring into emerging economies can be sustained, and thus be used for their long-term development. It will also help in adopting the right policies in the shorter run. Should these flows be only temporary, they would be of little use for these countries and only create short-run policy management problems. The first empirical studies attempting to uncover the factors causing the increase in flows found that low real interest rates in developed countries play a substantial role.[2] This evidence led some

---

2. See Calvo, Leiderman, and Reinhart (1996) and Frankel and Okongwu (1996) for surveys of these earlier studies.

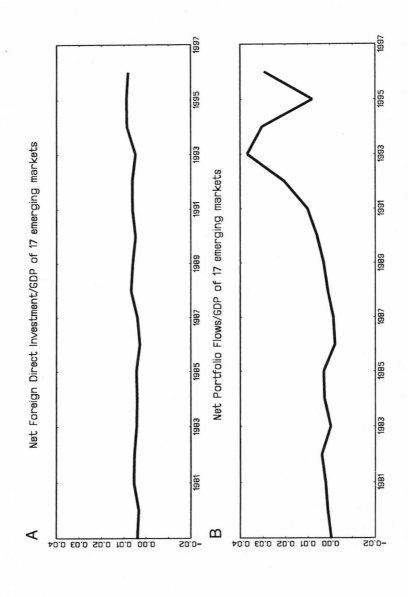

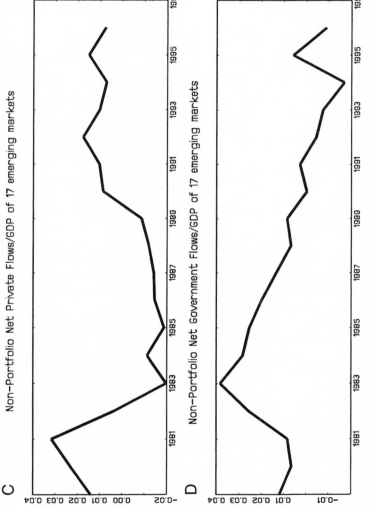

Fig. 3.2 Net foreign direct investment/GDP (*A*), net portfolio flows/GDP (*B*), nonportfolio net private flows/GDP (*C*), and nonportfolio net government flows/GDP (*D*), for seventeen emerging markets

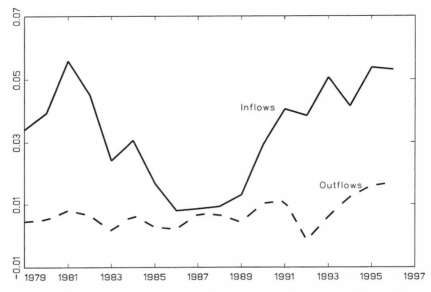

Fig. 3.3   Total capital inflows and outflows/GDP for seventeen emerging markets

analysts to conclude that the increase in inflows to emerging market countries was temporary and would decline with the subsequent increase in world interest rates. Developments in more recent years have shown this prediction to be incorrect.

Our contention is that there is one fundamental factor behind the increase in capital inflows to some developing countries: the wave of financial liberalization and structural reforms undertaken in recent years in emerging as well as industrialized countries. The changes in emerging market countries include the removal of capital controls, the liberalization of the domestic financial system, trade liberalization, macroeconomic stabilization, and privatization. Obviously, the dates, the extent, and the pace of liberalization differ across countries. Typically, liberalization measures were adopted progressively over several years. Moreover, most countries only liberalized partially. For example, Korea kept many restrictions in financial markets. Its partial liberalization measures, however, led to a surge in borrowing by domestic banks and, to a lesser extent, in some categories of portfolio flows.

Nevertheless, there is a clear trend toward liberalization in the 1990s. For example, an indication of capital account liberalization can be found by using the capital controls index computed by Bartolini and Drazen (1997) and based on the IMF Exchange Arrangements and Exchange Re-

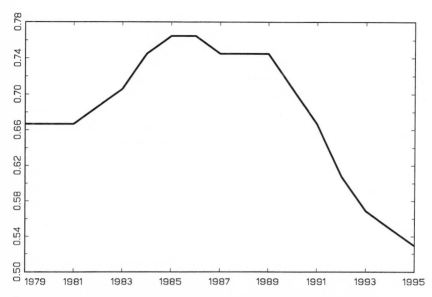

Fig. 3.4   **Average capital controls index for seventeen emerging markets**

strictions.[3] Figure 3.4 shows the average of this index for the seventeen emerging economies we consider. The degree of capital controls increased in the early 1980s only to decline dramatically in the 1990s. The profile of the capital controls index is strikingly similar to net lending depicted in figure 3.1.

It is also useful to put developments in emerging markets into perspective against the background of increased integration of industrialized countries. During the 1980s and 1990s we have seen a substantial increase in equity and bond flows among industrialized countries. This process, known as "securitization," is a result of domestic and international financial deregulation, financial innovation, and technological advances in communication and computing.[4] Nonetheless portfolio flows to emerging markets have grown even faster. Of total FDI plus portfolio outflows from the sum of twenty-one industrialized countries, we find that 2 percent was allocated toward our seventeen emerging markets in 1986 and 1987. This increased to an average of 16 percent during the 1990s.

Although the impact of the various reforms is not yet well understood, several studies have focused on equity markets and financial liberaliza-

3. We would like to thank Leonardo Bartolini for providing the data. See Bartolini and Drazen (1997) for more details on this index.
4. For further discussion on these developments, see World Bank (1997, ch. 2).

tion.[5] In particular, Henry (2000b) analyzes a group of eleven countries (a subset of our seventeen countries) and shows empirically that stock market liberalization has a significant positive impact on private investment. In a related paper, Henry (2000a) shows that equity prices significantly increase after a stock market liberalization. He also finds, however, that other economic reforms have an impact of the same order of magnitude. More specifically he constructs indexes of four types of reforms: macroeconomic stabilization, trade liberalization, privatization, and easing of exchange controls. This evidence shows that it is necessary to consider the set of all liberalizations and reforms to understand the recent developments (see also Bekaert and Harvey 1997). In this paper we will not attempt to disentangle the various liberalizations or reforms and simply assume that they jointly increase returns and give easier access to financial markets of these countries.

The increased attractiveness of emerging markets to foreign investors obviously preconditions the potential impact of other factors. For example, external developments such as movements in world interest rates are likely to have a larger impact on these economies. Domestic economic events will also have wider consequences. Thus, capital flows potentially become more sensitive to other variables and more volatile. Moreover, since the liberalizations represent in principle a permanent change, the increase in inflows should be seen as ultimately permanent. This should allow for an easier financing of emerging countries' development.

If one adopts the view that domestic liberalizations and reforms play a central role in the recent lending boom, it is important to understand their impact in both the short and the long run. One can easily think of a series of highly relevant questions: How much foreign capital can developing countries expect to receive in the long run? When are capital inflows "too large"? Is there a risk of sharp reversal in flows? Will volatility decline over time?

Before we attempt to address these questions, it is useful to consider figures 3.5 through 3.7 as they provide some interesting insights into the discussion. Figure 3.5 compares the cumulative inflows from 1989 to 1996 of individual countries. For each country it shows its fraction of total cumulative inflows to all the seventeen emerging market countries and compares it to the country's share in the 1992 capital stock of all seventeen countries.[6] When we look at total inflows, the countries that have experienced large inflows in comparison to the relative size of their capital stock are Argentina, Thailand, Korea, and Mexico. These countries have all experienced serious recent crises associated with a sharp drop in inflows. At

---

5. Stulz (1999) provides a nice survey. See also Bekaert (1995), Bekaert and Harvey (1997), and Henry (2000a, 2000b).
6. The capital stock data is computed by updating the estimates of King and Levine (1994). See section 3.4 for more details.

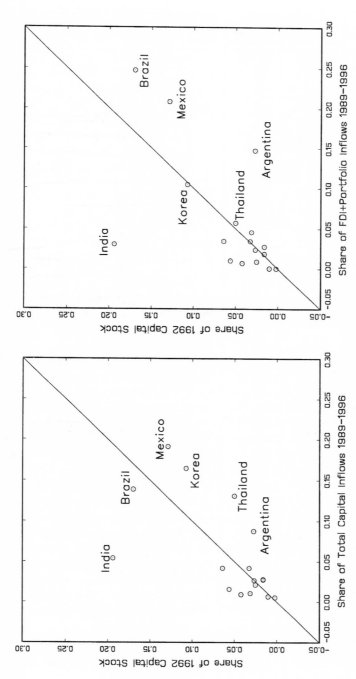

Fig. 3.5   Cumulative capital inflows (*left panel*) and share of FDI plus portfolio inflows (*right panel*) versus capital stock

Note: The share of 1992 capital stock (vertical axis) is the 1992 capital stock of a country divided by the total 1992 capital stock over all seventeen emerging markets. Similarly, the share of total capital inflows over 1989–96 is equal to total capital inflows during that period in a country divided by the sum of all those inflows over all seventeen emerging markets.

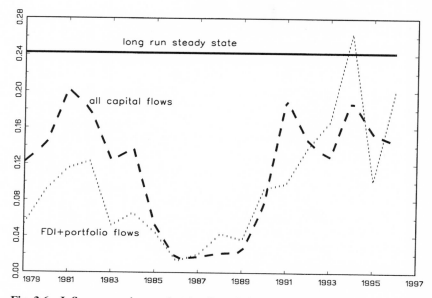

Fig. 3.6   Inflows emerging markets/outflows industrialized countries
Note: The figure shows the share of capital outflows from twenty-one industrialized countries going to the seventeen emerging markets.

the other extreme of the spectrum is India, whose capital stock is about 20 percent of the total emerging market capital stock, but whose inflows are only slightly over 5 percent of total inflows as a result of capital controls. When we only consider FDI plus portfolio flows,[7] Korea and Thailand have experienced "normal" inflows. These two countries received relatively large inflows to the banking sector, and faced reversals of these flows in 1997. It seems indeed that countries with large inflows tend to experience sharp corrections.[8]

Figure 3.6 shows the share of capital outflows from the sum of twenty-one industrialized countries that goes to the seventeen emerging economies. The straight line represents our estimate of the steady-state inflows based on a model that we develop in section 3.4. It corresponds to a scenario whereby the emerging markets are equally well integrated into world capital markets as the industrialized countries. In the 1990s emerging market countries have received somewhat less than 20 percent of total capital outflows from industrialized countries, which is similar to the peak during the previous lending boom. FDI plus portfolio flows peaked at 26 percent

7. Since most of FDI consist of equity claims above 10 percent of a firm's value, we add them to portfolio flows.
8. See Milesi-Ferretti and Razin (1997) for an econometric analysis of the determinants of net lending reversals.

of industrial country outflows during 1994, which is even slightly above our long-run steady-state estimate and far above the peak during the previous lending boom. On average, though, both portfolio and total flows during the 1990s remain below their long-run steady-state level.

Figure 3.7 presents the data in figure 3.6 on a country-by-country basis. For a particular country i, it shows the fraction of capital outflows from all other countries that is allocated to country i. Several conclusions can be drawn from these illustrations. First, inflows are highly volatile at the country level. Second, in many countries inflows overshoot our estimate of steady-state flows in some years. Third, in most cases the end of the overshooting period coincided with a crisis. This is particularly the case for Chile and Mexico in the early 1980s and for Mexico, Thailand, and Korea in the 1990s. Finally, we observe the overshooting for all different types of capital flows. Argentina, Brazil, and Mexico experienced sharp reversals of portfolio flows. Peru experienced a sharp reduction in FDI flows in 1995. Thailand and Korea faced a large drop in loans and deposits to banks and other financial institutions during 1997.

The countries that have experienced overshooting of capital inflows are also the ones where we have seen substantial capital account and financial liberalization. Argentina is an example of a country that liberalized capital flows at an early stage. Since 1989 foreigners may invest in Argentina without prior approval, on the same terms as investors who are resident in Argentina.[9] Capital flows to Argentina have been substantially above the long-run steady-state level since 1990. In Thailand major capital account liberalization measures were undertaken during 1990–92.[10] Direct investment was encouraged, new closed-end mutual funds were established, tax incentives were granted to foreign mutual funds for investment in the stock market, and authorities approved the establishment of the Bangkok International Banking Facility, which expanded short-term inflows. It is indeed during this period that we see a sharp increase in capital flows to Thailand, reaching above the long-run steady-state level. Korea has maintained significant capital account controls throughout the sample. The liberalizations have been very gradual and selective. In 1992 nonresidents were permitted limited access to the stock market and the limit on foreign direct investment was increased. In 1996 nonresidents were permitted to invest in domestic bonds through country funds. It has also become easier to attract short-term bank deposits from foreigners. Because the liberalizations were more limited and gradual, we see smaller overshooting of capital inflows than in countries that have more aggressively liberalized the capital account. Finally, there are countries such as India, Malaysia, South

---

9. See the 1990 and 1991 issues of *Exchange Arrangements and Exchange Restrictions* by the IMF.

10. See Johnston, Darbar, and Echeverria (1997) for details.

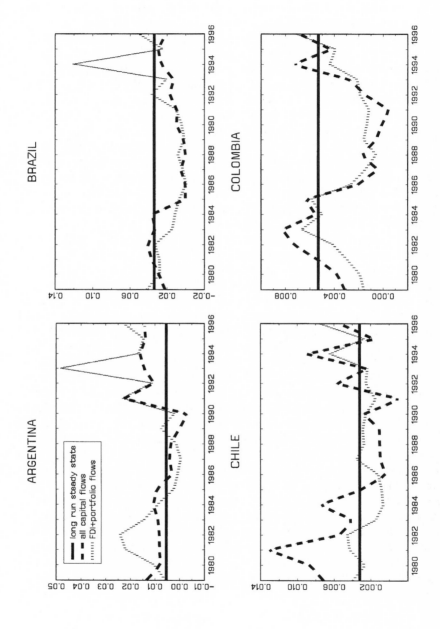

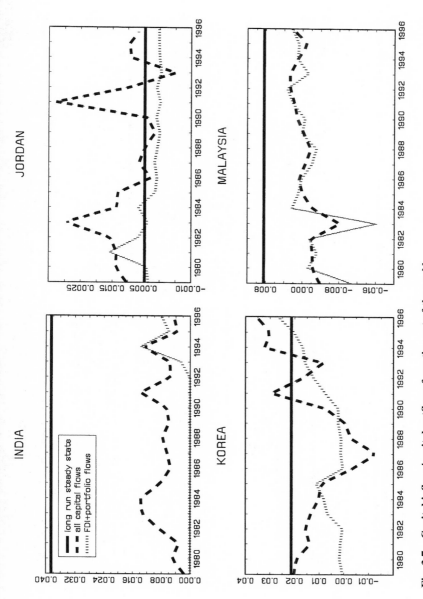

Fig. 3.7   Capital inflows/capital outflows from the rest of the world

Note: For each country, the figure shows the share of capital outflows from the rest of the world invested in that country.

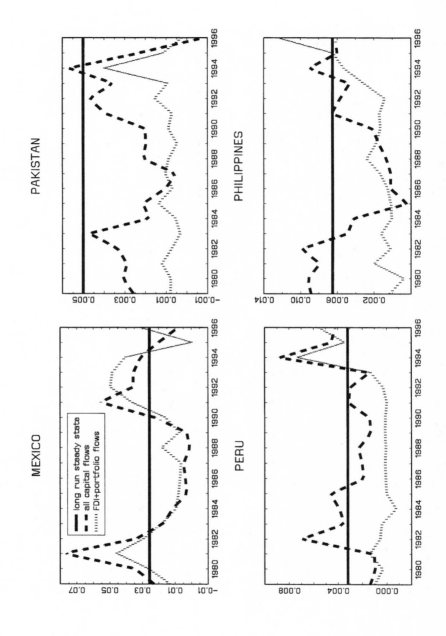

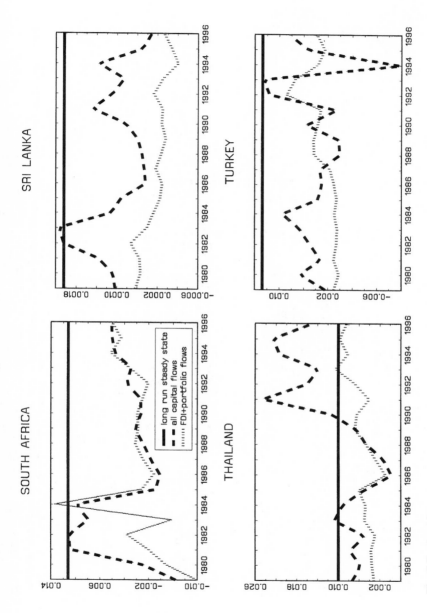

Fig. 3.7 (cont.)

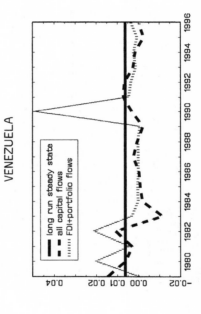

Fig. 3.7 (cont.)

Africa, and Sri Lanka whose capital markets remain largely closed to foreigners and where capital flows in the 1990s stayed significantly below the long-run steady state.

3.1.3   A Simple Framework

The above evidence shows that beside the general increase in capital flows to emerging market countries, there is a complex dynamic process. The objective of this paper is to shed some light on this process. More specifically, we address three issues: (1) What causes the overshooting? (2) Why can high volatility be associated with a period of liberalization? (3) How large can capital flows to developing countries be in the long run?

Since the impact of the liberalizations and structural reforms on the dynamics of capital flows has not been examined carefully in the previous literature, we study the implications of a simple dynamic model. We first consider a model in which the liberalization is completely deterministic. In other words, investors know when and how much emerging capital markets open up and macroeconomic reforms are adopted. This leads to portfolio adjustments and gives rise to a nonlinear relationship between capital flows and liberalization, with overshooting as a central feature. The nonlinear relationship between fundamentals and capital flows makes analysis of sustainability even more difficult than usually thought.[11]

We subsequently introduce incomplete information, from the point of view of foreign investors, about the extent of liberalization and economic reforms. Since the structural changes happening in reforming countries drastically alter the economic environment and since these countries may be new to investors, information on investment opportunities is often greatly limited. We argue that this incomplete information and the subsequent process of learning may have a substantial impact on the dynamics of capital inflows and can generate high volatility, consistent with that observed in the data. We illustrate this point by incorporating learning in our dynamic model and by simulating it.

Finally, we modify our model to examine the steady state. We compute some heroic estimates of long-run capital inflows in a world where emerging markets are "equally" integrated into world capital markets as industrialized countries.

Several explanations have been proposed in the literature to explain the volatility of capital flows, in particular in the context of the Southeast Asian crisis. These explanations rely on multiple equilibria, herd behavior, bubbles, or even irrational behavior. In contrast, our analysis shows that a simple macroeconomic model with optimal portfolio decisions can explain several important features of capital flows. Nevertheless, our focus

---

11. See Milesi-Ferretti and Razin (1996) for a discussion of sustainability.

on the impact of liberalizations is compatible with other approaches and should be seen as a complementary view.

3.2   A Model of Capital Flows

The impact of liberalizations and reforms is a complex issue that has been analyzed from different perspectives. McKinnon (1993) provides an interesting overview of many of the issues. In this paper, we argue that the dynamic implications of these structural changes are nonlinear and can explain some of the volatility of capital flows. Our approach is somewhat related to that of Bacchetta (1992), who uses an overlapping generation model to look at a joint liberalization of capital flows and of the domestic financial system. The latter is represented by a reduction in margins charged by the domestic financial system that implies both an increase in return to domestic savers and a decrease in the cost of capital for firms. It is shown that a joint liberalization generally leads to an initial period of large net capital inflows. Over time, however, net inflows decline and may be replaced by net outflows. Moreover, there is an overshooting in share prices. Nevertheless, Bacchetta's analysis only considers a small open economy, does not incorporate uncertainty, and only analyzes once-and-for-all liberalizations.

In this section, we consider a world economy with an arbitrary number of developed and emerging economies. We introduce uncertainty and the explicit portfolio decisions of investors.[12] We analyze both once-and-for-all and gradual liberalizations and study the impact on the dynamics of capital inflows. We also examine the impact of liberalization occurring simultaneously in all emerging markets. On the other hand, to keep the analysis tractable, we introduce some simplifying assumptions. In particular, we abstract from intertemporal consumption decisions[13] and assume that there are no capital outflows from emerging markets.[14] We also assume that capital can be costlessly moved across countries, although we do introduce an adjustment cost reflecting bottlenecks. Most of these assumptions can be relaxed in more complex and realistic models without altering the basic insights.

3.2.1   Basic Setup

Assume that the world is made up of N identical developed countries and J identical emerging economies. There is one capital good, which can

---

12. Calvo and Mendoza (1996, chap. 1 in this volume) also consider explicit portfolio decisions in a model of international capital flows.

13. Thus, we do not consider consumption booms that have been observed in some countries.

14. Figure 3.3 shows that this is not a bad approximation as most of the increase in the net inflows are due to gross inflows.

be invested in any country. At time 0 individuals in developed and emerging economies own respectively W^* and W capital goods. While capital goods depreciate at a constant rate δ, each year individuals receive a new endowment of capital goods equal to δW^* in developed countries and δW in emerging economies. Thus the endowment of capital goods in each country remains constant over time. The capital goods are lent to firms that produce a nonstorable consumption good in the following period. Firms have a random technology and shocks are country specific. Individuals receive the consumption good in proportion to their investment and consume it. Hence, this economy does not allow intertemporal substitution and individuals simply maximize each period the risk-adjusted return from their investment. This allows us to focus on the portfolio diversification aspect of capital flows to emerging markets.

It is assumed that emerging-country individuals invest only in domestic firms, while rich-country investors can diversify internationally. Allowing emerging-country residents to hold well-diversified portfolios does not qualitatively alter the results. It is therefore a simplifying assumption that allows us to focus on capital inflows, and, as figure 3.3 shows, it is also broadly consistent with the data. The return on investment in developed country i is $\mu_{it}^* \sim N(\overline{\mu}^*, \sigma^{*2})$. This means that with capital stock K_{it}^* production of the consumption good is $\mu_{it}^* K_{it}^*$. The return r_{it} on investment in emerging market i is composed of three elements:

$$r_{it} = \mu_{it} - \tau_{it} - c(I_{it}),$$

and the expected return is $\overline{r}_{it} = \overline{\mu} - \tau_{it} - c(I_{it})$. The variable $\mu_{it} \sim N(\overline{\mu}, \sigma^2)$ denotes the return from firms' production. We denote the correlation between returns in two countries by ρ_{EE} for two emerging economies, ρ_{DD} for two developed economies, and ρ_{ED} for a developed and an emerging economy. A tax τ_{it} is imposed on foreign investors. This tax captures the various barriers or costs to investment faced by investors (capital controls, illiquid markets, taxation, etc.). A liberalization is simply modeled by a decrease in τ_{it}.

Finally, there is an installation cost $c(I_{it})$ that is incurred when the capital stock is increased. A major element influencing capital inflows is that the liberalizing economies have difficulties absorbing large flows for various reasons. There may not be an efficient structure to channel funds to the most productive uses, in particular because of a weak financial system or thin markets.[15] Other reasons include incomplete information, lack of infrastructure or skilled labor, and various other bottlenecks. Without an installation cost the portfolio adjustment in response to a change in the tax is immediate. This would lead to an excessive, and unrealistic, realloca-

---

15. Gavin and Hausman (1996), World Bank (1997), and several others stress the role of weak domestic financial markets.

tion of resources between developed and emerging countries in response to a shock. We assume $c(I) = cI$, with c being a constant.[16]

Asset prices also fluctuate in presence of the installation cost $c(I)$. If we interpret $\mu - \tau$ as the return on installed capital, one can show that the price of installed capital in emerging market i minus the price of installed capital in industrialized countries, both at time $t - 1$, is equal to $c(I_{it})$ discounted at the implicit risk-free interest rate. An investment boom in emerging markets therefore leads to a rise in the relative price of emerging markets' capital. Asset price booms and busts associated with foreign capital inflows and outflows are indeed commonly seen in emerging markets and play a particularly important role in the Asian crisis. For simplicity, however, we do not introduce asset prices explicitly.

The basic decision variable is the proportion α_{it} that an individual in a rich country invests in country i. When the investment allocations are determined, the capital stock in emerging country i is given by

$$(1) \qquad K_{i,t} = W + N\alpha_{it}W^*,$$

while investment is given by

$$(2) \qquad I_{it} = K_{it} - (1 - \delta)K_{i,t-1}.$$

A liberalization, captured by a decline in τ_{it}, implies a change in portfolio allocations α_{it} and consequently in investment and the capital stock.

3.2.2   Portfolio Allocation

It is first necessary to derive the optimal portfolio allocation before determining the capital stock, investment, and capital inflows. Since there is no intertemporal allocation, individuals from developed countries maximize their utility each period through the optimal investment allocation across countries. Assuming an exponential utility function $U(C) = e^{-\theta C}$, and given that consumption is equal to portfolio return R_t times W^*, rich-country investors' optimization problem is

$$(3) \qquad \max_{\alpha_{jt}} E(R_t) - \frac{\gamma}{2}\text{var}(R_t),$$

where

$$R_t = \sum_{j=1}^{J}\alpha_{jt}r_{jt} + \sum_{i=J+1}^{J+N}\alpha_{it}\mu_{it}^*, \qquad \sum\alpha_{jt} = 1, \qquad \text{and } \gamma = \theta W^*.$$

---

16. We could also make the installation costs a function of I/K. But qualitatively this makes no difference for the results. We could have added an installation cost to the return in developed countries as well, but again omit it for the sake of simplicity. What is important is that the bottlenecks are greater for emerging markets than for industrialized countries.

The appendix derives the optimal investment allocations. Here we only consider the case where the correlation of returns across all countries is zero and $\sigma = \sigma^*$. The average expected return in emerging markets is denoted $\bar{r}_t = \Sigma_{j=1}^{J}\bar{r}_{jt}/J$. Then, the investment share in emerging country j is given by:

$$(4) \qquad \alpha_{jt} = \frac{1}{N + J} + \frac{\bar{r}_{jt} - \left[\dfrac{J}{N + J}\bar{r}_t + \dfrac{N}{N + J}\bar{\mu}^*\right]}{\gamma\sigma^2}.$$

The portfolio share depends on the expected excess return between emerging country j and the world return (equally weighting all countries).

The impact of a liberalization can readily be derived from equation (4). If the liberalization occurs in country j only we find:

$$\frac{\partial \alpha_j}{\partial \tau_j} = -\frac{N + J - 1}{(N + J)\gamma\sigma^2}.$$

If the liberalization occurs simultaneously in all emerging economies:

$$\frac{\partial \alpha_j}{\partial \tau_j} = -\frac{N}{(N + J)\gamma\sigma^2}.$$

Obviously the impact is larger when a country liberalizes alone because it has fewer competitors for the foreign capital. The difference increases with J. To attract a certain amount of foreign capital, the incentive to liberalize is greater the larger the number of other emerging countries that open up their markets. A larger reduction in τ is needed.

3.2.3   The Dynamics of Capital Flows

Once portfolio shares are known, capital flows can be derived. First consider the case where all countries liberalize simultaneously and have the same $\tau_{it} = \tau_t$. In that case we can write:

$$(5) \qquad \alpha_{jt} = x_0 + x_1(\bar{r}_t - \bar{\mu}^*),$$

where $x_0 = 1/(N + J)$ and $x_1 = N/[(N + J)\gamma\sigma^2]$. Using the definition of $\bar{r}_t$, the evolution of the capital stock is given by substituting equation (5) into equation (1):

$$(6) \quad K_{it} = W + N(x_0 + x_1(\bar{\mu} - \bar{\mu}^*))W^* - Nx_1W^*(\tau_t + cI_{it}).$$

Here we used the fact that all emerging countries have the same investment rate. Combining with equation (2) gives us a stable linear difference equation for the capital stock:

(7) $$K_{it} = f(\tau_t) + \frac{Nx_1W^*c}{1 + Nx_1W^*c}(1 - \delta)K_{i,t-1},$$

where

$$f(\tau_t) = \frac{N(x_0 + x_1(\overline{\mu} - \overline{\mu}^*))W^* + W - Nx_1W^*\tau_t}{1 + Nx_1W^*c}$$

is a negative function of τ_t. Since investment by domestic residents is a constant δW, capital inflows are equal to total investment minus δW. Using equation (2) this gives

(8) $$\text{Inflows}_{it} = f(\tau_t) - (1 - \delta)\frac{1}{1 + Nx_1W^*c}K_{i,t-1} - \delta W.$$

We can use these equations to determine the impact of a joint liberalization. We will also consider the case where only one country liberalizes. The equations are qualitatively similar. Assuming that the average tax rate across all emerging markets remains constant, it follows from aggregating equations (1), (2), and (4) that the aggregate capital stock, investment, and $\overline{r}_t$ remain constant. In that case, from equation (4),

(9) $$\alpha_{jt} = x_2 + x_3(\overline{r}_{it} - \overline{\mu}^*),$$

where

$$x_2 = \frac{1}{N + J} - \frac{(\overline{r}_t - \overline{\mu}_t)J}{(N + J)\gamma\sigma^2} \quad \text{and } x_3 = \frac{1}{\gamma\sigma^2}.$$

Substituting equations (9) and (2) into equation (1), the differential equation for the capital stock, and equation (8) for capital inflows, remain unchanged, with x_0, x_1, and τ_t replaced by x_2, x_3, and τ_{it}.

3.2.4 The Response to a Financial Liberalization

The dynamic impact of a liberalization can readily be derived. From equation (7) a permanent financial liberalization, as captured by a permanent decrease in the tax rate τ_{it}, leads to a gradual rise in the capital stock to a higher level since $f(\tau_t)$ increases. From equation (8) it follows that there will be an immediate rise in capital inflows, followed by a gradual decline to a higher steady-state level. Capital inflows therefore overshoot their new steady-state level after a liberalization. It can be easily verified that the overshooting is smaller, although more persistent, when the installation cost is larger. The precise dynamics of capital flows obviously changes with the form of installation costs, but even with a nonlinear cost function the qualitative results are the same.

However, examining a once-and-for-all liberalization does not appear very realistic. First, as we argue in section 3.1, it is a combination of various liberalizations and reforms that makes investment more attractive. They typically do not occur simultaneously. Second, even specific reforms are often gradual. For example, consider the stock market liberalizations that have been analyzed empirically. A useful measure of the stock market openness to foreign investors is the investability index computed by the International Finance Corporation (IFC). For each stock an investability index between 0 and 1 is computed, measuring the ease with which foreign investors can buy and sell the stock. The aggregate investability index is a weighted average of the index for each stock, with weights based on market capitalization. This index has been used in particular by Bekaert (1995) and Henry (2000a, 2000b) to measure liberalization. Figure 3.8 shows the evolution of this index for a subset of six countries.[17] While stock market liberalizations in Chile, India, and Mexico can best be characterized as once-and-for-all permanent liberalizations, those in Brazil, Pakistan, and Venezuela are more gradual.

Consequently it seems interesting to consider a gradual liberalization. The dynamic impact of such a liberalization obviously depends on its profile over time. In the next subsection we calibrate the model and numerically simulate a simple gradual liberalization.

3.2.5   Numerical Simulation

The gradual liberalization we consider is the case where the tax rate declines exponentially. We assume that τ_t decreases at a rate of 10 percent per year: $\tau_t = e^{-0.1t}\tau_0$. We set the model parameters as follows. First $\sigma = 0.05$ is the average standard deviation on a broad measure of capital return for the four industrialized countries in Baxter and Jermann (1997). Such a broad measure of capital return is not available for emerging markets. Harvey (1995) reports average returns on equity for industrial countries and emerging markets. The latter is on average 80 percent larger, so that we set $\sigma^* = 0.09$. We set $\mu = 0.07$, and $\mu^* = 0.106$ is set such that investment in emerging markets by industrialized countries is zero before the liberalization. The assumed correlations are $\rho_{EE} = 0.06$, $\rho_{ED} = 0.12$, and $\rho_{DD} = 0.35$. These are based on correlations for equity returns reported by Harvey (1995). We set $W = 1$ and $W^* = 4$. This reflects the fact that per capita capital stock in industrialized countries is on average about four times that of emerging markets.[18] We set the number of developed and emerging countries, N and J, both equal to 20. This implies that emerging markets hold 20 percent of global wealth. This corresponds closely to the share of emerging country capital stocks in the global capital stock. We set γ such that the rate of relative risk-aversion is 3 at the preliberalization

17. The other countries have either fewer observations or little change in the index.
18. This is based on the 1992 capital stock data discussed in section 3.1.

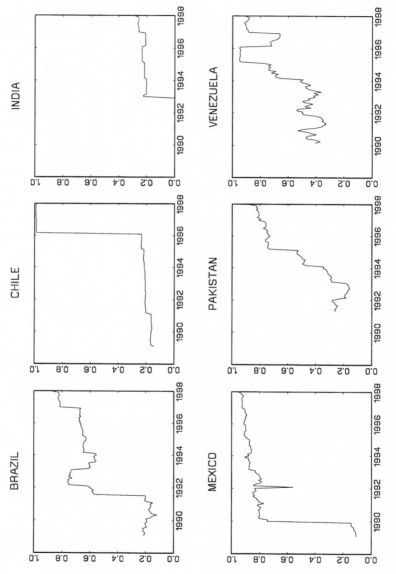

Fig. 3.8   IFC investability index

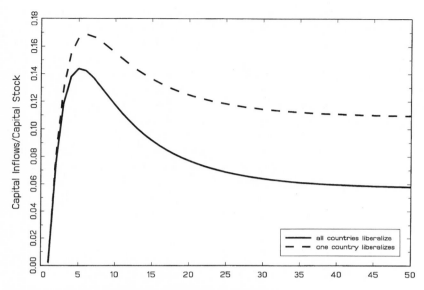

Fig. 3.9   Dynamic response to gradual liberalization

average level of industrial country consumption. The adjustment cost parameter c is set at 0.05. Finally, we set $\delta = 0.07$ to be consistent with the
depreciation rate assumed by King and Levine (1994) to compute the capital stock data we use.

Figure 3.9 shows the dynamic response of capital inflows relative to the
capital stock when the tax rate decreases exponentially at a rate of 10
percent per year, starting from a rate τ_0 of 0.05. The figure shows both the
case where only one country liberalizes and where all emerging market
countries liberalize. We clearly see an overshooting of the inflows in both
cases. The basic economic intuition is that there is a portfolio adjustment
that needs to take place once the tax rate drops. This is a stock adjustment
that requires relatively large flow adjustments in the short run. Foreign
investors buy a lot of emerging market equity in the short run to raise
exposure to that part of the world. Once most of the portfolio adjustment
has taken place, the portfolio flows decline. If the full liberalization takes
places instantaneously (permanent drop in the tax rate), inflows overshoot
immediately and then gradually fall back to their higher steady-state level.
In figure 3.9 portfolio flows rise during the first five years, after which they
gradually decline. The gradual rise of portfolio flows before they peak is
a result of the gradual liberalization. As discussed above, capital flows rise
more when only one country liberalizes. The difference is larger for the
new steady state than for the short-run response. In the short run there
are high adjustment costs, which prevent excessive overshooting.

The dynamics of capital flows presented in figure 3.9 depend on the specific profile assumed for τ_t. Other profiles obviously give different dynamics, but an overshooting is generally present. This overshooting is consistent with the data presented in figure 3.7. This result has potentially important implications. First, it shows that capital flows may be falling even when fundamentals are improving. Second, it shows that periods of large inflows and investment are likely to be followed by a downward correction.[19] This implies that periods of large inflows cannot be extrapolated. This considerably complicates policy decisions as they must take into account a potential future reversal. Edwards (chap. 7 in this volume) analyzes in detail the policy issues associated with overshooting. Third, the overshooting of capital flows will also give rise to an overshooting of asset prices because, as discussed above, the price of installed capital depends positively on the rate of investment. Asset price overshooting after a burst of capital inflows is commonly observed in emerging markets.

3.3   Incomplete Information and Learning

A crucial element in liberalization and reforms is incomplete information. Since the environment changes dramatically, investors do not have immediate full information on their new investment opportunities. The problem of incomplete information is likely to become less acute over time, however, as investors learn about their new environment. In this section we show that the presence of incomplete information can generate considerable volatility. We also argue that it can explain contagion across countries.

Incomplete information is obviously a pervasive phenomenon, but it can be far more acute in the case of liberalizing emerging economies. Foreign investors may have less information than domestic investors as these markets are new to them,[20] and there may only be incomplete information available to domestic investors and entrepreneurs. Further, there may be a large degree of uncertainty about how firms will succeed in the new environment. Bacchetta and Dellas (1997) and Fernandez and Rodrik (1991) consider examples where entrepreneurs are uncertain about their chances to succeed after a trade liberalization. Substantial liberalization and macroeconomic reforms imply a regime change. This creates an environment of uncertainty for foreign and domestic investors alike. Particularly in the beginning there is uncertainty both about the extent of the reforms and their success. In time, however, investors will learn and most of the initial uncertainty will be resolved.[21]

---

19. Notice that this is also consistent with the evidence present by Milesi-Ferretti and Razin (1997), who show empirically that high investment and large net inflows are significant in predicting reversals in net lending.

20. Frankel and Schmukler (1996) provide evidence of asymmetric information in the case of Mexico, while Coval (1995) and Brennan and Cao (1997) analyze its implications.

21. In a different context, but in a similar spirit, Lewis (1989) analyzes the process of learning about a shift in money demand.

In general there could be incomplete information about all components of total return: the underlying distribution of μ, the level of the tax τ, and the installation cost c. Although it does not matter much which of these is the source of incomplete information, we focus on uncertainty about τ. This could come from a lack of knowledge about the extent of economic reforms and liberalization, or uncertainty about the success of macroeconomic reforms. Although the government may announce that it has adopted far-reaching reforms, this may not fully convince foreign investors due to credibility problems. Given that investors only observe r_t, they cannot infer precisely the level of τ. Over time, however, investors continuously update their perception of τ by observing r_t. They find out the actual value of τ in the long run. This is similar to models of monetary policy credibility, whereby credibility is gradually established based on observed inflation rates, although there the government's policy is not always exogenous and changes with its reputation.[22]

Consider the following experiment. Assume that the tax rate in the emerging market is reduced permanently from $\tau = \bar{\tau}$ to $\tau = 0$ at time 0.[23] The government announces the reduction, but investors only give partial credibility to the announcement. Their prior is that with probability 0.5 τ has dropped to zero and with the same probability 0.5 it remains $\bar{\tau}$. Based on actual returns investors continuously update these probabilities. We introduce this feature in the model described above and assume that there is only one emerging market and one industrialized country, so $J = N = 1$.[24]

Let p_t be the probability investors attach to $\tau = 0$. At time t investors observe $x = \mu_t - \tau$. Through Bayesian learning, they update the probability that $\tau = 0$ as follows:

$$(10) \quad p_{t+1} = P(\tau = 0 | \mu_t - \tau = x) = \frac{P(\tau = 0, \mu_t - \tau = x)}{P(\mu_t - \tau = 0)}$$

$$= \frac{p_t P(\mu_t - \tau = x | \tau = 0)}{p_t P(\mu_t - \tau = x | \tau = 0) + (1 - p_t) P(\mu_t - \tau = x | \tau = \bar{\tau})}$$

$$= \frac{p_t \psi((x - \bar{\mu})/\sigma)}{p_t \psi((x - \bar{\mu})/\sigma) + (1 - p_t) \psi((x + \bar{\tau} - \bar{\mu})/\sigma)},$$

where $\psi(\cdot)$ is the density function of the $N(0,1)$ distribution.

---

22. See for example Backus and Driffill (1985a, 1985b). Persson (1988) and Rogoff (1987, 1989) provide surveys. In the context of international capital flows, Chari and Kehoe (1997) also consider a model with imperfect government credibility to explain capital flow volatility. But they rely on heterogeneity giving rise to herding. Investors decide sequentially whether to lend or not, which can give rise to informational cascades. We assume instead a simple representative agent framework, where everyone decides simultaneously how much to lend.

23. It would be far more difficult to analyze a gradual liberalization with learning.

24. Alternatively, we could examine the case where τ remains at $\bar{\tau}$ and investors give a probability of 0.5 to $\tau = 0$.

For a given probability p_t investors maximize their utility

(11) $-Ee^{-\theta C} = -Ee^{-\gamma R} = -Ee^{-\gamma(\alpha\mu+(1-\alpha)\mu^*-c\alpha I)}Ee^{\gamma\alpha\tau}$

$= -e^{-\gamma(\alpha\bar{\mu}+(1-\alpha)\bar{\mu}^*-c\alpha I)+0.5\gamma^2\,\text{var}(R)}[p_t + (1 - p_t)e^{\gamma\alpha\bar{\tau}}].$

Here we have used the fact that uncertainty about τ is independent of uncertainty about μ and μ^*. The first order condition with respect to α is

(12) $[-\gamma(\bar{\mu} - \bar{\mu}^* - cI) + 0.5\gamma^2(2\alpha\sigma^2 - 2(1 - \alpha)\sigma^{*2})](p_t + (1 - p_t)e^{\gamma\alpha\bar{\tau}})$

$+ (1 - p_t)e^{\gamma\alpha\bar{\tau}}\gamma\bar{\tau} = 0.$

Substituting

(13) $I_t = K_t - (1 - \delta)K_{t-1} = W + \alpha W^* - (1 - \delta)K_{t-1}$

into equation (12) we have a nonlinear equation in α. We solve this numerically. Equation (13) then gives us the investment rate, and therefore next period's capital stock. By subtracting δW we derive capital inflows.

An interesting feature of the model is that investors tend to pull out of a market that has faced a bad return as this signals a possibly high value of τ. Without incomplete information this is not what we would expect to happen. In that case a low return today (low value of μ) does not lead to a lower expected return tomorrow. The opposite could even be the case. During the recent Asian crisis we have seen a sharp drop in asset prices. To the extent that these prices dropped more than based on expected future dividends (the bursting of a bubble), it would lead to even higher expected returns for investors, which should lead to capital inflows. But instead we have witnessed large capital outflows. Our incomplete information story may play an important role here.

We simulate by drawing randomly from the normal distributions of μ and μ^*. After each draw the probability p_t is updated according to equation (10). Subsequently α_t and I_t are solved from equations (12) and (13). We still set $\bar{\tau} = 0.05$, $c = 0.05$, $\delta = 0.07$, $\sigma = 0.05$, $\sigma^* = 0.09$, and $\mu^* = 0.07$. We assume that $W = 20$ and $W^* = 80$, so that total wealth is still 100. The expected return on emerging market capital is set at $\mu = 0.083$, so that again investment in emerging market equity is zero before the liberalization.

Each random draw gives a different profile of capital flows. In figure 3.10 we show two random simulations. The behavior of capital flows is strikingly similar to the actual experience of various countries as shown in figure 3.7. Beyond this general impression, we can draw several conclusions from these results. First, incomplete information reduces the extent of overshooting. Without uncertainty about τ there should be an instantaneous increase in capital inflows followed by a gradual decline to the new

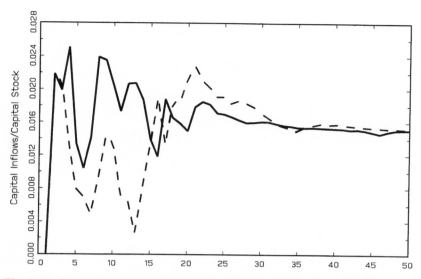

Fig. 3.10   Dynamic response to once-and-for-all liberalization with learning (two simulations)

steady-state value. In both simulations the initial increase is much smaller than it would be without uncertainty about τ. The reason is that investors are not sure in the beginning that τ has actually dropped, while in steady state they know that it has dropped to zero. Second, incomplete information can generate substantial volatility. A series of negative outcomes for r, followed by a series of positive outcomes implies huge swings in the first periods. Third, volatility declines over time as investors learn. This is reassuring for liberalizing economies as more stability ahead can be expected, as long as the other sources of uncertainty are not increasing. A fourth conclusion is that a simple model with a representative rational investor can easily explain the observed volatility, so that it is not necessary to rely on more sophisticated stories or models, such as informational cascades (see, e.g., Chari and Kehoe 1997) or multiple equilibria stories. Finally, the two simulations show that it is very easy to generate various profiles of capital flows. One should therefore not take too seriously specific simulations, including ours.

The model with incomplete information can easily be extended to generate contagion across countries.[25] Consider the same experiment as above of a partially credible decrease in τ, but assume that several emerging

25. See Chuhan, Perez-Quiros, and Popper (1996), Calvo and Reinhart (1995), or Eichengreen, Rose, and Wyplosz (1996) for some evidence on contagion. See also Agénor (1997) and Agénor and Aizenman (1997) for models consistent with the observed contagion.

countries liberalize at the same time. Moreover, assume that investors think (rightly or not) that events in one emerging country provide information about other countries. Thus, a very low return r_{it} in country i will lead to a decline in the subjective probability that $\tau_i = 0$, but it will also lead to declines in other countries. In this case we may observe a large decline in inflows to country i accompanied by declines in other countries. The extent of the declines in other countries will depend on the informational value attributed by investors to country i's return. This value will probably vary across countries. For example, a negative shock in Thailand may provide more informational value (in the eyes of the investors) about other Southeast Asian countries than a shock in Mexico.

3.4   Steady-State Capital Flows

An important question is to what extent developing countries can rely on foreign capital in the long run. Another natural question is how current capital inflows compare with their long-run values. These issues have been raised in section 3.1, where we used our estimates of long-run flows in figures 3.6 and 3.7. In this section we derive the steady-state values by considering a very simple model in the same line as the one presented in the previous sections.

By "steady state" we mean that emerging economies are perfectly integrated into international capital markets, or at least as much as industrialized countries are (defined below). This implies that, in contrast to the previous sections, there are also capital outflows from emerging market economies. Moreover, we assume no net capital flows and focus on gross capital inflows to emerging economies. First, consider a situation where all investors, of both emerging markets and industrialized countries, hold perfectly diversified portfolios. Assuming for simplicity that there is only one good, so that the real return of an asset is the same for all investors, and that there is no nontradable human capital, everyone holds the same portfolio.[26] Since the demand for assets equals supply, it follows that the fraction of each investor's portfolio allocated to a particular country is equal to the capital stock of that country relative to the world capital stock.

This benchmark of perfect diversification, however, is grossly violated in the data due to the well-known home bias. Figure 3.11 shows for four industrialized countries the fraction of their equity portfolio currently invested at home and what fraction they would have invested at home under the perfect diversification benchmark.[27] Based on the equilibrium under

26. See Bottazzi, Pesenti, and van Wincoop (1996) and Baxter and Jermann (1997) for an analysis of the effects of human capital on portfolio choice; and see Pesenti and van Wincoop (1998) and Baxter, Jermann, and King (1998) for the role of nontraded goods. Here we abstract from these complications.

27. The data are from Tesar and Werner (1997).

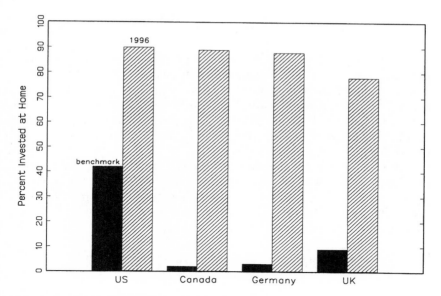

Fig. 3.11   Equity portfolio share invested at home
Note: Benchmark is the value of the domestic stock market divided by the value of the global stock market.

perfect diversification discussed above, the benchmark fraction invested at home is equal to the value of the domestic stock market divided by the value of the global stock market. It is clear that we are still very far from a world of perfect diversification. In 1996, U.S. investors allocated 90 percent of their portfolio toward domestic shares. This would have been only slightly over 40 percent under perfect diversification. British investors currently allocate 78 percent toward domestic assets, but would have invested 10 percent at home under the benchmark. The bias is even stronger for German and Canadian investors.

It is therefore necessary to take the home bias into account. Without trying to understand what drives this bias, we simply assume that a fraction ϕ of each country's capital stock is nontradable and owned by domestic investors. The remainder of their wealth is perfectly diversified. The portfolio of the "tradable" wealth is the same for all investors, so that for a country i in equilibrium

$$(14) \qquad (1 - \phi)K_i = \sum_{j=1}^{J} \alpha_i (W_j - \phi K_j).$$

Here J now refers to the total number of countries, not just emerging markets, and W_j is the wealth of country j. Since $\Sigma W_j = \Sigma K_j = K^w$ is the world capital stock, it follows that

(15)
$$\alpha_i = \frac{K_i}{K^w}.$$

So even when we allow for home bias, for the well-diversified component of portfolios we still find that the fraction invested in country i corresponds to the ratio of that country's capital stock to the world capital stock. We will focus on this ratio instead of the actual quantity of inflows as it is independent of the home bias coefficient ϕ. This is somewhat less informative, but we still have little understanding of the potential evolution of the home bias in the long run.

Now consider a particular emerging market i and the sum of claims on the rest of the world by all countries other than i. We would like to know what fraction of those claims is invested in country i. Making the additional assumption that $W_i = K_i$, which holds approximately in the data, we find that the fraction of external claims by other countries that is invested in country i equals

(16)
$$\frac{\left(1 - \dfrac{K_i}{K}\right)K_i}{\sum\limits_{j \neq 1}\left(1 - \dfrac{K_j}{K}\right)K_j}.$$

We only need a measure of the capital stock of all countries in order to compute this fraction for individual countries. We obtain this measure by extending the estimates of King and Levine (1994) for all seventeen emerging markets plus twenty-one industrialized countries.[28] We assume our "world" is made up of the sum of these thirty-eight countries.

It is hard to directly compare this to the data since for many countries, particularly the emerging markets, we do not have good data on the outstanding stocks of assets and liabilities. However, we can apply the same measure to flow data as well. If we assume, as we did in sections 3.2 and 3.3, that the rate of depreciation δ is the same for all countries, in steady state all flows are proportional to the corresponding stock, with proportionality factor δ. Therefore in steady state equation (16) should also be equal to capital inflows into country i divided by all capital outflows from countries other than i. This is shown in figure 3.7, where the horizontal line in each of the graphs is the steady state measure equation (16). Figure 3.6 shows the steady state for the sum of all emerging markets.

These estimates are clearly based on a set of strong assumptions. For

28. King and Levine (1994) estimate capital stock data until 1988 based on Summers and Heston (1991) investment data and using a perpetual inventory method. We use the same methodology and the updated Summers and Heston data (Mark 5.6) to extend the capital stock data until 1992. In a couple of countries we estimated the 1991 or 1992 investment data as they were not available.

example, we assume that all countries grow at the same rate. It would be useful to refine the analysis and extend the basic model in various directions. In any case, two conclusions arise from figures 3.6 and 3.7. First, at the aggregate level only FDI plus portfolio flows briefly rose above the steady-state level during the recent lending boom. Although the picture is perfectly consistent with the overshooting story of section 3.2, capital flows remain below the steady state. We can think of this as lowering τ, but not to zero. Many countries still have significant restrictions on capital flows. Moreover, all the liberalizations did not take place at the same time. Alternatively, there may have been uncertainty about τ as in section 3.3. Second, figure 3.7 shows that for many of the individual countries the inflows reached significantly above the steady-state level and then returned to close to that level. Examples are Argentina, Brazil, Mexico, Peru, and Thailand.

3.5 Conclusions

The recent increase in capital flows to emerging markets and its associated volatility generates difficulties for policy makers and academics alike. In this paper we hope to have contributed to a better understanding of the issues. We adopt a global perspective of capital flows, considering the whole set of industrialized and emerging countries, rather than focusing on a specific set of countries. We take the view that there has been a wave of financial liberalizations and other reforms making it much more attractive to invest in emerging markets. We show that by using a simple and rather standard model, we can easily reproduce the main features of capital inflows to emerging markets: overshooting, volatility, and contagion. The model can also account for the overshooting of asset prices. Our results show that it is not necessary to rely on irrational or herding behavior of investors to explain these features. Moreover, we provide estimates of long-run capital inflows and compare them with actual flows, which provides useful information about crisis situations.

While our analysis identifies some basic mechanisms related to capital flows, it abstracts from many other important factors. First, we need to better understand the problems associated with the absorption of the capital inflows. In this context the role of the financial sector, ignored in our model, is particularly important. Several of the issues mentioned in the debate about the Southeast Asian crisis could be incorporated in our analysis. For example, capital flow volatility may be exacerbated in presence of mechanisms leading to "overlending" by financial institutions, as in McKinnon and Pill (1997) or Dooley (1997). Another source of exacerbation would come from the role of maturity transformation of financial intermediaries as in Diamond and Dybvig (1983) (see Goldfajn and Valdés 1997 for such an approach).

Second, the capital inflows and outflows themselves generate significant turbulence in emerging market economies, affecting, among other things, asset prices, economic activity, and the exchange rate. This turbulence in turn affects capital flows. We have ignored such feedback channels in our model. For example, Aghion, Bacchetta, and Banerjee (1999) show that the interaction of capital flows and real exchange rate movements can generate considerable volatility in presence of capital markets imperfections. Finally, it would be useful to distinguish between the various types of liberalization and reform and more explicitly model the behavior of the government in this context.

Combining some of the above elements with our analysis may help elucidate why capital flow reversals are most often associated with a crisis. For example, is it due to policies that are inconsistent with a decline in inflows, such as a fixed exchange rate? Or is it due to some other fundamental characteristics linked for example to financial intermediation and lending to emerging markets firms? Finding an answer to these questions is obviously highly relevant to policymaking. Our understanding of these issues remains limited, however, and much further work should be done.

Appendix

This appendix derives the optimal investment in an emerging market based on equation (3). For convenience we omit the time subscript. With α_j the proportion of the portfolio invested in emerging market j, the total proportion invested in emerging markets is $\alpha = \Sigma_{j=1}^{J}\alpha_j$. Define the vectors $\mathbf{a}' = (\alpha_1, \alpha_2, \ldots, \alpha_J)$ and $\mathbf{r} = (r_1, r_2, \ldots, r_J)$. Then total return R can be written as

(A1) $$R = \mathbf{a}'\mathbf{r} + (1 - \alpha)\mu^*,$$

and its expectation is

$$E(R) = \mathbf{a}'\bar{\mathbf{r}} + (1 - \alpha)\bar{\mu}^*,$$

where $\bar{\mathbf{r}} = E(\mathbf{r})$. Define the following $J \times J$ variance-covariance matrix:

$$\Sigma = \begin{pmatrix} \sigma^2 & \rho_{EE}\sigma^2 & \cdots & \rho_{EE}\sigma^2 \\ \rho_{EE}\sigma^2 & \sigma^2 & & \rho_{EE}\sigma^2 \\ \cdots & & & \cdot \\ \rho_{EE}\sigma^2 & \rho_{EE}\sigma^2 & \cdots & \sigma^2 \end{pmatrix}.$$

The portfolio variance is then given by

$$\text{var}(R) = \mathbf{a}'\Sigma\mathbf{a} + (1 - \alpha)^2\sigma_D^2 + 2\alpha(1 - \alpha)\rho_{ED}\sigma\sigma^*,$$

where $\sigma_D^2 = (1/N)\sigma^{*2} + (1 - (1/N))\rho_{DD}\,\sigma^{*2}$.

Using

$$\frac{\partial \mathbf{a}'\Sigma\mathbf{a}}{\partial\alpha_i} = 2\{\alpha_i(1 - \rho_{EE}) + \rho_{EE}\alpha\}\sigma^2,$$

the first order conditions to equation (3) for all i are

$$\bar{r}_i - \bar{\mu}^* - \gamma\{\alpha_i(1 - \rho_{EE})\sigma^2 + \rho_{EE}\alpha\sigma^2 - (1 - \alpha)\sigma_D^2$$

$$+ (1 - 2\alpha)\rho_{ED}\sigma\sigma^*\} = 0.$$

Hence

(A2) $$\alpha_i = \beta_0 + \beta_1(\bar{r}_i - \bar{\mu}^*) + \beta_2\alpha,$$

where

$$\beta_0 = \frac{1}{\gamma\sigma^2(1 - \rho_{EE})},$$

$$\beta_1 = \frac{\sigma_D^2 - \rho_{ED}\sigma\sigma^*}{\sigma^2(1 - \rho_{EE})},$$

$$\beta_2 = \frac{-\sigma_D^2 + 2\rho_{ED}\sigma\sigma^* - \rho_{EE}\sigma^2}{\sigma^2(1 - \rho_{EE})}.$$

Aggregating equation (A2), we have

(A3) $$\alpha/J = x_0 + x_1(\bar{r} - \bar{\mu}^*),$$

where $x_0 = \beta_1/(1 - J\beta_2)$ and $x_1 = \beta_0/(1 - J\beta_2)$. Substituting back into equation (A2),

(A4) $$\alpha_i = x_2 + x_3(\bar{r}_i - \bar{\mu}^*),$$

where $x_2 = \beta_1 + \beta_2\alpha$ and $x_3 = \beta_0$. When the tax rate is the same across emerging markets, the differential equation for the capital stock (equation [7]) and the solution (equation [8]) for capital inflows are still the same, now using the more general expressions for x_0 and x_1. As before, when one emerging country changes its tax rate, holding the average tax rate constant, x_0, x_1, and τ_t replaced by x_2, x_3, and τ_{it}.

References

Agénor, P.-R. 1997. Borrowing risk and the tequila effect. IMF Working Paper no. WP/97/86. Washington, D.C.: International Monetary Fund.

Agénor, P.-R., and J. Aizenman. 1997. Contagion and volatility with imperfect credit markets. NBER Working Paper no. 6080. Cambridge, Mass.: National Bureau of Economic Research.

Aghion, P., P. Bacchetta, and A. Banerjee. 1999. Capital markets and the instability of open economies. CEPR Discussion Paper no. 2083. London: Centre for Economic Policy Research.

Bacchetta, P. 1992. Liberalization of capital movements and of the domestic financial system. *Economica* 59:465–74.

Bacchetta, P., and H. Dellas. 1997. Firm restructuring and the optimal speed of trade reform. *Oxford Economic Papers* 49:291–306.

Backus, D., and J. Driffill. 1985a. Rational expectations and policy credibility following a change in regime. *Review of Economic Studies* 52:211–21.

———. 1985b. Inflation and reputation. *American Economic Review* 75:530–38.

Bartolini, L., and A. Drazen. 1997. When liberal policies reflect external shocks, what do we learn? *Journal of International Economics* 42:249–73.

Baxter, M., and U. Jermann. 1997. The international diversification puzzle is worse than you think. *American Economic Review* 87:170–80.

Baxter, M., U. Jermann, and R. G. King. 1998. Non-traded goods, non-traded factors, and international non-diversification. *Journal of International Economics* 44 (2): 211–29.

Bekaert, G. 1995. Market integration and investment barriers in emerging equity markets. *World Bank Economic Review* 9:75–107.

Bekaert, G., and C. R. Harvey. 1997. Foreign speculators and emerging equity markets. NBER Working Paper no. 6312. Cambridge, Mass.: National Bureau of Economic Research.

Bottazzi, L., P. Pesenti, and E. van Wincoop. 1996. Wages, profits, and the international portfolio puzzle. *European Economic Review* 40 (2): 219–54.

Brennan, M. J., and H. H. Cao. 1997. International portfolio investment flows. *Journal of Finance* 52:1851–80.

Calvo, G. A., L. Leiderman, and C. M. Reinhart. 1996. Inflows of capital to developing countries in the 1990s. *Journal of Economic Perspectives* 10:123–39.

Calvo, G. A., and E. G. Mendoza. 1996. Mexico's balance-of-payments crisis: A chronicle of a death foretold. *Journal of International Economics* 41:235–64.

Calvo, S., and C. M. Reinhart. 1995. Capital flows to Latin America: Is there evidence of contagion effect? Department of Economics, University of Maryland. Mimeo.

Chadha, B., and D. Folkerts-Landau. 1999. The evolving role of banks in international capital flows. In *International capital flows,* ed. Martin Feldstein. Chicago: University of Chicago Press.

Chari, V. V., and P. Kehoe. 1997. Hot money. NBER Working Paper no. 6007. Cambridge, Mass.: National Bureau of Economic Research.

Chuhan, P., G. Perez-Quiros, and H. Popper. 1996. The capital flow mix: Foreign direct investment, short-term investment, and other ingredients. New York: Federal Reserve Bank of New York. Mimeo.

Coval, J. D. 1995. International capital flows when investors have local information. Anderson Graduate School of Business, UCLA. Mimeo.

Diamond, D., and P. Dybvig. 1983. Bank runs, deposit insurance, and liquidity. *Journal of Political Economy* 91:401–19.

Dooley, M. P. 1997. A model of crises in emerging markets. NBER Working Paper no. 6300. Cambridge, Mass.: National Bureau of Economic Research.

Eichengreen, B., A. K. Rose, and C. Wyplosz. 1996. Contagious currency crises. *Scandinavian Journal of Economics* 98:463–84.

Fernandez, R., and D. Rodrik. 1991. Resistance to reform: Status quo bias in the presence of individual specific uncertainty. *American Economic Review* 81: 146–55.

Frankel, J. A., and C. Okongwu. 1996. Liberalized portfolio capital inflows in emerging markets: Sterilization, expectations, and the incompleteness of interest rate convergence. *International Journal of Finance and Economics* 1:1–23.

Frankel, J. A., and S. L. Schmukler. 1996. Country fund discounts and the Mexican crisis of December 1994: Did local residents turn pessimistic before international investors? *Open Economies Review* 7:511–34.

Gavin, M., and R. Hausman. 1996. Make or buy? Approaches to financial market integration. Inter-American Development Bank. Mimeo.

Goldfajn, I., and R. O. Valdés. 1997. Capital flows and the twin crises: The role of liquidity. IMF Working Paper no. WP/97/87. Washington, D.C.: International Monetary Fund.

Harvey, C. R. 1995. The risk exposure of emerging equity markets. *World Bank Economic Review* 9:19–50.

Henry, P. B. 2000a. Stock market liberalization, economic reform, and emerging market equity prices. *Journal of Finance,* forthcoming.

———. 2000b. Do stock market liberalizations cause investment booms? *Journal of Financial Economics,* forthcoming.

Johnston, R. B., S. M. Darbar, and C. Echeverria. 1997. Sequencing capital account liberalization: Lessons from the experiences in Chile, Indonesia, Korea and Thailand. IMF Working Paper no. 157. Washington, D.C.: International Monetary Fund.

King, R. G., and R. Levine. 1994. Capital fundamentalism, economic development, and economic growth. *Carnegie-Rochester Conference Series on Public Policy* 40:259–92.

Lewis, K. K. 1989. Changing beliefs and systematic rational forecast errors with evidence from foreign exchange. *American Economic Review* 79:621–36.

McKinnon, R. I. 1993. *The order of economic liberalization.* Baltimore and London: Johns Hopkins University Press.

McKinnon, R. I., and H. Pill. 1997. Credible economic liberalizations and overborrowing. *American Economic Review Papers and Proceedings* 87:189–93.

Milesi-Ferretti, G. M., and A. Razin. 1996. *Current account sustainability.* Princeton Studies in International Finance, no. 81. Princeton, N.J.: Princeton University.

———. 1997. Sharp reductions in current account deficits: An empirical analysis. NBER Working Paper no. 6310. Cambridge, Mass.: National Bureau of Economic Research.

Persson, T. 1988. Credibility and macroeconomic policy: An introduction and broad survey. *European Economic Review* 32:519–32.

Pesenti, P., and E. van Wincoop. 1998. An international benchmark portfolio: The role of non-traded goods. New York: Federal Reserve Bank of New York. Mimeo.

Rogoff, K. 1987. Reputational constraints on monetary policy. *Carnegie-Rochester Conference Series on Public Policy* 26:41–82.

———. 1989. Reputation, coordination and monetary policy. In *Modern business cycle theory,* ed. R. Barro, 236–64. Cambridge, Mass.: Harvard University Press.

Schineller, L. M. 1997. An econometric model of capital flight from developing countries. International Finance Discussion Papers no. 579. Washington, D.C.: Federal Reserve Board.

Stulz, R. 1999. International portfolio flows and security markets. In *International capital flows,* ed. M. Feldstein, 257–93. Chicago: University of Chicago Press.

Summers, R., and A. Heston. 1991. The Penn World Table (Mark 5): An expanded set of international comparisons, 1950–1988. *Quarterly Journal of Economics* 106:327–68.

Tesar, L., and I. Werner. 1997. The internationalization of securities markets since the 1987 crash. Department of Economics, University of Michigan. Mimeo.

World Bank. 1997. *Private capital flows to developing countries.* New York: Oxford University Press.

Comment   Carmen M. Reinhart

The aim of this paper is to assess the impact of financial liberalization in emerging markets on the dynamics of capital flows to these countries. By positing a cost of absorbing these flows, the authors explain how liberalization can give rise to an "overshooting" of capital inflows and asset prices. In addition, the authors examine whether incomplete information can give rise to a high degree of volatility in capital flows as well as to contagion. They also suggest that deviations in capital inflows from their steady-state levels can be used as a potential signal of future crises.

These are important questions to ask in light of the close linkages between capital flows and financial crises. Furthermore, financial crises, particularly in the domestic banking sector, seem to be closely entwined with financial liberalization and asset price bubbles (see Kaminsky and Reinhart 1999). The Asian crises of 1997–98 certainly attest to the relevance of these issues. Financial liberalization, full or partial, did appear to help explain the cycle of capital inflows and the prolonged lending boom that left these economies highly leveraged and, thus, vulnerable to financial crises. During the boom phase of the capital flow cycle, the ex post evidence is also consistent with an asset price overshooting of the type discussed in this paper.

In what follows, I will suggest that the analytical framework presented in this paper is extremely useful in understanding foreign direct investment (FDI) and portfolio equity flows to emerging markets in the 1990s. It is also useful for delineating how efforts to liberalize capital markets may have contributed to the boom phase of the capital flow cycle and its ultimate overshooting. The model also provides insights into FDI's compar-

Carmen M. Reinhart is associate professor in the Department of Economics and the School of Public Affairs at the University of Maryland, College Park, and a research associate of the National Bureau of Economic Research.

ative resilience vis-à-vis other types of capital inflows following periods of turbulence. This resilience was evident following the Mexican crisis of 1994–95 and the recent Asian crisis as well. This framework, however, is less well equipped to explain the surge in short-term capital flows, be these short-maturity bonds (as in Mexico or Indonesia) or bank loans (as in Korea and Thailand) and their links to financial liberalization. Hence, the framework presented in this paper is, in my view, a very relevant but partial explanation of the capital flow episode of the 1990s.

I will divide my comments into two broad areas. The first briefly deals with the stylized facts alluded to in the paper, while the second focuses on the theoretical model.

The Stylized Facts

Section 3.1 of the paper provides some background information on the evolution of capital flows to emerging markets in the 1990s. This section highlights the increasing importance of portfolio flows to emerging markets and the role of FDI. These and other points made by the authors are indeed important, but some qualifications of the stylized evidence, as presented in this paper, are in order.

First, while FDI and portfolio flows did surge in the earlier part of this decade, the increase was not universal and much more pronounced in Latin America than in Asia. In the years prior to the crisis, short-term flows to Asia surged, as Japanese and European banks significantly stepped up their lending to this region. Hence, in light of the paper's goal of understanding the role financial liberalization plays in stimulating capital inflows, the authors should also consider discussing the role played by short-term capital inflows during the period they are analyzing. Other papers, which have also modeled the financial liberalization process (see, e.g., Goldfajn and Valdés 1995; McKinnon and Pill 1996) have often stressed the distinctive behavior of banks during the postliberalization period. In particular, it has been shown that, during those periods, banks are inclined to acquire short-term offshore liabilities (capital inflows), that are then lent at home at substantially higher interest rates and longer maturities for a substantial profit. Certainly, the severe liquidity problems that some Asian countries have faced in 1997–98 have only served to confirm the prominent role played by short-maturity debt; the widespread incidence of banking crises have also underscored the central role that banks play in intermediating capital inflows. The increasing skewness in the composition of capital flows toward the short end of the maturity spectrum has also been linked to the vulnerability of the Asian economies of financial crises (see Kaminsky and Reinhart 1998).

Second, a stylized fact, which is prominently stressed in the background discussion and filters through to the analytical framework, is the assertion that financial liberalization is primarily a feature of the 1990s. Galbis

(1993) and Kaminsky and Reinhart (1999) provide detailed chronologies of the process of financial liberalization in most of the emerging market economies considered here. Financial liberalization was well underway in most of these countries by the early 1990s. Among the most documented of these financial reforms were the "big bang" liberalizations of the late 1970s and early 1980s in the Southern Cone. More generally, the removal of interest rate ceilings and directed lending was an ongoing process in the 1980s for several of the Asian and Latin American emerging markets emphasized in this study.

Third, the authors seem to suggest that financial liberalization has been synchronous across the broad range of highly heterogeneous emerging market economies in the 1990s, and thus liberalization has been a key ingredient in the widespread flow of capital to emerging markets in the 1990s. While I fully share the authors' view of the key importance of financial liberalization as a pull factor, there is little evidence of such widespread cross-country synchronicity of reforms. By the time Argentina and Brazil implemented macroeconomic reforms, many of the Asian economies now in trouble and Chile had been far advanced in this process. China is particularly difficult to fit in this mold; neither its domestic financial sector nor its external accounts have been liberalized by any reasonable measure—its currency lacks convertibility and its banking sector is bankrupt. A synchronous rise in flows to emerging markets may have other explanations than those that are stressed in this paper. Several studies that have analyzed the determinants of capital flows to emerging markets have found conclusive evidence on the importance of common push factors (see Montiel and Reinhart 1999 for a summary of this literature). Specifically, the decline in U.S. interest rates in the early part of the 1990s and the more dramatic march toward zero of Japanese short-term interest rates were clearly forces that helped propel capital toward Asia and Latin America.

The Theoretical Model

Let us recall that this paper aims to assess the impact of financial liberalization in emerging markets on capital flows to these countries and to explain why liberalization can give rise to the "overshooting" of capital inflows and asset prices. To do so, the authors begin by modeling financial liberalization as the reduction in a tax, which in turn increases the rate of return on physical capital in emerging markets. This approach seems quite sensible, since even in the absence of explicit policy decisions, one can reinterpret the reduction in this tax as the decline in transactions costs associated with new "information-age" technology. Furthermore, some countries (like Chile and China) have gone to great lengths to encourage FDI through tax breaks and other forms of preferential treatment while shunning short-term and portfolio flows.

In what follows, my discussion of the model will mainly focus on why I think that this type of model is better suited to explain the behavior of FDI and equity flows than the broader capital flow dynamics that the authors discuss in the introduction. This is not to suggest that explaining FDI and equity flows is a trivial feat, since both FDI and portfolio equity flows showed marked increases in the 1990s. Also, while the authors do not actually interpret and exploit some of their findings in this light, this framework also allows us to understand in an intuitively appealing manner the problem of "overinvestment" that characterized many of the Asian economies on the eve of crisis.

The model, however, would have to be substantially amended to shed light on the issue of bond flows and other short-term flows, which were also extremely important in explaining the capital flow surge of the 1990s as well as its subsequent volatility. To understand these other types of flows, some of the assumptions that are made will have to be relaxed. For example, it is assumed that capital outflows from emerging markets are not possible—investment is assumed to be "irreversible." Table 3C.1 clearly highlights that reversibility of capital flows is a major issue for emerging markets. Nor is this issue a new one, as the experiences of the early 1980s shown in the table highlight. However, it is true that not all capital flows are equally vulnerable to these abrupt reversals. Indeed, the kind of physical capital flows that the authors model in this paper (FDI) appear to be relatively resilient following the Mexican 1994 crisis and the Asian crises of 1997–98. Bond flows and foreign bank loans, which are

Table 3C.1   **Selected Large Reversals in Net Private Capital Flows (as a percentage of GDP)**

Country, Episode	Reversal
Argentina, 1982–83	20
Argentina, 1994–95	4
Chile, 1981–83	7
Chile,[a] 1990–91	8
Ecuador, 1995–96	19
Hungary, 1995–96	7
Indonesia, 1996–98	5
Malaysia,[a] 1993–94	15
Mexico, 1981–83	12
Mexico, 1993–95	6
Philippines, 1996–97	7
Venezuela, 1992–94	9
South Korea, 1996–98	11
Thailand, 1996–98	26
Turkey, 1993–94	10

Source: Calvo and Reinhart (1999).
[a]Reversal owing to the introduction of controls on capital inflows.

not included in this model, appear to account for the bulk of the observed reversals.

It is also the case that the authors work with a real model, in which there is no money, credit, nor exchange rates. There is also no debt. The introduction of a second emerging market asset, be it money, debt, or both, would clearly allow for a more comprehensive modeling of the capital flows of the 1990s. While there are always trade-offs between tractability and breadth, to understand the capital flows of the 1990s we must also address the issue of debt and bank lending. As we have seen in the cases of Southeast Asia and Korea, bond financing and bank loans accounted for an important share of capital inflows to this region as well as other emerging markets.

A less pressing, but possibly interesting, extension of this framework would be to relax the assumption that consumption decisions are taken on a period-by-period basis. The reason that this may be a fruitful exercise has to do with the authors' introduction of incomplete information and learning. While I very much like their idea of incomplete information as a possible source of volatility and contagion, this uncertainty is not (in its present form) allowed to feed back so as to affect consumption decisions.

In sum, if the authors wish to address the links between financial liberalization, aggregate capital flows, asset price bubbles, and volatility, I would urge them to incorporate other assets, besides physical capital, in their framework. An interesting extension of this type of analysis could also be to build on the financial liberalization story and incorporate a financial intermediary, as in Edwards and Végh (1997) and Krugman (1998). Of course, attempting to do too many of these things in a single model will no doubt prove messy but it would be highly complementary to the interesting issues that are already addressed in the paper.

References

Calvo, Guillermo A., and Carmen M. Reinhart. 1999. When capital inflows come to a sudden stop: Consequences and policy options. In *Key issues in reform of the international monetary and financial system,* ed. P. Kenan, M. Mussa, and A. Swoboda. Washington, D.C.: International Monetary Fund, forthcoming.

Edwards, Sebastian, and Carlos Végh. 1997. Banks and macroeconomic disturbances under predetermined exchange rates. *Journal of Monetary Economics* 40 (November): 239–78.

Galbis, Vicente. 1993. High real interest rates under financial liberalization: Is there a problem? IMF Working Paper no. 93/7. Washington, D.C.: International Monetary Fund.

Goldfajn, Ilan, and Rodrigo Valdés. 1995. Balance of payment crises and capital flows: The role of liquidity. Cambridge, Mass.: Massachusetts Institute of Technology. Mimeo.

Kaminsky, Graciela, and Carmen M. Reinhart. 1998. Financial crises in Asia and

Latin America: Then and now. *American Economic Review* 88, no. 2 (May): 444–49.

———. 1999. The twin crises: The causes of banking and balance of payments problems. *American Economic Review* 89, no. 3 (June): 473–500.

Krugman, Paul. 1998. Bubble, boom, crash: Theoretical notes on Asia's crisis. Cambridge, Mass.: Massachusetts Institute of Technology. Mimeo.

McKinnon, Ronald, and Huw Pill. 1996. Credible liberalizations and international capital flows: The overborrowing syndrome. In *Financial deregulation and integration in East Asia,* ed. T. Ito and A. Krueger, 7–42. Chicago: University of Chicago Press.

Montiel, Peter, and Carmen M. Reinhart. 1999. Do capital controls influence the volume and composition of capital flows? Evidence from the 1990s. *Journal of International Money and Finance* 18, no. 4 (August): 619–35.

II

Cross-Country Evidence

4

What Explains Changing Spreads on Emerging Market Debt?

Barry Eichengreen and Ashoka Mody

4.1 Introduction

The number and value of bonds issued by emerging market borrowers grew enormously in the course of the 1990s (table 4.1). They were a major source of capital for developing countries and had significant implications for the operation of international capital markets. The value of the bonds issued by developing countries rose from negligible levels in the 1980s (less than $3.5 billion in 1989) to $24 billion in 1992, more than $50 billion per year in 1993–95, an unprecedented $102 billion in 1996, and even higher levels in 1997.[1] Equity issues, while the subject of much attention, never reached comparable heights.

The market's ability to discriminate among borrowers and to price risk accordingly has been controversial, to say the least. Some observers

Barry Eichengreen is the George C. Pardee and Helen N. Pardee Professor of Economics and Political Science at the University of California, Berkeley, a research associate of the National Bureau of Economic Research, and a research fellow of the Centre for Economic Policy Research in London. Ashoka Mody was visiting professor of public policy and management at the Wharton School, University of Pennsylvania, when this paper was written. He is now Lead Specialist for International Finance with the Development Prospects Group of the World Bank.

The authors are grateful to Steve Dunaway, Anne Jensen, and Ken Wood of the International Monetary Fund who helped assemble the data set; to Ananda Chanda and Freyan Panthaki for sterling research assistance; to Richard Parry for arranging an early informal discussion of the results at the International Finance Corporation; to conference participants; and especially to Sylvia Maxfield, the paper's discussant. Robert Hill, David Roberts, and Nina Shapiro also provided useful comments. The views expressed here are those of the authors and should not be attributed to the World Bank or to any other organization.

1. A preliminary estimate for the first three quarters of 1997 is $112.7 billion, or $150 billion at an annual rate. There is reason to anticipate a deceleration in the fourth quarter of 1997, of course, given the turmoil in Asian financial markets.

Table 4.1   Bond Issues, Equity Issues, and Syndicated Loans to Emerging Markets (gross, US$ billions)

	1991	1992	1993	1994	1995	1996	First Quarter 1997
Portfolio equity	5.6	7.2	11.9	18.0	11.2	16.4	3.2
Bonds	13.9	24.3	62.7	56.5	57.6	101.9	27.7
Western Hemisphere	7.1	12.9	28.8	18.0	23.1	47.1	11.9
Asia	4.1	5.9	22.0	29.9	25.3	43.1	12.7
Europe and Central Asia	2.1	4.8	9.7	3.5	6.6	7.4	2.8
Middle East	0.4	0	2.5	3.0	0.7	2.6	0.3
Africa	0.3	0.7	0.2	2.1	1.9	1.6	0
Syndicated loan commitments	50.7	42.5	43.0	55.1	74.9	79.7	21.3
Short-term commitments	5.2	8.2	11.9	14.3	21.6	30.5	7.4
Total	75.4	82.4	129.5	144.0	165.3	228.5	59.6

Source: IMF (1997).

emphasize that the information relevant for forecasting returns is costly to acquire and process. Investors, in this view, price bonds on the basis of incomplete knowledge of countries' economic and financial circumstances, a practice conducive to herding and market volatility.[2] Others insist that investors have powerful incentives to be informed and discriminating. As evidence they cite the differentials that exist between yields on bonds issued by countries with different credit ratings and economic characteristics.

Proponents of both views have advanced their preferred explanation for the decline in emerging market spreads that took place between 1995 and early 1997. The secondary-market spread between developing country sovereign bonds and high-yield U.S. corporate issues fell from 1,752 basis points in March 1995 to 537 basis points in December 1996.[3] (The declining spreads of stripped Brady bonds over U.S. treasury rates is shown in fig. 4.1.) Advocates of the "efficiently functioning markets" view explain this trend by pointing to improving macroeconomic and financial fundamentals in developing countries, which rededicated themselves to economic liberalization and structural reform and, following the Mexican crisis, redoubled their efforts to put their fiscal, monetary, and financial affairs in order. Better policies, in this view, implied reductions in the risk of investing in emerging market debt and justified the decline in spreads. Others, more skeptical of market efficiency, question whether fundamentals improved sufficiently to justify the striking decline in spreads and suggest that investors in their exuberance may have been snapping up emerging market debt in disregard of historical relationships between fundamentals and yields.[4]

2. Calvo and Mendoza (1995) suggest that the incentive to gather costly information is a declining function of opportunities for portfolio diversification, so the market's growth may reduce the information possessed by the individual investor about a particular country. (This result depends on the assumption that the cost of acquiring information about a country is independent of the size of the investment or that it at least involves significant fixed costs.) News can then disproportionately affect the allocation of funds across countries and the prices of particular bonds (assuming that portfolio diversification facilitates reallocation). Under these circumstances, one can imagine how investors might fail to raise the risk premium on a particular bond issue to reflect a gradual deterioration in economic conditions, how news about this trend could lead to a jump in prices, and how information about conditions in one country could lead investors to revise their expectations about the prospects of others with superficially similar characteristics. Chari and Kehoe (1997) argue that "hot money" results from "frictions" in information leading to herd-like behavior of investors in and out of countries on the margin, that is, countries that are not obviously attractive or definitely "no-no's." They contrast their model with that of Calvo and Mendoza where the ability to diversify limits incentives for information acquisition. Chari and Kehoe argue that their model predicts the types of countries that will experience hot money flows whereas Calvo and Mendoza predict only that hot money flows will occur. Herd behavior may also be observed for foreign direct investment (Kinoshita and Mody 1997).

3. Spreads continued to fall through the third week of February 1997, after which they reversed direction and began to fluctuate more widely.

4. One oft-heard justification for this view is that the Mexican rescue removed the need for investors to concern themselves with a potential borrower's credit worthiness, or at least left them with this belief, since the package engineered by the United States and the Interna-

The weight that should be attached to these interpretations is critical for how we regard the post-1995 surge of portfolio capital flows to emerging markets and its equally sudden halt (along with a sharp rise in spreads) toward the end of 1997. If increased lending and spread compression in the second half of 1996 and early 1997 reflected improved fundamentals in the borrowing countries, then there is no reason to think that these favorable trends cannot be sustained. As long as governments are richly rewarded for putting national policies on a firmer footing, there are few grounds for worrying that the trend toward policy reform will be reversed or that the demand for emerging market debt will dry up. But if the surge of capital flows and decline in spreads reflected mainly the effects of liberal credit conditions in the major money centers, then there was reason to worry about the effects of the eventual tightening of financial market conditions in the advanced industrial countries. Even more troubling would be evidence that the increased capital flows and reduced spreads of the period centered on 1996 reflected an arbitrary shift in pricing behavior, in which case there was no reason to rule out an equally sudden shift back and a corresponding curtailment of flows.

In this paper we analyze data on about 1,300 developing-country bonds launched in the years 1991–97, a period that spans the recent episode of heavy reliance on bonded debt. In contrast to previous studies, we pay special attention to problems of sample selection. We analyze both the issue decision of debtors and underwriters and the pricing decision of investors. We minimize selectivity bias by treating the two decisions jointly.

Overall, the results confirm that higher credit quality leads to a higher probability of issue and to lower spreads. This supports the presumption that the market discriminates among issuers according to risk. But the same explanatory variables have different effects in the principal debt-issuing regions (Latin America, East Asia, and Eastern Europe). And when it comes to changes in spreads over time, we find that these are explained mainly by shifts in market sentiment rather than by shifts in fundamentals. An obvious break point is the fourth quarter of 1994, when the Mexican crisis erupted and spreads moved sharply higher, before falling subsequently to lower levels than before. Comparing 1991:Q1 to 1994:Q3 with 1995:Q1 to 1995:Q4 (the pre– and post– Mexican crisis subperiods), we find that changes in spreads were dominated by sharp adverse shifts in market sentiment more than by changes in fundamentals. The same is true of the subsequent compression, which this time reflected favorable shifts in market sentiment.

Section 4.2 of the paper begins by reviewing the literature. Section 4.3

---

tional Monetary Fund (IMF) allowed them to escape the 1994–95 Mexican crisis scot-free. If the same "chain of guarantees" is likely to again come into play in the event of future debt-servicing difficulties, bondholders have little reason to invest the time and effort needed to discriminate among bonds according to risk.

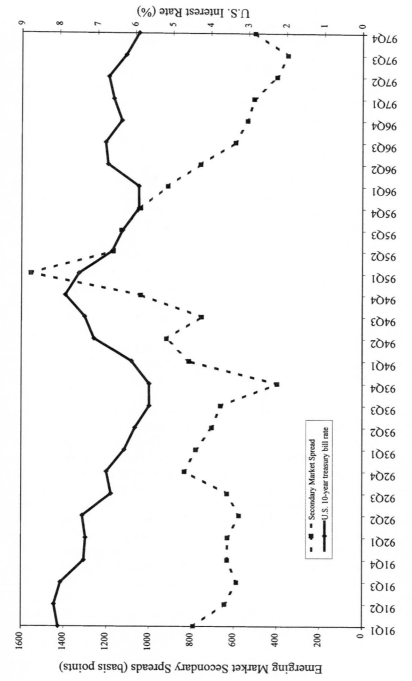

Fig. 4.1 Trends in emerging market secondary spreads and U.S. interest rates

describes the data and section 4.4 the issues of specification and estimation. Section 4.5 reports the basic results for both the issue decision and pricing behavior. Section 4.6 attempts to decompose the contributions of fundamentals and market sentiment to pricing behavior over time. Shifts in pricing behavior are also examined by comparing predicted and actual spreads both within the estimated sample and out of the sample. Section 4.7 draws out the implications of the analysis for how to think about emerging market debt.

4.2   The Literature

Despite the explosive growth of emerging market debt, there have been few systematic studies of the issue and pricing of developing-country bonds. This is in contrast to the secondary market for bank loans, about which there exist a significant number of studies (reflecting the dominance of banking lending in the period 1974–82).[5] But there is reason to think that the determinants of risk and therefore pricing behavior differ between bank loans and bonds. Models of delegated monitoring suggest that banks may have a comparative advantage in assembling and processing information about their clients and that this reputational asset may be incorporated into the secondary market prices of their claims. Pecking-order theories of finance suggest that claims with different degrees of seniority have different levels of risk and that their prices should bear a different relationship to fundamentals. Bonds typically have senior status, while the legal status of bank loans is more variable. Thus, the conclusions from studies of the market in bank loans may not carry over to the market in bonded debt.

The few extant studies of the market for developing-country bonds are subject to other limitations. For instance, Cantor and Packer (1995) analyze the determinants of spreads on sovereign bonds for forty-nine countries in 1995, relating spreads to per capita income, gross domestic product (GDP) growth, inflation, the fiscal balance, the external balance, and external debt, to indicators of economic development and default history, and to the average of Moody's and Standard & Poor's country credit ratings (CCRs). Limitations of this study include the fact that it considers developed as well as developing countries, that it analyzes only sovereign bonds and not also private issues, and that none of the macroeconomic variables is statistically significant when credit ratings are included. Cline (1995) limits his consideration to developing countries and includes corporate as well as government borrowers. However, he studies only highly indebted countries, whose representativeness may be questioned, and he considers only four economic determinants of interest rate spreads: inflation, per capita income, export growth, and GDP growth (along with dummy

---

5. See Hajivassiliou (1989) and Huizinga (1989) for examples and surveys of the literature.

variables for private issues and participation in Brady plan debt reduction schemes). Because his sample ends with the second quarter of 1993, he has only 92 bond issues, and some of his estimates are for just 68 bonds. Of his four economic variables, only export growth and GDP growth differ significantly from zero at standard confidence levels. A follow-up study (Cline and Barnes 1997) uses more recent data and a somewhat longer list of explanatory variables but is otherwise subject to many of the same limitations. In addition, it uses data for selected Western European borrowers as well as emerging markets, raising questions about the homogeneity of the sample.

Eichengreen and Portes (1989) analyze a larger sample of 375 international bonds issued in the 1920s, the last time bond markets were a leading vehicle for international lending. But the fact that their sample includes both developing and advanced industrial countries and that the information and regulatory structure of the market has changed over time limits the relevance of this study for present purposes. Edwards (1986) analyzes bond spreads in 1976–80, but since there did not then exist an active market in developing-country debt, he has data for only thirteen countries and 167 bonds. And it is not clear that we should expect pricing performance to remain the same over time.[6] New investors have entered the market since the period Edwards analyzes: while banks held fully 97 percent of all emerging market debt at the end of the 1980s, their share had fallen to less than two-thirds by the mid-1990s (Bernstein and Penicook 1996). New issuers entered as well.[7]

Finally, a study by Kamin and van Kleist (1997) analyzes launch spreads on 304 bonds (and 358 syndicated bank loans) issued in the 1990s. The authors relate spreads to Moody's and Standard & Poor's CCRs (as a summary measure of the macroeconomic determinants of country credit worthiness) and industrial country interest rates (as a measure of international financial conditions). They find that Latin American spreads are on average 39 percent higher than on otherwise comparable Asian issues, a result suggestive of market segmentation. Surprisingly they find that the coefficient on industrial country interest rates tends to be significantly negative or insignificantly different from zero, but never positive.

The fact that country participation in the bond market has risen over time suggests that ordinary least squares (OLS) estimates of the relationship between spreads and country characteristics will suffer from selectivity bias. The same changes in economic and financial conditions that affect the price of issues can also affect the decision to enter the market. Bond traders often remark that a rise in U.S. treasury rates raises spreads on

---

6. As emphasized above in section 4.1.

7. Potentially accentuating the trade-off between portfolio diversification and information acquisition emphasized by Calvo and Mendoza (1995).

developing-country bonds less than proportionately, for example, because high-risk borrowers are discouraged from coming to the market. Focusing exclusively on the determinants of the pricing decision to the neglect of the impact of those same factors on the decision to enter the market may therefore be a source of selectivity bias. In the next sections we employ a data set and methodology designed to ameliorate these problems.

4.3 Data and Sample Characteristics

The bonds we study are fixed income securities with a specified maturity, face value, and coupon.[8] While issued by emerging market borrowers, they are placed on international markets and are denominated in developed country currencies (dominantly in U.S. dollars). Although the bulk of this market consists of bonds placed in the Euromarkets (mainly the Eurodollar market), over our sample period a growing number of countries floated bonds on the U.S. public market for foreign issuers (the Yankee market) and the U.S. private placement market (under provisions of Rule 144a); there was also some growth in issues denominated in deutsche marks and yen. The bonds are typically underwritten by a syndicate of investment banks who commit to placing them with investors. After placement they trade on the secondary market and may be listed on an exchange.

4.3.1 The Bonds: Numbers, Spreads, and Issuers

Our data are initial offer or "launch" spreads for bonds offered between January 1991 and December 1997 by fifty-five countries, obtained from Capital Data Bondware and further processed by the Emerging Markets Division of the IMF. That they are launch spreads is important. Figure 4.2 shows that launch spreads move differently over time than spreads on secondary markets. While there is some tendency for primary spreads to follow secondary spreads with a lag of three of four quarters, the two series frequently diverge. In poor market conditions, when secondary spreads rise, primary spreads do not rise proportionately; indeed, sometimes they fall. This reflects the tendency for the number of issues to fall and for only the most credit worthy borrowers to remain in the market. In other words, factors that increase the risks of investing in emerging market debt, while raising secondary market spreads, may have the opposite effect on launch spreads insofar as riskier borrowers are rationed out of the market, leaving only low-risk, low-spread borrowers to launch new issues. This makes it important to control for the likelihood of new issues by different classes of borrowers.

---

8. The share of international bond issues with convertible and floating rates did in fact rise slightly after 1993, but we exclude these from the sample on the grounds that the risks and relationship to fundamentals are different and warrant a separate analysis.

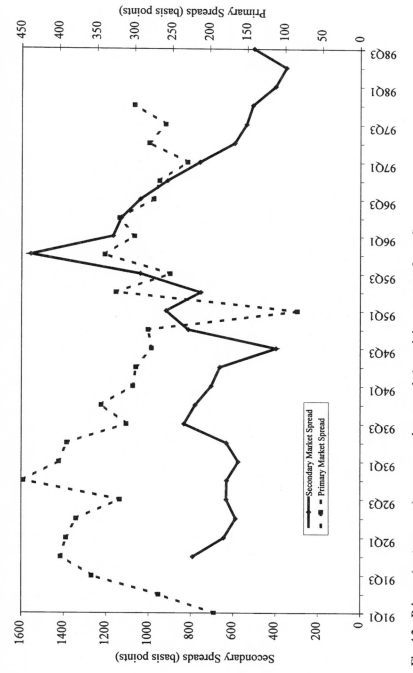

Fig. 4.2 Primary (contemporary) versus secondary spreads (moved three quarters forward)

Table 4.2   **Launch Spreads, 1991–97 (basis points)**

Region	1991	1992	1993	1994	1995	1996	1997	Average
Africa	200	166		197	151	140	94	159
East Asia	110	74	173	145	125	149	178	152
Eastern Europe	226	211	222	191	269	238	332	266
Latin America	376	448	410	369	413	390	307	384
Middle East			17	119	216	219	196	167
South Asia				385	190	233	174	212
Average	338	387	356	288	289	291	265	306
Number of bonds								
Bonds with spreads	52	118	239	163	170	302	314	1,358
Total bonds	84	165	332	202	203	342	369	1,697

Notes: A blank indicates that no bond was issued. A bond's spread is estimated by first calculating that bond's yield to maturity using the market price at the time of issue and then subtracting the yield on a "riskless" sovereign security of comparable maturity in the currency of issue.

Our source provides data for 1,697 bonds over the period 1991–97 (table 4.2). The number of bonds issued grew rapidly from 84 in 1991 to 332 in 1993 before falling to just over 200 in 1994 and 1995 (the Mexican crisis contributing to poor market conditions in 1995). Bond issuance rose sharply in 1996 and was set to record a banner year in 1997 before the Asian crisis hit. In our analysis we were able to use just over 1,300 bonds. No spreads were publicly available for 339 bonds. Also, for some bond issues ancillary information on country conditions was incomplete. Our results are based on data for 1991 through 1996, for which we have 1,033 usable bonds. We use 277 bonds issued in 1997 for out-of-sample forecasting.

Latin America accounts for about 60 percent of the bonds issued (1,000 of the 1,697). The main Latin issuers were Argentina, Brazil, and Mexico. East Asia is a distant second with 416 bonds (Korea being a leading issuer in that region). Eastern Europe had 180 bonds in this period, with 1997 an especially active year for the region.

Latin America has also had the highest spreads. Annual average spreads were more than 350 basis points in all the years from 1991 to 1996 and fell for the first time below that level to 307 basis points in 1997. In contrast, East Asian spreads were always less than 200 basis points even in 1997 when they rose to their highest level. That said, there is considerable variation within East Asia; the standard deviation of spreads relative to the mean is typically higher for East Asia than Latin America. Eastern European spreads have consistently been between those of Latin America and East Asia.

Table 4.3 summarizes sample characteristics by type of issuer. Three categories are distinguished: sovereign, other public, and private. The majority of the issues are by private borrowers, although public entities in East Asia have a relatively high propensity to issue bonds. Sovereign issues

Table 4.3   **Spreads and Bonds by Type of Issuer (basis points for spreads; numbers for bonds issued)**

| | Region | | | | | |
Sector	Africa	East Asia	Eastern Europe	Latin America	Middle East	South Asia
Sovereign	166	94	237	302	106	385
Bonds with spreads	6	32	88	127	30	1
Total number of bonds	10	38	130	175	37	1
Public	131	91	239	325	223	168
Bonds with spreads	5	147	20	131	9	3
Total number of bonds	11	194	27	181	10	4
Private	205	226	410	416	284	207
Bonds with spreads	2	145	21	572	11	8
Total number of bonds	6	184	23	644	11	11

dominate in Eastern Europe and the Middle East. Sovereign issues do not necessarily carry higher spreads than the other public issues, which partly reflects variations in country composition, although the regression analysis to follow suggests other factors may also be at work. We would expect private issues to carry higher spreads, reflecting the benchmark status of public issues and private bonds' greater perceived riskiness.[9] The averages for all regions except South Asia confirm this presumption, as does the regression analysis.

4.3.2   Explanatory Variables

We used a variety of macroeconomic indicators to analyze the determinants of the issue decision and the spread. As a proxy for the risk-free rate, we used the yield on ten-year U.S. treasury bonds (at time of issue). Several country characteristics were used to proxy for credit quality (for details, see the data appendix). Data were obtained principally from the World Bank's *World Debt Tables* and *Global Development Finance* and the IMF's *International Financial Statistics* and *World Economic Outlook* on the ratio of total external debt to gross national product (GNP), the ratio of debt service to exports, a dummy variable for whether a country concluded a debt restructuring agreement with either private or official creditors in the previous year, the ratio of international reserves to GNP, the growth rate of GDP (at constant 1990 prices, denominated in domestic currency), and the budget deficit as a share of GDP.

Sovereign credit ratings were gathered from *Institutional Investor*. Pub-

---

9. This is consistent with the procedures of bond rating agencies, which are reluctant to grant private borrowers higher credit ratings than sovereigns on the grounds that a sovereign with transfer problems will frequently interrupt the access of private domestic debtors to supplies of foreign exchange; see Levey (n.d.).

lished each March and September, these ratings are based on a survey of international bankers, who assign a numerical value ranging from 0 to 100 (with 100 indicating zero probability of default). For each observation we used the most recent credit rating prior to the bond's date of issue. But rather than include the raw CCR, we employ the residual from a first-stage regression of the credit rating on country and issuer characteristics. We utilize only the orthogonalized component because the credit rating is correlated with other issuer characteristics that are included separately as explanatory variables (see, e.g., Cantor and Packer 1994 and Haque et al. 1996).[10] Because a preliminary look at the data suggested different behavior on the part of issuers in Latin America and the Caribbean, we considered Latin American and East Asian issues separately as well as together.

4.4 Specification and Estimation

A standard model of spreads is a linear relationship of the form

$$(1) \qquad \log(\text{spread}) \; = \; fX \, + \, u_1,$$

where the dependent variable is the logarithm of the spread, X is a vector of issue and issuer characteristics, and u_1 is a random error. The vector X comprises *bond characteristics* (the maturity of the bond, principal amount, and whether it was privately placed); *global economic conditions* proxied by the ten-year rate on U.S. treasuries; *country characteristics* like the sovereign credit rating residual, the ratio of debt to GDP, the ratio of debt service to exports, a dummy variable if the country underwent a debt restructuring in the previous year, and the GDP growth rate; and *issuer characteristics* including the region of the borrower, whether the borrower is sovereign, other public, or private, and the currency in which the bond was issued.

The conditions under which this linear equation provides an unbiased estimate of the relationship of issuer characteristics to spreads may not be met, for not all potential issuers will be in the sample at all points in time.

---

10. The estimated equation was

credit rating = 36.93 + 12.45 reserves/GNP − 6.99 debt reschedule
             (59.42)   (19.04)   (− 5.04)

        − 11.75 debt/GNP + 252.96 GDP growth − 12.15 (reserves/GNP) ∗ LAC
        (−12.82)   (10.88)   (− 4.67)

        + 3.75 (debt reschedule) ∗ LAC − 10.28 (debt/GNP) ∗ LAC
         (1.98)   (−5.27)

        − 520.89 (GDP growth) ∗ LAC,
        (−7.38)

$R^2 \; = \; 0.48$, t-statistics are in parentheses.

The spread and its relationship to issue and issuer characteristics will be observed only when positive decisions to borrow and lend are made. We assume that spreads are observed when a latent variable β crosses a threshold β' defined by:

$$(2) \qquad \beta' = gX' + u_2,$$

where X' is the vector of variables that determines the desire of borrowers to borrow and willingness of lenders to lend (which we refer to as determinants of bond supply and demand, respectively), and u_2 is a second error term. If the error terms are bivariate normal with standard deviations s_1 and s_2 and covariance s_{12}^2 (where $\rho_2 = s_{12}^2/s_1 s_2$), this is a standard sample selection model, à la Heckman (1979). The model can be identified by the nonlinearity of the fitted probabilities in the selection equation and by the inclusion of elements in X' that are not also in X.[11]

Estimating the probit requires information on those who did not issue bonds. To address this problem we used the following approach. For each country we allowed for three types of issuers: sovereign, public, and private. For each quarter and country where one of these issuer types did not come to the market, we recorded a zero. Table 4.4 highlights the characteristics of issuers ($is = 1$) relative to non-issuers ($is = 0$). It suggests, plausibly, that issues are more likely when U.S. interest rates are low, when the borrower is of better quality credit (with higher credit rating residuals and lower debt levels), and when reserves are low and budget deficits are larger (creating a public-sector demand for foreign funds).

We estimate equations (1) and (2) jointly using maximum likelihood. Implemented with the full sample, the maximum-likelihood estimates converge nicely. When performing sensitivity tests using smaller samples, the full maximum-likelihood estimates do not always converge; in this case we perform the conventional two-step procedure, first estimating a maximum-likelihood probit model and then a regression using the estimated inverse Mills ratio (with full-information standard errors). Where estimates are obtained using both procedures, we find little difference in the results.

4.5   Results

The coefficients for the probit in table 4.5 are normalized to the partial derivative of the probability distribution function with respect to a small change in the independent variable evaluated at average values of the independent variables to facilitate interpretation of the coefficients. We report separate equations for the full data set and for the Latin American and

---

11. Ozler and Huizinga (1992) estimate a similar model on data for the secondary-market prices of bank loans.

Table 4.4   Descriptive Statistics of Issuers ($is = 1$) and Nonissuers ($is = 0$)

	All		Latin America and East Asia		Latin America		East Asia		Eastern Europe	
	$is = 1$	$is = 0$	$is = 1$	$is = 0$	$is = 1$	$is = 0$	$is = 1$	$is = 0$	$is = 1$	$is = 0$
Spread	305.94		319.10		384.25		152.18		265.82	
Amount	187.69		174.77		165.96		195.95		257.47	
Maturity	7.01		6.71		5.81		8.88		6.32	
Private placement	0.40		0.42		0.46		0.32		0.29	
U.S. treasury rate	6.50	6.77	6.50	6.79	6.50	6.78	6.49	6.81	6.51	6.75
Credit rating	43.82	37.12	44.46	40.42	37.10	28.97	62.15	63.14	40.67	33.34
Credit rating residual	6.93	−0.97	8.01	2.05	4.87	−2.15	16.41	11.12	2.69	−5.49
Debt/GNP	0.35	0.43	0.34	0.45	0.36	0.54	0.27	0.26	0.43	0.28
Dummy for debt rescheduling	0.20	0.13	0.22	0.21	0.30	0.28	0.05	0.08	0.08	0.07
Debt service/exports	0.36	0.19	0.38	0.22	0.48	0.28	0.12	0.11	0.31	0.12
GDP growth rate	0.01	−0.01	0.01	0.01	0.01	0.01	0.02	0.02	0.01	−0.05
Reserves/GNP	0.37	0.55	0.35	0.62	0.28	0.38	0.53	1.12	0.42	0.51
Deficit/GDP	−0.01	−0.02	0.00	0.00	0.00	−0.01	0.00	0.02	−0.05	−0.01
Latin America	0.59	0.26	0.71	0.66	1.00	1.00	0.00	0.00	0.00	0.00
Public	0.25	0.34	0.26	0.34	0.18	0.35	0.47	0.32	0.15	0.34
Private	0.52	0.33	0.58	0.30	0.64	0.31	0.44	0.29	0.13	0.35
Yen	0.16		0.14		0.05		0.37		0.30	
Deutsche mark	0.07		0.05		0.06		0.03		0.22	

Table 4.5   **Determinants of the Probability of a Bond Issue, 1991–96**

	All	Latin America and East Asia	Latin America	East Asia	Eastern Europe
Log of U.S.	−0.602	−1.340	−0.734	−1.270	−0.224
treasury rate	(−6.44)	(−6.79)	(−5.24)	(−6.79)	(−2.58)
Credit rating	0.018	0.00	0.023	0.00	0.003
residual	(16.65)	(0.00)	(9.66)	(0.00)	(2.18)
Debt/GNP	−0.289	−0.021	−1.251	−0.019	−0.018
	(−3.92)	(−0.11)	(−13.35)	(−0.11)	(−0.15)
Dummy for debt	−0.049	−0.190	0.024	−0.168	−0.034
rescheduling	(−1.09)	(−2.01)	(0.69)	(−2.01)	(−1.01)
Debt service/	0.721	−1.40	1.420	−1.327	0.446
exports	(6.53)	(−3.24)	(14.22)	(−3.24)	(4.20)
Reserves/GNP	−0.080	−0.504	−0.172	−4.780	−0.117
	(−3.44)	(−8.76)	(−1.99)	(−8.76)	(−2.82)
Deficit/GDP	−0.263	0.285	0.126	0.270	−0.471
	(−1.79)	(0.48)	(0.30)	(0.48)	(−2.24)
Public issuer	−0.035	0.403	−0.015	0.386	−0.117
	(−1.44)	(7.30)	(−0.36)	(7.30)	(−6.95)
Private issuer	−0.062	0.403	0.332	0.400	−0.144
	(−2.49)	(7.29)	(8.99)	(7.29)	(−7.59)
Latin America	0.154	−0.914			
	(0.54)	(−3.00)			
		Latin American Interactions			
Log of U.S.	0.027	0.618			
treasury rate	(0.18)	(2.57)			
Credit rating	0.0004	0.023			
residual	(0.17)	(5.61)			
Debt/GNP	−0.693	−1.21			
	(−6.65)	(−5.82)			
Dummy for debt	0.074	0.230			
rescheduling	(1.29)	(2.12)			
Debt service/	0.393	2.79			
exports	(2.19)	(6.32)			
Reserves/GNP	−0.055	0.334			
	(−0.77)	(3.25)			
Deficit/GDP	0.362	−0.161			
	(1.00)	(−0.22)			
Public issuer	0.024	−0.352			
	(0.57)	(−6.07)			
Private issuer	0.381	−0.078			
	(8.46)	(−1.17)			
Number of					
observations	4,120	2,504	1,744	760	689
Pseudo R^2	0.386	0.415	0.4642	0.2960	0.4863

Note: Numbers in parentheses are *t*-statistics.

Caribbean (henceforth referred to as Latin America), East Asian, and Eastern European subsamples.

When the U.S. treasury rate is high, the volume of new issues declines significantly. This finding is consistent with a "search for yield" view of the market—the idea that when U.S. interest rates fall there is a greater appetite for higher-yielding emerging market bonds. This appears to be uniformly the case, although the strength of the relationship varies across the regions. A sharp decline in issues following a rise in U.S. treasury rates is most evident for East Asia, suggesting the possibility that the East Asian issuers hold back the supply of bonds when U.S. interest rates rise and their borrowing costs go up.[12] The higher the credit rating residual, the greater the probability of issuance in all regions except East Asia, where the effect is insignificant. Higher debt levels reduce the probability of issue especially in Latin America. For East Asia, higher debt service is associated with lower probability of issue. On the supply side, low reserves, higher deficits, and, for Latin America and Eastern Europe, higher debt service levels tend to increase bond issuance.

Table 4.6 presents OLS estimates of the spread equation and table 4.7 the full model with the selectivity correction. The coefficients once again reveal differences in pricing across regions. For Latin America the coefficient on the issue amount indicates plausibly that larger issues command smaller spreads (consistent with the existence of economies of marketing and distribution and the greater liquidity of larger issues on the secondary market). Latin American private placements enter the spreads equation with a positive sign, consistent with the fact that these bonds are issued in markets with less stringent disclosure requirements. Disclosure requirements for private placements are less stringent because trading in those bonds is restricted to "qualified investors," that is, investors capable of managing the associated risk. Also, the bonds for this reason are less liquid. Because the private placement market is narrower and because information on issuer characteristics may be somewhat less complete, the presumption is that purchasers of bonds placed in that market will demand a higher spread. Latin American issues typically having been relatively short term; there is little evidence of a well-defined yield curve until 1996. The picture is different for East Asian issuers, who had by then placed several long-term issues for which they paid higher spreads. There is a large negative coefficient in the spreads equation on the dummy variable for Israel, reflecting the fact that its issues are guaranteed by the U.S. government. Supranational bonds (guaranteed by entities beyond the countries' borders) also have lower spreads.

Recent studies have found, somewhat surprisingly, a negative influence

---

12. We will have more to say on the identification of demand and supply effects of U.S. interest rates below when we consider the spread and issues decisions together.

Table 4.6 **Determinants of Spreads, 1991–96, OLS Regressions**

	All	Latin America and East Asia	Latin America	East Asia	Eastern Europe
Log amount	0.009	0.015	−0.054	0.074	−0.018
	(0.309)	(0.479)	(−1.898)	(0.878)	(−0.205)
Maturity	0.010	0.007	−0.006	0.019	−0.024
	(1.729)	(1.092)	(−0.897)	(1.368)	(−1.287)
Private placement	0.119	0.088	0.153	−0.061	0.029
	(2.492)	(1.787)	(3.774)	(−0.385)	(0.132)
Log of U.S.	−0.199	−0.160	−0.041	−0.703	−1.417
treasury rate	(−0.992)	(−0.728)	(−0.227)	(−1.059)	(−2.429)
Credit rating	−0.038	−0.043	−0.032	−0.033	−0.002
residual	(−14.118)	(−12.871)	(−7.945)	(−4.204)	(−0.183)
Debt/GNP	0.085	0.437	−0.067	−1.089	−1.255
	(0.488)	(2.054)	(−0.295)	(−1.529)	(−1.367)
Dummy for debt	0.211	0.147	0.155	0.100	0.124
rescheduling	(3.558)	(2.351)	(3.147)	(0.272)	(0.334)
Debt service/	1.355	1.400	0.929	5.323	1.237
exports	(7.201)	(6.381)	(4.565)	(4.055)	(1.765)
GDP growth	−4.799	2.253	−1.010	13.894	−14.250
	(−1.607)	(0.616)	(−0.325)	(0.922)	(−1.954)
Israel	−2.371				
	(−13.001)				
Supranational	−0.671	−0.710	−0.734		
	(−2.341)	(−2.467)	(−3.489)		
Public issuer	−0.231	−0.192	−0.215	0.325	−0.250
	(−3.161)	(−2.228)	(−2.759)	(1.422)	(−1.169)
Private issuer	0.156	0.182	0.057	0.882	−0.362
	(2.145)	(2.167)	(0.772)	(3.703)	(−1.366)
Yen issue	−0.180	−0.207	0.036	−0.339	0.266
	(−2.442)	(−2.504)	(0.370)	(−2.111)	(1.460)
Deutsche mark	−0.193	−0.259	0.070	−2.11	−0.105
issue	(−2.262)	(−2.541)	(0.842)	(−5.950)	(−0.669)
Latin America	0.229	0.221			
	(3.014)	(2.060)			
Constant	5.306	5.056	5.837	4.893	8.552
	(12.420)	(10.924)	(14.331)	(3.612)	(6.363)
Number of bonds	1,033	903	670	233	81
Adjusted R^2	0.5902	0.5920	0.2234	0.5035	0.0869

Note: Numbers in parentheses are *t*-statistics.

of the U.S. interest rate on emerging market spreads (see, e.g., Kamin and van Kleist 1997). The OLS results presented in table 4.6 are consistent with this finding. Among the possible interpretations of the negative sign is the change in composition of bonds issued when interest rates vary. Since higher interest rates are seen to reduce bond issuance (as in the probit above), it is possible that the bonds that do come to the market have some unobserved credit features that make them attractive and hence

Table 4.7   **Determinants of Spreads, 1991–96, with the Selectivity Correction**

	All	Latin America and East Asia	Latin America	East Asia
Log amount	0.017	0.018	−0.045	0.061
	(0.54)	(0.62)	(−1.80)	(0.75)
Maturity	0.008	0.006	−0.003	0.017
	(1.47)	(0.96)	(−0.52)	(1.26)
Private placement	0.121	0.084	0.114	−0.102
	(2.52)	(1.85)	(3.30)	(−0.67)
Log of U.S.	−0.169	0.173	0.342	−1.483
treasury rate	(−0.80)	(0.82)	(1.83)	(−2.03)
Credit rating	−0.041	−0.053	−0.041	−0.025
residual	(−11.00)	(−16.69)	(−10.39)	(−2.77)
Debt/GNP	0.357	1.043	1.386	−1.370
	(1.43)	(5.25)	(6.51)	(−1.93)
Dummy for debt	0.187	0.084	0.090	0.164
rescheduling	(3.09)	(1.41)	(1.80)	(0.45)
Debt service/	1.274	0.979	−0.028	5.690
exports	(4.95)	(4.78)	(−0.13)	(4.36)
GDP growth	−2.907	0.676	−0.74	21.32
	(−0.96)	(0.20)	(−0.28)	(1.41)
Israel	−2.37			
	(−13.02)			
Supranational	−0.679	−0.589	−0.650	
	(−2.35)	(−2.37)	(−4.74)	
Public issuer	−0.200	−0.231	−0.151	0.660
	(−2.65)	(−2.88)	(−2.02)	(2.55)
Private issuer	0.169	0.024	−0.096	1.170
	(2.24)	(0.311)	(−1.37)	(4.55)
Yen issue	−0.187	−0.214	−0.064	−0.389
	(−2.55)	(−2.86)	(−0.78)	(−2.47)
Deutsche mark	−0.198	0.278	0.069	−2.10
issue	(−2.35)	(−2.99)	(0.97)	(−6.02)
Latin America	0.188	0.133		
	(2.28)	(1.31)		
Constant	5.21	4.88	5.38	5.59
	(12.13)	(11.10)	(13.17)	(3.99)
ρ	−0.06	−0.55	−0.87	0.48
λ	−0.038	−0.368	−0.485	0.452
	(−0.42)	(−48.0)	(−18.25)	(2.62)
Number of bonds	1,033	903	670	233
Log likelihood	−2375.52	−1872.26	−989.10	−612.93

Note: Numbers in parentheses are t-statistics.

reduces observed spreads. If this interpretation is correct, then the negative sign should be significantly attenuated when we correct for the selection bias. Indeed, comparing the coefficients in tables 4.6 and 4.7, we find for Latin America that the negative coefficient on the U.S. treasury rate turns positive and significant at the 10 percent level. This is consistent with the idea that selection bias plays a role in driving the observed result.

For East Asia, in contrast, the negative coefficient on the U.S. interest rate persists even after correcting for selectivity. To interpret this finding, it is useful to consider the probit and the spreads equation together, for this leads to an intuitive interpretation in terms of supply and demand.[13] For Latin America, a higher interest rate reduces the probability of an issue and raises spreads (after correction for the selection bias). The implication is that when interest rates rise, the demand for Latin American bonds falls and their price therefore declines (equivalently, the spread rises). For East Asia, in contrast, a rise in U.S. interest rates appears to shift the supply curve inward, raising the price and reducing the spread.

For other variables that appear in both the issue and spreads equations, it is once again useful to ask whether they work in the same or opposing directions. In the regressions using the full sample of bonds, a larger credit rating residual (a better credit rating, other things equal) increases the probability of an issue and reduces the spread, as if countries with inferior credit ratings find it both more difficult and costly to borrow. Similarly, and especially in Latin America, a higher debt to GNP ratio both reduces the probability of an issue and increases the spread. In Latin America, debt rescheduling has a weak positive effect on the probability of an issue (i.e., those rescheduling debt are apt to come to the capital market quickly) while at the same time raising the spread that successful issuers are forced to pay. The dummy variable for Latin America behaves similarly: Other things equal, Latin American borrowers issue more bonds but pay higher spreads. Finally, although the magnitude and the significance of ρ—the correlation coefficient of the errors in the two equations—varies by time period and sample, it is generally negative. The implication is that unobserved factors that cause an issue to come to the market also reduce the spread and should be interpreted as unobserved determinants of demand.

In contrast, variables whose coefficients work in offsetting directions influence mainly the supply of bonds. For example, while countries that have recently rescheduled tend to have accumulated an unsatisfied appetite for borrowing and therefore supply additional new issues, the corresponding outward shift in the supply reduces the price of their bonds, increasing the spread. Similarly, the regional dummies suggest that Latin American countries have continent-specific characteristics, not otherwise quantified, that cause them to supply an unusually high volume of bonds; this works, other things equal, to drive down the prices of their issues and increase the spreads they are charged.

---

13. We invoke this interpretation sparingly and with caution, for in a market with imperfect information and enforcement, it is possible for the demand to bend back and for movements along that portion of the demand schedule to look like movements along a supply curve. (Note that we frame our discussion in terms of *bond* supply and *bond* demand, not in terms of *credit* supply and *credit* demand, as in textbook models of credit rationing. The distinction is of only terminological importance, but its significance is great; it leads us to speak of a "backward bending demand curve" rather than a "backward bending supply curve.")

The supply and demand effects vary noticeably by region. Note, for example, that the coefficients for issues denominated in yen and deutsche marks have significant negative signs for East Asia but not so elsewhere. Thus, for East Asia, it appears access to the yen-denominated markets (and to the deutsche mark markets) has proved an easy source of funds. With that source of funds available, the East Asian issuers are better able to time their bond issues. Another example of differential effects between East Asia and Latin America is the sign on ρ, the correlation between the error terms in the spread and probit equations. For Latin America this term behaves much like the credit rating residual—a low probability of issue is associated with a higher-than-predicted spread. For East Asia, in contrast, ρ is positive. An interpretation is that Asian bonds with a low probability of issue that come to the market anyway are not penalized with higher spreads. In fact, they are able to obtain lower-than-predicted spreads, perhaps reflecting the desire of investors, for reasons of diversification, to acquire East Asian bonds that are not in plentiful supply.

4.6   Changes in Spreads over Time

A central question in the literature on capital flows to emerging markets is whether changes in spreads are explicable by changes in fundamentals or whether there have been changes in pricing behavior over time. If a better credit rating, lower debt or debt service ratios, and fewer debt restructurings can explain the reductions in spreads that occurred between 1995 and 1997, then there may be reason to be relatively sanguine about the market's pricing behavior and, for that matter, about the sustainability of capital flows. If, on the other hand, recent capital inflows were encouraged by a not otherwise explicable shift in pricing in favor of developing country debt, then there is no a priori reason to rule out a sudden and equally dramatic shift back and a corresponding curtailment of flows.

4.6.1   The Contribution of Fundamentals and Sentiment

The change in spreads between two periods, denoted $S_1 - S_2$, can be expressed as follows:

$$(3) \qquad\qquad S_1 - S_2 = \beta_1 X_1 - \beta_2 X_2.$$

Adding and subtracting $\beta_1 X_2$ and rearranging, one obtains the familiar Oxaca decomposition:

$$(4) \qquad\qquad S_1 - S_2 = \beta_1 (X_1 - X_2) + X_2 (\beta_1 - \beta_2).$$

The first term on the right side of equation (4) is the contribution to the change in spreads of the change in their economic determinants $(X_1 - X_2)$; this can be thought of as the contribution of the change in fundamentals.

The second term is the contribution of the change in coefficients ($\beta_1 - \beta_2$). This can be thought of as the contribution of changes in market sentiment—in the way the markets regard the credit worthiness of countries with given characteristics. To aid interpretation, we further break these effects into subcategories. Among changes in sentiment, we distinguish the impact on spreads of changes in the constant term ($C_1 - C_2$), which can be thought of as blanket changes in sentiment as emerging market bonds come into or fall out of favor, from the impact of changes in the coefficients on the independent variables [$X_2(\beta_1 - \beta_2)$], which can be thought of as changes in sentiment toward countries with given macroeconomic characteristics (as, for example, the issues of relatively risky borrowers come to be regarded as more attractive). Similarly, we distinguish changes in the average inverse Mills ratio (which can be thought of as a measure of sample selectivity) versus changes in the average value of the other variables. Finally, we distinguish changes in the effect of a given level of the inverse Mills ratio (which can be thought of as the impact on spreads of having in the sample an issue that our selection equation predicts should not be included) from changes in the effect of other regressors. Intuitively, a rising coefficient on the inverse Mills ratio suggests that the market is growing more discriminating.

The decompositions are computed for two periods before and after the Mexican crisis, and before and during the 1996–97 period of spread compression (see table 4.8). Note that when the spread in the first period is larger than in the second (spreads are falling), a positive change in log spread is recorded. Launch spreads declined following the Mexican crisis;

Table 4.8   **Decomposition of the Change in Spreads**

	Change in Fundamentals	Change in β's	Change in Spread
The Mexican Crisis (1991:Q1–1994:Q3 to 1995:Q1–1995:Q4)			
Bond features	0.02	0.25	0.27
U.S. treasury rate	0.00	2.71	2.71
Country characteristics	1.13	0.17	1.30
Dummy variables	0.22	0.58	0.81
Inverse Mills ratio	0.00	−0.07	−0.07
Constant		−3.83	−3.83
Total	1.37	−0.18	1.18
Irrational Exuberance? (1995:Q1–1995:Q4 to 1997:Q1–1997:Q4)			
Bond features	0.00	−0.81	−0.81
U.S. treasury rate	0.04	−6.92	−6.88
Country characteristics	−0.70	0.06	−0.64
Dummy variables	−0.20	−0.24	−0.44
Inverse Mills ratio	0.01	0.31	0.32
Constant		8.22	8.22
Total	−0.85	0.62	−0.23

that decline was especially sharp in 1995, when only high-quality issues were brought to the market. (Recall that secondary spreads skyrocketed in 1995. That shift in sentiment against developing countries is reflected in issue behavior, as discussed below.)

Consider first the period preceding the Mexican crisis (1991:Q1–1994:Q3) compared to the period immediately following (1995:Q1–1995:Q4). While secondary market spreads rose sharply in 1995, launch spreads actually fell, as can be seen from the first panel of table 4.8 (again, according to our convention, a positive change in spread represents a decline in spreads from the first to the second period). This decline in spreads reflected five broad factors. First, market sentiment moved strongly against emerging markets: the constant term in the spread equation increased greatly and, all else equal, would have increased primary spreads considerably (in parallel with trends in the secondary markets). Second, this poorer market sentiment was offset by a change in the coefficient on U.S. treasury rates. For given U.S. treasury rates, in other words, the market was willing to charge lower spreads for the issues that were brought to the market. Third, the fundamentals of issuers coming to the market during the post-crisis period were better than those of issuers in the market prior to the crisis. Fourth, the market seems to have taken a more benign view of fundamentals immediately following the crisis. An exception to that was a more negative view of high debt service. Finally, there were compositional shifts in the issues that came to the market that lowered average spreads. Proportionately fewer Latin American issues and private issues and a greater share of yen-denominated and deutsche mark–denominated issues reduced the average level of spreads observed.

Secondary market spreads declined in 1996 and in the first half of 1997, a trend that was viewed by some as "irrational exuberance." But though secondary market spreads were falling, primary spreads show a small increase. But once again, this increase is composed of offsetting factors (see the bottom panel of table 4.8). Overall market sentiment (as summarized by the constant) improves. Again, as new, less credit worthy issuers came to the market, this shift in market sentiment was moderated by two offsetting factors: the reduced sensitivity of spreads to changes in U.S. interest rates, and a higher premium on the poorer risks entering the market.

4.6.2   Was the Market Irrationally Exuberant in 1996 and 1997?

The sharp decline in spreads in the second half of 1996 and continuing through at least the first half of 1997 led some observers to ask whether the market was irrationally exuberant. The decline in spreads was exceptionally rapid, and an unusual number of new issuers entered the market. Our estimates allow us to compare these outcomes with predictions.

We first estimated the equation for Latin America and East Asia up to

1995 and used the estimates to generate within-sample forecasts for 1995 and out-of-sample forecasts for 1996. The difference between predicted and actual spreads (in basis points) is presented in table 4.9. When the observed spread is less than predicted (an entry with a positive sign in table 4.9), we infer that the market is growing increasingly exuberant. Actual spreads were above predicted spreads and were especially high in late 1995 and early 1996. This is consistent with the earlier observation that primary launch spreads lag the changes in secondary market prices. Following a sharp decline in new issues as secondary spreads rose, primary issues started coming back to the market at higher spreads. In the second half of 1996, the divergence between actual and predicted spreads narrowed, foreshadowing the "irrational exuberance" of 1997.

We next repeated the estimates up to 1996 (as in table 4.7) and generated in-sample predictions for 1996 and out-of-sample predictions for 1997. The aggressive fall in spreads is evident for Latin America. Actual spreads fall below predicted with the gap increasing up to the third quarter of 1997. In the final quarter of 1997, the gap falls. With the East Asian crisis of the summer of 1997 spreading to Latin America, spreads rose, bringing them closer to the predicted spreads. For East Asia, we see clearly the effect of the crisis, with actual spreads rising rapidly above predicted spreads in the second half of 1997.

Table 4.9　　　　**The Swings in Market Sentiment**

	Predictions Based on Sample for 1991–95		Predictions Based on Sample for 1991–96	
	Latin America	East Asia	Latin America	East Asia
1995				
Q1	87	2		
Q2	−40	−23		
Q3	−6	−18		
Q4	−117	−59		
1996				
Q1	−61	−59	−4	−33
Q2	−69	15	−10	45
Q3	−33	−29	34	19
Q4	34	−30	84	3
1997				
Q1			145	60
Q2			134	−6
Q3			179	−70
Q4			147	−229

Note: Values represent differences between predicted and actual spreads in basis points.

4.7   Conclusions and Implications

We have studied the determinants of launch spreads on emerging market debt using a framework that accounts for the joint determination of the issue and pricing decisions and controls for selectivity. Factors that increase the probability of observing an issue and raise the spread we interpret in terms of the supply of bonds, while those that increase the probability of an issue while reducing the spread we interpret in terms of demand. The results confirm the importance of both blades of the scissors. But the results for Latin America and East Asia are different, especially toward the beginning of the 1990s. For example, there is evidence that the supply of bonds by Latin American issuers is less responsive to changing market conditions. There is some sign that the extent of this regional differentiation has narrowed as the market has grown deeper. Other signs of a maturing market include the appearance of a well-defined yield curve for Latin America, and evidence that borrowers are exploiting scale economies when issuing bonds.

Our most striking finding is that changes in market sentiment not obviously related to fundamentals have moved the market by large amounts over short periods. Changes in observable issuer characteristics and in the responsiveness of spreads and issues to those characteristics do not provide an adequate explanation for changes over time in the value of new bond issues and launch spreads. In important periods, such as the wake of the Mexican and Asian crises, blanket shifts in sentiment play the dominant role.

The obvious implication for policy is that governments should exercise caution when contemplating an economic policy strategy that relies on continuous inflows of foreign capital intermediated by the international bond market. Large quantities of foreign credit may be available when sentiment shifts in their favor, but it can also shift against them for reasons beyond their control, making it impossible to finance large current account deficits and forcing a difficult adjustment. There is an argument for insuring against the capriciousness of the bond market by diversifying sources of international borrowing to include foreign direct investment, equity investment, and syndicated bank loans. And it would be prudent to insure against the sudden evaporation of foreign financing and the sudden appearance of a painful adjustment burden by taking steps to limit the size of the current account deficit.

The first round of empirical work for this paper was done in the first half of 1997, a period of large-scale bond issues by emerging market borrowers and dramatic spread compression. There were but a few voices in the wilderness warning that this favorable state of affairs could come to a sudden end at any time. In a sense, this was the central prediction of our empirical work. It came true in the final quarter of that year.

Data Appendix

Bond Characteristics

The bond data set, obtained from Capital Data Bondware and further processed by the Emerging Markets Division of the IMF includes (a) spreads (in basis points, where one basis point is one-hundredth of a percentage point) over "risk-free" issue denominated in the same currency and of about the same maturity; (b) the amount of the issue (millions of US$); (c) the maturity in years; (d) a dummy variable taking the value 1 if the bond was "privately placed" and 0 otherwise; (e) currency of issue; and (f) whether the issuer was a sovereign, a public agency, or a private party.

Issuer Characteristics

The following variables were constructed from Bondware.

S	Sovereign
P	Private
O	Other

LAC	Latin America and Caribbean
ECA	Eastern Europe and Central Asia
AFR	Africa
SAS	South Asia
EAP	East Asia and Pacific

Country Characteristics

edt	total external debt (US$)
gnp	gross national product in current prices
reserves	total foreign reserves minus gold
gdp90	gross domestic product in 1990 prices and national currency
gdpnc	gross domestic product at current prices in national currency
gdp	gross domestic product in current prices and denominated in US$
deficit	total budget deficit (national currency)
dres	indicator variable to denote whether a debt rescheduling took place the previous year
edtgnp	ratio of edt to gnp
ggdp90	gross domestic product growth
defgdp	deficit/gdp
resgnp	reserves/gnp
tdsxgs	total external debt service/total exports
tb	10 yield of ten-years treasury bond
crtg	credit rating

Reserves, gdp90, gdpnc, and deficit are reported quarterly in the IMF's *International Financial Statistics.* Where quarterly data were not available, annual data were converted to quarterly figures by multiplying the "log difference" by one-fourth.

The two main sources for these variables were the World Bank's *World Debt Tables* (WBDT) and the International Monetary Fund's *International Financial Statistics* (IFS).

The exact series are

edt   WBDT vol. 2, series called "EDT"
gnp   WBDT vol. 2, series called "GNP"
tdsxgs WBDT vol. 2, series classified under Topic 4, Debt Indicators
resimf IMF IFS, series number "11.d"
gdp90   IMF IFS, series number "99b.p"
gdpnc   IMF IFS, series number "99b"
deficit IMF IFS, series number "80"
dres   WBDT vol. 1: table A3.3 "Multilateral debt relief agreements with official creditor, Jan. 80–Jan. 96," pp. 66–72 of the 1996 issue; table A4.4, "Multilateral debt relief agreements with commercial banks, Jan. 80–Dec. 95," pp. 78–82 of the 1996 issue

Credit ratings were obtained from the Bureau of Public Debt of the Department of Treasury, web address: http://www.publicdebt.treas.gov/of/ofrt102.htm.

Other specific sources included:

1. For Argentina, Hong Kong, Hungary, Israel, Korea, Singapore, and South Africa, data were obtained from IMF country desks.

2. Brazil's deficit/ratio was obtained from the Central Bank of Brazil, the Brazilian Ministry of Finance, and Garantia as reported by Dornbusch in *Brookings Papers on Economic Activity,* no. 1 (1997), 387, table 5.

3. For Hong Kong, additional data were obtained from the *Quarterly Report of Gross Domestic Product Estimates* published by the Census and Statistics Department, Hong Kong, August 1997.

4. Data for Taiwan were obtained from the December 1996/January 1997 *Balance of Payments of Taiwan District, the Republic of China,* published by the Central Bank of China (Taiwan).

Countries included in the analysis are Argentina, Bahrain, Barbados, Bolivia, Brazil, Chile, China, Colombia, Congo, Costa Rica, Croatia, Cyprus, Czechoslovakia, the Czech Republic, the Dominican Republic, Ecuador, Estonia, Guatemala, Hong Kong, Hungary, India, Indonesia, Israel, Jamaica, Kazakhstan, Latvia, Lebanon, Liberia, Lithuania, Malaysia, Malta, Mexico, Moldova, Morocco, Oman, Pakistan, Panama, Peru, the Philippines, Poland, Qatar, Romania, Russia, Singapore, Slovakia, South Africa, South Korea, Taiwan, Thailand, Trinidad and Tobago, Tunisia, Turkey, Ukraine, Uruguay, and Venezuela. Other countries included in the analysis but not recorded as having issued bonds are Ghana, Jordan, Mauritius, Saudi Arabia, and Sri Lanka.

References

Bernstein, Robert J., and John A. Penicook Jr. 1996. Emerging market debt: Practical portfolio considerations. Presented to the New York University Salomon Brothers Center Conference on Emerging Market Capital Flows, 23–24 May.
Calvo, Guillermo, and Enrique G. Mendoza. 1995. Reflections on Mexico's balance-of-payments crisis: A chronicle of a death foretold. University of Maryland, Department of Economics. Mimeo.
Cantor, Richard, and Frank Packer. 1994. The credit rating industry. *Federal Reserve Bank of New York Quarterly Review* 19, no. 2 (summer/fall): 1–26.
———. 1995. Determinants and impact of sovereign credit ratings. *Federal Reserve Bank of New York Economic Policy Review* 2 (October): 37–53.
Chari, V. V., and Patrick Kehoe. 1997. Hot money. Research Department, Federal Reserve Bank of Minneapolis. Mimeo.
Cline, William R. 1995. *International debt reexamined.* Washington, D.C.: Institute for International Economics.
Cline, William R., and Kevin J. S. Barnes. 1997. Spreads and risk in emerging market lending. Research Paper no. 97-1. Washington, D.C.: Institute of International Finance.
Edwards, Sebastian. 1986. The pricing of bonds and bank loans in international markets. *European Economic Review* 30:565–89.
Eichengreen, Barry, and Richard Portes. 1989. After the deluge: Default, negotiation, and readjustment during the interwar years. In *The international debt crisis in historical perspective,* ed. Barry Eichengreen and Peter Lindert, 12–47. Cambridge, Mass.: MIT Press.
Hajivassilious, V. 1989. Do secondary markets believe in life after debt? In *Dealing with the debt crisis,* ed. H. Ishrat and I. Diwan, 276–92. Washington, D.C.: World Bank.
Haque, Nadeem, Mammohan Kumar, Nelson Mark, and Donald J. Mathieson. 1996. The economic content of indicators of developing country creditworthiness. *IMF Staff Papers* 43:688–724.
Heckman, James. 1979. Sample section bias as a specification error. *Econometrica* 47:153–61.
Huizinga, Harry. 1989. Commercial bank claims on developing countries: How have banks been affected? In *Dealing with the debt crisis,* ed. H. Ishrat and I. Diwan, 129–43. Washington, D.C.: World Bank.
Kamin, Steven, and Karsten van Kleist. 1997. The evolution and determinants of emerging market credit spreads in the 1990s. Federal Reserve Board and Bank of International Settlements. Mimeo.
Kinoshita, Yuko, and Ashoka Mody. 1997. The usefulness of private and public information for foreign investment decisions. Policy Research Working Paper no. 1733. Washington, D.C.: World Bank.
Levey, David H. N.d. Evaluating sovereign risk. Moody's Investors Service. Mimeo.

Ozler, Sule, and Harry Huizinga. 1992. Bank exposure, capital, and secondary market discounts on developing country debt. NBER Working Paper no. 3961. Cambridge, Mass.: National Bureau of Economic Research.

Comment   Sylvia Maxfield

This paper fits into a growing body of literature exploring the determinants of capital flows into and from emerging market countries. One of the main points of debate is over when and to what extent "pull" and "push" factors or irrationality operate in the rapidly growing international market for developing country bonds. "Pull" refers to investors attracted by the fundamental characteristics of the issuing country. In this case one could assume a globally stable appetite for emerging market country bonds where demand, prices, and yields for a particular country's bonds depend on investors' careful evaluation of that country's past, present, and future creditworthiness. "Push" refers to investors turning to the emerging market asset class when their risk-free rate falls below a certain threshold. Here the price of bonds depends to a greater extent on the strength of demand for the emerging market bond asset class. When global liquidity falls and the risk-free rate rises, capital will move more or less indiscriminately out of emerging market bonds. These studies focus varyingly on bond prices, balance of payments, trade balances, actual flows as best as they can be measured, and other variables.

What is new in this paper is an effort to explain the likelihood of a new issue and variation in bond yields at the time of new issue launching. This emphasis should make the authors' effort interesting to Wall Street, but is perhaps not as exciting as an effort to predict variation in spreads as bonds trade in the secondary market. The authors have also assembled a huge number of observations. The paper is replete with interesting findings pointing to valuable follow-up work.

The authors' model includes a number of variables standard to Wall Street's own models of spread behavior. These capture the fundamental variables shaping credit worthiness such as the debt service ratio or GDP growth. These fundamentals are what is expected to motivate investors who are "pulled" into emerging market investment. U.S. Treasury yields are also included to control for changes in the risk-free investment rate and the "push" logic. The model explains cross-national variation better than change over time and points to some interesting differences between

Sylvia Maxfield is research associate at the David Rockefeller Center for Latin American Studies, Harvard University.

Latin America and Asia. The "pull" logic appears to operate more consistently in Asia than Latin America.

For example, the debt service ratio has the expected positive impact on spreads in Asia but not Latin America. Investors do not behave as though they expect conventional market discipline to operate in Latin America. One possible explanation is a belief that the higher the debt burden, the more likely an international bailout and the lower the default risk. Another explanation is that irrational exuberance operated to a greater extent in Latin America than Asia. Another result is that GDP growth has a negative effect on spreads in Asia and positive one in Latin America, suggesting that investors believe Asians will harness growth to help repay debt but Latin Americans might not. Overall these results could be interpreted as suggesting that, for the period studied, the market for Asian international bonds behaved more in line with expectations than the Latin American markets. This should not be surprising given that the period covers the Mexican peso crisis. The data on error term correlation suggest that unobservables are doing much of the work to explain new issue launch spreads in Latin America.

The authors also use their results to tell a novel story about demand and supply in international markets for developing-country bonds. They find that as U.S. interest rates rise, new issue launch spreads fall. This contravenes the "push" logic that investors buy emerging market assets when the risk-free rates falls. Their explanation is that when U.S. rates rise only the more credit worthy issuers come to the market. Supply is constricted and spreads compress.

This result suggests the need for more nuanced study of the interaction of supply and demand for emerging market assets. Wall Street refers to these considerations as "technical" factors, while determinants of credit worthiness such as debt service ratios are called "fundamentals." Most experienced fixed income traders will tell you that in any relatively illiquid market, technicals (supply and demand considerations) are key to price behavior. An interesting extension of Eichengreen and Mody's research would be to separate the sample according to the extent of liquidity. The conventional Wall Street wisdom is that technical factors matter more the less liquid the market. A related consideration is variation in the size of the issue and the issuers' total outstanding bond stock. Larger issues will be more liquid. If diversification is an important investor motive, demand could be unexpectedly high and spreads tight for issues from countries with few bonds outstanding.

The results also suggest a different and to me more plausible conclusion than the one offered by the authors. This explanation returns to the demand side and is simply that investor exuberance swamped the rate differential logic throughout the entire period studied. Perhaps the impact of the risk-free rate on investors' behavior corresponds not to simple variation in the rate but to accumulated changes in the risk-free rate over time. The authors might consider looking for threshold levels that trigger changes in demand; this would, however, require longer time series than we have available. The authors' suggestion about supply behavior is striking and counterintuitive, but on Wall Street and for issuing country debt managers the more interesting question would be whether spreads in the secondary market follow the same logic.

In summary this paper contributes to the debate on determinants of investment in foreign currency denominated emerging market bonds. It suggests that "pull" logic operated more strongly in Asia than Latin America. Future research should aim to illuminate whether this happened due to cross-regional differences, informational inefficiency, moral hazard, irrationality, or some other factor. The paper also suggests a need to explore the interaction between global liquidity, the risk-free rate, and exuberance.

Is There a Curse of Location?
Spatial Determinants of Capital
Flows to Emerging Markets

Swati Ghosh and Holger Wolf

5.1 Introduction

Walter Bagehot noted more than a century ago that "the same instruments which diffused capital through a nation are gradually diffusing it among nations" (1880, 71).[1] The trend toward enhanced financial integration has since continued, with frequent spurts and the occasional spectacular reversals. By and large, the 1990s have been associated with increased integration: private-to-private capital flows between mature and emerging markets have increased very substantially, rising from US$44 billion in 1990 to US$167 billion in 1995, with public sector flows remaining virtually unchanged at about US$60 billion. Indeed, prior to the dramatic Mexican and Asian reversals (themselves evidence of increased integration), the shift from public to private flows has led some observers to pronounce a new era in which official bilateral and multilateral development assistance would be increasingly replaced by direct private investments.

While the large-scale inflows (and the recent large-scale outflows) have received wide attention by both policy makers and the academic community,[2] the fact that the new private flows bypassed the vast majority of

Swati Ghosh is senior economist in the East Asia and Pacific region at the World Bank. Holger Wolf is assistant professor in the Center for German and European Studies and the Department of Economics at Georgetown University.

The authors thank Miguel Savastano, Sebastian Edwards, and conference participants for helpful comments. The assistance of the central banks and the statistical offices of the G7 economies in obtaining data is gratefully acknowledged.

1. Presciently, he also noted that while "the effect of this will be in the end much to simplify the problems of international trade . . . for the present, as is commonly the case with incipient causes whose effect is incomplete, it complicates all it touches" (Bagehot 1880, 71).

2. See Calvo, Leiderman, and Reinhart (1993a, 1993b), Chen and Kahn (1997) and Chuhan, Claessens, and Mamingi (1993), among others.

developing countries has received less notice. Of the 107 countries classified as either low income or middle income by the World Bank, forty-eight countries received less than US$100 million in net private inflows in 1995, while another fourteen received between US$100 and US$200 million. The remaining forty-five economies received the lion's share, with China (US$44,339 million), Brazil (US$19,097 million), Mexico (US$13,068 million), Malaysia (US$11,924 million), Indonesia (US$11,648 million), Thailand (US$9,143 million), Hungary (US$7,841 million), and Argentina (US$7,204 million) each receiving more than twice the *total* inflows of the forty-eight less developed countries (LDCs) with the smallest inflows.[3]

The concentration of flows to a select group of star emerging economies admits of two explanations. First, it might simply be the case that fundamentals in these stars dominated fundamentals in the also-rans. In particular, development thresholds may play a crucial role in deciding who does, and who does not, obtain foreign funds: Market size matters for foreign direct investment (FDI), while the existence and liquidity of asset markets are trivial determinants of portfolio flows. If threshold effects are indeed the crucial determinants, the laggards will gain access to world capital markets as an automatic side effect of development. Furthermore, whether such access will be obtained is at least partially dependent upon their own policies.

Alternatively, one may suppose that development, and hence the breaching of thresholds enabling full access to world capital markets, is significantly determined by accidents of history, and specifically by location, which are largely exogenous. There are good reasons to support such a conjecture. It is well known, for instance, that bilateral trade decreases strongly in distance; indeed, this relation is one of the sturdiest stylized facts of the empirical trade literature. It is also well known that trade and FDI linkages are reinforcing: Countries with relatively high bilateral trade shares tend to have relatively high bilateral FDI shares.[4] It is not unreasonable to suppose that financial links in turn depend on FDI and trade links. Foreign-owned firms may have an easier time accessing foreign capital markets, as may domestic firms linked through demand and supply channels to foreign firms. As such linkages develop and international familiarity with the country grows, domestic firms in turn may find easier access. To the degree that location drives trade, which in turn drives FDI and financial integration, the outlook for the laggards is less rosy: An improvement in access under this scenario requires compensation for the natural

3. These countries of course also account for the lion's share of LDC population, thus the concentration in flows per capita is somewhat less pronounced.

4. The link is not perfect. In some cases, notably in the presence of trade barriers, FDI may be a substitute for, rather than a complement to, trade. The empirical and theoretical consensus, however, point to a complementary nature of FDI and trade as the rule. See Mundell (1957), Helpman (1984), Neary (1995), and Markusen (1997) for some representative views.

disadvantage of location, which also impedes—through the trade-growth nexus—development itself.

In this paper, we aim to throw some light on the role of geography in determining financial flows. We proceed in two steps. We begin on the recipient side by examining the determinants of access, assessing whether, controlling for other factors, location matters for determining access.

We next turn to the source countries to examine the spatial distribution of *outward* financial flows in a standard gravity framework. Gravity models have been quite useful in accounting for the distribution of bilateral trade, with most of the explanatory power deriving from bilateral distance (negatively), dummies for common borders, common language, common trade bloc membership (positive), and market size (positive). Using a data set of capital outflows by type and destination for the G7 economies, we estimate identical gravity specifications for trade and for four types of capital flows: foreign direct investment, bank lending, portfolio debt, and portfolio equity. The approach permits two insights. First, it yields a direct estimate of the sensitivity of capital flows to distance, and hence of the importance of location, ceteris paribus. Second, it permits a comparison of the relative importance of distance, the possession of common borders, common language, common membership in trade blocs, and market size across the different types of capital flows.

5.2 Data

This paper draws on a fairly diverse set of data sources. The national aggregated and disaggregated inward capital flow data are taken from the World Development Indicators (World Bank 1997). G7 outward capital flows are taken from the Bank for International Settlements (BIS; bank lending), Organization for Economic Cooperation and Development (OECD; foreign direct investment), and correspondence with national central banks, ministries of finance, and financial market groups (portfolio flows). The core of the trade data, as well as the distance, common border, common language, and trade bloc variables, have been taken from Shang-Jin Wei's NBER web page (www.nber.org/~wei). Trade and distance data were augmented from the International Monetary Fund's *IMF Trade Statistics* and from Bali online (www.indo.com/distance/) to match our sample. Inward capital flows are the average for the 1990–95 period. All outward data are for a single year, 1994 for FDI and bank lending, and different years between 1990 and 1994 for the portfolio data.

5.3 Determinants of Access

Examining the determinants of access requires a definition of "access." Our main measure is based on the three access scores for alternative capital flow types reported by *Euromoney,* based on a mixture of observed capital flows and subjective assessments. The three measures are intended to capture, respectively, access to bank lending, short-term finance, and capital markets. The bank lending measure is based on reported long-term private nonguaranteed debt disbursements. The short-term finance measure is based on the U.S. Export-Import Bank assessment, while the capital market measure is based on syndicated loan and bond issues and a subjective judgment of the current ease of market access. To obtain the overall access score, we rank countries by their combined scores, then classify countries in the top third as having access and countries in the bottom third as lacking access; we drop the intermediate group.[5] As a test for robustness, we also considered a second measure based on the average *absolute* net inflow of private capital as a percentage of gross domestic product (GDP) during the 1990–95 period. The third of countries with the largest share are assigned to the access group, the third of countries with the smallest shares to the no-access group. The middle third is again dropped to obtain a sharper distinction.

The measures are not ideal. Large net flows are a sufficient but not a necessary condition for access to world financial markets. Two caveats arise. First, among perfectly integrated markets, adjustment may happen primarily through relative price adjustment rather than flows. Given that most countries in the present data set are far from fully integrated, however, this possibility is a lesser concern. Second, small net flows are consistent with large but offsetting gross flows. This is arguably a more serious concern, though there is little evidence that offsets are significant at the bottom of our access measure: For the subset of countries in this group for which both inflows and outflows are available, one of the two categories tends to dominate the other, so that absolute net flows provide a reasonably good proxy for gross flows. The *Euromoney* rating attempts to reduce the reliance on observed flows by taking account of subjective assessments by market participants, and hence it is our preferred measure.

A first look at the data reveals significant apparent location effects. Only one of twenty-one African countries, but fifteen of eighteen European countries, is classified as having access. The split is of course consistent with other spatially correlated determinants of access. We examine the linkages in two steps. We begin with a probit analysis before turning to classification trees to formally allow for threshold effects.

5.3.1 Probit Tests

To assess the importance of location for access, ceteris paribus, we first regress in a probit framework the access dummy on relative population

---

5. Our measure is solely based on the access subscore reported by *Euromoney,* and thus excludes the scores for "economic performance," "political risk," "debt indicators," and "credit ratings" that dominate in the overall country risk score reported by *Euromoney.*

size (measured by 1989 population as a fraction of the sample maximum); relative market size (measured by 1989 U.S.-dollar GDP, purchasing power parity [PPP] adjusted, as a fraction of the sample maximum); real development stage (measured by 1989 GDP per capita as a fraction of the sample maximum); growth (measured by 1985–89 GDP per capita growth as a fraction of the sample maximum); openness (the 1989 export-to-GDP ratio); and three measures of location—the distance to the closest G7 economy, the GDP-weighted average distance to all G7 economies (all expressed relative to the sample maximum), and continental dummies for Africa and the Western Hemisphere (except Canada and the United States).

To reduce the endogeneity problem, the explanatory variables are either for 1989, or for the average of the years 1985 to 1989, while the access rating is for 1993. Our interest is twofold: first, to assess whether the explanatory variables have power for predicting whether a country has access, and second, to determine whether after controlling for these factors, a residual effect remains for location. Table 5.1 presents the results. The first three columns present regressions of the access dummy on, respectively, the weighted distance, the individual distances, and the two continent dummies. The weighted distance, a rough proxy for a country's distance from "world GDP," enters negatively and is significant at the 10 percent level. Bilateral distances offer a more mixed picture, perhaps reflecting the high correlation between the four European series (0.988) and between Canada and the United States (0.965). Restricting the distances to Germany, Japan, and the United States yields negative effects for all three distances (Germany: −0.67 [0.79], Japan: −4.14 [3.70], United States: −0.54 [0.64]). Both of the continental dummies for Africa and the Western Hemisphere are negative and significant.

Location factors are thus correlated with access. The next four columns examine to what extent this correlation reflects spatially correlated fundamentals. Column (4) presents the regression on the four fundamentals. Only income per capita, a proxy both for productivity and spending power, enters significantly, with a positive sign. A higher number of consumers and a faster growth rate are positively correlated with access; however, both variables are insignificant. Openness controlling for these factors enters negatively, albeit also insignificantly. The last three columns add the location variables to examine whether, controlling for the fundamentals, location exerts an additional effect. The answer is negative: None of the location factors enters significantly, while GDP per capita remains significant. Within the probit framework, the development stage is thus the main determinant of whether a country has or does not have access to financial markets.[6]

---

6. Results are by and large similar for the flow measure, with the exception of the openness variable, which enters positive, but is also insignificant. GDP per capita is the most significant influence; adding location variables to the fundamentals yields insignificant effects.

Table 5.1   Access Determinants: Probit

	(1)	(2)	(3)	(4)	(5)	(6)	(7)
Constant	1.11	0.43	0.79	−2.07	−3.16	26.96	−1.85
	(1.85)	(0.29)	(3.64)	(2.98)	(1.95)	(1.31)	(2.08)
Average distance	−1.88				1.78		
	(1.92)				(0.75)		
Distance to:							
Canada		−2.40				3.39	
		(0.90)				(0.59)	
France		−18.06				−3,158.7	
		(0.25)				(1.30)	
Germany		−14.72				119.47	
		(0.58)				(0.95)	
Italy		22.92				390.42	
		(1.38)				(1.21)	
Japan		−2.29				−71.42	
		(1.11)				(1.35)	
U.K.		8.22				2,681.1	
		(0.12)				(1.30)	
U.S.		4.81				−47.09	
		(1.51)				(1.36)	

	(1)	(2)	(3)	(4)	(5)	(6)	(7)
Africa			−2.46 (4.76)				−0.85 (1.07)
Latin America			−1.55 (3.03)				0.006 (0.09)
Population size				2.46 (0.95)	2.67 (0.98)	−11.67 (1.11)	2.31 (0.91)
GDP per capita				26.28 (3.33)	28.44 (3.28)	174.2 (1.43)	24.39 (2.90)
GDP per capita growth				1.89 (1.51)	1.84 (1.45)	12.53 (1.42)	1.50 (1.13)
Openness				−2.02 (0.88)	−2.65 (1.07)	−32.23 (1.35)	−1.29 (0.52)
Log likelihood	−48.04	−37.15	−30.61	−11.55	−11.25	−7.80	−10.81
Number of observations	72	72	72	65	65	65	64

Note: Numbers in parentheses are *t*-statistics.

There are good reasons to take these results with a grain of salt, however. In particular, the implicit assumption of linearity underlying the estimations may not be warranted. For instance, while it stands to reason that there is a positive relationship between the development stage and access, the link may take the form of a threshold effect rather than a log linear relation, so that access is obtained once some threshold level of development is breached but, beyond that level, further increases in the development level do not lead to equal increases in access. Similar conjectures hold for several of the explanatory variables. With fixed costs of entry, foreign financial firms may require a minimum aggregate economy size before committing resources. Beyond threshold effects, context dependence may also play a role. Thus the relative export ratio may be a crucial determinant of which of a group of small economies has access to world financial markets, but may matter little for determining the access of larger countries whose home financial sector is of sufficient size to attract foreign interest.

By definition, the coefficients in the standard multivariate regression analysis reflect the marginal effect of a change in the explanatory variable, holding constant the other variables. As such, these regressions cannot readily capture threshold effects or complementarities. In principle, it would be possible to allow for such effects by including sufficiently many dummy variables and interactive terms in the regression. In the absence of clear-cut theoretical predictions about the shape of the interaction, however, let alone the level of thresholds, adding such terms becomes impractical. The presence of threshold effects and context dependence can nevertheless be readily examined within a classification tree context, to which we turn next.

5.3.2 Classification Trees

A classification tree provides a simple ordering of a set of potential explanatory variables by their ability to predict into which of two groups a binary dependent variable falls. In the present case, the dependent variable is simply the 0-1 dummy for access. The algorithm searches through all possible thresholds for all potential explanatory variables to identify the variable (with an associated threshold) that best separates the two groups of countries. Suppose, for instance, that the lowest export growth in countries with access was 15 percent, while the highest export growth in countries without access was 12 percent. In this case, "export growth above 13 percent" provides a perfect separation rule.

More generally, the split will not be perfect, there will be some countries that have high export growth but no access (type I errors) and others that have low export growth but enjoy access (type II errors). The algorithm searches through all observed values of all explanatory variables to find the variable-cum-threshold that minimizes the sum of the type I and type

II errors.[7] The sum of the errors then provides an (inverse) measure of the ability of the variable to predict access. This rule is then used to split the sample into two subsamples, and the algorithm is applied in turn to each of them. To enhance robustness, the original sample is split into a learning and a test sample, and the ability of the rules identified for the learning sample to predict the division of the test sample enters the evaluation function for the rule.

In principle, the process could continue until every observation has been placed into its own branch (akin to including as many explanatory variables as observations in a regression), thus getting a perfect, if meaningless, fit. To avoid this overfitting, a termination rule is required. The termination rule used resembles, loosely speaking, an *adjusted R^2* criterion. After each split, the improvement in the overall fit (which, just like the change in the raw R^2 upon adding an additional explanatory variable is always nonnegative) is combined with a penalty on the number of branches that promotes parsimony. If the penalty exceeds the improvement, the branch is terminated at the prior node; if not, the algorithm continues.

In essence, the technique thus uses the potential explanatory variables to produce an ordered sequence of criteria (a decision tree) determining the likelihood that a country will or will not have access. Since the sequence of criteria can depend upon previous branchings of the tree, the algorithm can readily accommodate cross-dependencies between the explanatory variables. As a side benefit, the technique also establishes a hierarchy of explanatory variables, based on their ability to discriminate between the two groups (access, no access) of countries. Finally, because the algorithm uses interior thresholds, it is by construction extremely robust to outliers.

Restricting the set of explanatory variables to the bilateral distances to each of the G7 countries yields a single split: Countries more than 11,353 miles from Japan are classified as having no access, those closer as having access. The simple rule works quite well: Twenty-four of the twenty-six countries (92.3 percent) with greater bilateral distances indeed have no access under the *Euromoney* classification, while thirty-four of the forty-six countries (73.9 percent) with shorter bilateral distances have access. Restricting the sample to continental dummies likewise yields a quite powerful simple rule for predicting access: Countries in Africa and countries in the southern and central Western Hemisphere are predicted to have no access; of these thirty countries, twenty-seven (90 percent) are correctly classified, with very similar results for the flow-based measure.

The location of a country is thus highly correlated with whether the country enjoys access to international financial markets. We examine to

7. Depending on the question examined, different weights can be attached to type I and type II errors. For the present application, both types were weighted equally.

what extent this correlation reflects spatially correlated fundamentals by expanding the set of explanatory variables to also include the fundamental variables. The results are striking: Knowledge of GDP per capita is almost sufficient to predict access, with a threshold of 2,800 comparable U.S. dollars. Of the thirty-two countries with lower income per capita, thirty-one (96.9 percent) are rated as having no access; of the forty countries above, thirty-five (87.5 percent) are rated as having access. Overall, the simple threshold allows correct classification of 92 percent of observations.

For the simple flow measure, income per capita is again the dominant discriminator (with a $1,501 threshold), but is followed, for both high and low income countries, by a threshold on the minimum share of industry in GDP (43 and 33 percent, respectively). The overall fit is again very good: Using the thresholds on income per capita and on the industry shares allows correct classification of forty-eight out of fifty-six observations. Controlling for fundamentals, the distance variables do not enter as useful discriminants, nor do continental dummies.

The classification tree analysis, viewed in conjunction with the probit results, yields three quite robust insights. First, access is highly correlated with location: Countries located in Asia and the Western Hemisphere (except Canada and the United States) have a much lower probability of having access to world financial markets. Second, access is highly correlated with income per capita and industry shares. Third, income per capita provides a better discriminant than distance to the G7 economies.

The findings permit two interpretations. First, it might be that income per capita is lower in Africa and the Western Hemisphere for reasons unrelated to location. In this case, addressing the obstacles to growth will permit the as yet excluded countries to breach the development threshold and gain access. Second, it might be that low income per capita is itself causally linked to location. Such a link is not ex ante unreasonable. For instance, two separate literatures establish a strong positive trade-growth nexus and a very strong negative trade-distance linkage. Joining these two stylized facts potentially gives rise to a negative link between growth and the "distance" to world GDP.

The strength of such exogenous location effects relative to policy actions in determining growth and thus income per capita is an open question for future research exceeding the scope of the present paper. We can note, however, that a simple regression for the present data set of per capita growth on income per capita, openness, the investment ratio, the average distance measure, and the Africa and Western Hemisphere dummies does yield a significant negative effect of the continental dummies, and a negative but insignificant effect of distance. Significant negative coefficients on continental dummies have also been reported in a number of other papers in the empirical growth literature dating back to Barro (1991) and have proved rather robust to the inclusion of new explanatory variables.

5.4 Determinants of Outward Financial Flows

The previous section examined the dependence between the probability of having access and properties of the recipient country, including location. We now turn to the source countries to examine the determinants of the spatial distribution of outward flows, including the location of the recipient country relative to the source country. Relative location has long played a major role in empirical trade. A substantial literature documents that bilateral trade increases strongly in proximity, is even higher between countries sharing borders, and is higher still between countries sharing a border and a common language.[8] In contrast, spatial factors have received much less explicit attention in international finance, perhaps reflecting a greater concentration on price rather than quantity effects.[9]

In this section, we aim to provide some initial stylized facts on the spatial nature of outward capital flows to guide further exploration. It is ex ante far from evident whether such linkages exist and which form they take. For instance, standard portfolio theory may well be taken to suggest a *positive* effect of distance on flows: The very presence of a strong *negative* effect of distance on trade suggests that business cycle (and thus, to an approximation, return) correlations decrease in distance, suggesting that optimally diversified portfolios allocate higher shares to geographically distant markets. Taking a contrary view, it is also reasonable to suppose that informational advantages arise from proximity, for instance, common language may facilitate assessment of potential investments, common borders may facilitate supervision, and so forth, suggesting a *negative* effect of distance on capital flows.

To learn more about the spatial determinants of capital flows we explore capital flows in a standard gravity model. The model is advantageous for our purposes both because of its excellent track record in accounting for the spatial distribution of bilateral trade flows and because of its compatibility with a wide range of modeling approaches, allowing us to explore spatial linkages in a fairly unrestricted setting.

The estimated gravity equations are standard: The variable of interest (the log of bilateral exports, FDI, bank loans, debt, and equity) is related to the log of bilateral distance, a dummy for common borders and common language, a measure of remoteness, as well as to the market size of the recipient (measured by GDP in comparable U.S. dollars) and its development level (measured by GDP per capita in comparable U.S. dollars).

---

8. See Frankel, Stein, and Wei (1993), Engle and Rogers (1994), Helliwell (1995), Helliwell and McCallum (1995), Linneman (1966), McCallum (1995), Rauch (1996), and Wei (1996) among others for recent evidence. Recent work has shown the major theoretical trade models to be able to accommodate gravity effects (Anderson 1979; Armington 1969; Bergstrand 1985; Deardorff 1995).

9. Exceptions include Bohn and Tesar (1996) and Eaton and Tamura (1994).

Where possible, regressions are performed on the level of the financial variables. For some of the portfolio series, only flow observations were available; here it is assumed that the flows in a given year are proportional to the stock.

The remoteness indicator is a fairly recent innovation in the gravity literature. It aims to capture a dependence of the effect of bilateral distance on the proximity of third trading partners (Deardorff 1995): Two countries located close to each other but "distant" from world output are likely to transact more with each other than two equally distant states closer to world output. Remoteness is simply the GDP-weighted average distance to the G7 and, under the null, is expected to enter with a positive sign: Controlling for bilateral distance (which enters separately), greater remoteness from alternative transaction partners enhances the incentive for bilateral transactions. For the current data set, Iceland is the least remote country, while the Pacific islands are most remote.

Tables 5.2 through 5.7 presents the results. All regressions are single equation ordinary least squares (OLS). With consistent data sources, panel estimation would have been preferable. Given the heterogeneity of the current data set, with flow and stock measures from different sources and somewhat different definitions, single equation estimation seemed preferable. Table 5.2 provides a summary measure of the results, reporting the median coefficient estimate for each variable for each of the five transaction measures. The results display considerable similarity. The median elasticity of bilateral transactions with respect to bilateral distance is always negative though often insignificant, ranging between −0.45 for equities and −0.96 for FDI. The negative relation between trade and bilateral distance thus extends to other types of bilateral transactions, including bank loans, debt, and equity. The median elasticity with respect to remoteness is always positive, ranging from 0.33 for debt to 2.89 for FDI. Controlling for bilateral distance, greater proximity to world GDP reduces transactions. Not too surprisingly, the elasticity of transaction with respect to the recipient country market size is uniformly positive and closely centered around unity. Indeed, judging from the medians, FDI and

Table 5.2   **Gravity Regression: Median Coefficients**

	Median Export	Median FDI	Median Loan	Median Debt	Median Equity
Log distance	−0.71	−0.96	−0.81	−0.62	−0.45
Log remote	1.51	2.89	2.10	0.33	1.92
Adjacent?	0.45	0.62	−0.34		
Language?	0.64	0.81	0.15		
Log GDP	0.79	0.97	0.96	1.09	0.95
Log GDP per capita	0.25	0.57	0.35	0.09	0.99

Table 5.3   **Gravity Regression: Exports**

	Canada	France	Germany	Italy	Japan	United Kingdom	United States
Constant	−42.28	−17.80	−18.57	−15.32	−29.65	−22.56	−32.42
	(7.58)**	(2.99)**	(3.62)**	(2.17)**	(4.25)**	(4.52)**	(5.78)**
Log distance	−1.59	−0.68	−0.58	−0.71	−1.36	−0.64	−1.17
	(3.95)**	(3.59)**	(3.40)**	(3.19)**	(4.17)**	(3.89)**	(2.45)**
Log remote	4.03	1.37	0.98	0.87	2.82	1.51	2.68
	(6.09)**	(1.99)*	(1.62)	(1.13)	(5.18)**	(2.54)**	(4.30)**
Adjacent?	0.62	0.16	0.17	0.28		1.20	0.84
	(0.46)	(0.29)	(0.47)	(0.48)		(1.56)	(0.81)
Language?	0.72	0.68	0.64	−0.27	−0.71	1.05	0.53
	(2.87)**	(2.52)**	(2.20)**	(0.27)	(0.56)	(5.49)**	(1.98)*
Log GDP	0.89	0.66	0.79	0.72	0.81	0.71	0.96
	(8.44)**	(8.81)**	(12.60)**	(7.47)**	(8.15)**	(10.96)**	(9.98)**
Log GDP per capita	0.31	0.15	0.25	0.22	0.40	0.30	0.25
	(2.86)**	(1.84)*	(3.57)**	(2.39)**	(3.51)**	(4.05)**	(2.40)**
Number of observations	66	67	71	65	68	71	67
R^2	0.76	0.75	0.87	0.74	0.72	0.81	0.74
Adjusted R^2	0.74	0.73	0.86	0.71	0.70	0.80	0.72

Note: Numbers in parentheses are *t*-statistics.

*Significant at the 10 percent level.
**Significant at the 5 percent level.

Table 5.4   Gravity Regression: FDI

	Canada	France	Germany	Italy	Japan	United Kingdom	United States
Constant	−28.92	−32.19	−28.83	−38.47	−59.22	−48.04	−47.50
	(1.86)*	(1.83)*	(1.90)*	(2.52)**	(5.23)**	(3.80)**	(4.80)**
Log distance	−1.53	−0.63	−0.21	−0.96	−1.70	−1.06	−0.49
	(1.39)	(1.24)	(0.48)	(1.89)*	(3.12)**	(2.00)*	(0.39)
Log remote	2.89	2.35	1.24	2.39	4.53	3.55	3.04
	(1.59)	(1.31)	(0.81)	(1.51)	(5.25)**	(2.50)**	(2.34)**
Adjacent?	−0.70	−0.01	0.62	0.62			1.05
	(0.27)	(0.01)	(0.48)	(0.34)			(0.46)
Language?	1.11	1.33	0.81	0.52	−2.77	2.17	0.57
	(1.58)	(1.26)	(0.90)	(0.23)	(1.53)	(1.98)*	(1.08)
Log GDP	0.68	0.73	0.89	0.97	1.36	1.29	1.09
	(2.52)**	(2.74)**	(3.86)**	(4.18)**	(7.32)**	(5.65)**	(5.65)**
Log GDP per capita	0.57	0.61	0.40	0.64	0.74	−0.24	0.53
	(2.00)*	(2.43)**	(1.90)*	(2.60)	(3.27)**	(0.44)	(2.50)**
Number of observations	19	30	32	33	32	13	32
R^2	0.70	0.57	0.61	0.61	0.76	0.86	0.71
Adjusted R^2	0.55	0.46	0.52	0.52	0.71	0.76	0.65

Note: Numbers in parentheses are *t*-statistics.
*Significant at the 10 percent level.
**Significant at the 5 percent level.

Table 5.5   Gravity Regression: Bank Loans

	Canada	France	Germany	Italy	Japan	United Kingdom	United States
Constant	-20.89	-34.04	-9.57	-27.92	-33.13	-32.34	-42.81
	(1.52)	(4.26)**	(1.52)	(2.96)**	(3.39)**	(5.39)**	(5.05)**
Log distance	-1.46	-0.57	-0.81	-0.22	-1.52	-0.09	-1.52
	(1.42)	(1.53)	(3.95)**	(0.69)	(3.05)**	(0.40)	(2.61)**
Log remote	2.43	2.14	0.43	1.13	2.10	1.27	3.95
	(1.57)	(1.97)*	(0.60)	(0.96)	(2.47)**	(1.70)*	(4.24)**
Adjacent?	0.30		-0.60				-0.34
	0.11		(1.41)				(0.25)
Language?	0.36	1.25	-0.05		-1.85	0.54	-0.04
	(0.57)	(2.98)**	(0.16)		(0.97)	(2.25)**	(0.11)
Log GDP	0.60	0.98	0.82	0.96	1.20	1.03	0.92
	(2.29)**	(9.69)**	(10.10)**	(7.63)	(8.03)**	(14.05)**	(5.60)**
Log GDP per capita	0.36	0.24	-0.04	0.13	0.60	0.35	0.63
	(1.37)	(1.89)*	(0.45)	(0.84)	(3.26)**	(3.41)**	(3.57)**
Number of observations	34	86	40	69	58	81	53
R^2	0.43	0.61	0.86	0.53	0.69	0.81	0.68
Adjusted R^2	0.30	0.58	0.84	0.50	0.66	0.80	0.63

Note: Numbers in parentheses are t-statistics.

*Significant at the 10 percent level.

**Significant at the 5 percent level.

Table 5.6   **Gravity Regression: Debt**

	Germany	Italy	United States
Constant	−1.46	−13.53	−57.61
	(0.16)	(0.97)	(5.38)**
Log distance	−0.11	−0.62	−1.30
	(0.65)	(1.39)	(2.44)**
Log remote	0.03	0.33	4.34
	(0.04)	(0.22)	(3.85)**
Adjacent?			
Language?			
Log GDP	0.38	1.11	1.09
	(2.71)**	(4.27)**	(5.88)**
Log GDP per capita	0.09	−0.71	1.14
	(0.32)	(1.67)	(5.50)**
Number of observations	20	21	47
R^2	0.41	0.63	0.73
Adjusted R^2	0.26	0.54	0.70

Note: Numbers in parentheses are *t*-statistics.
**Significant at the 5 percent level.

Table 5.7   **Gravity Regression: Equity**

	Germany	Italy	United Kingdom	United States
Constant	−40.51	−23.25	−31.48	−54.47
	(2.63)**	(1.45)	(1.22)	(5.92)**
Log distance	−0.47	−0.43	−0.89	−0.08
	(1.55)	(0.92)	(2.03)**	(0.18)
Log remote	0.98	−0.11	2.85	3.39
	(0.64)	(0.07)	(1.32)	(3.52)**
Adjacent?				
Language?				
Log GDP	1.03	0.98	0.51	0.92
	(4.10)**	(3.54)**	(1.33)	(5.72)**
Log GDP per capita	1.52	0.79	0.98	1.00
	(3.22)**	(1.52)	(0.67)	(5.49)**
Number of observations	19	20	10	49
R^2	0.77	0.70	0.61	0.72
Adjusted R^2	0.70	0.62	0.30	0.70

Note: Numbers in parentheses are *t*-statistics.
**Significant at the 5 percent level.

Table 5.8   **Gravity Regressions: Summary**

Canada	−1.53	FDI	−0.96
Japan	−1.52	Loans	−0.81
United States	−1.17	Exports	−0.71
United Kingdom	−0.76	Bonds	−0.62
France	−0.63	Equity	−0.45
Italy	−0.62		
Germany	−0.47		

financial flows appear to be more sensitive to recipient market size than is trade. The relative productivity of the recipient country likewise is always positively related to transaction size, with elasticities ranging from a low of 0.09 for debt (though only three individual estimates are available for debt) to a high of unity for equity transactions. The results complement our earlier finding that income per capita acts as a key determinant of access. The dummies for language and common borders are not significant but are, with one exception, of the expected positive sign.

Turning to the results for the individual transaction types, bilateral exports exhibit the familiar strong gravity pattern, decreasing strongly in bilateral distance but increasing in the remoteness of the partner country. The spatial determinants are of less significance for the FDI regressions; however, all seven distance elasticities are of the predicted negative sign, while all seven remoteness elasticities are positive.

The same pattern emerges for bank loans, debt, and equity, with the sole exception of the remote coefficient on Italy. The significance level of the coefficients is substantially lower compared to the export regressions; this may be at least partly attributable to the sharply reduced number of observations.

Table 5.8 summarizes the results on the distance elasticities. The first two columns report the median elasticity by country; the last two columns report the median elasticity by transaction type. Transactions of European countries are on average considerably less sensitive to distance, with elasticities ranging from 0.5 to 0.75. In contrast, the three non-European countries have elasticities above unity. A possible explanation may be sought in the greater openness of the European economies and the relatively low transactions costs for intra-European trade. On the transaction types, it is interesting to observe that the distance elasticity is larger for loans and FDI, both involving sizable commitments with limited liquidity, than for more liquid portfolio investment. This ordering is consistent with views emphasizing the importance of proximity for monitoring, arguably more important for less liquid assets.

5.5 Conclusion

The last decade has witnessed a resurgence in private-to-private capital flows from mature to emerging markets. To date, however, the flows have reached only a small group of developing countries. In this paper, we contrast two explanations for the continuing lack of access of many less developed countries. The first attributes lack of access to lack of development: Both FDI and portfolio inflow require functioning real and financial development. In this view, the as yet excluded markets will gain access as their domestic markets mature. The second view is less optimistic: If financial flows, just as trade flows, depend crucially on location, specifically on the proximity to mature markets, the access of disadvantageously located economies, particularly in Africa, may remain quite limited for the foreseeable future.

The provisional evidence presented here suggests that the second view cannot be rejected out of hand. Two pieces of evidence suggest that location may matter. First, looking across recipient countries, we found that economies located in Africa and the Western Hemisphere enjoyed less access to world capital markets than did countries located in other continents. This direct dependence of access on location vanished, however, once controls for other potential determinants of access were included, notably total and per capita GDP. An open issue for future research is whether the very high correlation between location and GDP per capita is accidental or whether low GDP per capita is itself a function of location, for instance through trade gravity linkages.

The second piece of evidence was gathered from gravity-type regressions of five different transaction types—exports, FDI, loans, debt, and equity—for the G7 economies. We found a strong uniform pattern across all five types: Every single estimated distance elasticity was negative, though significance levels are low. Importantly, the estimated distance effect was conditional on controlling for total and per capita GDP, a prima facie puzzle under standard capital market models, though one that can readily be reconciled if information flow is endogenized to distance. A better understanding of the causes of the distance effects is clearly desirable at this juncture. We simply note the implication that capital flows will decrease in the remoteness of a recipient country to "world GDP" even for similar fundamentals (as captured by GDP per capita). In this sense, the findings support the view that location matters in a fundamental sense for development prospects.

References

Anderson, James. 1979. A theoretical foundation for the gravity equation. *American Economic Review* 69:106–16.

Armington, Paul. 1969. A theory of demand for products distinguished by place of production. *IMF Staff Papers* 16 (1): 159–78.

Bagehot, Walter. 1880. *Economic studies.* Ed. Richard Holt Hutton. London: Longmans, Green.

Barro, Robert. 1991. Economic growth in a cross section of countries. *Quarterly Journal of Economics* 106:407–43.

Bergstrand, Jeffrey. 1985. The gravity model in international trade. *Review of Economics and Statistics* 67:474–81.

Bohn, Henning, and Linda Tesar. 1996. U.S. portfolio investment in Asian capital markets. Working paper, University of California, Santa Barbara.

Calvo, Guillermo, Leonardo Leiderman, and Carmen Reinhart. 1993a. Capital inflows and real exchange rate appreciation in Latin America: The role of external factors. *IMF Staff Papers* 40 (1): 108–51.

———. 1993b. Inflows of capital to developing countries in the 1990s: Causes and effects. *Journal of Economic Perspectives* 10 (2): 123–39.

Chen, Zhaohui, and Mohsin Khan. 1997. Patterns of capital flows to emerging markets. IMF Working Paper no. 97/13. Washington, D.C.: International Monetary Fund.

Chuhan, Punam, Stijn Claessens, and Nlandu Mamingi. 1993. Equity and bond flows to Latin America and Asia: The role of external and domestic factors. PRE Working Paper no. 1160. Washington, D.C.: World Bank, March.

Deardorff, Alan. 1995. Determinants of bilateral trade: Does gravity work in a neoclassical world? NBER Working Paper no. 5377. Cambridge, Mass.: National Bureau of Economic Research.

Eaton, Jonathan, and Akiko Tamura. 1994. Bilateralism and regionalism in Japanese and US trade and FDI pattern. NBER Working Paper no. 4758. Cambridge, Mass.: National Bureau of Economic Research.

Engle, Charles, and John Rogers. 1994. How wide is the border? NBER Working Paper no. 4829. Cambridge, Mass.: National Bureau of Economic Research.

Frankel, Jeffrey, Ernesto Stein, and Shang-Jin Wei. 1993. Continental trading blocs: Are they natural or supernatural? NBER Working Paper no. 4588. Cambridge, Mass.: National Bureau of Economic Research.

Helliwell, John. 1995. Do national borders matter for Quebec's trade? NBER Working Paper no. 5215. Cambridge, Mass.: National Bureau of Economic Research.

Helliwell, John, and John McCallum. 1995. National borders still matter for trade. *Policy Options* 16 (July/August): 44–48.

Linneman, Hans. 1966. *An econometric study of international trade flows.* Amsterdam: North-Holland.

Markusen, James. 1997. Trade versus investment liberalization. Working paper. University of Colorado, Department of Economics.

McCallum, John. 1995. National borders matter: Canada-US regional trade patterns. *American Economic Review* 85 (June): 615–23.

Mundell, Robert. 1957. International trade and factor mobility. *American Economic Review* 47:321–35.

Neary, Peter. 1995. Factor mobility and international trade. *Canadian Journal of Economics* 28:S4–S23.

Rauch, James. 1996. Networks versus markets in international trade. NBER
    Working Paper no. 5617. Cambridge, Mass.: National Bureau of Economic Re-
    search.
Wei, Shang-Jin. 1996. Intra-national versus international trade. NBER Working
    Paper no. 5531. Cambridge, Mass.: National Bureau of Economic Research.
World Bank. 1997. *Private capital markets.* Washington, D.C.: World Bank.

Comment   Miguel A. Savastano

Swati Ghosh and Holger Wolf want to put geography considerations at
the forefront of discussions of capital flows to emerging markets. To do
this, they examine the role that geographical factors have played on an
important and grossly overlooked regularity of the surge of private capital
flows to emerging markets in the last decade: the fact that a handful of
developing countries has received the lion's share of the flows and that, by
and large, those flows have bypassed the vast majority of the developing
world. The authors put forward two competing hypotheses to account for
the uneven distribution of capital flows to less-developed economies: a
"development threshold" hypothesis (i.e., the level of income and income
per capita in the recipient countries) and a "location" hypothesis (i.e.,
geographical factors, including the bilateral distance between the recipient
countries and the G7 economies). They then proceed to test the two hypotheses, first from the recipient countries' perspective by examining the
determinants of access to international financial markets (using a probit
regression and a "classification tree" procedure), and then from the source
countries' side by estimating gravity-type equations for exports and four
types of capital flows during the early 1990s using a fairly unconventional
set of data.

The results do not help the authors' case. What Ghosh and Wolf find is
that each hypothesis receives some empirical support when it is tested
separately, but that when they are tested jointly the development threshold
hypothesis (the GDP measures) overwhelmingly dominates the location
hypothesis. This is what the authors obtain from the probit estimates in
table 5.1 and from their original analysis of access based on "classification
trees," and this is also what they obtain from the gravity-type regressions
of outward capital flows reported in tables 5.4 to 5.7. In fact, not counting
the results for bilateral exports (table 5.3), the coefficients of the "location"

Miguel A. Savastano is deputy division chief at the Research Department of the International Monetary Fund.
The opinions expressed in these comments are exclusively those of the author and do not
represent those of the IMF.

or "spatial" determinants reported in those tables turned out to be statistically significant in less than one-third of the regressions (six out of twenty-one), whereas the coefficient of (the log of) GDP was significant in twenty out of the twenty-one regressions and that of GDP per capita in about half of the cases.

Somewhat surprisingly, however, Ghosh and Wolf have a different reading of their results. They downplay the fact that the majority of coefficients of the "spatial" variables lose their statistical significance once they control for the countries' size and per capita income, dismiss the severe problem of lack of degrees of freedom that plague their regression estimates, and make much of the negative sign of the (nonsignificant) distance elasticities in their gravity-type regressions (table 5.8). Thus, rather confidently, they conclude that "the[ir] findings support the view that location matters in a fundamental sense for development prospects." I fully agree that location matters for growth and development and that further research in this area that builds on the recent work by Robert Barro, Jeff Sachs, and others will be rewarding. But this is not a conclusion that follows from the paper. As I see it, the main conclusion that follows from this work by Ghosh and Wolf is that *distance* (and hence gravity-type equations) is probably not among the factors that will help us understand the geography of capital flows. This may be a negative conclusion, but is nonetheless a useful conclusion; and it is the correct one.

The reason why distance and gravity-type models are not likely to shed much light on the geography of capital flows is the same reason that makes distance and gravity models perform so well in explaining bilateral trade flows: transaction costs, and in particular transportation costs. It is well known that the costs associated with transporting physical goods across borders and regions is what explains the robustness of distance variables in gravity models of bilateral trade. While it is entirely plausible to assume that private capital flows to emerging markets are subject to a variety of transaction costs, which are often hefty and even punitive, the notion that those transaction costs are somehow related to the *geographical distance* between the recipient countries and the capital-exporting countries is far-fetched—and that is what the evidence in the paper shows. Transaction costs of cross-border capital movements may have been highly correlated with geographical distance one hundred or two hundred years ago, but this has not been the case in the last few decades, and surely not in the 1990s. The possibility of making physical and, especially, portfolio investments in remote and unfamiliar markets and countries is one of the few spheres where globalization is not a myth.[1] Distance is not the central issue

1. Whether that is a positive development is a different question altogether, one that is beyond of the scope of the paper as well as of these comments.

anymore. Other types of costs and sources of asymmetric information are far more important. A fuller grasp of the nature of those costs and of their relation with location and other geographical factors seems a more promising route than the one taken by Ghosh and Wolf to put the geography of capital flows back on the map.

Capital Flows and the Behavior of Emerging Market Equity Returns

Geert Bekaert and Campbell R. Harvey

6.1 Introduction

During the last decade, we have witnessed significant changes in the pattern of world capital flows with some of the most dramatic changes taking place in emerging markets. In the late 1980s and early 1990s, a number of developing economies initiated reforms to liberalize their capital markets. These reforms made it easier both for foreign investors to access the local market and for domestic investors to diversify their portfolios internationally. Foreign equity and bond purchases have become an increasingly important source of capital for developing countries.

The recent crises in Asia and in Mexico in 1994 emphasize the importance of understanding both the impact of capital market liberalizations and the role of foreign portfolio flows for a country's economic prospects. The views widely differ. On the one hand, there is a new stream of research that examines the role of the financial sector and economic growth prospects. King and Levine (1993a, 1993b), Levine and Zervos (1996), Rajan and Zingales (1997), and Bekaert and Harvey (1998) all find a positive relation between the development of the financial sector and economic growth. Obstfeld (1994) explicitly links financial market integration to economic growth. Moreover, Bartolini and Drazen (1996) describe free

Geert Bekaert is professor of finance at Columbia Business School, on leave from Stanford University's Graduate School of Business, and a research associate of the National Bureau of Economic Research. Campbell R. Harvey is the J. Paul Sticht Professor of International Business at Duke University's Fuqua School of Business and a research associate of the National Bureau of Economic Research.

The authors appreciate the suggestions of Sebastian Edwards and the comments of conference participants. The authors thank Andrew Roper and Diego Valderrama for their helpful research assistance.

capital mobility as a possible signal for the government to use to enhance the credibility of a broader reform program. On the other hand, Krugman (1993) is skeptical about the benefits of capital market liberalizations and Mathieson and Rojaz-Suarez (1992) describe how an open capital account may undermine structural reform programs. Worse, some have argued that "the integration of financial markets is dangerous and destabilizing."[1]

Our goal is to characterize the relation between U.S. equity flows to emerging markets and important financial and macroeconomic variables. We use data on net U.S. equity capital flows to seventeen emerging markets during 1977–96. Following Bekaert, Harvey, and Lumsdaine (1999), we identify the break point in net equity capital flows (either up or down). We view these break points as indicative of the date when the marginal investor may have changed from local to foreign or vice versa. With these dates, we examine the behavior of a wide variety of economic and financial indicators.

We examine four categories of indicators. The first group includes the cost of capital, correlation with the world market return, and volatility. The second group focuses on the structure of the market. We include indicators such as the asset concentration ratios, the size of the market, and liquidity indicators. The third category is the economy: Foreign exchange volatility, real exchange rates, real gross domestic product (GDP) per capita, the size of the trade sector, inflation, interest rates, and fiscal deficits are analyzed. The last category is country risk. We are interested in the international perceptions of political, economic, and financial (credit) risk before and after changes in capital flows.

It is important to remember that capital flows are endogenous. Generally speaking, they should be considered the endogenous outcome of a portfolio choice problem. While we report statistics based on pre- and post-capital-flow break points, at no point do we argue that increases in net capital flows "cause" changes in any of these indicators. The complex process of liberalization provides the foundation for increases in capital flows. It is likely that the components of this process account for the changes in the variables that we report.[2]

Our exploratory analysis remains useful in light of the many financial and economic woes ascribed to foreign investors by concerned policy makers. The nature of our exercise prevents us from testing formal hypotheses, but our results may guide future empirical and theoretical work. In addition, our results may cast doubt on some popular rhetoric regarding the implications of foreign capital inflows.

---

1. See "Capital goes global," *Economist,* 25 October 1997, pp. 87–88. Claessens, Dooley, and Warner (1993) examine whether one can distinguish "hot," speculative capital flows from long-run, stable flows.
2. See Bohn and Tesar (1996), Calvo and Mendoza (chap. 1 in this volume), and Bacchetta and van Wincoop (chap. 3 in this volume) for alternative models of capital flows.

The paper is organized as follows. Section 6.2 provides the setting for our investigation by describing the relation between capital flows and financial market integration. Section 6.3 provides a brief description of the capital flow data that we use and some summary statistics. In this section, we describe our calculation of the break points. Section 6.4 details the behavior of the returns, financial structure, economy, country risk, and liquidity around capital flow breaks. Some concluding remarks are offered in the final section.

6.2   Capital Flows and Financial Market Integration

It is useful to distinguish between economic integration and financial integration. Economic integration is associated with the reduction in trade barriers (see Sachs and Warner 1995 for an extensive survey). Financial integration is associated with barriers to portfolio investments. It is often the case that these two concepts are linked. Indeed, Bekaert and Harvey (1995) use the size of the trade sector as an instrument for financial integration. While our focus is on financial integration, we will track the behavior of the trade sector to investigate whether financial integration coincides with economic integration in our sample.

A market is financially integrated if a project with identical risk has identical expected returns across different markets. The opposite of market integration, market segmentation, can cause fundamental distortions in an economy. In the segmented market, local investors are restricted to investing in local securities and foreign investors are not allowed (or the cost is high) to invest in the local market.

Obstfeld (1994) and Stulz (1999) detail some of the distortions that occur in the segmented market. Local investors are unable to diversify their equity portfolios because they can only invest in local securities. Further, the local market is usually very small with only a small number of securities. Since investors will pay a premium for diversification, new local firms will arise that inefficiently operate in industries that provide diversification. Current firms may also diversify away from their core activities by accepting negative net present value projects that make them more attractive to investors. One can see that segmentation directly leads to an inefficient allocation of productive resources.

The process of integration should reverse these inefficiencies. Investors will no longer be interested in investing in inefficient domestic companies when they can purchase a foreign stock that is efficient. If the economic liberalization occurs at the same time, the inefficient companies will likely be driven out of business because of price and quality competition from foreign producers. Similarly, the current producers in the local economy may reallocate capital from the inefficient conglomerate divisions to the divisions that have a comparative advantage. Nevertheless, Bekaert and

Harvey (1995, 1997, 2000) argue that it is particularly difficult to pin down the exact date when the local market becomes integrated with world markets. Using the legislative dates of capital market liberalizations is fraught with danger. For example, a country might initiate widespread reforms—but foreign investors ignore the country's equities because of market imperfections, because the reforms are incomplete, or because they deem the reform program not credible. Hence, while technically open, the market is effectively segmented.

The patterns in net capital flows should reveal much information about market integration. After legal reforms are initiated and the market structure is satisfactory—that is, if the market becomes truly integrated—we should see an increase in capital flows. It is also possible that the market moves in the other direction, that is, toward segmentation. If restrictive measures are initiated or the political and economic environment is not conducive to international investors, capital flows should "dry up." It is therefore also important to carefully consider the particular economic and political environments within each country. We have formed chronologies of important events that might impact capital flows for twenty countries. The timelines for each country are available at www.duke.edu/~charvey/Country_risk/couindex.htm.

Our investigation does not address the question of whether a developing country should prefer direct investment flows to portfolio flows. We choose to concentrate on the portfolio flows, more particularly on equity flows. However, we can indirectly shed some light on this question. It is popularly believed that since portfolio investment is more mobile than direct investment, increased portfolio investment could destabilize an economy and its financial markets. This leads us directly to our investigation of capital flows and equity returns. Destabilization might manifest itself through increased equity volatility. Early work by Bekaert (1995), Tesar and Werner (1995a), and Bekaert and Harvey (1997) suggests that this is not the case, but the results in Bekaert and Harvey (2000) are more mixed. We reassess these results and expand the scope of examination to other sensitive measures such as foreign exchange volatility and turnover.

The behavior of equity returns also includes any change in the cost of equity capital. Clark and Berko (1997) find that surprise purchases of Mexican equity lead to a significant and substantial price rise. They conclude that the price rise is permanent, reflecting greater risk sharing and improved liquidity, and hence induces a reduction in the cost of equity capital. Similarly, Henry (2000) documents a substantial positive price response to capital market liberalizations. Following Bekaert and Harvey (2000), we argue that the dividend yield is directly related to the cost of capital. We find that the dividend yield is sharply lower after increases in capital flows. Even if the change constitutes an actual change in the cost of capital, it is important to realize that foreign investment may not be the only causal factor. For example, Henry (2000) ascribes 50 percent of the price response to macroeconomic reforms (which may affect the growth rate of dividends as well), but Bekaert and Harvey (2000) find that an important part of the total drop in the dividend yield is accounted for by capital market liberalizations. We also find that correlations with the world market return are doubled after capital flow breaks. A decrease in expected returns and an increase in correlations suggests that the process of market integration leads to reduced diversification benefits for international investors, confirming the results in Bekaert and Urias (1996).

The rest of our paper details the association of capital flow breaks with financial and economic fundamental variables. We find that there are changes in almost every measure we examine moving from a low capital flows period to a high capital flows period.

Our focus on equity flows is potentially quite restrictive. Equity capital may flow into an emerging market while bond flows are drying up. After a general market opening, of course, we expect both bond and equity flows to increase more or less simultaneously as foreign investors adjust their portfolios. We therefore obtained data on bond flows and examine how they correlate with equity flows.

6.3   Capital Flows Data

6.3.1   World Capital Flows

The ideal data for the study of capital flows is a monthly world matrix of flows. Each element would detail the net flow from (row) a country to (column) another country. However, the task of constructing such a matrix is extraordinarily difficult. First, the United States is one of the few countries that has detailed monthly measurements for sixty-five countries. Even the United Kingdom, a country with bountiful economic data, does not report flows to individual countries. Second, even if two countries report flows, they are not easily reconciled because of different collection conventions. For example, Tesar and Werner (1994) do some basic cross-checking of U.S. treasury and Canadian data and find that the average quarterly net purchases of U.S. shares reported by Statistics Canada is less than half of those reported by the U.S. Treasury, while no similar magnitude of discrepancy is found for the reported U.S. net purchases of Canadian equity. Third, the country of origin is not necessarily the final destination for the capital flows. For example, much of the flow to the United Kingdom is channeled to other European and world investments because London is the leading world clearinghouse for non-U.S. transactions.[3]

Some attempts have been made to reconcile and create a flow matrix.

---

3. Similar problems exist for measuring bond flows. Ito (chap. 8 in this volume) reports that bank lending both in Asia and Latin America is dominated by European banks, not U.S. banks.

Indeed, there is great practitioner interest in this exercise. Empirical evidence from U.S. data on stock inclusions in a major index (Shleifer 1986; Harris and Gurel 1986) or flows to mutual funds (Warther 1995) suggests that flows affect prices. Presumably a superior measure of flow could lead to excess profits in the context of a trading strategy. Howell (1993) and Howell and Cozzini (1991, 1992) undertake the construction of a capital flow matrix.

We have obtained the Howell matrices for the years 1986–92.[4] Unfortunately, these matrices are only prepared on an annual basis. Furthermore, emerging markets are coarsely organized into three categories: Latin America, Asia, and other. Finally, many of the liberalizations were taking place in the early 1990s and these data end in 1992.

The Howell data, however, can give some insight into what we are missing by focusing on purely U.S. Treasury data. For example, in 1992 the total net equity flows to emerging markets was US$15.95 billion as reported in Howell. Of that amount, $8.97 billion originated from the United States. The next most important country is the United Kingdom, with $2.85 billion in flows (some of which is probably U.S. originated). The Department of Treasury (DOT) data suggest that the U.S. equity flows to emerging markets in 1992 were $5.54 billion. This comparison suggests that the Treasury data capture a sizable portion of the flows to emerging markets.

6.3.2   U.S. Capital Flows

Tesar and Werner (1994) provide a detailed analysis of the components of the U.S. capital flows data. The U.S. international portfolio investment transactions are reported through the DOT's International Capital Form S. Operationally, the twelve district Federal Reserve Banks, principally the Federal Reserve Bank of New York, collect these data, maintain contact with the respondents, and ensure the accuracy and integrity of the data (Kester et al. 1994). Tabulation of the data, however, is done by the DOT and is presented in its *Quarterly Bulletin*. The reporting is done on a monthly basis.

By law, banks, brokers, dealers, other financial institutions, and individuals are required to report the value of any long-term security transaction involving a foreign resident. American depositary receipt (ADR) transactions are included in the figures. Securities transactions are reported on a transaction basis. They are recorded by the nationality of the person with whom you are carrying out the transaction, not by the country that originally issued the security. A foreigner is any individual, branch, partnership, association, corporation, or other organization located outside the United States. Additionally, securities are recorded according to the residency of the issuer and not their currency denomination.

---

4. We are grateful to Michael Howell for providing us with this information.

Exceptions for reporting are given when the total purchases and the total sales of securities are less than $2 million for the reporting month. There are penalties for failing to report that can result in a civil penalty of up to $10,000 and up to a year in prison for willful failure to report (see DOT International Capital Form S).

As mentioned earlier, there are several problems with the data. The increasing complexity of financial transactions and the development of new financial instruments makes it harder to record all the appropriate information. Kester et al. (1994) detail three potential problems related to the reporting procedures themselves. These problems involve recording of information of U.S. residents living abroad, financial transactions carried out in foreign financial centers, and stocks of securities held by U.S. residents that are classified geographically by the counterparty and not by the issuing country.

Our data come directly from the DOT's *Quarterly Bulletin,* table CM-V-4, "Foreign Purchases and Sales of Long-Term Securities by Type and Country." This table reports "Gross purchases by foreigners," which we classify as a U.S. sale, and "Gross sales by foreigners," which we classify as a U.S. purchase. We focus on foreign equity securities (columns 7 and 14) and bond securities (columns 6 and 13).

6.3.3   Accumulating Capital Flows and Break Points

The capital flow data have been extensively studied before in a portfolio allocation context by Bohn and Tesar (1996) and Tesar and Werner (1994, 1995a, 1995b). We begin by accumulating the capital flows to obtain an approximate measure of the ratio of U.S. ownership to market capitalization. This process must include local market equity appreciation realized by the U.S. investor. The dollar position of U.S. investors in emerging equity market i is

$$(1) \qquad \text{Ownership}_{i,t} = \text{Flow}_{i,t} + \text{Ownership}_{i,t-1}(1 + R_{i,t}),$$

where $\text{Flow}_{i,t}$ is the net capital flow in period t and $R_{i,t}$ is the market i return in U.S.-dollar terms from the International Finance Corporation (IFC).[5] We also calculate the cumulative net capital bond flows. Since we do not have information on bond returns in each market, we present a simple accumulation of the net bond flows. While our statistical analysis concentrates on equity ownership using equation (1), figure 6.1 presents the simple accumulation of equity and bond flows. The correlations that are reported in the figure are also based on the simple accumulations.

---

5. Tesar and Werner (1995a) do not take into account the capital gains on the equity investments for emerging markets. They report a simple accumulation of the net capital flows. However, Tesar and Werner (1994) do adjust for capital gains.

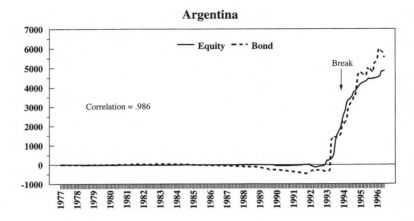

Fig. 6.1 Cumulative U.S. net equity and bond flows for seventeen emerging markets

Note: US$ millions unadjusted for local returns. Equity breaks based on flows adjusted for market returns divided by market capitalization.

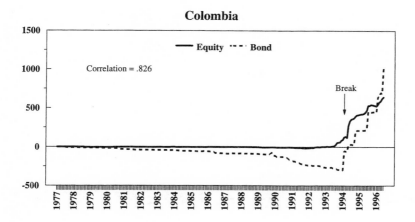

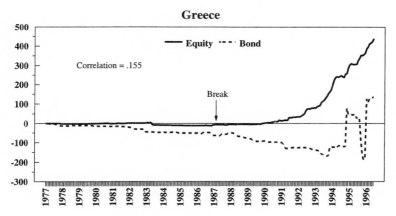

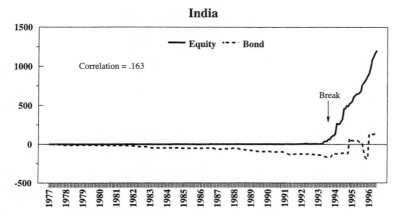

Fig. 6.1   (cont.)

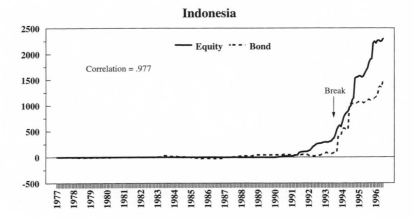

Indonesia

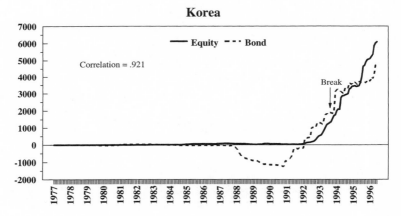

Korea

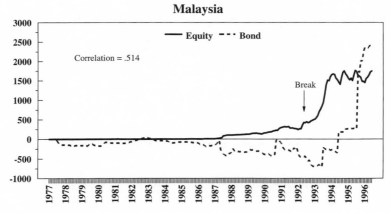

Malaysia

Fig. 6.1   (cont.)

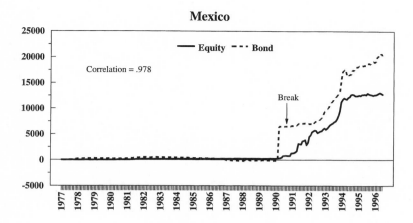

Mexico

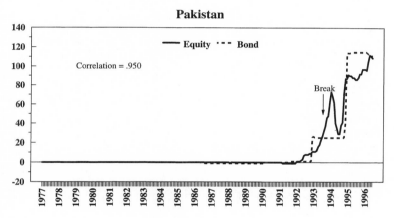

Pakistan

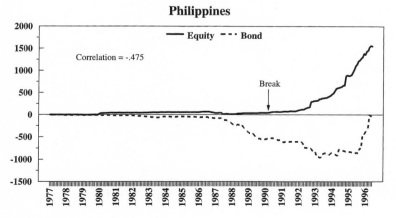

Philippines

Fig. 6.1   (cont.)

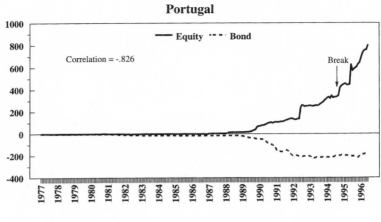

Portugal

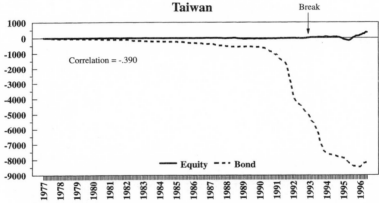

Taiwan

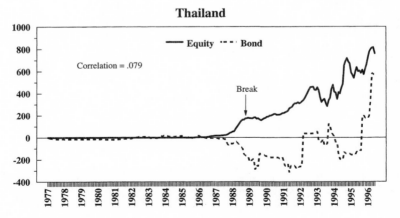

Thailand

Fig. 6.1   (cont.)

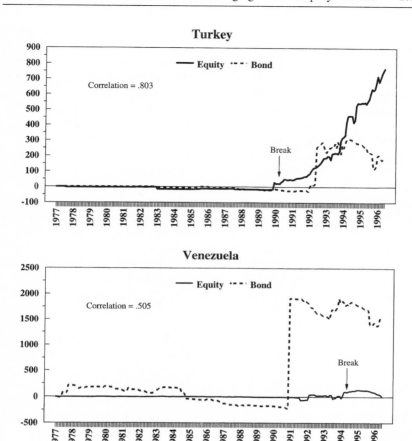

Fig. 6.1   (cont.)

One problem that we face is the starting point. The capital flow data from the DOT's *Quarterly Bulletin* begins reporting in January 1977. However, for many countries there are zero entries for a number of years. In addition, we rely on the IFC data to calculate the increase in equity ownership resulting from a rise in the local market index. Hence, the starting point for equation (1) differs across many countries. Further, we do not know the initial stock of U.S. capital in the emerging stock market. Hence, it is possible that we calculate some of the early ownerships as small negative numbers. The negative ownerships do not concern us too much given the nature of our examination. Our focus is on the more recent flow data. In addition, we are concerned with the patterns in the flows—not the levels. Finally, it also may be the case that foreigners hold portfolios different than the IFC index. Kang and Stulz (1997) show that foreign investors are more likely to invest in securities that are large and well known. The IFC indices have some advantage here over more comprehensive local indices because of the IFC's focus on large, relatively liquid securities.

Our first task is to assess the break points in the equity flows. We use the break points that are reported in Bekaert and Harvey (2000). We examine seventeen emerging markets that are tracked by the IFC. The IFC also tracks Jordan, Nigeria, and Zimbabwe; however, the Treasury *Bulletin* does not include data on these countries.[6]

We use the endogenous break point tests detailed in Bai, Lumsdaine, and Stock (1998). We report the 90 percent confidence interval for the break as well as the median point. In some countries, for example Taiwan, there is a wide confidence interval. In other countries, for example the Philippines, the interval is extremely tight. The technique tells us whether there is a break in the time series—but it does not tell us if the break is up or down. A visual inspection of the data suggests that sixteen of the seventeen are associated with increases in capital flows and only one, the Philippines, is associated with a decrease in capital flows.

Table 6.1 also reports the mean levels of ownership five years before and five years after (and including the break month). For some of the countries, we do not have data for five years after. We then report the average to the end of the sample. Table 6.1 confirms that foreign ownership is greater in the postbreak period for every country except the Philippines. It may be the case that foreign equity ownership is increased at the expense of foreign bond ownership. However, this does not necessarily appear to be the case. Table 6.1 reports the mean levels of cumulative bond flows before and after the equity break. In eleven of the sixteen countries, the bond flows increase (often sharply) after the equity break.

We report four types of test statistics over two different samples. In the first sample, the Philippines (the only country where the capital flows break in a downward direction) is excluded. In the second sample, all countries with insignificant breaks, from the first column of table 6.1, are excluded. The first statistic is a simple difference in means across the seventeen countries. This test allows for different variances in the prebreak and postbreak data, but imposes independence across countries and across time.

The second set of tests is country specific. We conduct heteroskedasticity-consistent tests of the hypothesis of no change in each time series for each country. These tests also correct for a first-order moving average process in the residuals for all series that are available on a monthly basis. For those series that have components that are observed at an annual

6. The IFC currently follows more than twenty markets. We use the full sample of countries that are available in 1992. Our statistical tests require a minimum number of observations. As a result, we do not include Eastern European countries and others that were added after 1992.

Table 6.1   Analysis of Net U.S. Capital Flows

Country	Net Equity Holdings Break Point			Level of Equity Holdings		Cumulative Net Bond Flows		Correlation of Equity and Bond Flows	
	Fifth Percentile	Median	Ninety-fifth Percentile	Five Years Before	Five Years After[a]	Five Years Before	Five Years After[a]	Full Sample	Post-1990
Argentina	Apr-93	May-93***	Jun-93	-0.0201	0.1519****	-285.9	3,642.7***	0.986	0.985
Brazil	Nov-87	Jul-88***	Mar-89	0.0013	0.0399****	-16.6	71.6	0.924	0.914
Chile	Jan-86	Feb-88	Mar-90	0.0003	0.0230***	-269.7	-906.3***	-0.789	-0.741
Colombia	Aug-93	Sep-93***	Oct-93	-0.0103	0.0206****	-174.9	187.3***	0.826	0.939
Greece	May-85	Jan-87***	Sep-88	-0.0177	-0.0065****	-44.3	-84.2***	0.155	0.645
India	Mar-93	May-93***	Jul-93	0.0006	0.0059****	-251.0	-183.2***	0.163	0.846
Indonesia	Feb-93	Jul-93	Dec-93	0.0124	0.0603****	42.6	861.6***	0.977	0.967
Korea	Sep-91	Apr-93*	Nov-94	0.0080	0.0321***	-469.0	3,159.5***	0.921	0.908
Malaysia	Feb-91	May-92	Aug-93	0.0082	0.0162***	-300.8	284.2***	0.514	0.581
Mexico	Jul-89	Jun-90**	May-91	0.0753	0.1526***	213.7	10,765.4***	0.978	0.962
Pakistan	Apr-93	May-93***	Jun-93	0.0001	0.0090****	1.6	67.8***	0.950	0.929
Philippines	Feb-90	Feb-90****	Feb-90	0.3240	0.1513***	-195.8	-717.8***	-0.475	0.226
Portugal	Jun-93	Sep-94	Dec-95	0.0231	0.0497***	-161.3	-197.8***	-0.826	-0.468
Taiwan	Sep-88	Sep-92		0.0001	0.0008****	-1,287.4	-7,209.2***	-0.394	-0.432
Thailand	Feb-88	Aug-88***	Feb-89	0.0076	0.0322***	-6.1	-145.5***	0.080	0.634
Turkey	May-88	Jan-90	Sep-91	-0.0300	0.0067***	-10.4	125.4***	0.803	0.616
Venezuela	Dec-93	Mar-94***	Jun-94	-0.0072	0.0082***	1,044.1	1,668.8***	0.505	0.230
Mean[b]				0.0032	0.0377	-123.5	756.7	0.423	0.532
P-value				0.01	0.01	0.17	0.17	0.31	0.31

(*continued*)

Table 6.1   (continued)

Country	Net Equity Holdings Break Point			Level of Equity Holdings		Cumulative Net Bond Flows		Correlation of Equity and Bond Flows	
	Fifth Percentile	Median	Ninety-fifth Percentile	Five Years Before	Five Years After[a]	Five Years Before	Five Years After[a]	Full Sample	Post-1990
Mean[c]				0.0038	0.0446	1.2	1,915.0	0.649	0.799
P-value					0.03		0.06		0.15
P-value[b,d]					0.00		0.56	NA	NA
P-value[c,d]					0.00		0.87	NA	NA
P-value[b,e]					0.00		0.00	NA	NA
P-value[c,e]					0.00		0.00	NA	NA

Note: Bond flows are reported in millions of U.S. dollars. All multivariate regression tests are corrected for group-wise heteroskedasticity and group-wise moving average processes in the residuals. NA = not available.

[a]Probability values based on Newey-West corrected t-statistics from the regression

Series $= B0 + ($Indicator for Five Years after Break$) * B1$.

[b]Excludes the Philippines which has a break down in capital flows

[c]Excludes the Philippines and countries with breaks that are not significant.

[d]t-statistic significance on a panel estimation with fixed effects of the regression

Series$[i,t] = B0[i] + ($Indicator for Five Years after Break$)[i,t] * B1$.

[e]χ^2 joint test that all of the coefficients are zero in the pooled time series regression with fixed effects

Series$[i,t] = B0[i] + ($Country Specific Indicator for Five Years after Break$)[i,t] * B1[i]$.

*Significant at the 10 percent level.
**Significant at the 5 percent level.
***Significant at the 1 percent level.

frequency, we correct for a twelfth-order moving average process. The test statistics' *p*-values are denoted with asterisks.

The third set of tests involves a multivariate estimation with a single indicator variable that is activated after the break dates. The coefficient on this variable represents the average difference in the postbreak period. We test whether this single coefficient is different from zero. This estimation is groupwise heteroskedasticity consistent (allows for different variances across the countries). We also allow the errors to follow panel-specific moving average processes. Finally, we allow for fixed effects in the estimation.

The final test is another version of the multivariate test. In this test, we add country-specific indicator variables that pick up the country-specific difference between the prebreak and postbreak means. We conduct a groupwise heteroskedasticity- and moving-average-consistent Wald test that these coefficients equal zero.

Not surprisingly, equity flows increase significantly in all countries but the Philippines and U.S. ownership on average increases from less than 0.5 percent to 4–5 percent of local market capitalization. The changes are significant in every country. Except for Brazil, the change in cumulative bond flows is statistically significant. The χ^2 tests reveal a significant increase in cumulative bond flows that appears to be economically substantial.

Figure 6.1 allows a comparison of the patterns in equity and bond capital flows. In many countries, for example Argentina, there is a striking correlation between the equity and bond capital flows. In some countries (Brazil, Colombia, India, Indonesia, Malaysia, Thailand, and Turkey), the equity capital flows "lead" changes in the bond capital flows. In some other countries (Korea, Mexico, Pakistan, and Venezuela), the bond market distinctively changes before the equity market.

The final columns of table 6.1 report the correlations between the equity and bond flows. For the purpose of this table, we calculate the cumulative net equity flows, unadjusted for local market returns. This puts the equity flows on the same footing as the bond flows (which also do not include local market returns). The correlation is very high. There are six countries (Argentina, Brazil, Indonesia, Korea, Mexico, and Pakistan) with correlations above 90 percent. The correlations are even higher if we focus on the post-1990 period. In this sample, the average correlation between the equity and bond flows is 51 percent. In general, the evidence points to the bond and equity markets being complementary sources of foreign funding rather than substitutes.[7]

---

7. Negative correlations are found for Chile, Portugal, and Taiwan, which would suggest that the equity and bond markets might be substitutes in these countries.

6.4   Finance, Economics, and Changes in Capital Flows

There are significant challenges in measuring equity volatility, correlation, and the cost of capital for emerging markets. We choose to follow the path of Bekaert and Harvey (1997) for volatility and correlation and Bekaert and Harvey (2000) for the cost of capital.

6.4.1   The Cost of Capital

Bekaert and Harvey (2000) argue that a change in the marginal investor and the different equity valuation it entails should have discrete effects on the price level of stocks (see also Korajczyk 1996). They argue that a technique exploiting information in price levels, as reflected in dividend yields, may be more powerful than trying to directly model expected returns. Indeed, the dividend yield has the advantage of being directly measurable—that is, it need not be pre-estimated—and being a stationary random variable. Moreover, shocks to prices should dominate its variation over time. Finally, the dividend yield is intricately linked to the cost of capital.

Consider a simple example from Bekaert and Harvey (2000). Assume rational expectations and a discounted dividend model for the stock price, P_t:

$$(2) \qquad P_t = E_t\left[\sum_{i=1}^{\infty} \delta^i_{t+i} D_{t+i}\right],$$

where D_t are the dividends and δ_t is the discount factor. Let

$$L_t = \begin{cases} 0, & \text{before liberalization;} \\ 1, & \text{after liberalization.} \end{cases}$$

Further assume that the liberalization is a one-time, unexpected event. When the market is segmented, the required rate of return is constant and equal to r. When the market opens up, the required rate of return drops to $\bar{r}$. We can represent this simple model for expected returns as

$$(3) \qquad \delta_t = \frac{1}{1 + r - \eta L_t},$$

where $\eta = r - \bar{r}$, the drop in the cost of capital. Under this set of assumptions, the relation between the change in the dividend yield $\overline{D}_t/P_t - D_t/P_t$ and the change in the cost of capital η depends on the dividend process.

In the standard Gordon model, which assumes $E_t D_{t+i} = (1 + g)E_t D_{t-1+i}$, this relation is virtually one to one.[8] It is straightforward to show:

---

8. The Gordon model is not a realistic model for stock price determination, but Bekaert and Harvey (2000) show that its main intuition remains valid with more general models.

(4)
$$\eta = r - \bar{r}$$
$$= (1 + g)\frac{D_t}{P_t} - (1 + \bar{g})\frac{\overline{D_t}}{P_t} + g - \bar{g}.$$

If the growth rate of dividends is not affected by the capital market liberalization, a regression of D_t/P_t onto the liberalization indicator variable, L_t, yields $-\eta/(1 + g)$. Hence, the slope coefficient provides a slight underestimation of the true response of the cost of capital.

Bekaert and Harvey (2000) detail the potential problems in using this measure in cost of capital estimation. Nevertheless, it is a reasonable starting point. Table 6.2 shows that the dividend yield decreases in ten of sixteen countries after the capital flow break point (with capital flow increases). On average, the dividend yield decreases from 3.86 percent to 2.65 percent, implying a statistically significant (at the 10 percent level) reduction in the cost of capital. This analysis includes all countries except the Philippines, where a significant down break in capital flows occurred. If we specialize the analysis to the set of countries that experienced a significant increase in equity capital flows, the dividend yield moves from 4.27 percent to 2.47 percent. This decrease is also statistically significant across all of our tests.

Although much noisier, it is also possible to gain some insights from the log ex post returns. We find that the average U.S.-dollar returns in the five-year period before the capital equity flow break is 20.00 percent and 13.36 percent following the break. While this is a large absolute difference in average returns, the multivariate test is only significant at the 10 percent level. This is consistent with the simulations in Bekaert and Harvey (2000) that show it is much more difficult to observe a shift in the cost of capital by examining the behavior of equity returns.

6.4.2   Volatility and Correlation

We follow the work of Bekaert and Harvey (1997) and estimate a sophisticated time-series model for volatility for each country that allows both the conditional mean and the conditional variance to vary through time.[9] We condition on both world and local information to capture the changes in the degree of market integration. This model delivers a time series of conditional volatilities for each country as well as conditional correlations of each country's return with the world market return.

Define the arithmetic excess return on the national equity index of country i in U.S. dollars as $r_{i,t}$. Our model has three components. First, the conditional mean, $\mu_{i,t-1}$, is assumed to be time varying:

---

9. For other related work on volatility, see De Santis and İmrohoroğlu (1996), Aggarwal, Inclan, and Leal (1999), Kim and Singal (2000), and Richards (1996).

Table 6.2   Behavior of Equity Returns

Country	Dividend Yield		Fitted Correlation with World		Fitted Volatility (annual)		Ex Post Log Returns (annual)		Ex Post Volatility (annual)		βs	
	Five Years Before	Five Years After[a]	Five Years Before	Five Years After[a]	Five Years Before	Five Years After[a]	Five Years Before	Five Years After[a]	Five Years Before	Five Years After	Five Years Before	Five Years After
Argentina	1.99	2.94***	0.12	0.26***	119.67	60.34***	46.74	18.02	99.31	33.67	−0.93	1.31
Brazil	5.00	3.81	0.06	0.06	61.69	79.24***	23.48	13.35	61.94	79.21	0.26	1.22
Chile	5.22	6.38**	0.12	0.09***	33.55	31.86**	19.00	39.23	34.60	24.72	0.58	−0.09
Colombia	5.04	1.89***	0.04	−0.02***	27.37	25.45	35.06	14.77	33.22	27.44	0.16	0.03
Greece	9.91	4.24***	0.12	0.16***	26.46	46.86***	−10.80	30.46	25.36	50.56	−0.11	0.62
India	1.67	1.09***	−0.02	−0.18***	33.57	27.77	14.37	5.60	38.22	28.36	−0.47	0.25
Indonesia	0.84	1.40**	0.06	0.32***	73.17	56.43	−7.80	19.20	32.07	28.19	0.20	0.78
Korea	1.33	1.33	0.22	0.21	27.78	25.95**	2.42	5.83	29.74	22.64	0.68	0.51
Malaysia	2.14	1.68***	0.48	0.49	21.42	22.87	10.74	17.82	28.22	24.87	1.10	0.72
Mexico	3.62	1.82***	0.15	0.32***	46.38	35.79*	43.69	12.17	63.32	40.19	1.15	0.78
Pakistan	5.23	1.80***	0.02	0.12***	32.29	30.87	17.70	5.59	26.34	26.34	0.03	−0.11
Philippines	2.75	1.05***	0.29	0.39***	35.69	34.90	63.32	11.04**	35.56	34.64	0.57	0.87
Portugal	3.09	3.20	0.51	0.50	26.67	19.30	3.35	13.23	24.52	14.26	0.90	0.48
Taiwan	0.56	1.08***	−0.04	0.21***	73.12	69.68	12.16	11.95	62.32	36.18	0.91	0.94
Thailand	7.52	3.21***	−0.10	0.38***	28.07	27.76	27.14	19.16	28.45	28.11	0.71	0.55
Turkey	7.13	4.00***	−0.39	0.02***	96.80	68.40*	59.38	−5.31	74.41	64.37	0.47	0.09
Venezuela	1.41	2.55***	0.08	0.00***	52.77	58.07	23.36	−7.30	48.37	61.11	−0.39	−0.35

Mean[b]	3.86	2.65	0.09	0.18	48.80	42.91	20.00	13.36	44.40	36.89	0.33	0.48
P-value		0.07		0.10		0.21		0.13		0.15		0.11
Mean[c]	4.27	2.47	0.07	0.13	44.81	40.00	22.32	11.76	45.43	39.76	0.11	0.48
P-value		0.00		0.25		0.12		0.02		0.24		0.04
P-value[b,d]		0.08		0.19		0.09		0.73		NA		NA
P-value[c,d]		0.11		0.37		0.08		0.61		NA		NA
P-value[b,e]		0.00		0.00		0.27		0.97		NA		NA
P-value[c,e]		0.07		0.00		0.25		0.94		NA		NA

Note: All multivariate regression tests are corrected for group-wise heteroskedasticity and group-wise moving average processes in the residuals. NA = not available.

[a] Probability values based on Newey-West corrected t-statistics from the regression

Series = B0 + (Indicator for Five Years after Break) * B1.

[b] Excludes the Philippines which has a break down in capital flows.
[c] Excludes the Philippines and countries with breaks that are not significant.
[d] t-statistic significance on a panel estimation with fixed effects of the regression

Series$[i,t]$ = B0$[i]$ + (Indicator for Five Years after Break)$[i,t]$ * B1.

[e] χ^2 joint test that all of the coefficients are zero in the pooled time series regression with fixed effects

Series$[i,t]$ = B0$[i]$ + (Country Specific Indicator for Five Years after Break)$[i,t]$ * B1$[i]$.

*Significant at the 10 percent level.
**Significant at the 5 percent level.
***Significant at the 1 percent level.

(5) $$r_{i,t} = \mu_{i,t-1} + \varepsilon_{i,t}.$$

Second, the unexpected return, $\varepsilon_{i,t}$, is determined by both a common world shock, $\varepsilon_{w,t}$ and a purely idiosyncratic (country-specific) shock, $e_{i,t}$,

(6) $$\varepsilon_{i,t} = v_{i,t-1}\varepsilon_{w,t} + e_{i,t},$$

where $v_{i,t-1}$ is a time-varying weight that reveals the relative importance of world versus local information. Finally, the local idiosyncratic conditional variance, $(\sigma_{i,t}^{\ell})^2$, follows an asymmetric GARCH $(1,1)$ model which follows from the work of Glosten, Jagannathan, and Runkle (1993):

(7) $$(\sigma_{i,t}^{\ell})^2 = E[e_{i,t}^2|I_{t-1}] = c_i + \alpha_i(\sigma_{i,t-1}^{\ell})^2 + \beta_i e_{i,t-1}^2 + \gamma_i S_{i,t} e_{i,t-1}^2,$$

where I_{t-1} is the information available at time $t-1$ and $S_{i,t}$ is an indicator variable that takes on the value of 1 when the idiosyncratic shock is negative and 0 otherwise. We also assume that

(8) $$e_{i,t} = \sigma_{i,t}^{\ell} z_{i,t},$$

where $z_{i,t}$ is a standardized residual with zero mean and unit variance. We investigate two distributional assumptions for the standardized residual, $z_{i,t}$: the normal distribution and a mixture of normal distributions. The latter distribution allows for both skewness and kurtosis.

The conditional mean of country i's return is assumed to be linear in a set of global and local information variables. The global information variables include a constant, the world market dividend yield in excess of the thirty-day Eurodollar rate, the default spread (Moody's Baa minus Aaa bond yields), the change in the term structure spread (U.S. ten-year bond yield minus three-month U.S. bill), and the change in the thirty-day Eurodollar rate. These variables are designed to capture fluctuations in expectations of the world business cycle (see Harvey 1991). The local information variables include a constant, the equity return, the exchange rate change, the dividend yield, equity market capitalization to (GDP), and trade to GDP. All of the information variables are known at time $t-1$. The financial variables are lagged by one month and the macroeconomic variables are lagged by one year to allow for reporting delays.

The world market expected returns and variances are a special case of equations (1)–(5), with $i = w$, $\sigma_{i,t}^{\ell} = \sigma_{w,t}$, $v_{w,t-1} = 0$. The conditional mean of the world market return, $\mu_{w,t-1}$, is assumed to be a linear function of global information variables. Finally, the relative importance of world versus local information in the variance equation is defined as

(9) $$v_{i,t-1} = \mathbf{q}_{i,0} + \mathbf{q}_{i,1}'\mathbf{X}_{i,t-1}^{*\prime},$$

where, following Bekaert and Harvey (1997), $X^*_{i,t-1}$ includes the subset of the local information variables that might proxy for the degree of market integration: market capitalization to GDP and the size of the trade sector (exports plus imports divided by GDP). The data for this exercise are U.S.-dollar total return indices for twenty countries provided by the IFC and the sample covers 1976–95. These data are described in more detail in Bekaert and Harvey (1995).

The results are contained in table 6.2. In eleven of seventeen countries, the fitted correlation with the world increases. On average the correlation increases from 0.09 to 0.18, which is significant in the multivariate tests that allow for country-specific coefficients. We also calculated ex post βs with the Morgan Stanley Capital International world market portfolio. The βs increase from an average of 0.33 to 0.48, which is significant at the 11 percent level. When we examine only the countries with significant increases in equity flows, the βs increase from an average of 0.11 to 0.48. This change is significant at the 5 percent level and suggestive of higher correlations with world aggregates.[10]

The results for volatility are more ambiguous. The fitted volatility declines in nine of seventeen countries. On average, volatility falls from 49 percent (on an annual basis) to 43 percent after the break in net capital flows, but the difference is not significant. On the other hand, when we look at the ex post volatility of the returns, there is more of a change. In the early period, the volatility is 44 percent, which falls to 37 percent in the later period. This decrease in volatility is not significant. These results suggest that volatility neither systematically increases nor decreases after capital flow breaks.

6.4.3   Financial Market Indicators

Table 6.3 details the behavior of a number of financial market indicators. We find that on average the number of stocks included in the IFC index significantly increases from thirty-five to fifty-seven after the break in capital flows. The IFC index attempts to cover 70 percent of market capitalization (see Bekaert and Harvey 1995). It seems like more stocks are being included in the country indices to attain the 70 percent minimum.

This suggests a pattern in stock market growth in the emerging markets. It is not as simple as the largest firms getting larger. Additional firms are entering the equity market and smaller current firms are becoming larger. This is consistent with the data on concentration ratios. The concentration ratio (modified Herfindahl ratio) declines, albeit insignificantly, after the

---

10. The pooled regression tests are not available for the βs or the ex post volatility because only two observations are available for each country, prebreak β (volatility) and postbreak β (volatility).

Table 6.3 **Financial Indicators**

Country	Number of Companies		Concentration Ratio		Market Capitalization to GDP		Cross-Sectional Standard Deviation		Exchange Rate Volatility		Value Traded to GDP		Turnover	
	Five Years Before	Five Years After[a]	Five Years Before	Five Years After[a]	Five Years Before	Five Years After[a]	Five Years Before	Five Years After[a]	Five Years Before	Five Years After[a]	Five Years Before	Five Years After[a]	Five Years Before	Five Years After[a]
Argentina	25.78	32.10***	0.28	0.29	0.04	0.08***	0.25	0.12***	0.38	0.03***	2.09	2.55	0.47	0.30***
Brazil	21.42	56.93***	0.29	0.18***	0.04	0.05***	0.21	0.26**	0.06	0.14***	1.47	2.04**	0.42	0.38
Chile	23.90	29.62***	0.22	0.22	0.09	0.46***	0.14	0.10***	0.05	0.02***	0.86	2.67***	0.08	0.09
Colombia	20.25	24.42***	0.19	0.20**	0.07	0.19***	0.13	0.12	0.02	0.02***	0.36	1.40***	0.06	0.10***
Greece	10.00	21.57***	0.57	0.27***	0.02	0.09***	0.09	0.13***	0.04	0.03*	0.04	1.46***	0.04	0.14***
India	58.63	118.78***	0.18	0.12***	0.07	0.21***	0.12	0.10*	0.02	0.02	3.53	2.91**	0.75	0.18***
Indonesia	62.51	45.71***	0.19	0.20	0.08	0.13***	0.12	0.11	0.01	0.00***	1.80	4.11***	0.44	0.36
Korea	70.07	152.27***	0.18	0.21***	0.27	0.31**	0.07	0.09**	0.01	0.01***	18.80	31.40***	0.84	1.08**
Malaysia	55.32	90.17***	0.19	0.19	0.64	1.70***	0.09	0.09	0.01	0.01***	7.77	51.72***	0.13	0.33***
Mexico	34.13	66.56***	0.16	0.26***	0.07	0.23***	0.19	0.11***	0.07	0.02***	2.41	9.85***	0.71	0.46***
Pakistan	52.50	71.00***	0.16	0.15*	0.05	0.15***	0.09	0.11**	0.01	0.02***	0.42	3.25***	0.08	0.36***
Philippines	18.00	32.82***	0.31	0.29*	0.05	0.25***	0.14	0.13	0.02	0.02	1.56	4.73***	0.30	0.19***
Portugal	30.02	31.38*	0.22	0.20***	0.11	0.14***	0.09	0.07**	0.04	0.04	1.82	3.20***	0.20	0.31***
Taiwan	57.58	84.13***	0.19	0.16***	0.62	0.50*	0.11	0.08***	0.01	0.01***	172.44	100.03***	2.84	1.97***
Thailand	9.72	37.90***	0.32	0.23***	0.04	0.21***	0.08	0.11***	0.02	0.01***	2.12	14.23***	0.49	0.71**
Turkey	15.14	27.95***	0.23	0.25	0.03	0.12***	0.17	0.18	0.02	0.03**	0.23	3.90***	0.10	0.55***
Venezuela	15.25	16.70***	0.25	0.34***	0.10	0.07***	0.16	0.12**	0.04	0.09***	3.12	1.09***	0.33	0.18***

Mean[b]													
35.14	56.70	0.24	0.15	0.22	0.29	0.13	0.12	0.16	0.11	13.70	14.74	0.50	0.47
P-value	0.03			0.22	0.11		0.24		0.24		0.47		0.44
Mean[c]													
31.78	59.82	0.26	0.08	0.23	0.16	0.14	0.13	0.07	0.04	3.43	7.02	0.42	0.39
P-value	0.05			0.24	0.02		0.33		0.25		0.16		0.42
P-value[b,d]	0.02			0.20	0.00		0.20		0.36		0.00		0.01
P-value[c,d]	0.00			0.06	0.00		0.86		0.64		0.07		0.03
P-value[b,e]	0.00			0.00	0.00		0.00		0.00		0.00		0.00
P-value[c,e]	0.00			0.00	0.03		0.00		0.00		0.00		0.00

Note: All multivariate regression tests are corrected for group-wise heteroskedasticity and group-wise moving average processes in the residuals.

[a] Probability values based on Newey-West corrected t-statistics from the regression

$$\text{Series} = B0 + (\text{Indicator for Five Years after Break}) * B1.$$

[b] Excludes the Philippines which has a break down in capital flows.

[c] Excludes the Philippines and countries with breaks that are not significant.

[d] t-statistic significance on a panel estimation with fixed effects of the regression

$$\text{Series}[i,t] = B0[i] + (\text{Indicator for Five Years after Break})[i,t] * B1.$$

[e] χ^2 joint test that all of the coefficients are zero in the pooled time series regression with fixed effects

$$\text{Series}[i,t] = B0[i] + (\text{Country Specific Indicator for Five Years after Break})[i,t] * B1[i].$$

*Significant at the 10 percent level.

**Significant at the 5 percent level.

***Significant at the 1 percent level.

break in capital flows. This is consistent with some smaller firms increasing in size at a rate faster than the larger firms. The cross-sectional average may also be influenced by a number of countries (e.g., Mexico) where privatizations introduced a number of large firms to the market.

Market capitalization to GDP increases after the flows break point. Market capitalization to GDP increases in fourteen of sixteen countries. On average the equity market accounts for 15 percent of GDP before the break and 29 percent of GDP after the break. The multivariate tests suggest that this increase is significant, leaving little doubt that the size of the equity market relative to GDP increases.

We also examine the cross-sectional volatility of the individual security returns. This is a monthly measure of dispersion. If all of the securities were in one particular industry, the returns would be highly correlated and the cross-sectional volatility would be low. With industrial diversification, the cross-sectional volatility would be high. The results in table 6.3 show no particular pattern.

We examine two liquidity indicators: average value traded divided by GDP and turnover. Average value traded is the average monthly value of the shares traded in millions of U.S. dollars. We divide this by the previous year's GDP. This ratio sharply increases in a number of countries. The overall ratio's change is significant at the 10 percent level for those countries that had a significant break in capital flows. The turnover ratio is the total value of shares traded during the month divided by the average market capitalization. Some countries show significant increases in turnover and some show significant decreases. Overall, there are no particular patterns when examining the turnover ratio. Of course, some caution needs to be exercised in comparing the ratios across countries. Taiwan, for example, is an extremely influential observation. For interpretation, the emphasis should be placed on our multivariate tests that tend to downweight these influential observations in a generalized least squares framework.

Finally, we look at the foreign exchange (FX) market. We calculate a trailing annualized three-year standard deviation of exchange rate changes. The multivariate test that allows for country-specific coefficients suggest significant changes in FX volatility. The volatility of the FX rate is almost cut in half after the break in capital flows. The most dramatic decreases in FX volatility are found in Argentina and Mexico. Of course, dramatic changes in FX volatility could be induced by moving from a float to a pegged regime or by stabilization plans in countries with rampant inflation. A chronology of the currency regimes in the emerging markets can be found at www.duke.edu/~charvey/Country_risk/couindex.htm.

6.4.4   The Economy

Table 6.4 details the association of capital flow breaks and fundamental economic variables. There are a number of interesting features. First, in

Table 6.4   Macroeconomic Indicators

Country	Real GDP per Capita Growth — Five Years Before	Real GDP per Capita Growth — Five Years After[b]	Average (exports and imports)/GDP (%) — Five Years Before	Average (exports and imports)/GDP (%) — Five Years After[b]	Average Trade Surplus/GDP (%) — Five Years Before	Average Trade Surplus/GDP (%) — Five Years After[b]	Average Inflation (annual %) — Five Years Before	Average Inflation (annual %) — Five Years After[b]	Interest Rate (lending)[a] — Five Years Before	Interest Rate (lending)[a] — Five Years After[b]	Real Exchange Rate — Five Years Before	Real Exchange Rate — Five Years After[b]	External Debt (% GDP) — Five Years Before	External Debt (% GDP) — Five Years After[b]	Long-Term External Debt (% GDP) — Five Years Before	Long-Term External Debt (% GDP) — Five Years After[b]	Government Surplus (% GDP) — Five Years Before	Government Surplus (% GDP) — Five Years After[b]
Argentina	0.757	1.314	19.45	26.56***	0.63	3.43***	1,410.35	4.87***	3,822.78	10.42***	95.08	50.72***	47.1	29.0***	37.4	24.2***	-0.78	0.00***
Brazil	2.404	-1.741***	15.57	18.97***	3.29	-1.31***	220.88	1,475.31***	304.35	3,867.19***	187.06	125.11***	44.1	30.1***	37.9	24.4***	-10.01	-7.76*
Chile	2.783	5.779***	55.94	67.42***	3.18	-0.54***	23.50	19.08***	36.20	31.70**	94.66	100.12*	108.1	61.8***	92.0	49.1***	-1.67	1.22***
Colombia	1.795	3.510***	34.76	46.82***	-2.56	4.37***	27.56	22.05***	42.26	40.56	96.97	72.10***	39.7	28.7***	35.1	21.9***	0.36	-0.55**
Greece	0.852	1.161	42.91	61.93***	-6.94	0.29***	20.51	16.73***	20.12	24.80***	138.25	109.39***	NA	NA[c]	NA	NA[c]	-12.65	-20.28***
India	3.137	3.673	15.18	17.87***	-0.49	0.59***	9.87	9.09	17.25	16.30***	99.08	97.30	30.5	32.9*	26.7	30.1***	-7.09	-6.29***
Indonesia	6.103	5.788	42.89	47.27***	-0.13	-1.10	7.91	9.19***	21.90	18.34***	109.47	135.56***	60.8	55.1***	50.3	44.4***	-0.59	0.61***
Korea	6.832	6.604	75.44	90.11***	3.90	4.55	7.32	5.17***	10.23	8.70***	100.76	100.84	NA	NA[c]	NA	NA[c]	-0.25	0.31***
Malaysia	5.540	6.046*	140.16	182.51***	5.82	6.21	2.71	4.26***	7.62	8.47***	106.47	94.55***	47.3	39.8***	42.0	31.0***	-1.41	1.87***
Mexico	-1.041	0.281*	35.61	51.00***	3.28	9.16***	81.03	16.14***	66.39	19.28***	90.38	95.29***	61.6	39.3***	54.5	28.3***	-10.25	NA[c]
Pakistan	2.534	0.590***	31.77	34.08***	-1.73	1.19***	9.59	11.45***	NA	NA[c]	98.63	105.75***	48.9	50.0	39.0	43.1***	-7.03	-6.82
Philippines	0.141	-0.284	52.62	70.43***	1.15	4.37***	10.06	11.77	18.92	19.30	98.79	91.42***	83.0	66.3***	63.7	54.4***	-2.89	-2.06***
Portugal	0.019	1.594	83.00	94.18***	10.75	15.41***	9.76	3.91***	20.12	14.33***	96.48	92.18*	NA	NA[c]	NA	NA[c]	-4.21	NA[c]
Taiwan	4.349	5.281	80.27	75.93***	8.78	3.47***	3.28	3.55	NA	NA[c]	NA	NA[c]	NA	NA[c]	NA	NA[c]	NA	NA[c]
Thailand	4.801	8.687***	53.18	77.91***	-2.06	2.93***	2.38	4.90***	17.22	16.63	98.57	98.98	39.8	35.2***	30.2	24.4***	-3.35	3.24***
Turkey	2.436	1.726	32.61	40.74***	-0.95	3.79***	50.85	72.10***	45.47	65.55***	131.52	105.68***	42.4	38.0***	34.1	30.2***	-3.63	-4.61***
Venezuela	0.319	-2.588**	47.00	49.56***	-1.82	-8.32***	46.33	65.35***	33.08	39.30**	93.85	79.31***	66.1	55.5***	55.3	46.5***	-0.33	-4.14***
Mean[d]	2.73	2.98	50.36	61.43	1.43	2.76	21.61	18.78	28.19	25.33	104.24	99.00	53.04	41.28	44.54	33.12	-4.19	-3.32
P-value		0.40		0.20		0.22		0.37		0.17		0.16		0.03		0.34		0.00
Mean[e]	2.24	2.15	37.09	47.48	-0.45	1.69	25.57	18.86	29.56	23.65	102.06	94.87	47.23	37.59	39.52	30.35	-5.14	-4.70
P-value		0.47		0.15		0.12		0.29		0.03		0.02		0.04		0.44		0.00

(continued)

Table 6.4 (continued)

Country	Real GDP per Capita Growth		Average (exports and imports)/ GDP (%)		Average Trade Surplus/GDP (%)		Average Inflation (annual %)		Interest Rate (lending)[a]		Real Exchange Rate		External Debt (% GDP)		Long-Term External Debt (% GDP)		Government Surplus (% GDP)	
	Five Years Before	Five Years After[b]	Five Years Before	Five Years After[b]	Five Years Before	Five Years After[b]	Five Years Before	Five Years After[b]	Five Years Before	Five Years After[b]	Five Years Before	Five Years After[b]	Five Years Before	Five Years After[b]	Five Years Before	Five Years After[b]	Five Years Before	Five Years After[b]
P-value[d,f]		0.76		0.00		0.62		0.41		0.37		0.58		0.00		0.00		0.75
P-value[e,f]		0.85		0.00		0.70		0.29		0.24		0.92		0.02		0.00		0.61
P-value[d,g]		0.99		0.00		0.66		0.23		0.00		0.00		0.00		0.00		0.00
P-value[e,g]		0.98		0.00		0.77		0.10		0.00		0.00		0.01		0.00		0.00

Note: Inflation and interest rate calculations exclude Argentina and Brazil. Taiwan is not included in some of the macroeconomic analysis because it is not a member of the IMF and we lack the relevant data. All multivariate regression tests are corrected for group-wise heteroskedasticity and group-wise moving average processes in the residuals. NA = not available.

[a] Deposit rates used for Argentina, Brazil, Mexico, and Turkey.

[b] Probability values based on Newey-West corrected t-statistics from the regression

$$\text{Series} = B0 + (\text{Indicator for Five Years after Break}) * B1.$$

[c] Indicates that the regression was not estimated due to data problems.

[d] Excludes the Philippines, which has a break down in capital flows.

[e] Excludes the Philippines and countries with breaks that are not significant.

[f] t-statistic significance on a panel estimation with fixed effects of the regression

$$\text{Series}[i,t] = B0[i] + (\text{Indicator for Five Years after Break})[i,t] * B1.$$

[g] χ^2 joint test that all of the coefficients are zero in the pooled time series regression with fixed effects

$$\text{Series}[i,t] = B0[i] + (\text{Country Specific Indicator for Five Years after Break}[i,t] * B1[i].$$

*Significant at the 10 percent level.

**Significant at the 5 percent level.

***Significant at the 1 percent level.

the analysis that excludes only the Philippines, real per capita GDP growth increases from 2.73 percent to 2.93 percent after flow break points. Examining the countries with significant breaks, GDP per capita does not significantly change. On a country-by-country basis, Chile, Colombia, Mexico, and Thailand have significant increases in real GDP per capita. There are increases in Argentina, Greece, India, Malaysia, Portugal, and Taiwan, but they are not significant.

There is a sharp reduction in inflation in many countries. The overall average is skewed by Argentina and Brazil. Excluding these two countries, inflation drops from 21.61 percent to 18.78 percent after the flow break point. Similar results are found for local interest rates.

Capital flow breaks are also associated with changes in trading patterns. Table 6.4 indicates that the size of the trade sector is larger after portfolio flows break. On average the trade sector accounts for 61.4 percent of GDP after a flow break point compared to 50.4 percent before. These results are consistent with a joint process of financial market and economic integration. Indeed, as Feldstein and Horioka (1980) point out, in a world with free capital flows, savings and investment should be delinked and large current account imbalances can be run since they can be feasibly financed. However, the data do not seem to support the notion that larger capital mobility has led to emerging markets running large current account deficits. On average, there is a trade surplus as a percentage of GDP of about 1.4 percent before the capital flows break point, which increases to 2.8 percent on average after the break.

External debt to GDP also significantly decreases on average. While the long-term external debt decreases, the change is not significantly different from zero. With government deficits going down on average as well, it is tempting to conclude that the developing countries have reduced their external debt burden by improving their trade balances and freeing up resources from lower government deficits. In addition, despite the inflowing equity capital, they are on average actually exporting rather than importing capital. This may suggest that developing countries are not relying on more foreign capital at all but have simply replaced debt with equity. Consider the case of Chile in figure 6.1. There is a clear negative correlation between equities and bonds and the largest decrease in external debt of all the countries in our sample. This is consistent with a substitution effect.[11] Nevertheless, given the large cross-country differences, we should

---

11. It is well known that many emerging markets have reduced their reliance on commercial bank debt and some, like Chile, have also reduced their reliance on foreign fixed income.

There is some interesting theoretical and empirical work on the various sources of financing. For example, Boyd and Smith's (1996) model suggests that as an economy develops, the aggregate ratio of debt to equity will generally fall, yet debt and equity remain complementary sources for the financing of capital investments. See the empirical work in Demurgüç-Kunt and Maksimovic (1996).

caution against such generalized inference. For example, more than half of the average increase in trade surplus to GDP in the postbreak period can be attributed to two European countries: Portugal and Greece.

We also compiled real exchange rate indices for the various countries by dividing the exchange rate in local currency to the dollar by the ratio of the local consumer price index to the U.S. consumer price index. These data are from the International Financial Statistics of the International Monetary Fund. Hence, an increase in the index suggests a real exchange rate depreciation. We find a significant real appreciation of the local currencies in nine of the sixteen countries after equity flow breaks, and a significant drop in only four countries. Overall, foreign capital flows seem to lead to real exchange rate appreciations, as is often claimed. The change is highly statistically significant when we allow for country-specific coefficients in the multivariate regressions.

6.4.5   Country Risk

We examine five different measures of country risk: Institutional Investor's Country Credit Rating (IICCR), International Country Risk Guide (ICRG) Economic Risk, ICRG Political Risk, ICRG Financial Risk, and ICRG Composite Risk. The ICRG Composite Risk is a weighted average of the three preceding components (see Erb, Harvey, and Viskanta 1996a, 1996b). A higher country rating means lower risk. These measures are all ex ante. That is, in the case of the IICCR, participants are asked to make an assessment of the future riskiness of a country.

The results in table 6.5 suggest an unambiguous increase in rating across the different measures. For example, the ICRG Composite Risk rating increases in every country except Venezuela. The average rating increases from 61.1 to 69.7, which is a statistically significant change. Erb, Harvey, and Viskanta (1996a) link expected returns and country ratings. An 8.6-point increase in rating would translate into a 2.4 percent decrease in the expected returns. Overall, the message is that capital flow inflows are associated with investor perceptions of lower country risk.

6.4.6   Portfolio Results

In a final experiment, we create two equally weighted portfolios. At each month, the first portfolio, which we call the "segmented portfolio," includes the returns of the countries that have not experienced a significant break in the equity capital flows. At each month, the second portfolio, which we call the "integrated portfolio," includes the returns of the country that have already experienced a significant break in the equity capital flows. The number of countries in each portfolio shifts through time as a number of countries move from the segmented portfolio to the integrated portfolio. As such, it is possible that the results could be heavily influenced by one or two countries when there are a small number of countries in the

Table 6.5   **Country Risk**

Country	Institutional Investor's Country Credit Rating		ICRG Economic Index		ICRG Financial Index		ICRG Political Index		ICRG Composite Index	
	Five Years Before	Five Years After[a]	Five Years Before	Five Years After[a]	Five Years Before	Five Years After[a]	Five Years Before	Five Years After[a]	Five Years Before	Five Years After[a]
Argentina	21.9	36.3***	21.2	32.4***	25.1	36.6***	62.4	74.0***	54.5	71.9***
Brazil	32.7	27.5***	20.7	22.6***	23.9	32.2***	63.4	66.5***	54.1	60.8***
Chile	28.1	36.4***	23.9	31.6***	25.6	39.1***	45.9	62.0***	47.9	66.5***
Colombia	36.4	44.4***	33.3	34.9***	35.3	38.4**	56.4	58.0	62.6	65.1*
Greece	53.1	47.5***	30.0	30.1	25.9	29.9***	60.7	61.8*	58.5	61.1***
India	47.7	51.7***	35.1	36.7***	35.0	40.2***	49.5	63.4***	49.4	67.0***
Indonesia	43.7	42.6	28.8	34.9***	27.7	36.4***	42.3	63.0***	60.6	69.8***
Korea	67.3	70.4***	37.7	40.6***	47.2	46.5***	66.8	77.3***	76.1	82.0***
Malaysia	32.3	44.3***	27.4	31.2***	31.9	40.4***	67.9	68.7	69.8	79.8***
Mexico	58.4	63.7***	38.7	40.9***	30.8	44.2***	62.8	70.8***	58.2	70.5***
Pakistan	29.5	29.4	31.7	31.1**	23.1	32.7***	34.7	54.2***	44.9	59.2***
Philippines	22.2	27.0***	28.6	31.5***	21.6	29.1***	42.4	48.5***	46.5	54.6***
Portugal	64.5	67.9***	39.3	41.5***	42.8	43.2	71.2	80.6***	76.8	82.7***
Taiwan	77.0	78.8***	43.5	43.5	48.2	47.3	75.2	78.6***	83.6	85.2***
Thailand	53.1	60.6***	35.1	37.0***	29.6	41.6***	56.9	59.5***	61.0	69.1***
Turkey	38.7	43.3***	27.8	28.0	24.1	29.6***	52.5	57.0**	52.3	57.4***
Venezuela	36.0	33.6***	31.6	32.2	35.1	34.6	67.3	64.9**	67.2	66.3
Mean[b]	45.02	48.65	31.61	34.33	31.96	38.31	58.48	66.25	61.09	69.65
P-value		0.26		0.11		0.01		0.02		0.01

(continued)

Table 6.5 (continued)

Country	Institutional Investor's Country Credit Rating		ICRG Economic Index		ICRG Financial Index		ICRG Political Index		ICRG Composite Index	
	Five Years Before	Five Years After[a]	Five Years Before	Five Years After[a]	Five Years Before	Five Years After[a]	Five Years Before	Five Years After[a]	Five Years Before	Five Years After[a]
Mean[c]	43.61	46.51	31.50	33.85	31.10	37.69	58.08	65.01	58.64	67.31
P-value		0.33		0.14		0.00		0.03		0.00
P-value[b,d]		0.22		0.00		0.00		0.00		0.00
P-value[c,d]		0.33		0.00		0.00		0.00		0.00
P-value[b,e]		0.00		0.00		0.00		0.00		0.00
P-value[c,e]		0.00		0.00		0.00		0.00		0.00

Note: All multivariate regression tests are corrected for group-wise heteroskedasticity and group-wise moving average processes in the residuals.

[a] Probability values based on Newey-West corrected t-statistics from the regression

Series = B0 + (Indicator for Five Years after Break) * B1.

[b] Excludes the Philippines, which has a break down in capital flows.

[c] Excludes the Philippines and countries with breaks that are not significant.

[d] FE indicates the t-statistic significance on a panel estimation with fixed effects of the regression

Series$[i,t]$ = B0$[i]$ + (Indicator for Five Years after Break)$[i,t]$ * B1.

[e] χ^2 joint test that all of the coefficients are zero in the pooled time series regression with fixed effects

Series$[i,t]$ = B0$[i]$ + (Country Specific Indicator for Five Years after Break)$[i,t]$ * B1$[i]$.

*Significant at the 10 percent level.

**Significant at the 5 percent level.

***Significant at the 1 percent level.

Table 6.6   **Integration/Segmentation Portfolio Analysis: January 1987 to September 1994**

Moment	Segmented Portfolio	Integrated Portfolio
Significant countries		
Annualized mean %	25.88	24.13
Annualized volatility %	20.73	35.16
Correlation with world	0.132	0.355
β with world	0.174	0.771
All countries		
Annualized mean %	20.78	25.52
Annualized volatility %	18.70	33.01
Correlation with world	0.365	0.320
β with world	0.423	0.652

Note: Significant countries include all countries in the analysis except for Chile, Turkey, Malaysia, Taiwan, Indonesia, and Portugal. The Philippines is always excluded.

portfolio. To address this problem, we restrict the sample period to January 1987–September 1994.

The portfolio results are contained in table 6.6. Consistent with our analysis of the cost of capital and our tests on the ex post returns, there is little difference in the ex post observed returns (25.9 percent compared to 24.1 percent on an annual basis for the significant countries). We also find evidence of higher volatility. In the segmented portfolio, the average annualized volatility is 20.7 percent, whereas in the integrated portfolio the volatility is 35.2 percent. The volatility analysis contrasts with the inconclusive results in the ex post volatility analyzed in table 6.2.

We also calculated the correlations and βs of the two portfolios with world returns. The correlation with the world portfolio increases from 0.13 to 0.36 moving from the segmented to the integrated portfolio. We also find that the β increases from 0.17 to 0.77. The increase in correlation is consistent with integrated markets being relatively more affected by world information than segmented markets.

6.5 Conclusions

The idea of our paper is that patterns in capital flows can reveal information about market liberalizations. In a segmented capital market, there are unlikely to be significant foreign capital flows. An effective capital market liberalization may be associated with significant new foreign capital flows. Our starting point is to identify breaks in equity capital flows. In sixteen of the seventeen countries we examine, such a break is associated with an increase in net capital flows. We then compare measures of both the financial system and the economy in the prebreak and postbreak regimes.

Ours is the first paper to compare and contrast the behavior of both equity and bond capital flows. For many countries, the patterns of equity and bond flows are very similar. In a few countries, it seems that bond flows precede equity flows.

We find that expected returns decrease after significant breaks in capital flows. In addition, risk decreases, at least as measured by country rating, and the correlation of equity returns with the world market is higher. This seems consistent with a "one-time" portfolio adjustment associated with the movement from segmented to integrated markets. It does not seem to be consistent with the "return chasing" hypothesis postulated by Bohn and Tesar (1996).

In addition, we find that the increase in capital flows is associated with marginally higher per capita GDP, a larger trade sector, less long-term country debt, lower inflation, and lower foreign exchange rate volatility.

Although not all of these changes are statistically significant, the general picture is one that contradicts the view that foreign portfolio investors are detrimental to a developing country's economy. Of course, our methods do not allow us to distinguish between the scenario where foreign equity investment is responsible for the improved macroeconomic and financial outlook and the scenario where it is simply attracted by the prospect of these improvements. Nevertheless, our suggestive findings of lower expected returns and risk and higher loadings on world factors are consistent with international investors rebalancing their portfolios in response to a wider opportunity set (see also Bohn and Tesar 1996). If this is the case, policy makers across the world would be well advised to create an environment that attracts, rather than repels, foreign portfolio investors.

References

Aggarwal, Reena, Carla Inclan, and Ricardo Leal. 1999. Volatility in emerging stock markets. *Journal of Financial and Quantitative Analysis* 34 (1): 33–55.

Bai, Jushan, Robin L. Lumsdaine, and James H. Stock. 1998. Testing for and dating breaks in stationary and nonstationary multivariate time series. *Review of Economic Studies* 65 (3): 395–432.

Bartolini, Leonardo, and Allan Drazen. 1996. Capital account liberalization as a signal. NBER Working Paper no. 5925. Cambridge, Mass.: National Bureau of Economic Research.

Bekaert, Geert. 1995. Market integration and investment barriers in emerging equity markets. *World Bank Economic Review* 9 (1): 75–107.

Bekaert, Geert, and Campbell R. Harvey. 1995. Time-varying world market integration. *Journal of Finance* 50:403–44.

———. 1997. Emerging equity market volatility. *Journal of Financial Economics* 43:29–78.

————. 1998. Capital markets: An engine for economic growth. *Brown Journal of World Affairs* 5 (1): 33–58.

————. 2000. Foreign speculators and emerging equity markets. *Journal of Finance* 55, no. 2 (April): 565–613.

Bekaert, Geert, Campbell R. Harvey, and Robin Lumsdaine. 1999. Dating the integration of world capital markets. Unpublished working notes, Stanford University and Duke University.

Bekaert, Geert, and Michael S. Urias. 1996. Diversification, integration and emerging market closed-end funds. *Journal of Finance* 51:835–70.

Bohn, H., and L. Tesar. 1996. U.S. equity investment in foreign markets: Portfolio rebalancing or return chasing? *American Economic Review* 86, no. 2 (May): 77–81.

Boyd, J., and B. Smith. 1996. The coevolution of the real and financial sectors in the growth process. *World Bank Economic Review* 10 (May): 371–96.

Claessens, S., M. Dooley, and A. Warner. 1993. Portfolio capital flows: Hot or cool? In *Portfolio investment in developing countries,* ed. S. Claessens and S. Gooptu, 18–44. Washington, D.C.: World Bank.

Clark, J. M., and E. Berko. 1997. Foreign investment fluctuations and emerging market stock returns: The case of Mexico. Unpublished working paper. New York: Federal Reserve Bank.

Demurgüç-Kunt, Asli, and V. Maksimovic. 1996. Stock market development and financing choices of firms. *World Bank Economic Review* 10 (May): 341–69.

De Santis, Giorgio, and Selahattin İmrohoroğlu. 1996. Stock returns and volatility in emerging financial markets. Unpublished working paper, University of Southern California, Los Angeles.

Erb, Claude B., Campbell R. Harvey, and Tadas E. Viskanta. 1996a. Expected returns and volatility in 135 countries. *Journal of Portfolio Management* 22, no. 3 (spring): 46–58.

————. 1996b. Political risk, economic risk and financial risk. *Financial Analysts Journal* 52, no. 6 (November/December): 29–46.

Feldstein, M., and C. Horioka. 1980. Domestic saving and international capital flows. *Economic Journal* 90:314–29.

Glosten, Lawrence R., Ravi Jagannathan, and David E. Runkle. 1993. On the relation between the expected value and the volatility of the nominal excess return on stocks. *Journal of Finance* 48:1779–1802.

Harris, L., and E. Gurel. 1986. Price and volume effects associated with changes in the S&P 500 list: New evidence for the existence of price pressure. *Journal of Finance* 41:815–29.

Harvey, Campbell R. 1991. The world price of covariance risk. *Journal of Finance* 46:111–57.

Henry, Peter Blair. 2000. Equity prices, stock market liberalization, and investment. *Journal of Financial Economics,* forthcoming.

Howell, Michael. 1993. Institutional investors and emerging stock markets. In *Portfolio investment in developing countries,* ed. S. Claessens and S. Gooptu. Washington, D.C.: World Bank.

Howell, Michael, and Angela Cozzini. 1991. *International equity flows—Games without frontiers: Global equity markets in the 1990s.* International Equity Research, Salomon Brothers.

————. 1992. *International equity flows.* London: Barings Securities.

Kang, Jun-Koo, and René M. Stulz. 1997. Why is there a home bias? An analysis of foreign portfolio equity ownership in Japan. *Journal of Financial Economics* 48, no. 1 (October): 3–28.

Kester, Annie Y., et al. 1994. *Following the money: US finance in the world economy.* Washington, D.C.: National Academy of the Sciences.

Kim, E. Hand, and Vijay Singal. 2000. Stock market openings: Experience of emerging economies. *Journal of Business,* forthcoming.

King, Robert, and Ross Levine. 1993a. Finance and growth: Schumpeter might be right. *Quarterly Journal of Economics* 111:639–71.

———. 1993b. Finance, entrepreneurship, and growth. *Journal of Monetary Economics* 32 (3): 513–42.

Korajczyk, Robert A. 1996. A measure of stock market integration for developed and emerging markets. *World Bank Economic Review* 10:267–90.

Krugman, Paul. 1993. International finance and economic development. In *Finance and development: Issues and experience,* ed. Alberto Giovannini, 11–23. Cambridge: Cambridge University Press.

Levine, Ross, and Sara Zervos. Stock market development and long-run growth. *World Bank Economic Review* 10:323–40.

Mathieson, Donald J., and Liliana Rojaz-Suarez. 1992. Liberalization of the capital account: Experiences and issues. Unpublished working paper. Washington, D.C.: International Monetary Fund.

Obstfeld, Maurice. 1994. Risk taking, global diversification and growth. *American Economic Review* 84:1310–29.

Rajan, Raghuram G., and Luigi Zingales. 1997. Financial dependence and growth. Unpublished working paper. Graduate School of Business, University of Chicago.

Richards, Anthony J. 1996. Volatility and predictability in national markets: How do emerging and mature markets differ? *IMF Staff Papers* 43 (3).

Sachs, J., and A. Warner. 1995. Economic reform and the process of global integration. *Brookings Papers on Economic Activity,* no. 1: 1–118.

Shleifer, A. 1986. Do demand curves for stocks slope down? *Journal of Finance* 41:579.

Stulz, R. M. 1999. International portfolio flows and security markets. In *International capital flows,* ed. Martin Feldstein, 257–93. Chicago: University of Chicago Press.

Tesar, L., and I. Werner. 1994. International equity transactions and U.S. portfolio choice. In *The internationalization of equity markets,* ed. J. Frankel, 185–215. Chicago: University of Chicago Press.

———. 1995a. U.S. equity investment in emerging stock markets. *World Bank Economic Review* 9 (1): 109–30.

———. 1995b. Home bias and high turnover. *Journal of International Money and Finance* 14 (4): 467–92.

Warther, V. A. 1995. Aggregate mutual fund flows and security returns. *Journal of Economics* 39:209–35.

III

Capital Flows to Latin America, Asia, and Eastern Europe

Capital Flows, Real Exchange Rates, and Capital Controls
Some Latin American Experiences

Sebastian Edwards

7.1 Introduction

The East Asian crisis of 1997–98 has generated a stream of stunning news about bankruptcies, dwindling international reserves, weak banks, and plunging currencies. In the midst of this ever growing debacle, many observers have been surprised by Latin America's resilience and by the absence of a major contagion effect into the region. Some private sector analysts have argued that Latin America's insulation from the Asian crisis has been the result of the major reforms implemented in the region in the last decade or so. Since these reforms have created a lean productive structure, the argument goes, Latin America will continue to receive a substantial flow of capital from abroad. This view is nicely captured by the following quote from ING Barings (1998, 64): "The general resilience of Latin America to a more difficult global economic backdrop has much to do with . . . an improving microeconomic base. The region has benefited from strong liquidity flows (both FDI and portfolio capital)." And according to Santander Investment (1998, 5–6), "regional economies should continue to perform well . . . capital flows in 1998, however, will be a key variable . . . privatization related capital flows . . . should continue going into the region this year, with portfolio inflows trailing off amid prevailing market instability." Although other observers are less sanguine, they agree on the important role of capital inflows in determining the region's eco-

Sebastian Edwards is the Henry Ford II Professor of International Economics at the Anderson Graduate School of Management, University of California, Los Angeles, and a research associate of the National Bureau of Economic Research.

The author is indebted to Alejandro Jara, Rajesh Chakrabarti, and Kyongchul Kim for assistance. He is particularly grateful to José De Gregorio, his discussant at the conference, for comments.

nomic future. For example, according to Goldman Sachs (1998, 5), "the global financial shocks affecting Asia . . . forced us to downgrade significantly the economic outlook for Latin America in 1998. This is so because [of] lower capital inflows . . . [and] higher bond spreads." This dependence on capital flows is not new. Even a cursory analysis of Latin America's economic history in the second half of this century would show that capital flows—both their level and volatility—have greatly affected the region's performance.

Mexico's experience during the last twenty years captures in a nutshell the story of the Latin American region. After facing a serious external crisis in the early 1980s, Mexico embarked on ambitious reforms aimed at modernizing its economy during the late 1980s. The country was opened to international competition, a massive privatization process was undertaken, and most economic transactions were deregulated. Largely as a result of these reforms the international financial community rediscovered Mexico in the early 1990s, and a significant volume of capital started flowing into the country.

The Mexican currency crisis of December 1994, however, generated considerable anxiety among policy analysts, financial operators, and international civil servants. Some asked whether Latin America was indeed ready to adopt market-oriented policies, while others questioned the appropriateness of specific policies, including the use of a rigid nominal exchange rate as a way to reduce inflation. The behavior of capital inflows has been at the center of almost every analysis of the Mexican crisis. Some authors have argued that massive flows allowed Mexico to increase consumption in spite of weak fundamentals. According to others, the predominantly "speculative" nature of these flows signaled, from early on, that the Mexican experience was bound to run into a serious external crisis. Yet others argued that Mexico's mistake was to have lifted capital controls too early, allowing these "speculative" flows to disturb the country's macroeconomic foundations. According to these analysts a more appropriate policy stance in Mexico would have been to maintain some form of capital controls, as a number of emerging economies—including Chile, Colombia, and Israel, among others—have done for some time. The proponents of this view argue that capital controls will isolate these young economies from volatile short-run capital flows, helping them reduce their overall degree of vulnerability to external shocks, including speculative attacks.[1]

The purpose of this paper is to discuss some of the most important aspects of Latin America's experience with capital flows. The paper is organized as follows: In section 7.2 I discuss, from a historical perspective,

1. On the Mexican crisis, see, e.g., Dornbush and Werner (1994), Dornbusch, Goldfajn, and Valdés (1995), Bruno (1995), and Calvo and Mendoza (1996). On the benefits and costs of capital controls, see, e.g., the essays collected in Edwards (1995b).

Latin America's experience with capital flows during the last twenty-five years. In section 7.3 I discuss, within the context of the sequencing of reform literature, the relationship between capital flows, real exchange rates, and international competitiveness. Section 7.4 focuses on the role of capital controls as a device for isolating emerging economies from the volatility of international capital markets. I begin by reviewing the policy issues and the current debate on the subject. I then present an empirical analysis of Chile's recent experiences with capital controls, and I make some comparisons to the recent experiences of Colombia. The analysis of the Chilean experience is particularly important since its practice of imposing reserves requirements on capital inflows has been praised by a number of analysts, including senior staff of the multilateral institutions, as an effective and efficient way of reducing the vulnerability associated with capital flows volatility. Section 7.5 presents my conclusions. In that section I also provide some reflections, based on recent Latin American historical episodes, on the role of banks in intermediating capital inflows and on financial crises.[2]

7.2 Twenty-Five Years of Capital Flows to Latin America

7.2.1 Capital Hunger in the 1970s

During the 1960s and early 1970s Latin America was basically cut off from private international financial markets.[3] With the exception of limited amounts of foreign direct investment (FDI), very little private capital moved into the region. Throughout this period Latin America relied on official capital flows—largely from the World Bank, the Inter-American Development Bank (IADB), and the International Monetary Fund (IMF). In a way, the region was the captive customer of the multilateral institutions. During this period, and following the then-dominant "two gaps" approach to economic development, most analysts believed that an increase in the availability of foreign financing would allow the region to relax the "foreign constraint" and accelerate the rate of growth (Eaton 1989).

In the mid- and late 1970s, and largely as the result of the oil price shocks, international private liquidity increased significantly, and Latin America became a major recipient of recycled "petrodollars." In 1981 alone the region received (net) private capital inflows in excess of 21 per-

---

2. It is important to stress at the outset that Latin America is an extremely diverse region with sophisticated as well as backward economies, with large and very small countries, and with stable and volatile economic systems. This means that broad generalizations are bound to be misleading and to provide oversimplified views of the region. For this reason, then, in this paper I make an effort to make distinctions across countries as well as to discuss broad regional trends.

3. Parts of this section draw on Edwards (1999).

cent of exports. Individual country cases, however, differed significantly during this period. While in Brazil, Mexico, and Venezuela a majority of these flows were captured by the government and were used to finance large (and increasing) fiscal deficits, in Argentina and Chile—two nations embarked at the time on early market-oriented reforms—they were largely channeled to the private sector.[4]

7.2.2   The Debt Crisis and the Lost Decade

During 1979–81, and in spite of major commodity price shocks, most countries in Latin America continued to grow at healthy rates, and a handful of them in the Southern Cone were even experimenting with market-oriented reforms. What most observers missed at the time—as they would again a dozen years later in Mexico—was that in most countries three worrisome developments were taking place: (1) real exchange rates became significantly overvalued, seriously hurting exports' competitiveness; (2) domestic saving remained flat, at rates inconsistent with sustainable rapid growth; and (3) a large proportion of the capital inflows were being used to finance consumption or investment projects of doubtful quality. Most of these funds were intermediated by banks that were subject to little supervision, which quickly became the Achilles' heel of these economies.[5]

In August 1982, Mexico's Finance Minister Jesus Silva Herzog informed a stunned international community that his country was not able to meet its financial obligations. In late 1982 and early 1983, country after country saw the access to international financial capital markets disappear. Even Chile and Colombia, two countries that played by the rules of the game and did not attempt to reschedule their debts, experienced a drying up of private international financing. They were subject to what Ocampo (1989) has called the Latin "neighborhood effect."

Between 1982 and 1989 most of the Latin American nations muddled through, while they tried to negotiate debt reduction deals with their private creditors. The initial reaction by the creditor countries was that the debt crisis represented a temporary liquidity problem that could be solved with a combination of macroeconomics adjustment, debt rescheduling agreements, and some structural reforms. Two years after the eruption of the crisis, optimism had returned to the creditor countries. The IMF *World Economic Outlook, 1984* and the World Bank's *World Development Report, 1984* included optimistic projections, predicting a steady decline of the debt/export ratio in the Latin American countries until 1990. The facts, however, proved both institutions wrong. By 1987, five years into the crisis,

---

4. On the behavior of the Latin American economies during this period, see, e.g., Edwards (1995a).

5. Naturally, since funds are fungible it is very difficult to know exactly how the capital inflows were finally used. The above description, however, is an accurate picture of the economic developments in the region at that time.

it was becoming increasingly clear even to the most recalcitrant observers that the debt burden had greatly reduced the incentives for reforming the region's economies. Between 1985 and 1987 net resource transfers—defined as net capital inflows minus interest and dividends payments to the rest of the world—were significantly negative, averaging almost 28 percent of exports.

In March 1989, the creditor nations and the multilateral institutions recognized that, in many cases, it was in everyone's interest to provide (some) debt forgiveness. This approach was based on the idea that for highly indebted countries partial debt forgiveness would encourage the type of market-oriented reform conducive to higher exports and faster growth. Higher growth, in turn, would allow them to accelerate the payment of the (remaining) debt. In March of that year, U.S. Secretary of the Treasury Nicholas Brady announced a new initiative based on *voluntary* debt reduction. This basic proposal amounted to exchanging old debt for new long-term debt, with a lower face value. The exact conversion ratios, and the detailed characteristics of the new instruments, were to be negotiated between the debtor countries and their creditors—mostly U.S. banks. In order to make this new approach feasible and attractive to creditor banks, the advanced nations and the multilateral institutions devoted a substantial amount of resources—on the order of US$30 billion—to guarantee the new "Brady" concessional bonds. Typically, principal payments on these new securities were backed by thirty-year zero coupon U.S. treasury bills, and interest payments were subject to rolling three-year guarantees. Between 1989 and 1997 Costa Rica, Mexico, Venezuela, Uruguay, Argentina, Brazil, and Peru reached agreements with their creditors to reduce their debt burdens.

In order to be eligible for Brady plan negotiations, countries had to show willingness "plus some prior action" to engage in serious market-oriented economic reform. This plan was seen as a way of rewarding countries truly committed to implementing modernization reforms, and it was expected that it would lift the debt overhang burdens associated with extremely high payments. In 1989 Mexico and Costa Rica were the first countries within the Brady plan framework to reach broad agreements with their creditors to reduce the value of their debt. Venezuela and Uruguay followed in 1990 and 1991, and Argentina and Brazil signed draft agreements in 1992. In 1996 Peru became the latest country to come to terms with its creditors within the context of the Brady plan.

By 1990 the vast majority of the countries in the region had embarked on market-oriented reforms. Although programs varied across countries, they exhibited three common components: (1) The implementation of stabilization programs aimed at reducing inflation and generating a sustainable current account balance. In most countries fiscal retrenchment, including major tax reform, were at the core of these programs. (2) The opening up of these economies to international competition. While every country reduced its trade barriers substantially, the approach toward capital account liberalization was very diverse. While in some nations—Mexico and Argentina, for example—capital controls were abolished, in others such as Brazil, Chile, and Colombia some form of capital controls—especially on capital inflows—was maintained. (3) Major privatization and deregulation programs, aimed at reducing the importance of the state in economic affairs. As the reforms proceeded, many countries added the implementation of social programs targeted to the poor as a fourth component of the new development strategy (Edwards 1995a).

7.2.3 The World Financial Market's Rediscovery of Latin America in the 1990s

Starting in 1990 the majority of the Latin American countries were able, once again, to attract private capital. By 1992 the net volume of funds had become so large—exceeding 35 percent of the region's exports—that a number of analysts began to talk about Latin America's "capital inflows problem" (Calvo, Leiderman, and Reinhart 1993; Edwards 1993). To many analysts this sudden change from capital scarcity and negative resource transfers to foreign capital overabundance was surprising and reflected a surge in speculation in international markets. To others, the fact that merely a dozen years after a major crisis these countries were able to tap the international market reflected the success of the market-oriented reforms. If the market is willing to reward these countries with plentiful funds, the argument went, it must reflect that the reforms are bearing fruit.

Figure 7.1 presents the evolution of net total capital flows (in billions of dollars) into Latin America during the period 1975–96. As may be seen, the cyclical—almost paranoid, one could say—nature of capital inflows into Latin America comes out clearly. This figure shows the abundance of the late 1970s and early 1980s, followed by the collapse in inflows during

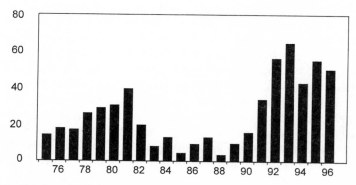

Fig. 7.1   Total capital inflows into Latin America, 1975–96 (US$ billions)

most of the 1980s, and the remarkable return to abundance in the last few years. The crunch of the 1980s, when the region as a whole was transferring (in net terms) almost 30 percent of its exports to the rest of the world, was extremely severe. One of the most important features of the new reality in the 1990s has been the significant decline (in relative terms) of official capital flows—and in particular funds coming from the multilateral institutions such as the IMF and the World Bank. The year 1995, however, was characterized by a major jump in net official flows, when as a result of the Mexican crisis, the IMF, the World Bank, the IADB, and the U.S. government transferred very large amounts of funds to Mexico. This is a vivid reflection of the significant change experienced by official financing during the last few years. It has gone from being the most important provider—and in some countries, the sole provider—of foreign funds, to being a provider of stabilizing funds. In a way the multilateral official institutions have become insurance companies of sorts, whose main role is to provide relief when a bad state of nature occurs.

Figure 7.2 presents data on *net* capital inflows for eight selected countries. Figure 7.3, on the other hand, contains data on the composition of capital inflows in these Latin American countries for 1975–96. Three types of flows are distinguished: (1) foreign direct investment, which reflects, at least in principle, a long-term commitment on behalf of the investor in the host country; (2) portfolio investment, which includes transactions in equity and debt securities; (3) other types of flows, a rather broad category that includes trade credit (both long and short term) and official (bilateral and multilateral) loans. Several important trends emerge from these figures. First, portfolio investment is a relatively new phenomenon in these countries. Until the late 1980s, "other" constituted the dominant form of inflows in most countries. Second, in some countries portfolio flows were by far the dominant form of inflows after 1991. This has particularly been the case in Argentina and Mexico. Figure 7.3 also shows that Brazil has experienced a tremendous surge in portfolio funds in the last few years. These portfolio flows take two basic forms: equities acquisitions—mostly in the form of American depositary receipts (ADRs)—by foreign investors, and bond issues in international markets. The World Bank (1997) has reported that an increasing number of institutional investors (including pension funds) in the advanced countries are adding emerging economies' equities to their portfolios. This heavy reliance on equities and bonds contrasts with the 1970s, when syndicated bank loans constituted the dominant form of private capital inflows into Latin America. Third, figure 7.3 shows that the importance of FDI varies significantly across countries. Chile, Colombia, and Peru have received particularly large volumes of FDI in the last few years. In all three cases these funds have been largely devoted to natural resources–intensive sectors—mining in Chile and Peru, and oil in Colombia.

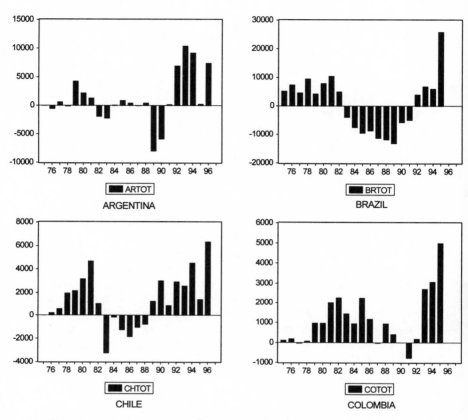

Fig. 7.2   Total net capital flows in selected Latin American countries, 1975–96 (US$ millions)

The recent surge in capital inflows—and in particular of portfolio inflows—to Latin America has been the result of two basic forces. First, developments in international financial conditions, and in particular the decline in U.S. interest rates since in 1990–91, have encouraged investors in the advanced countries to seek higher returns in other markets, including Latin America. Calvo, Leiderman, and Reinhart (1993) provided an early, and very influential, study of the determinants of capital inflows into the region. These authors argue that cyclical external factors have been by far the most important determinant of these flows. These results have recently been confirmed by the World Bank's (1997) massive study on private capital inflows to the developing countries. Second, the improvement in Latin America's economic prospects—including the reduction in country risk that has been associated with the implementation of market-oriented reforms—has increased the attractiveness of these countries to

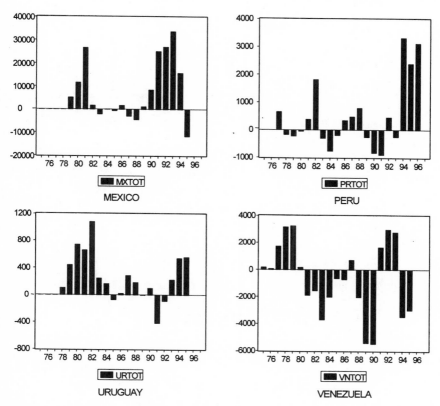

Fig. 7.2   (cont.)

international investors. In an extension of the Calvo, Leiderman, and Reinhart (1993) study, Chuhan, Claessens, and Mamingi (1993) found that the recipient country's own fundamentals were as important as cyclical factors in explaining the surge in portfolio flows into Latin America. In a recent analysis of the determinants of capital inflows into Chile, Larrain, Laban, and Chumacero (1997) argue that while interest rate differentials play a key role in determining short-term flows, they are unimportant in determining longer ones. These are affected by longer-term structural variables, and in particular the country's impressive market-oriented reforms.

7.2.4   Policy Issues and Dilemmas in a Volatile Era

The surge in capital flows in the last few years has raised a number of important policy issues. It has been argued, for example, that under capital mobility the national authorities lose (some) control over monetary policy, and that the economy will become more vulnerable to external shocks. In

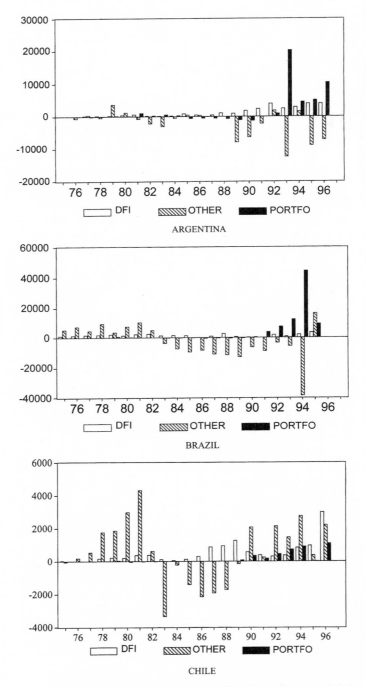

Fig. 7.3   Composition of capital flows in selected Latin American countries, 1975–96 (US$ millions)

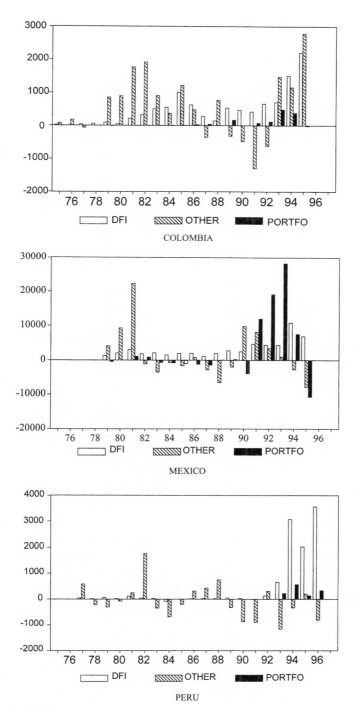

Fig. 7.3 (cont.)

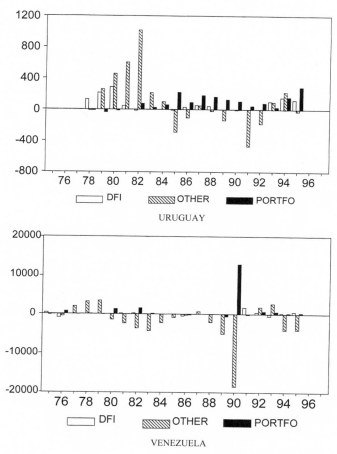

Fig. 7.3   (cont.)

particular there have been increasing concerns that major reversals in capital flows will trigger—as in East Asia—major currency collapses. Also, policy makers have often expressed concerns over their (effective) freedom for selecting the exchange rate regime, if capital is highly mobile. Moreover, sometimes it has been argued that full capital mobility will result in "overborrowing" and, eventually, in a major debt crisis. This preoccupation has been heightened in countries with a weak banking system and a limited capacity for implementing modern supervisory and regulatory systems. The impact of large capital inflows on domestic saving has also become an issue of concern among policy makers and analysts. Other concerns regarding the liberalization of capital movements relate to increased real exchange rate instability and potential losses of international competitiveness stemming from real exchange rate appreciations. Still other analysts have pointed out that the premature opening of the capital account could lead to massive capital flight from the country in question. This type of discussion has led to a growing literature on the most adequate sequencing and speed of liberalization and stabilization reforms. The extent of actual—as opposed to legal—capital mobility has been the subject of intense policy debate in Latin America. This discussion is directly related to the important question of the effectiveness of capital controls, an issue I address in some detail in section 7.4 of this paper.

7.3 The Sequencing of Liberalization, Capital Inflows, and Real Exchange Rates

The increase in capital inflows into Latin American during the first half of the 1990s allowed the countries in the region to increase aggregate expenditure substantially. This generated pressure on domestic prices, large real exchange rate appreciations, and, thus, a loss in international competitiveness. This phenomenon, which has generated concern among academics, policy makers, and financial sector operators, has been at the center of debates on the appropriate sequencing of economic reform. In particular, analysts have asked whether the capital account should be opened (relatively) early in the liberalization process, or whether its reform should be postponed until the reform process has reached a certain level of maturity.

The academic and policy debate on the sequencing of reform has largely been prompted by previous Latin American attempts to open up to international competition. This issue was first considered in the 1980s in discussions dealing with the Southern Cone's (Argentina, Chile, and Uruguay) experiences, which emphasized the macroeconomic consequences of alternative sequences (see, among others, McKinnon 1982; Frankel 1989; Edwards 1984, 1985; and Harberger 1985). The outcome of that debate was a generalized acceptance that the following sequencing was, in most cases, the preferred one: Major fiscal imbalances have to be tackled, and a minimal degree of macroeconomic stability should be attained very early in the reform process. Most analysts also agree that the liberalization of the capital account should only take place once trade liberalization reform has been implemented, and that financial reform (including the relaxation of capital controls) should only be implemented once a modern and efficient bank regulatory and supervisory framework is in place. Finally, there is an increasing agreement that an effort should be made to ease labor market regulations as early as possible in the reform process. Three ideas are at the heart of this analysis. First, in a newly liberalized environment poorly regulated banks will tend to finance questionable projects, creating the potential for a financial meltdown. Moreover, with poor bank regulation—and particularly in the presence of implicit deposit insurance—serious moral hazard issues will arise. Second, labor market flexibility will facilitate the reallocation of resources that follow major relative price changes. And third, real exchange rate appreciations induced by major capital inflows may frustrate a trade liberalization reform by reducing the export sector's ability to compete internationally.

The notion that the capital account should be liberalized toward the end of the reform effort has acquired renewed prominence in the aftermath of the 1997–98 East Asian crisis. For example, in an interview in the *Financial Times* (9 February 1998), the IMF's managing director Michel Camdessus said: "We need to be audacious but sensitive. We need to push ahead with capital flow liberalisation but in an orderly manner" (1). He added: "The last thing you must liberalize is the very short term capital movements" (13).

In the rest of this section I discuss the relationship between capital flows and real exchange rates within the context of the recent Latin American experiences. The potential role of capital controls and bank supervision in the liberalization process are taken up in the following sections. Figure 7.4 presents the evolution of bilateral real exchange rate (RER) indexes for a selected group of Latin American countries for the period 1970 through mid-1997.[6] An increase in the values of these indexes represents a real depreciation and, thus, an increase in the country's degree of international competitiveness. A number of characteristics of real exchange rate behavior in Latin America emerge from these figures. First, RERs have historically been very volatile in Latin America. Comparative analyses on real exchange behavior have indeed shown that, for long periods of time, RER variability has been greater in Latin America than in almost any other part of the world. Second, these figures show that in all eight countries the RER depreciated drastically after the 1982 debt crisis, only to experience very large appreciations in the 1990s. These appreciations were largely caused, as I will argue later, by the surge of capital inflows in the 1990s. Third, these figures show that for the majority of the countries in the sample the appreciation trend has slowed down in the last two or three quarters and, in some of them, it even seems to have ended.

In figure 7.5 I provide a first look at the relationship between aggregate (net) capital inflows and the real exchange rate for a selected group of countries.[7] As may be seen, in each of them there is a negative relationship between capital inflows and the real exchange rate: Increases in capital inflows have been associated with real exchange rate appreciation, while

6. These bilateral indexes are relative to the U.S. dollar and have a base of 1990 = 100. In their construction, the U.S. producer price index (PPI) and each individual country's consumer price index (CPI) were used.

7. These are the countries for which the IMF provides quarterly data on aggregate capital inflows. In order to have a larger sample, in table 7.1 below I have used data on quarterly changes in international reserves as a proxy for capital inflows.

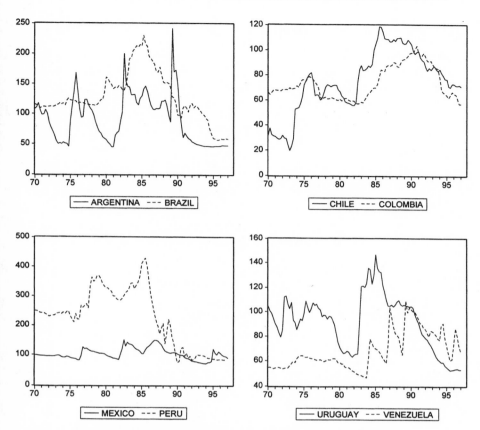

Fig. 7.4   Real exchange rate indexes for selected Latin American countries, 1970–97

declines in inflows are associated with RER depreciation. Correlation co-efficients between a proxy for quarterly capital inflows and the RER indexes support the view that for all countries in the sample there has been a negative association between these two variables (Edwards 1999). Table 7.1 contains summary results for Granger causality tests for these two variables. These show that in seven out of the eight cases it is not possible to reject the hypothesis that capital flows *cause* real exchange rate. In three of the seven countries it is not possible to reject two-way causality, and in none of the seven cases analyzed was it found that real exchange rate caused capital inflows. When these tests were performed for alternative sub-samples, similar findings were obtained. These results, then, provide preliminary support for the view that the recent surge in capital flows have been (partially) responsible for generating the loss in real international competitiveness reported above.

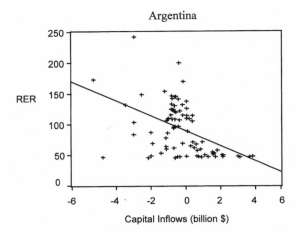

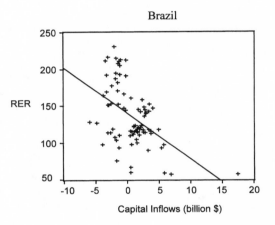

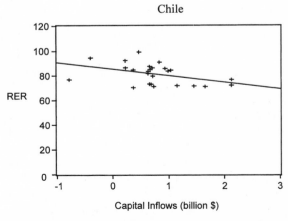

Fig. 7.5   Real exchange rates and capital inflows in selected Latin American countries, 1970–97

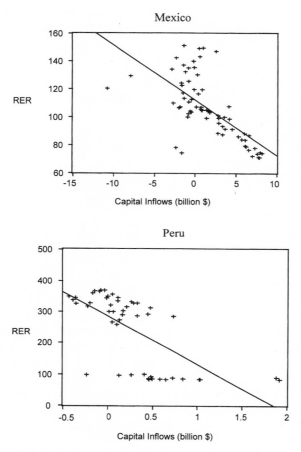

Fig. 7.5   (cont.)

The exact way in which capital inflows will be translated into a real exchange rate appreciation will depend on the nature of the nominal exchange rate system and on the way the monetary authorities react to changes in the key macroeconomic variables. Under a fixed exchange rate regime, the increased availability of foreign resources will result in the accumulation of international reserves at the central bank, monetary expansion, and increased inflation. This, in turn, will pressure the RER toward appreciation. As I have discussed in greater detail in Edwards (1999), many countries have tried to tackle this problem by attempting to sterilize these flows. Under a flexible exchange rate regime, on the other hand, large capital inflows will generate a *nominal*—as well as real—appreciation.

A number of analysts have argued that the appreciation of the real

Table 7.1   Capital Inflows and Real Exchange Rates in Selected Latin American
                   Countries: Some Basic Statistical Relations (quarterly data, 1980–97)

	Correlation Coefficient	Do Capital Inflows "Cause" Real Exchange Rates?	Do Real Exchange Rates "Cause" Capital Inflows?
Argentina	−0.723	Yes	No
Brazil	−0.727	Yes	Yes
Chile	−0.382	Yes	Yes
Colombia	−0.145	No	No
Mexico	−0.656	Yes	No
Peru	−0.478	Yes	Yes
Venezuela	−0.146	Yes	No

Note: Quarterly changes in international reserves were used as a proxy for capital inflows. Granger causality tests were performed. The results for Colombia and Venezuela are sensitive to the sample considered. If 1985–97 is used, the correlation coefficient is larger (in absolute terms), and in the case of Colombia it is not possible to reject the hypothesis that capital inflows "cause" real exchange rates.

exchange rate following a surge in capital inflows is an equilibrium phenomenon, that is, one generated by fundamentals. This was, for example, the approach taken by the Mexican authorities during 1991–94 when a number of independent observers argued that the real appreciation of the peso was not sustainable and was bound to generate a major currency crisis.[8] A limitation of this interpretation, however, is that it fails to incorporate the stock flows dynamics of adjustment following a major capital inflows episode. Most developing countries have traditionally faced an external credit constraint. This constraint, however, is usually relaxed when the country in question begins implementing what is perceived to be a successful market-oriented reform process. This relaxation in the external credit constraint will, in turn, have two implications. First, it will result in an increase in the long-run sustainable volume of capital inflows. In general, this long-run sustainable level will depend on the *stock* demand for the country's securities by foreigners, the country's real rate of growth, and the world interest rate. Second, the relaxation of the capital constraint will generate a short-run overshooting in the *inflow* of capital into the country. The reason for this is that in order for the new (stock) demand for the country's securities to become effective in the short run—while the additional credit that has become available to the country is disbursed— capital inflows (and the current account deficit) will have to exceed their long-run equilibrium volume. In most instances, this adjustment process will not be instantaneous; in some cases it will even take a few years. His-

8. For discussions on Mexico's real exchange rate appreciation in 1991–94 see, e.g., Dornbusch (1993), Dornbusch and Werner (1994), and Edwards (1993). On Mexico's official position regarding these developments see, e.g., Banco de Mexico (various years).

torically, episodes of capital inflows surges have been characterized by increases in the demand for the small country securities on the order of 20 to 30 percent of gross domestic product (GDP), and by peak annual inflows on the order of 7 to 9 percent of GDP (World Bank 1997).

One of the most important dynamic effects of the transition described above is on the real exchange rate. As capital flows in, there will be an increase in expenditure and an appreciation in the real exchange rate. The extent of this appreciation will vary from country to country and will depend, largely, on two sets of key variables: the intertemporal elasticity of aggregate demand, on the one hand, and the income elasticity of demand and supply elasticity for nontradable goods, on the other. The intertemporal elasticity will determine the extent of consumption smoothing and the distribution of the expenditure increase through time; the elasticities for nontradables, on the other hand, will determine the extent to which the surge in capital inflows will exercise pressure on nontradable prices (see Edwards 1989 for a formal treatment of these issues using an optimizing intertemporal model). Once capital stops flowing in, or even when the rate at which it flows slows down and moves down toward its (new) long-run equilibrium level, the real exchange rate will be "overly" appreciated and, in order to maintain equilibrium, a massive adjustment may be required. The dynamics of capital inflows and current account adjustment will require, then, that the equilibrium real exchange rate first appreciates and then depreciates. And while during the surge in inflows the real exchange rate appreciates without any impediment, when the availability of foreign capital declines nominal wage and price rigidity will make the required real depreciation difficult under a pegged exchange rate.[9]

In order to gain further insights into the dynamic interactions between capital flows and real exchange rates, I estimated a series of unrestricted vector autoregressives (VARs) for a subgroup of countries using quarterly data. This analysis poses a number of data-related challenges, however, and the results obtained should be interpreted with caution. First, given the tumultuous nature of recent Latin American history, the length of useful time series is rather limited. This problem is particularly serious in Argentina and Brazil, where bouts of hyperinflation during the late 1980s and early 1990s introduced significant noise into the data. Second, until the late 1980s, most countries in the region faced severe external credit constraints and were unable to attract foreign capital. This reduces the time span of available data even further. Third, many of these countries do not have detailed data on capital flows at the quarterly frequency. For this reason, I have focused on aggregate capital inflows, and in some of them I have followed Calvo, Leiderman, and Reinhart (1993) and have used

---

9. This type of analysis has been made in relation to the sequencing of reform debate. See, e.g., Edwards (1984).

quarterly changes in international reserves as a proxy for aggregate capital flows. Although it would have been ideal to use disaggregated quarterly data, some comfort can be drawn from the fact that, as argued by Calvo, Leiderman, and Reinhart (1993, 1995), in most countries changes in international reserves are a fairly good proxy of capital flows. In the appendix I present a detailed description of the data and their sources. Fourth, in some of these countries there were important changes in the nature of capital controls in the last few years. The way in which these controls potentially affected the relationship between capital inflows and real exchange rates is addressed in some detail in section 7.4 of this paper.

The VAR analysis reported below attempts to address the following questions. (1) Do innovations to capital flows generate an appreciation in the real exchange rate, as predicted by standard real exchange rate models? (2) How pronounced and persistent are these effects? (3) Is it possible to identify differences across countries in the dynamic response of the real exchange rate to capital flows shock? The following variables were included in these quarterly VARs: the log of a bilateral real exchange rate index relative to the United States; a measure of capital flows (see the appendix for exact definitions for each country); the rate of growth of domestic credit; interest rate differentials adjusted by a proxy for expected devaluation (see the discussion in section 7.4 for the methodology used to measure expected devaluation); and the rate of inflation. In addition, in Brazil, Chile, and Colombia a measure of the importance of capital controls was also included in some of the estimates. In the case of Colombia I also included a terms of trade index and an index of the extent of trade protection.[10] In all cases the analysis was undertaken using the cyclical component of the series; this, in turn, was obtained by filtering the series using the Hodrick-Prescott procedure. In all cases the cyclical components of the series exhibited stationarity.[11]

Figure 7.6 shows, for a selected group of Latin American countries, the impulse response functions of the cyclical component of the log of the bilateral real exchange rate index to a one standard deviation innovation to capital flows. As may be seen in all cases, the capital flows shock generated an appreciation in the real exchange rate, as predicted by the theory. Interestingly enough, both the magnitude and dynamics of the response varies across countries. More important for our analysis, however, is the surprisingly small effect these capital flows innovations have on the (log of the) real exchange rate. As may be seen, these effects range from a 4.0 percent appreciation in Argentina to a 0.8 percent appreciation in Chile and Brazil, in response to a one standard deviation shock in capital in-

10. In the case of Colombia, the domestic credit variable was excluded due to the lack of a complete time series.

11. Due to the small number of observations it was not possible to consider very long lag structures. In most VARs two to four lags were considered.

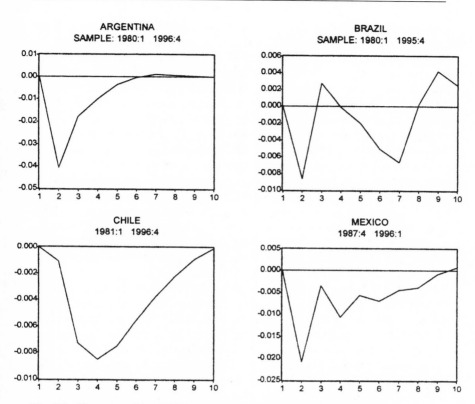

Fig. 7.6   Response of log(RER) to one standard deviation innovation in capital flows

flows. Interestingly enough, these results are largely independent of the variables' ordering in the VAR estimation (see the discussion below, however). There are a number of possible explanations for these results. First, the data on capital flows are measured with error and it is possible that, as a result, the impact of an aggregate capital inflow is underestimated by the statistical analysis. Second, it is possible that while shocks to aggregate flows have a limited effect on the real exchange rate, some type of capital movements—portfolio flows, for instance—will have a greater impact. Unfortunately, the lack of appropriate quarterly data does not allow us to investigate this possibility. Third, it is possible that the magnitude of the effect has changed over time, and that by using a relatively longer time series these effects are being missed. More specifically, from a policy perspective, it is particularly important whether these relationships have differed in periods with and without capital controls. This possibility is explored in greater detail in section 7.4 using data on Chile.

An analysis of the variance decomposition of these VARs, not presented here due to space considerations, indicates that in spite of the small effect on the real exchange rate discussed above, capital inflows have indeed played an important role in explaining changes in real exchange rate indexes in these countries. As is customary, in estimating these VARs the different series were ordered in a way that takes into account their degree of exogeneity. As mentioned, when alternative orderings were tried, however, most of the results reported here were not altered.

During the 1990s most Latin American countries tried to minimize the macroeconomic—and in particular the real exchange rate—consequences of capital inflow surges. Two basic approaches have been used to deal with this phenomenon: (1) The imposition of some form of capital controls aimed at slowing down the rate at which foreign funds come into the country. Brazil, Chile, and Colombia have made a fairly extensive use of this policy (see the discussion in section 7.4 for details). (2) Sterilized intervention, aimed at offsetting the monetary—and inflationary—consequences of the capital inflows. Almost every country in the region has attempted this approach.

The extent to which countries in the region have relied on sterilization has varied, however, with Colombia and Chile being particularly active. This is illustrated in figure 7.7, which contains the impulse response functions of domestic credit creation to a one standard deviation innovation of capital inflows in Chile during different periods. As may be seen, in all cases the original response has been to tighten domestic liquidity. Although it has been widely used, sterilized intervention is not free of problems. In particular, if undertaken in a systematic fashion, as has been the case in many Latin American countries during the last few years, it can be very costly for the central bank. This is because interest earnings on international reserves are rather low, while the central bank has to pay a relatively high interest rate to persuade the public to buy its own securities. Calvo (1991), for example, has argued that this cost can become so high that it may threaten the sustainability of the complete reform effort. Moreover, as Frankel (1989) has pointed out, in an economy with capital mobility and predetermined nominal exchange rates it is not possible for the monetary authorities to control monetary aggregates in the medium to long run. This view has been confirmed by econometric estimates of the monetary "offset" coefficient for a number of countries (see, e.g., the studies in Steiner 1995).

Colombia's experience with sterilization during the early 1990s illustrates very clearly what Calvo (1991) has called "the perils of sterilization." In 1990 the newly elected President Gaviria announced a trade liberalization program aimed at eliminating import licensing and greatly reducing import tariffs. At the same time, a twenty-year-old exchange and capital controls mechanism was eliminated. By March 1991, however, it was

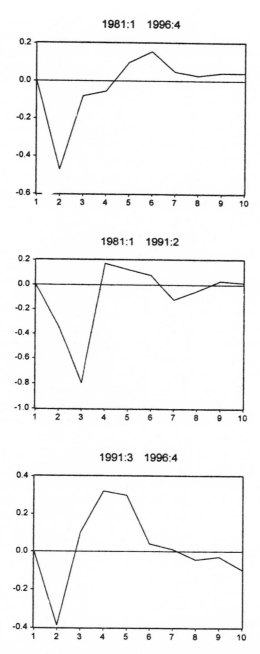

Fig. 7.7   Response of domestic credit growth to one standard deviation innovation in capital flows to Chile

becoming increasingly clear that the trade reform was not having the effects the economic team had anticipated. Perhaps the most surprising fact was that imports were not growing and that, as a result, the country was experiencing an increasing trade surplus. This, in conjunction with larger inflows of capital, was exerting pressuring on money supply, making macroeconomic management very difficult. As inflation increased, the real exchange rate began to lose ground, and both exporters and important competing sectors began to lose competitiveness. The Banco de la Republica reacted to this situation by implementing a series of policies that in retrospect appear to have been contradictory among themselves. First, an aggressive policy of sterilizing reserve accumulation was undertaken. This was done by issuing indexed short-term securities (the *obligaciones monetarias* [*OMAs*]). In the first ten months of 1991 the stock of this instrument shot up from US$405 million to US$1.2 billion, or 85 percent of the total monetary base. Naturally, this policy resulted in an increase in domestic (peso denominated) interest rates and a significant interest rate differential. This attracted further capital into the country, frustrating the sterilization policy itself. Second, the authorities decided—as they had in the past when facing coffee booms—to postpone the monetization of export proceeds. For this reason, in 1991 the monetary authority stopped buying foreign exchange in the spot market. Instead it started issuing "exchange certificates" (*certificados de cambio*) in exchange for export foreign currency proceeds. These certificates could be transacted in the secondary market and initially had a three-month maturity, which was later extended to one year. Moreover, the central bank established a maximum discount for the certificates in the secondary market of 12.5 percent. All of this, of course, amounted to an attempt at controlling too many variables—the spot and future exchange rates, the nominal interest rate, and the stock of money— at inconsistent levels. During the first ten months of 1991 Colombia had been trapped in a vicious circle: A very rapid process of reserve accumulation generated high inflation and a real exchange rate appreciation; but the policies put in place to combat these phenomena created incentives for capital inflows and a further appreciation of the real exchange rate.

7.4   Capital Controls: How Extensive? How Effective?

7.4.1   Issues and Measurement

Historically, most Latin American countries have relied heavily on different forms of capital controls. While throughout most of the post–World War II period these have been aimed at avoiding capital "flight," more recently—and for the reasons discussed above—countries have tried to avoid (or at least slow down) large inflows of capital. There has long been a recognition, however, that legal impediments on capital mobility are not always translated into actual restrictions on these movements. This distinction between *actual* and *legal* capital mobility has been the subject of intense policy debate in Latin America. Naturally, this discussion is directly related to the important question of the effectiveness of capital controls. There is ample historical evidence suggesting that there have been significant discrepancies between the legal and the actual degree of capital controls. In countries with severe legal impediments to capital mobility—including countries that have banned capital movement—the private sector has traditionally resorted to the overinvoicing of imports and underinvoicing of exports to sidestep legal controls on capital flows. The massive volumes of capital flight that took place in Latin America in the wake of the 1982 debt crisis clearly showed that, when faced with the "appropriate" incentives, the public can be extremely creative in finding ways to move capital internationally. The question of how to measure, from an economic point of view, the degree of capital mobility and the extent to which domestic capital markets are integrated to the world capital market continue to be the subject of extensive debate (see Dooley, Mathieson, and Rojas-Suarez 1997 for a comprehensive recent treatment of the subject).

In two early studies Harberger (1978, 1985) argued that the effective degree of integration of capital markets should be measured by the convergence of private rates of return to capital across countries. In trying to measure the effective degree of capital mobility, Feldstein and Horioka (1980) analyzed the behavior of savings and investments in a number of countries. They argue that if there is perfect capital mobility, changes in savings and investments will be uncorrelated in a specific country. That is, in a world without capital restrictions an increase in domestic savings will tend to "leave the home country," moving to the rest of the world. Likewise, if international capital markets are fully integrated, increases in domestic investment will tend to be funded by the world at large and not necessarily by domestic savings. Using a data set for sixteen member countries of the Organization for Economic Cooperation and Development (OECD), Feldstein and Horioka found that savings and investment ratios were highly positively correlated, and they concluded that these results strongly supported the presumption that *long-term* capital was subject to significant impediments. Frankel (1989) applied the Feldstein-Horioka test to a large number of countries during the 1980s, including a number of Latin American nations. His results corroborated those obtained by the original study, indicating that savings and investment have been significantly positively correlated in most countries. In a comprehensive analysis of the degree of capital, Montiel (1994) estimated a series of Feldstein-Horioka equations for sixty-two developing countries, including fifteen

Latin American nations.[12] Using the estimated regression coefficient for the industrial countries as a benchmark, Montiel concluded that the majority of the Latin American nations exhibited a relatively high degree of capital mobility—indeed much larger than what an analysis of legal restrictions would suggest.

In a series of studies, Edwards (1985, 1988) and Edwards and Khan (1985) argued that time series on domestic and international interest rates could be used to assess the degree of openness of the capital account (see also Montiel 1994). The application of this model to a number of countries (Brazil, Colombia, Chile) confirms the results that, in general, the actual degree of capital mobility is greater than what the legal restrictions approach suggests. Haque and Montiel (1991), Reisen and Yeches (1991), and Dooley (1995) have provided expansions of this model that allow for the estimation of the degree of capital mobility even in cases when there are not enough data on domestic interest rates and when there are changes in the degree of capital mobility through time. Their results once again indicate that in most Latin American countries "true" capital mobility has historically exceeded "legal" extent of capital mobility. More recently, Dooley, Mathieson, and Rojas-Suarez (1997) have developed a method for measuring the changes in the degree of capital mobility in developing countries. They argue that in countries with capital controls and interest rates ceilings, traditional approaches such as the Edwards and Khan (1985) approach can generate misleading results. They develop a model that recognizes the costs of undertaking disguised capital inflows. The model is estimated using a Kalman filter technique for three countries, including Mexico. The results suggest that Mexico—as well as the Philippines and Korea—experienced a very significant increase in the degree of capital mobility between 1977 and 1989.

7.4.2   Some Evidence: Chile's Experiences with Capital Restrictions during the 1990s

Chile and Colombia have been the heaviest users of restrictions on capital mobility in Latin America during the last few years. In both countries these controls have been part of a concerted effort to avoid some of the destabilizing short-term effects—and in particular the real exchange rate appreciation—of capital inflow surges. In their current form capital controls were introduced in 1991 in Chile and in 1993 in Colombia.[13] In both countries the restrictions have been based on an unremunerated reserve requirement that importers of capital have to deposit in the central bank.

12. The Montiel study was based on time series estimates. The Feldstein-Horioka approach, on the other hand, was devised as a cross-sectional procedure.

13. It should be noted that both of these countries had a long tradition with capital controls before the 1990s. See, e.g., Edwards (1999). Brazil has also relied on capital controls during the 1990s. See Cardoso and Goldfajn (1997).

The specific aspects of both of these schemes are presented in detail in this section (see also Budnevich and LeFort 1997; Cardenas and Barrera 1997; and Edwards 1999).

The Chilean experience with capital restrictions has received considerable attention by policy makers and media analysts in the aftermath of the East Asian currency crises of 1997–98. Some observers have argued that Chile's approach to capital movements has been effective in reducing vulnerability to speculative periods and reducing the real exchange rate "deprotection" effect of large capital inflows. For example, Joseph Stiglitz, the World Bank's chief economist, has been quoted by the *New York Times* (1 February 1998) as saying: "You want to look for policies that discourage hot money but facilitate the flow of long-term loans, and there is evidence that the Chilean approach or some version of it, does this." Not everyone, however, is as enthusiastic with this scheme. According to the *Financial Times* (January 1988), for instance, "Chile's controls are on inflows rather than outflows of capital, but the new figures suggest that the controls have *not been successful* in preventing the entry of speculative capital" (7, italics added). Even if the Chilean type of restrictions have been successful in reducing the extent of real appreciation, the issue of "permanence" still has to be addressed. For how long are these restrictions to be maintained? Are they a transitional device, or are they a permanent feature of the Chilean economy? When is an economy mature enough to open its cross-border capital transactions fully? Some of these issues are addressed toward the end of this section, while other are tackled in the rest of the paper.

In this subsection I provide an empirical evaluation of Chile's experience with capital controls during the 1990s.[14] It should be stated at the outset that evaluating the effectiveness of capital restrictions is an exceedingly difficult task. First, as already pointed out, the length of the available time series is rather limited. Second, data for some important variables are not readily available and, thus, proxies have to be constructed. Third, it is not always clear what criteria should be used to evaluate whether a particular set of restrictions has been effective.[15] In fact, it is possible that while according to specific criteria the policy has been appropriate, according to an alternative perspective it has been ineffective. It is particularly important to avoid methodological traps—into which some media analysts and even senior observers of the international scene seem to fall so easily—of the type: "Chile has grown very fast avoiding a currency crisis,

---

14. Mexico still maintains some (minimal) restrictions on FDI. Argentina also has free capital mobility. Its experience is more recent, however, and the highly unstable macroeconomic environment of the 1980s and early 1990s reduces greatly the length of time series data.

15. Notice that I have used the word *effective* and not *successful*. This is deliberate, as I have made no attempt to provide a comprehensive cost-benefit analysis of Chile's capital restrictions.

Table 7.2   **Restrictions on Capital Inflows into Chile**

Type of Capital Inflow	Restriction
Foreign direct investment	Minimum stay of one year. No restrictions on repatriation of profits.
Portfolio inflows: Issuing of ADRs	The issuance of ADRs by Chilean companies is strictly regulated. Only companies that meet a certain risk classification requirement (BBB for nonfinancial companies, and BBB+ for financial institutions) can issue ADRs. There is also a minimum amount requirement: Until September 1994, this was US$50 million; at that time it was lowered to US$25 million; and in November 1995 it was further reduced to US$10 million.
Other portfolio inflows	All other portfolio inflows—including secondary ADR inflows, foreign loans, bond issues—are subject to a nonremunerated 30 percent reserve requirement. This reserve requirement is independent of the length of stay of the inflow. In the case of loans and bonds, the recipient may choose to pay the financial cost of the reserve requirement.
Trade credit	Credit lines used to finance trade operations are also subject to the 30 percent deposit.

Source: Budnevich and LeFort (1997).

and has capital restrictions. Ergo, capital restrictions of the Chilean type are desirable!"

In Chile restrictions to capital movements have taken two basic forms: minimum stay requirements for FDI flows and nonremunerated reserve requirements on other forms of capital inflows. Table 7.2 contains details on these regulations, as of the third quarter of 1997. It is interesting to compare Chile's experience with that of Colombia, where capital controls have taken the form of a variable reserve requirement on foreign loans—except trade credit—obtained by the private sector. Initially this reserve requirement was set in Colombia at a rate of 47 percent and was only applicable to loans with a maturity shorter than eighteen months. During 1994, and as the economy was flooded with capital inflows, the reserve requirements were tightened. In March they were made extensive to all loans with a maturity below three years; in August they were extended to loans of five years or less. Moreover, the rate of the reserves requirement became inversely proportional to the maturity of the loan: thirty-day loans were subject to a stiff 140 percent reserve requirement, making them virtually prohibitive, while five-year loans had to meet a 42.8 percent deposit. In both Chile and Colombia restrictions to capital movements act as an implicit tax on foreign financing.

In evaluating Chile's recent experience with capital restrictions I have focused on three issues. First, is there evidence that capital controls have affected the composition of capital flows? Second, is there evidence that the imposition of restrictions to capital mobility has affected the dynamic response of the real exchange rate to capital flows shocks? The importance of this question stems from the fact that the restrictions were deliberately imposed to reduce the real exchange rate deprotection associated with the surge in capital inflows (Valdes-Prieto and Soto 1996a). I tackle this question by estimating a series of unrestricted VARs on quarterly data and analyzing the real exchange rate impulse response functions. Third, is there evidence that the impositions of the unremunerated reserve requirements affected in a significant way the relationship between Chile's and international interest rates? More specifically, I inquire whether these restrictions affected the time series process of interest rate differentials (corrected by expected devaluation) in Chile. In general one would expect that impediments to free capital mobility would affect both the speed at which interest rate differentials decline as well as the level to which they converge. I address this third question through the analysis of impulse response functions and the estimation of a series of univariate equations using rolling regression techniques.

In a recent study Valdes-Prieto and Soto (1996b) have calculated the tax equivalence of Chile's unremunerated reserve requirement on capital inflows and have evaluated their effect on a number of variables including real exchange rates. The authors conclude that these restrictions have not been (fully) evaded and that for a 180-day loan their annual tax equivalence has fluctuated between 1.29 and 4.53 percent. The implicit tax equivalence of longer-term funds has been, since mid-1992, proportional, with loans with longer maturities paying a lower implicit tax (see also Cowan and De Gregorio 1997). According to Valdes-Prieto and Soto (1996a, 1996b) these capital restrictions altered the composition of capital inflows: They discouraged short-term capital inflows but had no significant effects on the aggregate volume of capital entering the country.

In table 7.3 I present data on the composition of capital flows into Chile between 1988 and 1996. As may be seen, there has indeed been a marked change in the composition of capital inflows, with shorter (that is less than a year) flows declining steeply relative to longer-term capital. The fact that this change in composition happened immediately after the time when the capital restrictions were imposed supports the view that the controls policy has indeed affected the composition of inflows. These data also show that, with the exception of a brief decline in 1993, the total volume of capital inflows into the country has continued to increase.

In the rest of this section I analyze the effect of (net) flows and capital controls on real exchange rates and on interest rate differentials.

Table 7.3   Gross Capital Inflows to Chile

Year	Short-Term Loans	Percentage of Total	Long-Term Loans	Percentage of Total	Total	Deposits[a]
1988	916,564	96.3	34,838	3.7	951,402	—
1989	1,452,595	95.0	77,122	5.0	1,529,717	—
1990	1,683,149	90.3	181,419	9.7	1,864,568	—
1991	521,198	72.7	196,115	27.3	717,313	587
1992	225,197	28.9	554,072	71.1	779,269	11,424
1993	159,462	23.6	515,147	76.4	674,609	41,280
1994	161,575	16.5	819,699	83.5	981,274	87,039
1995	69,675	6.2	1,051,829	93.8	1,121,504	38,752
1996	67,254	3.2	2,042,456	96.8	2,109,710	172,320

[a]Deposits in Banco Chile due to reserve requirements.

Capital Restrictions and Real Exchange Rates in Chile

One of the fundamental purposes—if not the main purpose—of Chile's restrictions on capital inflows has been to reduce their volume and, in that way, their pressure on the real exchange rate. According to a recent paper coauthored by a former senior Ministry of Finance official, "growing concerns about inflation and the exchange rate pressure of capital inflows have led policymakers to introduce specific capital controls" (Cowan and De Gregorio 1997, 3). Valdes-Prieto and Soto (1996b), on the other hand, have argued that the imposition of these restrictions in mid-1991 responded to the authorities' attempt to balance two policy objectives: reducing inflation and maintaining a competitive real exchange rate. According to these authors, by implementing these unremunerated reserve requirements the authorities hoped to reduce—or at least delay—the real exchange rate appreciation effects of these flows, while at the same time maintain a higher differential between domestic and international interest rates (corrected by expected devaluations). This higher differential, in turn, was expected to help achieve the anti-inflationary objective. In this subsection I evaluate the real exchange rate objective, while in the next I address the interest rate differential objective.

I used two approaches to evaluate the real exchange rate objective of Chile's capital controls policy. First, using quarterly data I reestimated the VARs from section 7.3 for two different subsamples—one with and one without capital controls—and evaluated the real exchange rate impulse response to capital inflows innovations. Under an effective policy one would expect that the real exchange rate response to a capital flow innovation would be less pronounced—both in terms of its maximum effect as well as its dynamics—in the period with controls. Second, I used the longer period VARs (1987–96) estimates to evaluate the impulse response to a shock to the tax equivalence of the unremunerated reserve requirement.[16]

Figure 7.8 contains the impulse response functions for the log of the real exchange rate for the complete period (1981–96), a subperiod with no restrictions on capital inflows (1987–91:Q2), and a subperiod when the capital restrictions have been put into effect (1991:Q3–96). The same data definitions as in the preceding section were used. Figure 7.9, on the other hand, contains the real exchange rate response to an innovation to the (implicit) tax on capital inflows.[17] Two important facts emerge from these figures. First, the effect of the capital innovation on the (log) of the real exchange rate are extremely similar across periods. As may be seen, the maximum appreciation is almost the same in the with-restrictions period and in the period where there were restrictions to capital inflows. However, the (log) of the real exchange rate returns to equilibrium somewhat faster in the with-restrictions period. This result is confirmed by the impulse response function in figure 7.9.[18] As may be seen, an innovation to restrictions on inflows results in a slight real depreciation. The effect is short lived, however, and disappears after four quarters. The ordering of the variables is, as usual, important. In determining the ordering, one could be tempted to argue that capital controls are exogenous. This, however, could be highly misleading since in Chile, as in other emerging markets, the extent and coverage of controls have been adjusted in response to changes in the magnitude of capital flows. For this reason, alternative orderings—including one where capital controls are allowed to respond endogenously—were considered. Overall, the results under alternative orderings confirm the results from figure 7.9. The variance decomposition of the forecast errors of the (log of the) real exchange rate, not presented here due to space considerations (results available on request), confirms that the restrictions on capital inflows have not been effective in affecting the real exchange rate behavior: The capital restrictions variable explains no more than 3 percent of the forecast error.

Although these results are subject to some limitations—the experience with capital restrictions is rather short, limiting the availability of data points, and a proxy for aggregate capital flows was used—they do provide preliminary evidence suggesting that the impact of this policy on the real exchange rate has been very limited and short lived. These results confirm

16. The tax equivalences estimated by Valdes-Prieto and Soto (1996b) were updated to the end of 1997.

17. Cardoso and Goldfajn (1997) analyze a series of impulse response functions to a capital controls innovation in Brazil.

18. As Cardoso and Goldfajn (1997) have argued, capital controls in Latin America are likely to be endogenous. Thus, care should be taken in establishing the vector ordering in the VAR estimation.

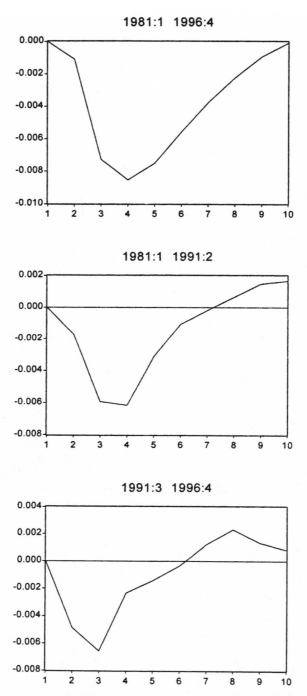

Fig. 7.8 Response of log(RER) to one standard deviation capital flows innovation in Chile

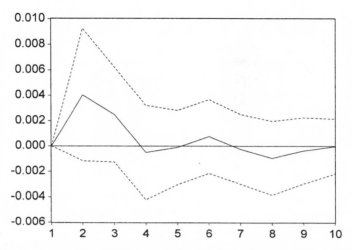

Fig. 7.9   Response of log(RER) to controls ± 2 standard errors, 1988:1–1996:4

previous findings by Valdes-Prieto and Soto (1996b), who, using a very different technique and a shorter sample to estimate a real exchange rate equation for Chile, concluded that "the unremunerated reserve requirement does not affect in any way the long run level of the real exchange rate. . . . In addition . . . these reserve requirements have an insignificant effect on the real exchange rate in the short run" (99).

Capital Restrictions and Interest Rate Differentials in Chile

Since the mid-1980s Chile's monetary authorities have used interest rate targeting as one of the main—if not the main—anti-inflationary tools (Fontaine 1996). More specifically, as a way to reduce inflation, the central bank has systematically attempted to maintain relatively high interest rates. This policy, however, became increasingly difficult to sustain during the late 1980s and 1990s when, as a result of Chile's improving stance in international financial markets, higher domestic rates started to attract increasingly large volumes of capital. A fundamental objective of the capital restrictions policy in effect since 1991, then, has been to allow the country to maintain a higher interest rate. According to Cowan and De Gregorio (1997, 16), "capital controls allowed policy makers to rely on the domestic interest rate as the main instrument for reducing inflation. . . . The reserve requirement has permitted maintaining the domestic interest rate above the international interest rate, without imposing excessive pressure on the exchange rate." In this subsection I use a battery of time series estimates to formally investigate the way in which capital restrictions have, in fact, affected interest rate differentials, and thus the ability to perform independent monetary policy, in Chile.

In the absence of restrictions to capital mobility, and under the assumption of risk neutrality and in the absence of country risk, the uncovered interest arbitrage condition will hold, and deviations from it would be white noise and unpredictable. The speed at which these deviations from interest arbitrage are eliminated is an empirical question, but in a well-functioning market it would be expected to happen very fast. The existence of restrictions to capital mobility and of country risk, however, alter this basic equation in a fundamental way. In this case there will be an equilibrium interest rate differential (δ):

$$(1) \qquad \delta_t = r_t - r_t^* - E\Delta e_t = k + R + u_t,$$

where r_t is the domestic interest rate, r_t^* is the international interest rate for a security of the same maturity, $E\Delta e$ is the expected rate of devaluation, k is the tax equivalence of the capital restriction, R is the country risk premium, and u_t is an identical independently distributed (i.i.d.) random variable. As in the case of free capital mobility, if at any moment in time the actual interest rate differential exceeds ($k + R$), there will be incentives to arbitrageurs to move funds in or out of the country. This process will continue until the equilibrium interest rate differential is reestablished. The speed at which this process takes place will, in principle, depend on the degree of development of the domestic capital market, as well as on the degree of capital mobility existing in the country in question. Countries with stiffer restrictions will experience slow corrections of deviations from the equilibrium interest rate differential (Edwards and Khan 1985; Dooley 1995; Dooley, Mathieson, and Rojas-Suarez 1997). Additionally, as equation (1) shows, the degree of capital restrictions (that is, k) will also affect the value toward which the interest rate differential will converge.[19]

In a world with changing policies, k is not constant through time. In fact, as has been documented in the preceding sections, the value of k has changed markedly in most Latin American countries during the last few years. With other things given, it would be expected that the imposition (or tightening) of capital restrictions will have two effects on the behavior of the interest rate differential. First it will increase the value toward which this differential converges; second, it will reduce the speed at which this convergence takes place. This means that under stricter restrictions on capital mobility, the monetary authority gains greater control over domestic interest rates in two ways. First, it can maintain a higher interest rate differential—that is, the steady-state value of δ will be higher than what it would have been otherwise. Second, δ can deviate from its long-run equilibrium for longer periods of time. In this subsection I use quarterly and

---

19. The tax equivalence of a Chile-style reserve requirement will be a function of the international interest rate.

monthly data on interest rate differentials for Chile to investigate the way in which the imposition and tightening of capital restrictions affected their behavior.

A problem with equation (1) is that there are no long reliable series on expectations of devaluation.[20] In order to address this problem I constructed a series of expected devaluations as the one-step-ahead forecasts obtained from an autoregressive moving average (ARMA) process for the actual rate of devaluation. After identifying the possible processes, several plausible representations were estimated. Finally, those that provided the better forecasts—measured according to standard criteria—were used. In the case of quarterly data I used an ARMA(2,1), while for monthly data I used an autoregressive (AR[1]) process to construct the expected devaluation series.[21]

As a first step, unrestricted VARs estimated on quarterly data were used to estimate impulse response functions of interest rate differentials to a one standard deviation innovation of themselves: Figure 7.10 presents these impulses for two subsamples: 1981–91, when there were no capital restrictions; and 1991–96, when the restrictions were in place. As may be seen, in both periods the deviation of δ from its equilibrium tended to disappear quite rapidly. This adjustment process seemed to have been somewhat faster in the period with no capital restrictions. As may be seen from the figure, during this early period δ has essentially gone back to trend after two quarters; for the later period, the adjustment is cyclical and after four quarters there is still a slight differential. This result is, in some ways, what one would have expected: In a period of capital restrictions interest rate differentials are somewhat more sluggish than in periods with no controls. A potential problem with this interpretation, however, is that during part of the earlier period (1986–87) Chile was still facing a severe foreign credit constraint and had very limited access to international capital markets. Unfortunately, due to the brevity of the experiments we are analyzing, the issue of "restrictions" versus "access" cannot be addressed in an adequate way using quarterly data. Monthly data, however, allow us to use additional information and explore the behavior of interest rate differentials further.[22]

Assume that interest rate differential can be represented by the following univariate process:

20. In the last few years, however, there has been a forward market for foreign exchange, but the data available do not cover a long enough period for our purposes.
21. The interest rate differentials series used in the VARs reported above were also constructed using this procedure.
22. A shortcoming of using monthly series, however, is that there are no data on many of the other variables of interest. For this reason, in the analysis that follows I have restricted myself to univariate methods.

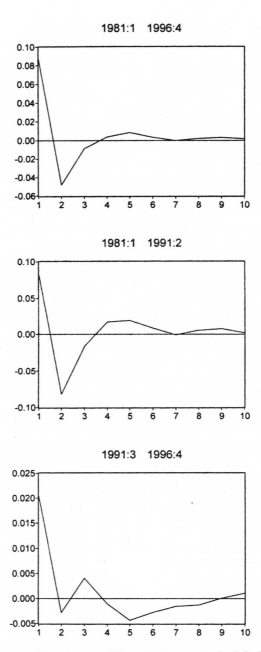

Fig. 7.10 Response of interest rate differential to one standard deviation innovation in interest rate differential in Chile

(2) $$B(L)\delta_t = \alpha + G(L)u_t,$$

where L is the lag operator, $B(L)$ and $G(L)$ are polynomial functions of L, and α is a coefficient. The form of these polynomials will determine the dynamics of δ_t, including whether it will converge to a steady-state value. This steady state, in turn will be determined by the form of the two polynomials and by α. The simplest case is obtained when

$$B(L) = 1 - \beta L; \quad A(L) = 1.$$

In this case interest rate differentials are characterized by an AR(1) process, and to the extent that β lies inside the unit circle, δ will converge to $[\alpha/(1 - \beta)]$. In the absence of controls and with a zero country risk premium, we would expect $[\alpha/(1 - \beta)] \cong 0$, with interest rate differentials converging to zero. Moreover, in this case, we would expect that β would be very low, with interest rate differentials disappearing very rapidly. With country risk and capital restrictions, however, α would be different from zero, β will be rather high, and interest rate differentials will converge to a positive value.

If there are policy changes—and, in particular, if there are changes in the extent of capital restrictions—we would expect that the parameters in equation (2) will change. The extent and importance of these changes can be analyzed empirically by identifying and estimating univariate models of interest rate differentials for different periods of time. Table 7.4 presents the results obtained for Chile from the estimation of a number of alternative ARMA processes for δ for four different time periods. Since in all cases the AR(1) representation proved to be adequate, in the discussion that follows I will concentrate on these results.[23] It is particularly interesting to compare the no-restrictions period (1988:1–1991:6) with the restrictions period (1991:7–1996:12). As may be seen, the AR coefficient is slightly lower in the second (no capital restrictions) subsample (0.40), than in the first one (0.46). This is contrary to what was expected; however, the difference is not statistically significant, as a test statistic strongly rejects the hypothesis of different AR coefficients across samples. According to these results the point estimate of the α coefficient is higher in the first subsample, although once again the difference is not statistically significant.

The results obtained from this specific splitting of the sample, then, may be interpreted as suggesting that there are very few, if any, differences in the dynamics of interest rate differentials in these two periods. These results, however, should be interpreted with care, since they are subject to at least two limitations. First, during the period under analysis the country

---

23. It should be noted, however, that the interpretation of the results is not very different if any of the alternative representations is considered.

Table 7.4   Measure of Persistence: Chile, Different Samples

Model Specification	Constant	Inverted AR Roots	Inverted MA Roots	Q-Statistic $p = 5$	$p = 10$
1982:11–1996:12					
AR(1)	0.06	0.45		1.35	4.56
AR(2)	0.06	0.42 / 0.04		1.20	4.25
MA(1)	0.06		−0.40	8.65	10.65
MA(2)	0.06		−0.23+0.37i / −0.2−0.37i	1.35	4.27
ARMA(1,1)	0.06	0.43	−0.03	1.24	4.35
ARMA(2,)	0.06	0.31 / −0.12	−0.14+0.26i / −0.14−0.26i	0.93	3.99
1982:11–1991:6					
AR(1)	0.05	0.18		8.35	18.87
AR(2)	0.04	0.13−0.29i / 0.13+0.29i		8.18	19.51
MA(1)	0.04		−0.26	6.73	17.31
MA(2)	0.04		−0.14+0.24i / −0.14−0.24i	5.46	15.77
ARMA(1,1)	0.04	−0.02	−0.28	6.85	17.46
ARMA(2,2)	0.04	0.05+0.32i / 0.05−0.32i	−0.09+0.37i / −0.09−0.37i	5.06	15.75
1988:1–1991:6					
AR(1)	0.12	0.46		2.30	4.83
AR(2)	0.12	0.26−0.31i / 0.26+0.31i		1.00	3.29
MA(1)	0.12		−0.61	0.25	2.13
MA(2)	0.12		0.05 / −0.64	0.38	2.25
ARMA(1,1)	0.12	−0.31	−0.84	2.05	3.86
ARMA(2,2)	0.17	0.87 / −0.55	0.97 / −0.98	4.19	8.54
1991:7–1996:12					
AR(1)	0.09	0.40		7.65	9.82
AR(2)	0.09	0.25+0.4i / 0.25−0.4i		5.33	6.90
MA(1)	0.09		−0.44	8.18	10.02
MA(2)	0.09		−0.26−0.22i / −0.26+0.22i	6.10	7.92
ARMA(1,1)	0.09	0.15	−0.35	6.62	8.34
ARMA(2,2)	0.09	0.53+0.28i / 0.53−0.28i	0.80 / −0.17	1.96	3.81

risk premium associated with Chile experimented some important changes. This means that α in equation (2) will tend to change over time. Additionally, α will also tend to change since the implicit tax on the restriction capital mobility (k) is a function of r^*. Second, it is possible that the dynamics of interest rate differentials did not change exactly at the time of the imposition of the restrictions. After all, the implicit tax was rather small at first and there was substantial evasion.

These issues were addressed in two ways. First, I added Chile's ranking in *Euromoney*'s Country Risk Ratings as a proxy for the country risk premiums (see fig. 7.11 for the evolution of such ratings, where a higher number means increased country risk), as well as the U.S. interest rate to the regression. Second, I considered two alternative dates for splitting the sample: July 1992 and January 1993. Both of these dates correspond to a tightening of the inflows restrictions. The inclusion of the country risk proxy and of the international interest rates had no significant effects on the estimation; in fact, the sign of the country risk proxy was the opposite of what was expected and nonsignificant, while that of the international interest rate was nonsignificant. Changing the dates did, on the other hand, have an effect on the estimation. This may be seen in table 7.5, where the results from an augmented equation for the dynamics of interest rate differentials are presented. In this equation, dummy variables that take the value of one for the postrestrictions period have been included. Two interesting features emerge from this table. First, the coefficient of lagged differentials is higher for both postrestrictions periods. Moreover, as may be seen, the results indicate that the (δ dummy) variable is marginally sig-

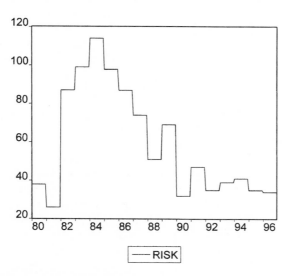

Fig. 7.11   Country risk premium for Chile

Table 7.5   Dynamics of Interest Rate Differential: 1988–96 (monthly data)

	Equation (2.1)[a]	Equation (2.2)[b]
Constant	0.12	0.15
	(1.76)	(1.85)
Dummy	−0.042	−0.051
	(−1.239)	(−1.323)
δ_{t-1}	0.311	0.324
	(2.763)	(2.792)
δ_{t-1}*dummy	0.218	0.152
	(1.887)	(1.787)
Risk	−0.002	−0.003
	(−1.081)	(−1.049)
r^*	1.183	0.807
	(1.343)	(0.822)
DW	1.18	1.81
R^2	0.23	0.23
N	108	108

[a]The dummy took a value of 1 from January 1993 onward.
[b]The dummy took a value of 1 from June 1992 onward.

nificant. This suggests that during at least some of the postrestrictions period, interest rate differentials were more sluggish than in the prerestrictions period. This supports the notion that the restrictions allowed the monetary authorities greater short-term control over domestic interest rates. The fact, however, that the estimated valued of the constant experienced a slight decline in the postrestrictions period suggests that the authorities may not have had as much control over interest rates in the longer run.

In order to investigate the dynamic behavior of interest rates further, I estimated the following equation using a rolling regressions technique:

$$(3) \qquad\qquad \delta_t = \alpha + \beta \delta_{t-1} + u_t.$$

Two alternative windows of twenty-four and thirty-six months were considered. The estimated coefficients were then used to estimate a rolling value of the steady-state interest rate differential. These results are presented in figures 7.12, 7.13, and 7.14. In constructing these figures I dated each coefficient by the last observation included in the sample. For example, in the case of the twenty-four-month window, the observation for 1995:6 corresponds to the respective coefficient estimated using a sample spanning from 1993:6 through 1995:6. To the right of the vertical lines, then, the complete sample used to estimate the coefficients corresponds to the postrestrictions period. These results suggest that in the postrestrictions period the degree of persistence of interest rate differentials (the estimated value of β) has increased slightly. This happened after a period

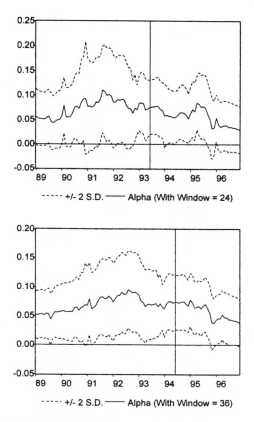

Fig. 7.12   Chile: Alpha in AR(1) process

(1990–93) of gradual decline in persistence, which largely corresponded to the decline in Chile's risk premium (see fig. 7.11). Although the increase in β has been rather small, the trend is quite clear and supports the view that, as the authorities had intended, the imposition of restrictions on capital movements increased their short-term control over domestic interest rates. The results in figure 7.14 on the rolling estimates of the steady-state interest rate differentials are less clear cut. Regarding the postrestrictions period, however, these estimates (and in particular the twenty-four-month window estimates) suggest that the steady-state differential trended gently upward until mid-1995; from that time onward a decline is observed. The most likely explanation for this reduction in the equilibrium differential is the recent improvement in Chile's country risk position. Although these results cannot be considered as conclusive or definitive, they do provide a note of skepticism on Chile's ability to control interest rate differentials over the longer run.

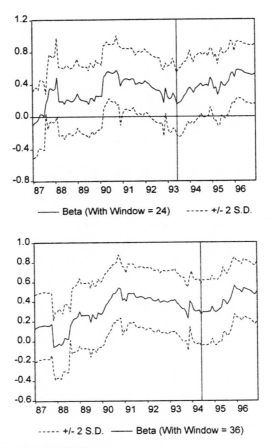

Fig. 7.13   Chile: Beta in AR(1) process

Capital Restrictions and Financial Vulnerability:
Chile in Historical Perspective

In the aftermath of the East Asian crisis a number of observers have argued that capital controls—and in particular restrictions on short-term capital inflows—will help reduce the degree of vulnerability of the domestic financial sector. Once again, it has been argued that the Chilean experience provides support for this policy view. The problem, however, is that from a methodological point of view it is not possible to know whether the absence of financial crises in Chile during the last few years has been the result of the capital controls policy or of other characteristics of the Chilean economy.

As it turns out, Chile has relied on capital controls on two occasions during the last twenty years: in 1978–82 and, more recently, after 1991.

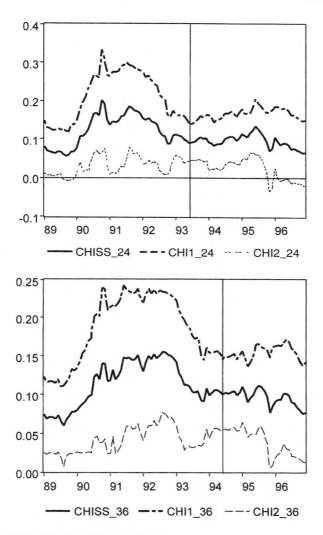

Fig. 7.14   Chile: Steady state in AR(1) process

During both episodes capital restrictions took the form of unremunerated reserve requirements on short-term capital entering the country, and on both occasions the main goals of the policy were to protect the economy from currency speculation and to avoid the appreciation of the real exchange rate. In spite of the existence of restrictions on capital mobility, in 1981–82 Chile went through a traumatic crisis, when the peso was devalued by almost 90 percent and a large number of banks had to be bailed out by the government. The main difference between then and now was not capital controls—virtually identical controls were in place during both episodes—but had to do with banking sector regulations. In the early years Chilean banks were mostly unregulated and were allowed to speculate in real estate and make questionable loans to their owners. It is a picture that strongly resembles crony capitalism in East Asia! A massive banking reform implemented in 1986 put an end to all of that. It established strict guidelines on banks' exposure and activities and instituted a broad system of onsite inspections. This reform helped create a healthy, strong, and efficient banking system. The main purpose of this subsection is to provide a brief analysis of this earlier Chilean experience with restrictions on capital inflows.

In 1976, as in 1991, the Chilean authorities became concerned about the increasing flow of capital *into* the country. For a variety of reasons—including the effect on the real exchange rate and on the financial sector—the authorities decided to restrict capital inflows through an array of mechanisms. All capital moving into the country had to be registered with the central bank. Foreign lenders who wanted to have access to foreign exchange in the future faced additional restrictions in the form of minimum maturities and maximum interest rates. Loans with maturities below twenty-four months were forbidden, and those with maturities from twenty-four to sixty-six months were subject to unremunerated reserves requirements ranging from 10 percent to 25 percent of the value of the loan. These reserve requirements were deposited in the central bank for the complete stay of the loan. Given the steepness of these deposits, until 1982 the overwhelming majority of loans had maturities in excess of sixty-six months: the average maturity was fifty-four months in 1979, sixty-four months in 1980, and sixty months in 1981. For all practical purposes, then, starting in 1976 Chile had in place a capital controls system that closely resembled the one implemented in 1991, and discussed in detail in the preceding section. In fact, it may be argued that, since flows of less than one year were prohibited, capital controls during the early years were stricter than during the more recent period.

During the earlier episode Chilean banks faced important restrictions on the intermediation of foreign funds. These restrictions operated in two ways. First, there was a limit on the level of banks' foreign liabilities. Second, and more importantly, there was a maximum amount by which banks could increase their foreign liabilities each month. Until December 1978 foreign currency (gross) liabilities could not exceed 1.6 times the bank's equity. At that time this limit was increased to 1.8 times the bank's equity.

In June 1979 a major step toward liberalizing the banking system was taken when the restriction on banks' maximum ratio of foreign liabilities to equity was eliminated, and the *level* of foreign liabilities became subject to banks' overall maximum debt to equity ratio of twenty. As a result of this, foreign funds intermediated by domestic banks increased by almost 100 percent during that year. However, banks were still subject to a severe restriction on the maximum *increase* in the level of foreign liabilities permitted per month. In late 1979 the maximum monthly increase in bank's (gross) foreign liabilities was "the largest of 5% of equity or US $2 million." At this time this restriction on the maximum monthly increase in foreign liabilities became binding, as banks could obtain from abroad large sums that could be brought only slowly into the country. In April 1980 this flow restriction was eliminated and banks could increase their foreign liabilities as fast as they wanted.

The vast majority of loans were obtained by private banks without government guarantee. In fact, it was thought at the time by the economic authorities and other observers that since most of the debt had been contracted by the private sector without any government guarantee, the very rapid increase in foreign debt did not represent a threat for the country as a whole: If a domestic private borrower could not pay its foreign obligations, that was a *private* problem, between it and the foreign creditor, which would be solved through a regular bankruptcy procedure.

In his 1981 Report of the Nation's Economic Conditions, Minister de Castro even argued that private indebtedness from abroad should be actively encouraged since it represented higher foreign savings. According to de Castro, "There is no doubt that the current account deficits . . . are highly beneficial for the country, and that we should make an effort to maintain them at the highest possible level and for the larger possible period of time."

A major problem, however, was that at the time banks were very poorly regulated. This situation had already become apparent in 1976, when a medium-size bank—Banco Osorno—failed. The government decided to bail depositors out, ex post guaranteeing deposit and, thus, creating a classical moral hazard situation. But perhaps the most significant problem was that banks were owned by major conglomerates that used them to shore up their firms, finance dubious investment projects, and fuel a major real estate boom. It has been estimated, for example, that in some banks more than 40 percent of the loan portfolio was concentrated on conglomerate-owned firms (Edwards and Edwards 1991). In spite of the 1976 crisis, very little was done to put an end to this situation and the banks' practice of channeling foreign funds to the conglomerates continued. In mid-1981, as international interest rates increased rapidly, asset prices in Chile began to fall and the demand for deposits experienced a significant decline. Some firms had difficulties in paying their debts, and in November 1981 two major banks—Banco Español and Banco de Talca—ran into serious difficulties and had to be bailed out by the government. During late 1981 and early 1982, aggregate production collapsed, domestic interest rates continued to increase, and the number of bankruptcies increased greatly. In the first half of 1982 deposits in the Chilean banking system—and especially deposits by foreigners—continued to decline steeply. During the first five months of 1982 alone, foreign deposits in commercial banks dropped by 75 percent. In June 1982 the government decided to devalue the peso, in the hope of alleviating the speculative pressure on the economy. The devaluation, however, affected negatively the financial conditions of many firms that had borrowed heavily in dollars. Depositors decided to fly from peso-denominated assets, commercial banks continued to accumulate bad loans, and the central bank had to inject large amounts of funds into the economy. In January 1983 the government concluded that the costs of this muddling through strategy were too high and pulled the rug from under some of the major commercial banks. By mid-1983 a number of banks had gone bankrupt, and Chile's financial crisis was in full swing. At the end of the road, the massive bank bailout that followed cost the country (in present value terms) in excess of 20 percent of GDP. What makes this story fascinating is its parallel to the 1997–98 crises in Indonesia and Korea. All the key elements are there: a rigid exchange rate policy, marked overvaluation, a high current account deficit, reckless lending by conglomerate-controlled banks, poor bank supervision, and a major asset bubble. Perhaps more importantly, Korea, as Chile, had restrictions on capital mobility. In neither case, however, did these help to prevent the crisis. One cannot avoid thinking that, had watchers of East Asia studied the Chilean financial crisis of 1982, they would not have been so shocked by the turns of events in the Asian "tigers."

7.5   Conclusions

The resurgence of capital inflows into Latin America has raised some important questions: Will there be another reversal? Are institutional investors likely to behave in a herd fashion, as in the past? How vulnerable are the Latin American countries to a contagion effect coming out of East Asia or other emerging markets? The analysis presented in the preceding sections suggests that the conditions behind capital flows have changed. These appear to be less volatile that in the past, and investors are becoming increasingly sophisticated and understand that there are significant differences across regions and countries. However, the issue of vulnerability still remains. What makes the situation particularly difficult is that in many Latin American countries commercial banks—which (ultimately) intermediate the capital inflows—continue to be financially weak, even in the aftermath of the Mexican crisis. Moreover, in most nations supervisory systems are inefficient and unable to monitor effectively the quality of the portfolio and the extent to which banks indeed abide by existing rules and regulations.

Latin America's own history justifies the current concern with banks' vulnerability. As previous episodes in the region have shown, when banks fail the effects of financial crises are greatly magnified. Past experiences in Chile and Mexico illustrate this point vividly. Banks were at the center of the Chilean crisis of 1982. After intermediating very large volumes of capital inflows during 1978–80, commercial banks had become increasingly vulnerable to negative shocks stemming from the international economy.

In a similar way it is possible to argue that both the magnitude and timing of the 1994 Mexican crisis were affected by the behavior of the banking system. Throughout 1994, as international interest rates increased and Mexico was hit by a series of political shocks, the Mexican authorities made great efforts to maintain domestic (peso-denominated) interest rates at a relatively low level. A two-pronged approach was followed: On the one hand, a cap was imposed on peso-denominated interest rates; on the other, the authorities issued increasingly large amounts of dollar-denominated securities—the so-called *tesobonos.* The investment house J. P. Morgan summarized this state of affairs in its newsletter of 22 July 1994: "Half of the 28-day and 91-day Cetes [peso-denominated securities] were issued; the central bank would not accept the high yields required by the market to auction the full amount." And on 23 July the *Economist* pointed out that "the central bank has also had to issue plenty of tesobonos—dollar linked securities that are popular with investors that worry about currency risk." This strategy—which in retrospect has mystified so many analysts—partially responded to the Mexican authorities' concerns regarding the financial health of Mexican banks. Their concerns had begun in late 1992, when a large increase in past-due loans became evident. In 1990, nonperforming loans were estimated to be only 2 percent of total loans; that ratio increased to 4.7 percent in 1992, to 7.3 percent in 1993, and to 8.3 percent at the end of the first quarter of 1994. With the fourth largest bank—Banca Cremi—in serious trouble, the authorities tried to buy additional time as they worked out an emergency plan. By the end of the first semester, the State Development Banks had developed a relief program based on some write-offs of commercial banks' past-due interests and government-issued loan guarantees. In the belief that the peso was sustainable and that they had superior information, Mexican banks engaged in aggressive derivatives operations, accumulating sizable dollar-denominated off-balance-sheet liabilities (Garber 1996). On 19 December 1994, however, with the banks of Mexico having virtually run out of reserves, the Mexican authorities decided to widen the exchange rate band. It was, however, too little, too late. In the months to come it became increasingly clear that a key element in the stabilization policy would be to contain the extent of the banking crisis.

Data Appendix

Data are from the IMF's *International Financial Statistics* (IFS, various issues), unless otherwise indicated.

Capital Inflows. Financial Account (line 78bjd, IFS) plus Net Errors and Omissions (line 78cad, IFS), for Argentina, Brazil, and Mexico. Change in Total Reserves minus Gold (line 11.d, IFS), for Chile and Colombia.

Real Exchange Rate. Bilateral real exchange rate estimated using the nominal exchange rate (line rf, IFS), the CPI (line 64, IFS), and the US Producer Price (line 63, IFS).

Capital Controls. Calculated using the methodology in Valdes-Prieto and Soto (1996a).

Domestic Credit. Line 32, IFS.

Expected Devaluation. The fitted values from the estimated AR process of actual devaluation rate as explained in the text.

Domestic Interest Rate. Deposit Rate (line 601, IFS).

International Interest Rate. US Treasury Bill Rate (line 60c, IFS).

Interest Rate Differential. Domestic Interest Rate minus International Interest Rate minus Expected Devaluation.

Risk. *Euromoney*'s Country Risk Rating (several issues).

References

Banco de Mexico. Various years. *Informe sobre la Politica Monetaria.* Mexico City: Banco de Mexico.
Bruno, Michael. 1995. Currency crises and collapses: Comment. *Brookings Papers on Economic Activity,* no. 2: 271–94.
Budnevich, Carlos, and Guillermo LeFort. 1997. Capital account regulation and macroeconomic policy: Two Latin American experiences. Working Paper no. 6. Santiago: Banco Central de Chile.
Calvo, Guillermo A. 1991. The perils of sterilization. *IMF Staff Papers* 38, no. 4 (December).
Calvo, Guillermo, Leonardo Leiderman, and Carmen Reinhart. 1993. Capital in-

flows and real exchange rate appreciation in Latin America: The role of external factors. *IMF Staff Papers* 40 (March): 108–51.

————. 1995. Capital inflows to Latin America with reference to the Asian experience. In *Capital controls, exchange rates and monetary policy in the world economy,* ed. Sebastian Edwards. Cambridge: Cambridge University Press.

Calvo, Guillermo, and Enrique Mendoza. 1996. Petty crime and cruel punishment: Lessons from the Mexican debacle. *American Economic Review* 86, no. 2 (May): 170–75.

Cardenas, Mauricio, and Felipe Barrera. 1997. On the effectiveness of capital controls: The experience of Colombia during the 1990s. *Journal of Development Economics* 54, no. 1 (October): 27–57.

Cardoso, Eliana, and Ilan Goldfajn. 1997. Capital flows to Brazil: The endogeneity of capital controls. IMF Working Paper no. 97/115. Washington, D.C.: International Monetary Fund.

Chuhan, Punam, Stijn Claessens, and Nlandu Mamingi. 1993. Equity and bond flows to Latin America and Asia: The role of global and country factors. Policy Research Working Paper no. 1160. Washington, D.C.: World Bank, International Economics Department.

Cowan, K., and J. De Gregorio. 1997. Exchange rate policies and capital account management: Chile in the 1990s. Working paper. Santiago: Universidad de Chile, Departamento de Ingenieria Industrial.

Dooley, Michael. 1995. A survey of academic literature on controls over international capital transactions. IMF Working Paper no. 95/127. Washington, D.C.: International Monetary Fund.

Dooley, Michael, D. Mathieson, and L. Rojas-Suarez. 1997. Capital mobility and exchange market intervention in developing countries. NBER Working Paper no. 6247. Cambridge, Mass.: National Bureau of Economic Research.

Dornbusch, Rudiger. 1993. Inflation, exchange rates, and stabilization. In *The international monetary system: Highlights from fifty years of Princeton's Essays in International Finance,* 369–92. Boulder and Oxford: Westview Press.

Dornbusch, Rudiger, Ilan Goldfajn, and Rodrigo Valdés. 1995. Currency crises and collapses. *Brookings Papers on Economic Activity,* no. 2: 219–70.

Dornbusch, Rudiger, and Alejandro Werner. 1994. Mexico: Stabilization, reform and no growth. *Brookings Papers on Economic Activity,* no. 1.

Eaton, Jonathan. 1989. Foreign public capital flows. In *Handbook of development economics,* vol. 3, ed. H. Chenery and T. N. Srinivasan. Amsterdam: North-Holland.

Edwards, Sebastian. 1984. The order of liberalization of the external sector in developing countries. Essays in International Finance, vol. 156. Princeton, N.J.: Princeton University.

————. 1985. Money, the rate of devaluation, and interest rates in a semi-open economy: Colombia, 1968–82. *Journal of Money, Credit and Banking* 17 (1): 59–68.

————. 1988. *Exchange rate misalignment in developing countries.* Baltimore: Johns Hopkins University Press.

————. 1989. *Real exchange rates, devaluations and adjustment.* Cambridge, Mass.: MIT Press.

————. 1993. *Latin America and the Caribbean: A decade after the debt crisis.* Washington, D.C.: World Bank.

————. 1995a. *Crisis and reform in Latin America: From despair to hope.* New York: Oxford University Press.

————, ed. 1995b. *Capital controls, exchange rates and monetary policy in the world economy.* Cambridge: Cambridge University Press.

———. 1999. Capital inflows into Latin America: A stop-go story? In *International capital flows,* ed. Martin Feldstein, 5–42. Chicago: University of Chicago Press.

Edwards, Sebastian, and Alejandra Edwards. 1991. *Monetarism and liberalization: The Chilean experience.* Chicago: University of Chicago Press.

Edwards, Sebastian, and M. Khan. 1985. Interest determination in developing countries: A conceptual framework. *IMF Staff Papers* 32, no. 3 (September): 377–403.

Feldstein, Martin, and Charles Horioka. 1980. Domestic saving and international capital flows. *Economic Journal* 90 (June): 314–29.

Fontaine, Juan A. 1996. *La construccion de un mercado de capitales en Chile.* Washington, D.C.: World Bank, Economic Development Institute.

Frankel, J. 1989. Quantifying international capital mobility in the 1980s. NBER Working Paper no. 2856. Cambridge, Mass.: National Bureau of Economic Research, February.

Garber, Peter. 1996. Managing risk to financial markets from volatile capital flows: The role of prudential regulation. *International Journal of Finance and Economics* 1, no. 3 (July): 183–95.

Goldman-Sachs. 1998. *Emerging Markets Biweekly,* 7 January.

Haque, Nadeem, and Peter Montiel. 1991. Capital mobility in developing countries: Some empirical tests. *World Development* 19 (October): 91–98.

Harberger, Arnold. 1978. Perspectives on capital and technology in less developed countries. In *Contemporary economic analysis,* ed. M. Artis and A. Nobay, 151–69. London: Croom Helm.

———. 1985. Observations on the Chilean economy, 1973–1983. *Economic Development and Cultural Change* 33, no. 3 (April).

ING Barings. 1998. *Global Investment Strategy,* first quarter.

Larrain, Felipe, Raul Laban, and Romulo Chumacero. 1997. What determines capital inflows? An empirical analysis for Chile. Development Discussion Paper no. 590. Cambridge, Mass.: Harvard Institute for International Development.

McKinnon, Ronald. 1982. The order of economic liberalization: Lessons from Chile and Argentina. *Carnegie-Rochester Conference Series on Public Policy* 17 (autumn): 159–86.

Montiel, Peter. 1994. Capital mobility in developing countries: Some measurement issues and empirical estimates. *World Bank Economic Review* 8, no. 3 (September): 311–50.

Ocampo, Jose Antonio. 1989. Colombia and the Latin American debt crisis. In *Debt, adjustment and recovery,* ed. Sebastian Edwards and Felipe Larrain. Oxford: Basil Blackwell.

Reisen, H., and H. Yeches. 1991. Time-varying estimates on the openness of the capital account in Korea and Taiwan. Technical Paper no. 42. Paris: Organization for Economic Cooperation and Development, August.

Santander Investment. 1998. *Global Economic Research, Economic Weekly,* January, 15–23.

Steiner, Roberto. 1995. *Flujos de capitales en America Latina.* Bogota: Tercer Mundo-Fedesarrollo.

Valdes-Prieto, Salvador, and Marcelo Soto. 1996a. New selective capital controls in Chile: Are they effective? Working paper. Santiago: Catholic University of Chile.

———. 1996b. Es el control selectivo de capitales efectivo en Chile? Su efecto sobre el tipo de cambio real. *Cuadernos de Economia* 33 (April): 77–108.

World Bank. 1997. *Private capital flows to developing countries: The road to financial integration.* New York: Oxford University Press.

Comment   José De Gregorio

Edwards's paper is an interesting effort to discuss with rigor and empirical content capital movements in Latin America and the effects of capital controls. In these comments I will focus on the Chilean experience during the 1990s. As Edwards argues, "The . . . Chilean experience is particularly important since its practice of imposing reserve requirements has been praised by a number of analysts, including senior staff of the multilateral institutions, as an effective and efficient way of reducing vulnerability associated with capital flows volatility." I will briefly discuss how it has worked. Then I will review the effects it has had on interest rates, the real exchange rate, and debt structure. Then I will comment on some aspects of the Chilean experience usually ignored in the literature and finish with some lessons that can be drawn.

The most important and well-known restriction applied in Chile is the unremunerated reserve requirement (URR, or *encaje*) introduced in June 1991 and set to zero, but not eliminated, in late 1998. The Chilean case is interesting because the controls were applied in a period of massive inflows, during which the country experienced very strong economic performance (see table 7C.1). Output and exports grew strongly. Savings and investment were also high by Chile's historical standards. Finally, inflation declined and the fiscal position was strong.

Chile has been a country characterized by widespread foreign exchange and capital controls. This was particularly important after the debt crisis, when many controls were put in place to prevent outflows and to secure external financing. In this context, with the surge of capital flows to emerging markets in the late 1980s and early 1990s, the economy started opening up the capital account and easing many restrictions. For example, restrictions on international investment by pension funds, mutual funds, and other institutional investors had been relaxed. However, a minimum holding period for foreign investment remained in place and the unremunerated reserve requirement was introduced.

The specifics of the reserve requirement have changed over time, but from 1992 to 1998 they basically imposed the obligation for most inflows to deposit 30 percent in the central bank.[1] This deposit would not be remunerated, resulting in a financial cost for the investor. In practice this works as a fixed cost of entry. Therefore, the longer the inflow stays in Chile the less the relative cost of this entry fee is. Hence, the URR penalizes more short-term inflows compared to long-term inflows, since the for-

José De Gregorio is professor at the Center for Applied Economics, Universidad de Chile. The author is very grateful to Rodrigo Valdés for very helpful discussions.

1. For a description and discussion of the evidence, see Nadal de Simone and Sorsa (1999). For a recent assessment, see De Gregorio, Edwards, and Valdés (1998).

Table 7C.1   **Chile: Macroeconomic Indicators**

	1990	1991	1992	1993	1994	1995	1996	1997	1987–97 Average
GDP growth (%)	3.7	8.0	12.3	7.0	5.7	10.6	7.4	7.1	7.8
Inflation (Dec.–Dec.)	27.3	18.7	12.7	12.2	8.9	8.2	6.6	6.0	14.0
Fiscal surplus[a] (% GDP)	0.8	1.5	2.3	2.0	1.7	2.6	2.3	1.9	1.8
Gross national saving (% GDP)	23.2	22.3	21.5	20.9	21.1	23.8	20.8	21.4	21.6
Fixed investment (% real GDP)	24.2	22.4	24.7	27.2	27.4	30.6	31.2	33.0	26.0
Current account (% GDP)	−1.6	−0.3	−2.3	−5.7	−3.3	−2.1	−5.4	−5.3	−3.0
Quantum of exports (%)	11.5	9.9	16.7	3.3	11.1	7.7	17.2	10.8	10.9
Real exchange rate (86 = 100)	112.8	106.4	97.6	96.9	94.2	88.9	84.7	78.2	98.5
Terms of trade (80 = 100)	95.9	95.4	94.5	86.2	97.7	116.0	94.4	98.3	98.5

Source: Central Bank, Ministry of Finance, and Instituto Nacional de Estadísticas.

[a]Central government.

mer can spread the cost along a longer horizon.[2] The minimum holding period for foreign investment is currently one year, and it was reduced from three years in 1995. This minimum holding period has barred many investment funds from investing in Chile because of regulations that do not allow them to invest in countries with this type of restriction.

The URR was introduced with the purpose of allowing interest rates higher than those abroad, limiting the extent of capital inflows and the appreciation of the exchange rate (Zhaler 1998).[3] Because the interest rate is the main instrument used to control aggregate demand and to reduce inflation, and because Chile is a country with a large exports base and a strong pro-export orientation, authorities thought that with the URR the objectives of remaining competitive and having high interest rates could be made compatible. So, the URR attempted to delink tight domestic monetary policy, with an exchange rate objective, from monetary conditions abroad. This explains the evolution of the URR. First it was used only for bank credit. Then, as other forms of inflows exempted from the URR were taking advantage of high interest rates, authorities started extending this restriction to other capital inflows, such as portfolio investment.

Therefore, a first evaluation of the URR must look at its effects on interest rates and the real exchange rate. The evidence at this juncture is still controversial, but one can conclude that no strong effects on the real exchange rate have been found. There are some short-term effects, but they are small compared to the ex post evolution of Chile's real exchange rate. Of course, it is always possible that the empirical work done until now has not been performed properly. However, during the period 1990–97 the real exchange rate appreciated at an annual rate of about 4–5 percent per year (see table 7C.1), and no theory could support the argument that the URR could have prevented this from happening.

Regarding real interest rates some effects have been found. For example, Edwards's paper shows that despite the fact that the URR may affect the short-run response of interest rates, it does not appear to have long-run effects. Similarly, De Gregorio, Edwards, and Valdés (1998) also find in VARs that "transitory shocks" to the URR have "transitory" effects on the real interest rate. This is not surprising, since most fluctuations of the URR are due to changes in international interest rates; but the most important effect is a once-and-for-all impact on arbitrage conditions when the URR is introduced, and this effect could be permanent. The fixed cost of entry generates an option value of investing and liquidating that investment in Chile, which could reduce the direct cost of the fee. Indeed, Her-

---

2. Calculations by De Gregorio, Edwards, and Valdés (1998) indicate that for a London Inter-Bank Offering Rate (LIBOR) of 6 percent, the URR is equivalent to an additional annual financial cost of 23 percent for operations at the one-month holding period, 8 percent at three months, and 1 percent at two years.

3. See also De Gregorio 1997.

rera and Valdés (1997) made this point and they have shown that the URR could support at most interest rate differentials between 1 and 2 percent. If the authorities overestimated its effect, they could have increased interest rates beyond the cost of the URR inducing more capital inflows.

Another objective for the URR, which began to be emphasized some time after its introduction, was to "discourage hot money." Official declarations were that Chile was very open, and opening up, to all long-term investment, but that it was not interested in short-term "speculative inflows." This was an important objective, but its importance has changed over time. For example, when the URR was reduced to zero in 1998 it was done to stimulate inflows and to defend the currency from depreciating. Whether capital inflows in 1998–99 are speculative or not, it is no longer an issue.

There is no evidence that the URR would have reduced the magnitude of capital inflows. But there is strong evidence that shows that the URR has changed the maturity structure of Chile's external debt, tilting the composition toward longer maturities. A cursory look at the evidence confirms this conclusion. In table 7C.2 it can be observed that there has been a sharp decline in the share of short-term debt. There has been some discussion about the central bank figures, since the Bank for International Settlements (BIS) reports that Chile's share of short-term debt is much higher than is shown by official figures (see Eichengreen et al. 1998). But a look at BIS figures, which effectively show more short-term debt, reveals two facts that support the view that in Chile the maturity has tilted toward the longer term. First, the share of Chile is one of the smallest among emerging markets, and second, it is the country with the smallest increase in the share of short-term debt among emerging markets during the 1990s (see De Gregorio, Edwards, and Valdés 1998).

Therefore, one can argue that effectively the URR has lengthened the maturity of Chile's external debt. However, when using Chile's example to argue in favor of controls in other countries, several issues, often ignored in the discussion, have to be taken into account:

- The Chilean economy had strong fundamentals, solid public finances, an independent central bank, and a very open and competitive economy when the URR was introduced and applied. The international environment was very positive and there were massive amounts of capital available to be invested in emerging markets. All of that can explain the impressive performance achieved during 1990–97. Capital controls did not signal any problems in the economy. In fact, they may have signaled very strong conditions, which ultimately could have increased incentives for inflows (Cordella 1998). The lesson is that being heterodox when the economy is doing well and is attempting to smooth the boom is not the same as introducing controls to stop an imminent crisis.

Table 7C.2   External Debt (US$ millions)

	1990	1991	1992	1993	1994	1995	1996	1997
Total external debt	17,425	16,364	18,242	19,186	21,478	21,736	22,979	26,701
Private	5,633	5,810	8,619	10,166	12,343	14,235	17,816	21,613
Public	11,792	10,554	9,623	9,020	9,135	7,501	5,163	5,088
Long and medium term	14,043	14,165	14,767	15,699	17,613	18,305	20,344	25,414
Short term	3,382	2,199	3,475	3,487	3,865	3,431	2,635	1,287
Short term/total (%)	19.4	13.4	19.0	18.2	18.0	15.8	11.5	4.8

Source: Central Bank.

- Capital flows play an important role so there are clear welfare losses. They provide financing in capital scarce countries. They allow consumption smoothing, especially in economies that are subject to strong volatility of income, such as Chile because of the importance of copper. Some of these flows take the form of short-term capital. Restricting those flows has clear implications for welfare losses as the extent of consumption smoothing and investment is limited.
- There are other distortions that need to be taken into account when evaluating the URR. In Chile, small and medium-size firms without access to long-term international financing are the most affected by this restriction. Large firms that can borrow long term abroad can avoid the URR, while small and medium-size firms have to pay high domestic interest rates. Thus, the URR, despite being a market-based control, introduces an artificial distortion that makes domestic short-term borrowing vis-à-vis long-term foreign borrowing more expensive.
- Policy makers can rely too heavily on the URR under the mistaken belief that it is very efficient. Indeed, it is possible that they overstate their power in Chile. As argued above, some of the benefits expected when the URR was introduced, providing monetary autonomy, are limited. Therefore, financial policies may be implemented under the assumption that they will not strongly affect the real exchange rate or capital inflows.

The main effect capital controls have had in Chile is the lengthening of maturity of external debt. Vulnerability has been reduced since it is not necessary to roll over a significant part of external debt every quarter or year. However, its effects in allowing monetary independence and in preventing a steep appreciation are less clear. For this reason, and given the distortions that the URR generates, it does not seem necessary to extend it to all capital flows, as suggested by the need of monetary independence. It is advisable not to use the URR as an instrument to significantly increase interest rates and avoid an appreciation. Its main function is to avoid liquidity problems by lengthening the maturity of foreign liabilities, in particular, external debt. Of course, the problem is that using the URR only on external debt may induce loopholes and short-term debt may take other forms to avoid paying the URR. However, these loopholes appear precisely when interest rates are very high, under the assumption that the economy is protected, which usually is not the case. Of course the URR is not the only instrument for avoiding liquidity problems. In particular, the URR does not help if liquidity problems arise domestically. For this reason establishing tight liquidity requirements on the banking system, such as those applied in Argentina, may be an alternative to capital controls. In general, prudential supervision and sound regulation of the banking system are a key to reducing vulnerability and avoiding the welfare costs of capital controls.

References

Cordella, T. 1998. Can short-term capital controls promote capital inflows? Washington, D.C.: International Monetary Fund. Mimeo.

De Gregorio, J. 1997 Macroeconomic and financial policy in Chile. In *The banking and financial structure in NAFTA countries and Chile,* ed. G. von Furstenberg. Boston: Kluwer Academic.

De Gregorio, J., S. Edwards, and R. Valdés. 1998. Capital controls in Chile: An assessment. Santiago: Universidad de Chile. Mimeo.

Eichengreen, B., et al. 1998. Capital account liberalization: Theoretical and practical aspects. IMF Occasional Paper no. 172. Washington, D.C.: International Monetary Fund.

Herrera, L. O., and R. Valdés. 1997. The effects of capital controls on interest rates differentials. Santiago: Central Bank of Chile. Mimeo.

Nadal de Simone, F., and P. Sorsa. 1999. Capital account restrictions in Chile in the 1990s. Washington, D.C.: International Monetary Fund. Mimeo.

Zhaler, R. 1998. Chile's macroeconomic policies in the 1990s as seen from the vantage point of the central bank. Santiago: Economic Commission for Latin America and the Caribbean. Mimeo.

Capital Flows in Asia

Takatoshi Ito

8.1 Introduction

It was just a few years ago that capital flows to Asian emerging markets were praised as a model for the rest of the world. A majority of capital flows to Asia took the form of foreign direct investment (FDI) rather than portfolio investment. Although portfolio investment is quick to come and quick to go, it is less likely, many believe, for FDI to reverse direction. Capital flows to Asia increased investment, which in turn contributed to Asian nations' achieving higher growth. Then high growth performances attracted further capital inflows. A virtuous cycle of capital flows and economic growth was indeed an important part of the Asian miracle. In the wake of the Asian crisis, however, the praises all but disappeared. Even Asia could not withstand the shocks of volatile capital outflows caused by a sudden change in investors' expectations.

When the baht was floated on 2 July 1997, it was hardly a surprise for many foreign exchange dealers, treasury officials and central bankers of G7, and academic economists. However, few predicted that the exchange rates would depreciate as much as they actually did or that the crisis would spread to other countries in the region, especially to Korea, in the following months. Indonesia had been praised by the World Bank until just before the Thai devaluation. There was little sign of trouble in Korea until three months after the baht devaluation. There was no warning of con-

Takatoshi Ito is professor in the Institute of Economic Research at Hitotsubashi University, Tokyo, and a research associate of the National Bureau of Economic Research.

Comments from Sebastian Edwards, Martin Feldstein, Carmen Reinhart, Dani Rodrik, Aaron Tornell, and other conference participants were extremely helpful. All views and opinions expressed in the paper are the author's and do not necessarily reflect those of institutions that the author is and has been affiliated with at present or in the past.

tagion in the International Capital Markets report of 1997 (published in September 1997). The International Monetary Fund (IMF) financial support package was negotiated and accepted by the Thai authorities in August, followed by Indonesia in November and Korea in December. After six months, there is no clear assessment whether the contagion has stopped. It turns out that the Asian currency crisis of 1997 is broader and deeper than the Mexican peso crisis of 1994–95.

From the end of June to the end of December 1997, the Indonesian rupiah depreciated more than 140 percent, while the Korean won and the Thai baht depreciated more than 80 percent, vis-à-vis the U.S. dollar. The Malaysian ringgit and Philippine peso depreciated about 50 percent. Even the Singaporean dollar and Taiwanese dollar depreciated close to 20 percent. The least affected were the Hong Kong dollar and Chinese renminbi, both of which kept the nominal exchange rate to the U.S. dollar.

Stock prices in these countries have also plummeted. In the ASEAN-4 (Thailand, Malaysia, the Philippines, and Indonesia) and Korea, stock prices fell by more than one-half from January to December of 1997. Withdrawal of funds from the stock market by foreign investors at least partly explains a simultaneous collapse of stock and currency markets.

These exchange rate and stock price movements reflect the strong outflow of capital from these Asian countries. Even relatively large foreign reserves, in terms of import months, were not enough in Thailand and Korea. In the case of Thailand, speculations in the forward market exhausted foreign reserves (in terms of spot-forward net positions) and, in the case of Korea, refusal of rollovers to Korean commercial banks by foreign banks exhausted the "usable" Korean foreign reserves.

The Asian cases of 1997 also suggest a strong contagion. Countries in the region are greatly affected by a currency crisis in any one of them. Although there are similarities among countries in crisis, differences are also pronounced. Common features include external shocks, the yen-dollar exchange rate movement, and internal factors such as a weak banking system and large short-term borrowings. One cannot deny the possibility that a crisis in one country suddenly changes investors' minds about the prospects of other countries.

The rest of this paper is organized as follows. The next section describes how capital flowed into Asia from 1991 to 1996. Section 8.3 summarizes the crisis of 1997. The similarities and differences between Mexico and Asian countries, and also those among Asian countries, will be shown. In section 8.4, lessons from this episode of currency crises will be drawn. Section 8.5 concludes.

8.2   Capital Flows to Asia

8.2.1   Overview

Capital flows to Asia have been a focus of intensive study in the last several years, especially after the currency crisis of the 1997. Figure 8.1 shows the total gross capital inflows—direct investment, portfolio investment, and other capital flows (78bed, 78bgd, 78bid lines of International Financial Statistics, IMF)—to the ASEAN-4 and China for the period 1976–97. Several characteristics are evident. First, capital flows to these countries increased markedly in the 1990s (until the crisis of 1997). Second, capital flows to China after 1993 dwarf the flows to other countries. Third, among ASEAN countries, Thailand was the largest recipient of capital flows between 1988 and 1996. However, with the currency crisis, Thailand's inflows became outflows in 1997. Fourth, capital flows to Indonesia and Malaysia were larger than those to other countries from 1982 to 1984, but have declined since then.

Let us focus on net private capital flows in the 1990s and compare Asia with other regions. Table 8.1 shows global capital flows to developing and transition economies. Net private capital flows to emerging markets increased sevenfold from 1990 to 1996. In 1990, total capital flows to emerging markets (developing countries and transition economies) were about $30 billion, of which two-thirds went to Asia and one-third to Latin America. In 1993, the total amount of capital flows was up to $160 billion, of which Asia and Latin America received about 40 percent each. A majority of flows to Asia took the form of direct investment and an overwhelming portion of flows to Latin America took the form of portfolio investment.

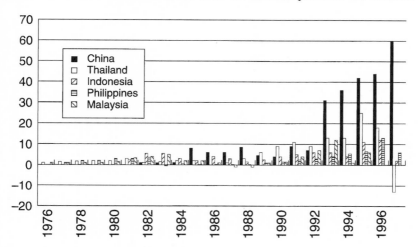

Fig. 8.1   Capital flows to Asia: All types

Table 8.1   Net Private Capital Flows to Emerging Markets (US$ billions)

	1990	1991	1992	1993	1994	1995	1996	1997
Emerging markets								
Total	31.0	126.9	120.9	164.7	160.5	192.0	240.8	173.7
FDI	17.6	31.3	37.2	60.6	84.3	96.0	114.9	138.2
Portfolio	17.1	37.3	59.9	103.5	87.8	23.5	49.7	42.9
Others	-3.7	58.4	23.8	0.7	-11.7	72.5	76.2	-7.3
1. Asia								
Total	19.1	35.8	21.7	57.6	66.2	95.8	110.4	13.9
FDI	8.9	14.5	16.5	35.9	46.8	49.5	57.0	57.8
Portfolio	-1.4	1.8	9.3	21.6	9.5	10.5	13.4	-8.6
Others	11.6	19.5	-4.1	0.1	9.9	35.8	39.9	-35.4
1a. Affected								
Total	24.9	29.0	30.3	32.6	35.1	62.9	72.9	-11.0
FDI	6.2	7.2	8.6	8.6	7.4	9.5	12.0	9.6
Portfolio	1.3	3.3	6.3	17.9	10.6	14.4	20.3	11.8
Others	17.4	18.5	15.4	6.1	17.1	39.0	40.6	-32.3
2. Latin America								
Total	10.1	26.1	56.0	64.3	47.4	35.7	80.5	91.1
FDI	6.7	11.0	13.6	12.8	24.3	25.3	36.9	51.2
Portfolio	17.5	14.7	30.4	61.1	60.6	-0.1	25.2	33.5
Others	-14.0	0.3	12.0	-9.5	-37.5	10.5	18.5	6.5
3. Transition economies								
Total	3.5	-2.4	7.2	12.2	18.4	29.8	21.3	34.5
FDI	-0.3	2.4	4.2	6.0	5.4	13.2	13.1	18.2
Portfolio	0.0	0.0	0.1	4.5	4.1	2.9	2.9	7.3
Others	3.7	-4.8	2.9	1.7	8.9	13.6	13.6	9.0
4. Other regions								
Total	-1.7	67.4	36.0	30.6	28.5	30.7	28.7	34.3
FDI	2.2	3.5	5.9	5.9	7.9	7.9	7.9	11.0
Portfolio	1.1	20.7	16.3	16.3	13.7	10.2	8.9	10.8
Others	-5.0	43.3	8.4	8.4	7.0	12.5	11.8	12.6

Source: IMF, *International Capital Markets*, September 1998.

Notes: "Others" includes short- and long-term credits, loans (not including use of IMF credit), currency and deposits, and other accounts receivable and

The large ratio of portfolio flows to Latin American countries in 1991–93 became a source of instability in the wake of, if not a trigger of, the Mexican peso crisis. In 1995, net portfolio investment to Latin America became negative in the wake of the Mexican peso crisis. The total private flows also declined sharply. Capital flows to Latin America recovered sharply only in 1996, contributing to a new record high for the capital flows to emerging markets exceeding $240 billion, of which about one-half went to Asia and one-third to Latin America.

Several reasons for the sharp rise in capital flows from 1990 to 1996 have been pointed out in the literature. First, a declining trend of the interest rates in the advanced countries prompted institutional investors to search for high-yield opportunities in many emerging markets.[1] The pursuit of high yield was reinforced by the investors' desire to diversify their portfolio internationally. Second, on the recipient side, emerging markets liberalized restrictions on inward investment. Some developing countries introduced economic reforms including financial sectors. Others allowed direct investment into various industries. These factors are analyzed in IMF (1995).

During the episode of strong capital inflows, several host countries complained that the volume of capital inflows was too great and was causing adverse side effects, overheating domestic economies to speculative appreciation pressure. Thailand and Malaysia in particular received inflows amounting to more than 10 percent of gross domestic product (GDP). Thailand was accumulating foreign reserves as a result of intervention to prevent appreciation even with current account deficits of 8 percent (of GDP) in 1995–96. Without intervention, the currency would have appreciated. Intervention was probably only partly sterilized. There are some signs that capital inflows contributed to a real estate boom in Thailand and Malaysia. More detailed discussions on the inflow problem are found in IMF (1995).

The picture changed sharply in 1997. The Thai baht was effectively devalued in July of that year and the Thai government asked the IMF for assistance in August. The currency crisis spread to Indonesia, Malaysia, the Philippines, and Korea in the subsequent months. Private capital fled from these countries. In the end net private capital flows to Asia fell from $110 billion in 1996 to a mere $14 billion in 1997. Net portfolio investment to Asia became negative in 1997 for the first time since 1990. If the affected countries—Indonesia, Korea, Malaysia, the Philippines, and Thailand—

---

1. An influence of the U.S. interest rate on global capital flows to the emerging markets was pointed out in the Mexican crisis of 1994–95. The declining interest rate in the United States from 1992 to 1994 prompted a large volume of capital flows to Latin America and other emerging market economies. The rapid interest rate hike in the United States from February 1994 to the summer of 1994 is thought to be one of the many reasons for capital outflows from Mexico, which finally caused the currency devaluation in December 1994.

were singled out, the net private capital that fled was on the order of $11 billion. Even during the crisis, FDI to Asia did not decline from 1996 to 1997. This reflects both investors' confidence in the long-run prospects of Asian economies and host countries' willingness to be acquired in hard times. It is also notable that portfolio flows declined sharply in both the Latin American countries in 1995 and the Asian economies in 1997. However, the drop in portfolio flows was much more dramatic among Latin American countries in the aftermath of the Mexican crisis.

In terms of total net private capital flows, the decline among Asian countries from 1996 to 1997 was much more dramatic than the decline for Latin American countries from 1994 to 1995. There are two factors to consider. First, in the Mexican crisis of 1994–95, the crisis was effectively stopped by the IMF packages to Mexico at the end of January 1995 and to Argentina in March 1995. In contrast, the Asian currency crisis spread from Thailand to Indonesia to Korea. This contributed to a much larger decline in net capital flows to Asia in 1997 than to Latin America in 1995. Second, in both crises, bank lending and credits were sharply reversed (see "Others" line in table 8.1) among Asian economies.

8.2.2   Scenario: Virtuous and Vicious Cycles

Net capital inflows make it possible for a host country to run current account deficits without running down foreign reserves. They increase the resources that the host country can use. In Asia, capital inflows were mostly used for investment. The saving rate is already high in many Asian countries, especially in Malaysia and Singapore, but the investment rate is even higher. Investment, both FDI and domestic companies and government projects, is believed to have contributed to higher growth. Higher growth in turn invites more investment.

One of the factors that helped exports and economic growth of the East Asian countries in the last two decades was a long-term trend of yen appreciation. There are at least two ways yen appreciation contributes to economic growth of the Asian economies. First, as the yen appreciates, Asian products become more price competitive against Japanese goods in the world markets, especially in the Japanese and U.S. markets. For example, Korean shipbuilding, steel, and semiconductors are direct competitors to Japanese counterparts in the world market. Although they may not compete directly in the same quality category, they indirectly compete in the same product category. Hence, yen appreciation promotes business chances for manufacturing companies based in East and Southeast Asian economies.

Second, yen appreciation has convinced many Japanese companies of the benefits of moving production facilities out of Japan. Looking for production sites where high-quality workers are available at low wages, Japanese manufacturing companies shifted production abroad, mainly to

Asia.[2] Technological transfers with Japanese management helped the Asian countries increase productivity in manufacturing. Some of the facilities in Asia became productive enough to export to the United States, Japan, and the rest of the world.

Hence, the low interest rate and yen appreciation were external shocks to the Asian economies in 1994–96. Yen appreciation produced more Japanese direct investment in Asia. Foreign direct investment from Japan and other advanced countries provided the host countries with technology transfer and export capability. Asian exports grew at the rate of 20 to 30 percent. Low interest rates in the industrial countries including Japan produced the portfolio flows to the Asian economies. Those portfolio flows were used for investment rather than consumption. Asian economies were totally confident in their export-led growth strategy and the World Bank's "East Asian miracle" gave a seal of approval.

The currency "stability" vis-à-vis the U.S. dollar was instrumental in bringing in direct and portfolio investment. The investors had confidence in Asian countries that were virtually pegged to the U.S. dollar. The currency risk was considered by the investors and borrowers to be minimal, and the credit risk was also considered minimal due to high economic growth. The interest rates in the Thailand were higher than in the United States, and that invited bank deposits and short-term bond investment.

Growth in one Asian country is further amplified by growth in other countries in the region, as countries are connected by trade and investment flows. The "multiplier" of growth among countries in the region was considered to be rather high.

Large current account deficits in some countries were a source of concern for some economists. But high economic growth made it possible to assert that the "grow-out-of-debt" scenario would work. The low total productivity growth pointed out by Young (1992, 1994) and Krugman (1994) raised some doubts about the sustainability of high growth. But industrialization and sophistication of the industries were impressive enough to erase these doubts. Essentially, high growth invited more capital inflows, which produced even higher exports and economic growth. This is the virtuous cycle, as schematically depicted in figure 8.2. Until 1996, almost all observers were confident that the virtuous cycle would work for the foreseeable future.

The virtuous cycle was suddenly interrupted in 1996–97. Exports from most Asian countries sharply declined for several reasons. The yen depreciation from 1995 to 1997 reduced Asian goods' competitiveness. Slow growth produced lower economic growth. However, even before the crisis, there had been growth recession: From 1995 to 1996, the growth rate in

---

2. Japanese manufacturing companies also shifted their production to North America, partly to avoid trade conflicts and partly to prepare for NAFTA.

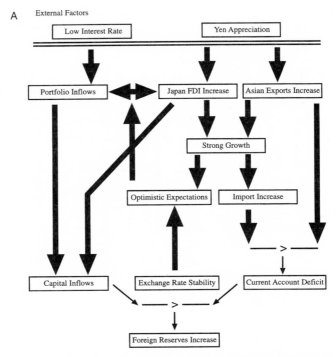

Fig. 8.2 *A*, **Capital inflow phase, 1990–95;** *B*, **Capital outflow phase, 1996–98**

Thailand was down from 8.8 percent to 5.5 percent, in Malaysia from 9.5 percent to 8.6 percent, in Singapore from 8.7 percent to 6.8 percent, and in Korea from 8.9 percent to 7.1 percent. On the other hand, growth was hardly affected in Indonesia, the Philippines, China, and Taiwan.

The growth rate of Japanese FDI and portfolio flows to Asia was slowing down due to the yen depreciation, but capital flows to Asia continued to be strong because of increased flows from Europe and the United States in 1996. In fact, there was no significant change in FDI and capital flows until the devaluation in July 1997.

Japanese FDI to Asia, mostly assembly plants of finished products, has stimulated industrialization. Factories built by Japanese FDI, however, continue to require imports of parts and semifinished goods from Japan. The domestic production of parts has become a challenge for Asian countries, which have recorded large trade deficits against Japan. (An exception is Indonesia, which records surpluses against Japan.)

Once the currency was destabilized in July–August 1997 among ASEAN countries, capital inflows to the region were cut substantially. As discussed above, net private capital flows to the Asian region in 1997 became only one-tenth that of 1996. Most of the outflows took place in

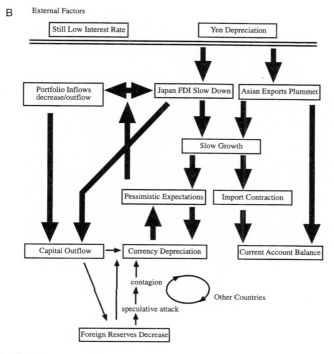

B   External Factors

Fig. 8.2   (cont.)

banking flow reversal. All the logic of the virtuous cycle worked in reverse. The vicious cycle (see fig. 8.2) set in after September 1997: Capital outflows caused the currency to depreciate; depreciation made the real economy and the banking sector weaker; weak economies made investors pessimistic; and pessimism encouraged further capital outflows.

8.2.3   FDI to Asia

Foreign direct investment to Asia has increased steadily during the 1990s. Table 8.2 shows the FDI flows to selected Asian countries and economies measured by host countries' authorities.[3]

From table 8.2 (panel A), it is evident that all Asian countries significantly increased FDI inflows during the 1990s. The increases are most

3. Precise definitions of FDI are different from country to country. Some countries include reinvestment, others do not; some countries count both the foreign investment and domestic partners' contributions in the case of joint ventures; most countries are on the reporting basis, while China is on the disbursement basis; and for Singapore and Malaysia, only manufacturing sectors are included, while for other countries, all sectors are included. For precise definitions, see the comparative table of definitions in Economic Planning Agency (1998, 80). Therefore, numbers are not exactly comparable across countries.

Table 8.2   **Gross FDI Inflows (US$ millions)**

A. Time-Series of FDI Inflows

	1990	1991	1992	1993	1994	1995	1996	1997
China	3,500	4,400	11,000	27,500	33,800	37,500	42,400	45,300
Korea	803	1,396	895	1,044	1,317	1,941	3,203	6,971
Taiwan	2,302	1,778	1,461	1,213	1,631	2,925	2,461	4,267
Singapore	1,224	1,425	1,678	1,966	2,833	3,423	4,054	3,979
Indonesia	8,751	8,778	10,323	8,144	23,724	39,915	29,931	33,833
Thailand	8,029	4,988	10,022	4,285	5,875	16,492	13,124	10,616
Malaysia	6,517	6,202	6,975	2,443	4,321	3,652	6,812	4,018
Philippines	961	778	284	520	2,374	1,871	967	1,993
Vietnam	512	1,147	1,926	2,615	3,722	6,524	8,497	5,550

B. Cross-Section by Source Country, 1995

	Korea 1995	Taiwan 1994	Hong Kong 1995	China 1995	Singapore 1995	Malaysia 1994	Philippines 1995	Thailand 1995	Indonesia 1995	Total
Total	1,914.4	1,523.9	566	37,520.5	4,852.4	4,242.5	1,871	16,492	39,914.7	108,897.4
United States	644.9	293.7	198	3,083	2,075.8	473.6	627.9	2,582.2	2,770.5	12,749.6
Japan	418.3	391	514.1	3,108.5	1,152.5	667.1	101.2	7,891.4	3,792	18,036.1
Germany	44.6	91.5		386.4		247.6	0.9	174.7	1,344.6	2,290.3
United Kingdom	86.7	29.2	−85.5	914.1		35.5	125	301.8	6,322.1	7,728.9
France	35.2	15.5		287		18.9		26.2	498.4	881.2
Italy				263.3		20		49.6	22.8	355.7
Netherlands	170.1	79.9	34.7	114.1		12.1	5.6		360	776.5
Switzerland	9.8		−39.6	63.5	13.2			100.3	44.9	192.1
Other EU		0						37.2	345.5	382.7
EU total	346.4	216.1	−90.4	2,028.4	13.2	334.1	131.5	689.8	8,938.3	12,607.4
Others	504.8	623.1	−55.7	29,300.6	1,610.9	2,767.7	1,010.4	5,328.6	24,413.9	65,504.3

Source: Panel A: Economic Planning Agency, Japan, *Asian Economies 1998* (in Japanese), 1998. Panel B: Economic Planning Agency, *Keizai Bunseki* (*Economic Analysis*), no. 156, "Applied General Equilibrium Analysis of Current Global Issues—APEC, FDI, New Regionalism and Environment" (by Kanemi Ban et al.), March 1998.

Notes: Based on each country's direct investment figures. China's figure is based on disbursement basis. Others are on the approval basis.

significant in China, where there was a fifteenfold increase in six years (1990 to 1996, before the East Asian crisis). Other countries—Korea, Singapore, Indonesia, Thailand, and Vietnam—saw from twofold to fourfold increases in the first six years of the 1990s.

Panel B of table 8.2 shows the source countries of FDI to Asia in 1995. Japan provided the most FDI to the total of nine Asian countries (the four newly industrializing economies [NIEs], ASEAN-4, and China). In some countries (Korea, Taiwan, Singapore, and the Philippines), the United States is the leading FDI source country, while for others, Japan is the leader. Europe collectively was investing into Asia in an amount similar to the U.S. investment. However, for most Asian countries, the impact of FDI is dictated by the behavior of Japanese and U.S. investors.

As the largest investor in the region, the role of Japan in FDI into Asia is crucial. The data are collected by the Japanese Ministry of Finance and are compiled on a voluntary (formerly mandatory) reporting basis. Table 8.3 shows changes in the Japanese FDI to the nine Asian economies in the 1990s.[4] The Japanese FDI to the world was below $5 billion a year until 1980. It grew to more than $10 billion in 1984. Only two years later, the amount had doubled, exceeding $22 billion. It reached $67 billion in 1989. In the beginning of the 1990s, FDI in fact declined to $36 billion before rising again to about $50 billion. Out of the total FDI in the postwar period—$617 billion—more than half took place in the 1990s. The largest recipient is Indonesia, closely followed by Hong Kong and China. Japan invested in the NIEs (Korea, Taiwan, Singapore, and Hong Kong) during the 1980s as well as the 1990s (the ratio of FDI investment in the 1990s to all the other years is below 60 percent). In contrast, more than 60 percent of Japanese FDI to Thailand, Malaysia, and the Philippines was made in the 1990s, reflecting both the rapid rise of these economies and the sharp rise in Japanese investment in them. At the beginning of the 1990s, Indonesia, Thailand, and Malaysia were the preferred destinations of Japanese FDI. On average Indonesia has received more than ¥150 billion (about $1.3 billion) annually in the 1990s. By the mid-1990s, however, China had become the top host of Japanese FDI. In 1995, China received more than ¥430 billion (about $4 billion) of Japanese FDI.

Foreign direct investment is often said to be a preferred form of investment for host countries. (Direct investment is usually defined as a purchase of more than 10 percent in equities of a particular company.) Compared with bank credits, bank deposits, or bonds, it is more difficult and costly to withdraw investments that have become factories and other real assets. Moreover, direct investment brings foreign management and tech-

---

4. These numbers do not necessarily agree with host countries' data presented in table 8.2, panel B. Possible reasons are mentioned in n. 3.

Table 8.3 FDI from Japan, Time-Series across Countries (US$ billions)

	1990	1991	1992	1993	1994	1995	1996	1997	1990–97 Total	1951–97 Total	1990s (%)
Total	56,911	41,584	34,138	36,025	41,051	51,478	48,101	54,025	363,312	617,206	58.9
Asia	7,054	5,936	6,425	6,637	9,699	12,380	11,634	12,194	71,958	112,423	64.0
Malaysia	725	880	704	800	742	576	573	792	5,792	8,298	69.8
Singapore	840	613	670	644	1,054	1,187	1,117	1,826	7,951	13,664	58.2
Thailand	1,154	807	657	578	719	1,242	1,406	1,869	8,432	11,701	72.1
Indonesia	1,105	1,193	1,676	813	1,759	1,608	2,419	2,517	13,089	23,524	55.6
Philippines	258	203	160	207	668	719	560	524	3,299	4,620	71.4
Hong Kong	1,785	925	735	1,238	1,133	1,149	1,489	696	9,150	17,215	53.2
Taiwan	446	405	292	292	278	456	522	450	3,141	5,427	57.9
Korea	284	260	225	245	400	450	416	443	2,723	6,577	41.4
China	349	579	1,070	1,691	2,565	4,485	2,515	1,989	15,243	17,716	86.0

Source: Annual Report of International Finance, 1999, Tokyo: Ministry of Finance.

Notes: FDI from Japan in this table is on the "reporting basis" of cross-border investment. It may not match with actual disbursement because some reported investment may be canceled and some will be carried out without reporting (no penalty). New FDI financed locally or reinvestment from past FDI is not covered by this table. FDI numbers are announced in yen after 1995. They are converted to the U.S. dollar using the average exchange rate of the year.

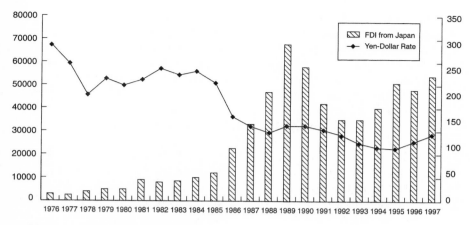

Fig. 8.3   FDI and the yen-dollar rate

nology transfers, which are expected to contribute to improving industrialization levels of a host country.

8.2.4   FDI Determinants

According to the virtuous cycle hypothesis, FDI from Japan is motivated by optimistic expectations of the prospects for the Asian economies and yen appreciation. The Japanese firms moved production to Asian economies as the yen appreciated. The level of the yen-dollar rate influences the flow of FDI from Japan to Asian countries. Figure 8.3 shows the correlation between the level of the yen-dollar rate and FDI from Japan to Asian countries.[5] This shows the rapid rise of FDI from 1986 to 1989, which appears to be a lagged response to the sharp yen appreciation (drop in the yen-dollar rate) from 1985 to 1988.

Foreign direct investment flows from Japan to Asia, in aggregate or in individual countries, can be analyzed in a more rigorous manner. For example, the yen-dollar exchange rate is an important motivation for FDI flows from cost-conscious Japanese manufacturing firms. For each industry, there seems to be a threshold value of the yen such that, when the firm judges that the yen is persistently above the threshold, it moves its production facility to Asia. It may take a year to convince the firm that the yen is "persistently" above a certain level, so the yen-dollar rate is lagged one period. But in this way generally the yen-dollar exchange rate can be understood to determine the locations of production facilities for

5. The Asian countries in this illustration include the four NIEs, ASEAN-4, China, and other broadly defined Asian countries. The category follows "Asia" in the Ministry of Finance data source.

Japanese exporters. The most labor-intensive portion of the production process is often outsourced first, after which the semifinished or finished products are then exported back to Japan or other countries.

Japanese FDI is also motivated by the prospect of the growth of Asian economies, as some of the products are intended to be consumed locally. Japanese auto makers have set up production, sometimes in joint ventures, in Thailand, Indonesia, and Malaysia, for example, mainly to sell autos in those countries. This is done primarily to avoid high tariffs on auto imports.

With these considerations, the log of FDI flow from Japan to Asia is regressed on the log of the yen-dollar exchange rate (lagged one year) and growth rate, in aggregate or the individual countries. Unfortunately, the FDI data are only available annually, and the sample period is from 1976 to 1997. Table 8.4 shows regression results.

In the aggregate specification, the log of aggregate FDI flows from Japan to eight Asian countries (four NIEs and ASEAN-4), FDI8, is regressed on the log of the yen-dollar exchange rate of year $t - 1$ and the average growth rate of these eight countries. The negative coefficient of the yen-dollar rate implies that FDI from Japan to the eight Asian economies tends to increase as the yen appreciates (drop of the yen-dollar rate). The positive coefficient of the growth rate implies that an increase in growth rates of the Asian economies tends to increase FDI from Japan to these economies.

For individual countries, the log of aggregate FDI flows from Japan to an Asian country is regressed on the log of the yen-dollar exchange rate of year $(t - 1)$, and the growth rate of year (t). Results in general confirm effects of the yen-dollar exchange rate and the optimistic expectation, driven by actual growth rate, on the FDI flows from Japan. In each economy, either the yen or the growth rate is statistically significant (at least at 5 percent, except for Taiwan, where there is significance only at 10 percent) with expected signs. In Korea, the Philippines, and Malaysia, both variables are significant.

8.2.5   Effects of FDI on the Economy

When foreign capital flows in as direct investment, it has at least two positive effects on the economy. First, it adds to the domestic saving to become funds for investment. Second, it often comes with technology spillovers.

There are many studies of the impact of FDI on the host country.[6] Recent studies, such as Belderbos, Capannelli, and Fukao (2000) and Urata

---

6. For an overview of the theory of FDI and its surge in the 1980s, see Graham and Krugman (1991, 1993). A seminal work on Japanese FDI is Kojima (1978).

Table 8.4   **Determinants of FDI**

Dependent Variable	Constant	Trend	Log(Yen($t - 1$))	Growth (of respective economy)	R^2 D.W.
Log(FDI8)	12.439	0.058	−1.111	0.068	0.86
	(3.02)	(1.38)	(−1.71)	(2.41)	1.65
	[0.003]	[0.168]	[0.087]*	[0.015]**	
Log(FDIKor)	10.842	0.024	−1.335	0.128	0.74
	(2.50)	(0.58)	(−1.83)	(7.18)	1.55
	[0.013]	[0.013]	[0.068]	[0.000]***	
Log(FDITai)	4.534	0.147	−0.397	0.069	0.81
	(1.32)	(4.33)	(−0.67)	(1.87)	0.59[a]
	[0.186]	[0.000]	[0.500]	[0.061]*	
Log(FDIHon)	12.854	0.056	−1.425	0.010	0.68
	(2.98)	(1.33)	(−2.03)	(0.18)	0.96[a]
	[0.003]	[0.184]	[0.042]**	[0.855]	
Log(FDISin)	15.820	0.022	−1.915	−0.027	0.81
	(2.76)	(0.46)	(−1.99)	(−1.38)	1.44[a]
	[0.006]	[0.643]	[0.047]**	[0.169]	
Log(FDITha)	6.520	0.164	−0.880	0.146	0.92
	(1.52)	(4.00)	(−1.25)	(4.26)	2.02
	[0.129]	[0.000]	[0.213]	[0.000]***	
Log(FDIInd)	5.673	0.057	−0.156	0.145	0.36
	(0.65)	(0.66)	(−0.11)	(2.37)	1.95
	[0.515]	[0.509]	[0.912]	[0.012]**	
Log(FDIPhi)	30.05	−0.101	−4.604	−0.060	0.86
	(4.38)	(−1.70)	(−3.98)	(−1.95)	2.16
	[0.000]	[0.089]	[0.000]***	[0.051]*	
Log(FDIMal)	−8.392	0.260	1.804	0.132	0.84
	(−1.37)	(4.54)	(1.80)	(4.27)	1.81
	[0.172]	[0.000]	[0.072]*	[0.000]***	

Note: Sample period, 1976:1–1996:1. Estimations are executed by RATS with the "Rubusterrors" option, using a consistent covariance matrix allowing for heteroskedasticity and autocorrelation (LAGS = 2), when necessary.

FDI8 = the sum of FDI from Japan to the four NIEs and ASEAN-4.

Log(Yen) = log of the yen-dollar rate, average of the year.

Growth rate = growth rate of the respective economy of the equation. In the case of FDI8, the growth rate is the weighted average of growth rates of the eight economies, with nominal GDP in dollars as weights, in percent.

t-statistics are in parentheses. Significance levels are in brackets.

[a]Sample period 1977:1–1996:1.

*Significant at the 10 percent level.

**Significant at the 5 percent level.

***Significant at the 1 percent level.

and Kawai (2000), show the significant technological spillovers to the subsidiaries in Asia from the Japanese manufacturing firms.[7]

The growth rate of the Asian economy is regressed on the level of FDI in year $(t - 1)$, the change in the yen-dollar exchange rate, Japan's growth rate, and the U.S. growth rate. Yen appreciation (drop in the yen-dollar rate) will enhance competitiveness of Asian exporters that compete with Japan's exporters. Therefore the change in the exchange rate will promote exports of the Asian economies, contributing to their economic growth. The coefficient of the change in the yen-dollar exchange rate is expected to be negative. The two most important markets for most Asian economies are Japan and the United States. Therefore, the income effects of Japanese and U.S. economic growth should appear in the economic growth of Asian economies as positive coefficients on Japan's economic growth rates and U.S. economic growth rates.[8]

Our main interest here is whether the lagged FDI will increase economic growth rate, controlling for the exchange rate and the economic growth rates of the two most important trading partners. The specification that only FDI of year $(t - 1)$ is included assumes a high dissemination of technology transfer and a temporary boost of productivity. The statistically significant positive coefficient on the FDI term is indicative of growth-enhancing technology transfers.

Table 8.5 shows the regression results. For the aggregate of the eight economies, results are consistent with the theoretical predictions mentioned above. The first row shows the result for the aggregate of the eight Asian economies (the four NIEs and ASEAN-4). The weighted average of growth rates of the economies tends to increase when the level of FDI from Japan

---

7. Belderbos, Capannelli, and Fukao (2000) examined the determinants of local contents among 157 Japanese electronics manufacturing subsidiaries in Asia. Local contents, the sum of in-house value added, and local outsourcing are considered to be a key for benefits to host countries, as they yield technology transfers. The authors found that local contents are lower in greenfield subsidiaries, subsidiaries of R&D-intensive parents, and export-oriented subsidiaries in ASEAN-4 and China. In contrast, local contents are higher in export-oriented subsidiaries located in the NIEs in those subsidiaries that have a higher domestic sales ratio, and in subsidiaries of a vertical keiretsu firm with strong intrakeiretsu supplier relationships. Urata and Kawai (2000) attempt to measure the intrafirm spillovers by comparing total factor productivity changes in the parent and subsidiaries. They found that capability to absorb technologies, reflected in educational level and in experiences in industrial production, in the host countries is very important for them to absorb technology transfer from foreign firms, both in the forms of intrafirm technology transfer and local technology transfers.

8. The major channel to growth from the exchange rate, Japanese growth, and U.S. growth is considered to be through exports. The "East Asian miracle" (World Bank 1993) was very much a story of tremendous export growth. In the 1980s and the first half of the 1990s, many economies in Asia achieved sustained export growth of 20 percent or more. Export promotion, instead of import protection, was a successful incentive. All Asian countries, which were agrarian economies only decades ago, rapidly modernized manufacturing firms and began to export more sophisticated manufactured goods. See Ito (1998b) for a detailed analysis of Asian export deceleration in 1995–96.

Table 8.5   Impact of FDI on Growth Rate

Dependent Variable	Constant	Log(FDIx(t − 1))[a]	YenChg	Japangr	USgr	$\bar{R}^2$ D.W.
Asia8gr	0.422 (0.20) [0.838]	0.589 (2.30) [0.021]**	−0.058 (−3.25) [0.001]***	0.361 (3.02) [0.003]***	0.237 (3.41) [0.001]***	0.14 1.79
Korea	0.603 (0.13) [0.212]	0.827 (1.25) [0.212]	−0.080 (−2.36) [0.018]**	0.445 (1.98) [0.235]	0.468 (1.19) [0.235]	0.14 1.89
Taiwan	5.598 (2.95) [0.003]	−0.241 (−0.77) [0.442]	−0.116 (−3.99) [0.000]***	0.474 (2.15) [0.032]**	0.497 (4.18) [0.000]***	0.51 2.74
Hong Kong	16.945 (4.68) [0.000]	−1.813 (−4.05) [0.000]***	−0.035 (−0.66) [0.512]	0.113 (0.40) [0.686]	0.268 (0.98) [0.327]	0.25 2.15
Singapore	8.925 (2.79) [0.005]	−0.056 (−0.14) [0.890]	0.073 (1.17) [0.238]	−0.216 (−0.55) [0.585]	0.097 (0.57) [0.566]	0.17 1.32
Indonesia	9.173 (1.24) [0.215]	−0.352 (−0.35) [0.720]	0.021 (0.73) [0.460]	−0.175 (−0.72) [0.469]	0.141 (0.54) [0.590]	0.21 1.22

(continued)

Table 8.5   (continued)

Dependent Variable	Constant	Log(FDIx(t − 1))[a]	YenChg	Japangr	USgr	$\bar{R}^2$ D.W.
Thailand	−1.250	1.108	−0.078	0.795	0.117	0.32
	(−0.66)	(3.88)	(−1.68)	(3.40)	(0.70)	1.00
	[0.508]	[0.000]***	[0.092]*	[0.001]***	[0.482]	
Malaysia	2.690	0.888	0.102	0.061	0.008	0.16
	(1.30)	(3.06)	(2.42)	(0.24)	(0.06)	1.24
	[0.193]	[0.002]***	[0.015]**	[0.810]	[0.951]	
Philippines	0.953	0.270	−0.012	0.497	−0.388	0.18
	(0.25)	(0.37)	(−0.16)	(1.09)	(−0.68)	0.95
	[0.803]	[0.710]	[0.875]	[0.276]	[0.493]	

Note: YenChg is the percent of the yen rate change from year (t − 1) to year (t).
Japangr is the growth rate of Japan.
USgr is the growth rate of the United States.
t-statistics are in parentheses. Significance levels are in brackets.

[a] x stands for the country.
*Significant at the 10 percent level.
**Significant at the 5 percent level.
***Significant at the 1 percent level.

in the preceding year is high, implying the boost to productivity associated with FDI. The growth rate becomes higher if the yen appreciates (a negative sign denotes yen appreciation) from the preceding year. Higher growth in Japan and the United States helps the growth of these economies. Estimates are that a 10 percentage point appreciation in the yen increases the average Asian growth rate by 0.5 percent in these economies. A 1 percentage point increase in Japanese and U.S. growth rates increases the average Asian growth rate by 0.4 and 0.2 percent respectively.

For individual economies, results are not as prominent as the aggregate equation. The FDI effect on growth is evident for Hong Kong, Thailand, and Malaysia. The yen-dollar exchange rate seems to influence growth in Korea, Taiwan, Thailand, and Malaysia. In these economies, a 10 percentage point appreciation in the yen boosts the economic growth rate by 1 percent. Japanese economic growth has a positive spillover effect on Korea, Taiwan, and Thailand, while U.S. economic growth has a positive effect only on Taiwan. Regressions for Singapore, Indonesia, and the Philippines did not produce any meaningful result.

8.2.6   Portfolio Flows

Portfolio investment consists of equities, bonds, and other securities investment. Bank deposits and lending and cross-border transfers between bank branches are usually classified as "other types" of capital flows. Table 8.6 shows three types of gross capital flows—FDI, portfolio, and other—to Korea, ASEAN-4, and China. The values are in terms of their percentage of GDP so that the relative impact to the economy can be assessed. Between 1994 and 1996 (that is, after the Mexican crisis and before the Asian crisis), these countries received a large amount of capital inflows, but composition was very different across countries.

China and Malaysia are the two countries that encouraged and received FDI. Their portfolio inflows are minimal or even negative in the case of Malaysia. Except for Malaysia in 1992 and 1993, other types of capital inflows were also very small.

Thailand received the most capital inflows measured as a percentage of GDP between 1993 and 1996. The total capital inflows were about 10 percent of GDP between 1993 and 1996. Most notably, portfolio inflows and other types of inflows were higher than FDI. Since portfolio or other types of capital flows are considered to be much more mobile than FDI, this feature was an ominous sign of the coming currency crisis, at least in retrospect. The precise mechanism of movement of "hot money," however, is debatable.

In the case of the Mexican crisis in December 1994, it has been argued that sudden and massive outflows in the days after the "surprise" 15 percent devaluation is to blame for bringing down the peso by almost 50 percent in one week. Mostly, short-term securities investment, especially

Table 8.6   Different Types of Capital Flows as a Percentage of GDP

Year	Korea			Thailand			Indonesia			Philippines			Malaysia			China		
	FDI	POR	OTH	FDI	POR	OTH	FDI	POR	OTH	FDI	POR	OTH	FDI	POR	OTH	FDI	POR	OTH
1990	0.31	0.09	2.17	2.85	-0.04	8.17	1.03	-0.09	3.29	1.20	-0.11	3.56	5.44	-0.59	-0.21	0.90	0.00	0.28
1991	0.40	0.79	2.38	2.04	-0.08	9.77	1.27	-0.01	3.62	1.20	0.28	5.00	8.31	0.35	1.03	1.08	0.14	1.11
1992	0.24	1.61	1.60	1.89	0.83	5.81	1.39	-0.07	3.47	0.43	0.29	5.55	8.89	-1.92	5.46	2.31	0.08	-0.85
1993	0.18	3.17	-0.44	1.44	4.36	5.38	1.27	1.14	1.38	2.28	1.65	4.52	7.80	-1.10	11.59	4.58	0.61	-0.10
1994	0.21	2.14	3.58	0.95	1.72	6.82	1.19	2.19	-0.87	2.48	1.41	5.56	5.99	-2.28	-2.64	6.25	0.73	-0.28
1995	0.39	3.04	4.70	1.23	2.43	11.53	2.16	2.04	1.20	1.99	3.53	4.10	4.73	-0.50	3.72	5.14	0.10	0.73
1996	0.48	4.37	5.07	1.29	1.98	6.55	2.72	2.20	0.11	1.82	6.14	7.63				4.93	0.29	0.16
1997	0.64	2.78	-1.88	1.97	2.80	-13.13	2.18	-1.23	-0.21	1.51	0.67	5.18				4.91	0.85	0.94

Source: IMF, International Financial Statistics, 1998.

Notes: FDI = foreign direct investment, line 78bed.
POR = portfolio investment, 78bgd.
OTH = other capital flows, 78bid.

tesobonos, by mutual funds and institutional investors were quickly withdrawn. Large portfolio investments have the potential to cause such a sudden reversal of capital flows when investors' assessments of the country change.

8.2.7 Bank Lending

In order to understand further what kind of money is invested, cross-border bank lending is investigated. Table 8.7, panel A, shows the balance of cross-border bank lending from industrial countries to developing countries. Total liabilities and short-term liabilities of recipient countries, as of end-June 1997, are shown in the first two columns. The breakdown of total lending, by countries of lending banks to each borrowing country is shown. The general tendency is for Japanese and European banks to lend to Asian countries, while U.S. and European banks lend to Latin American countries. Among the Asian countries, Japanese banks have higher shares in Thailand (54 percent), Indonesia (39 percent), and Malaysia (36 percent), while European banks, collectively, have more than 40 percent of shares in China, India, Malaysia, and Taiwan. Among the Latin American countries, U.S. banks' share is between 20 and 28 percent, while that of European banks is about 50 percent.

As a percentage of GDP, total bank liabilities are highest in Thailand (0.381), followed by Malaysia, Indonesia, and Korea. These countries have higher ratios of bank liabilities to GDP than any Latin American countries.

Bank lending behavior is supposedly different from securities investment. Although they are short term, bank loans are often made with the implicit understanding of rolling over indefinitely. If the interest rate spread is maintained, bank lending is usually rolled over. However, once banks suspect that credit (default) risk has become critical, any interest rate spread may not keep the bank lending.

In order to assess the vulnerability to potential problems with bank lending, such as a sudden refusal of roll-overs, short-term lending to the foreign reserves is examined. The ratio of the stock of short-term liabilities to foreign reserves represents one possible measure of this type of vulnerability. If the ratio is higher than one, it implies that if all banks refuse to roll over the short-term loans, foreign reserves will be exhausted. Among Asian countries, the ratio exceeds one in Korea, Indonesia, and Thailand. These three countries needed IMF assistance later in 1997. In retrospect, this indicator would have been effective in predicting the Asian currency crisis. Among Latin American countries, the ratio exceeds one in Argentina and Mexico.

In table 8.7, panel B, the changes in these bank liability indicators from 1993 to 1997 are shown. For Asian countries, bank liabilities tended to increase for both the total liability to GDP ratio and the short-term liability to foreign reserve ratio. The exception is China for the latter indicator.

Table 8.7   Cross-Border Bank Lending

A. International Bank Lending to Selected Emerging Markets, June 1997

	Total Liability (US$ millions)	By Maturity Short (Up to 1 year)	By Nationality of Lending Banks			Total/GDP (96)	Short-Term Liability/Foreign Reserves
			Japan	United States	Europe		
China	57,922	30,137	32	5	48	0.071	0.234
Indonesia	58,726	34,661	39	8	38	0.265	1.629
Korea	103,432	70,182	23	10	35	0.213	2.106
Malaysia	28,820	16,268	36	8	44	0.293	0.609
Philippines	14,115	8,293	15	20	48	0.162	0.726
Taiwan	25,163	21,966	12	10	57	0.092	0.243
Thailand	69,382	45,567	54	6	28	0.381	1.411
Asia	389,441	242,273	32	8	40		
Argentina	44,445	23,891	4	23	59	0.158	1.303
Brazil	71,118	44,223	7	23	45	0.096	0.772
Chile	17,573	7,615	8	23	51	0.146	0.447
Colombia	16,999	6,698	8	20	59	0.105	0.674
Mexico	62,072	28,226	7	28	43	0.185	1.187
Latin America	251,086	131,304	6	24	50		

B. Comparison of 1993 and 1997

	Total Liability/GDP		Short-Term Liability/Foreign Reserves		Japanese Share (%)		U.S. Share (%)		European Share (%)	
	1993	1997	1993	1997	1993	1997	1993	1997	1993	1997
China	0.047	0.071	0.509	0.234	40	32	2	5	36	48
Indonesia	0.192	0.265	1.622	1.629	55	39	8	8	27	38
Korea	0.119	0.213	1.397	2.106	30	23	10	10	33	35
Malaysia	0.166	0.293	0.210	0.609	41	36	10	8	34	44
Philippines	0.108	0.162	0.499	0.726	17	15	44	20	32	48
Taiwan	0.069	0.092	0.175	0.243	27	12	16	10	41	57
Thailand	0.207	0.381	0.733	1.411	55	54	8	6	24	28
Asia					40	32	9	8	34	40
Argentina	0.107	0.158	1.193	1.303	7	4	32	23	49	59
Brazil	0.118	0.096	0.930	0.772	17	7	17	23	43	45
Chile	0.227	0.146	0.557	0.447	9	8	33	23	42	51
Colombia	0.140	0.105	0.433	0.674	17	8	28	20	31	59
Mexico	0.138	0.185	1.029	1.187	7	7	35	28	42	43
Latin America					10	6	28	24	45	50

Source: Bank for International Settlements, *The Maturity, Sectoral and Nationality Distribution of International Bank Lending,* Basle, January 1998.

Notes: Europe includes Austria, Belgium, France, Germany, Italy, Luxembourg, Netherlands, Spain, and the United Kingdom. Total liability/GDP and short-term liability/foreign reserves are June 1993 and June 1997; the country shares are December 1993 and June 1997.

The cases of Thailand and Malaysia stand out in their increases in the latter indicator. Asian countries relied on bank lending for their economic development.

For Latin American countries, movements are mixed. Between 1993 and 1997, some countries increased the total liability to GDP ratio and the short-term liability to foreign reserve ratio, while other countries decreased these ratios.

The salient feature of the country share movement is the rapid expansion of European banks in both Asia and Latin America. In aggregate, European banks increased their share of lending to Asia by 6 percentage points, while the Japanese banks decreased lending by 8 points. In the case of Latin American countries, the European banks increased their share from 45 percent to 50 percent, while both the Japanese and U.S. banks decreased their shares by 5 percent. If the lending boom to Asia was to be blamed, which is a controversial "if," then the European banks were the ones that seemed to lay the last brick in Asia.

In China, Indonesia, Korea, Malaysia, and Taiwan, European banks increased their share markedly at the expense of Japanese banks, while in the Philippines, European banks increased their share at the expense of the United States. Only in Thailand did Japanese banks maintain a significant share.

8.2.8   Too Much Capital Flows?

As explained in the beginning of this section, capital flows, especially FDI, are in general part of a "virtuous cycle" in developing countries. However, when the volume of capital flows, especially short-term flows, becomes too large, monetary policy becomes difficult. (See Khan and Reinhart 1995 for one of the earliest studies of this topic. See also IMF 1995.) Capital flows to Asian countries have been sometimes massive, sometimes exceeding 10 percent of GDP.

When the size of capital inflows becomes larger than current account deficits, there is an appreciation pressure on the currency. Having adopted the de facto dollar peg, many Asian countries have resisted the appreciation pressure by intervening in the foreign exchange market. The stability in the exchange rate was considered to be important for nurturing exporting industries and inviting FDI inflows. As intervention continued, levels of foreign reserves among Asian countries soared in the 1990s. Intervention can be sterilized or left unsterilized. Unsterilized intervention will increase the monetary base, resulting in lower interest rates. The stimulating effect of lower interest rates may cause inflation if the economy is already at the full capacity of production, which is often the case for emerging market economies that attract massive capital inflows.

In order to avoid inflation, intervention can be sterilized. Sterilized intervention is a combination of foreign exchange intervention and domestic open market operation to keep the monetary base constant (in levels or in proportion to GDP in a growing economy). Sterilized intervention will, in theory, keep the interest rate level. In practice, however, the interest rate may rise. Suppose the initial capital inflows were in the form of FDI. The domestic end of sterilization is most likely done in the short-term money market. Then, the short-term interest rate may increase, while the long-term interest rate will decline. The higher short-term interest rate will invite more capital inflows in the form of portfolio investment. Hence, sterilized intervention may increase capital inflows.

Of course, a story related in terms of a policy decision tree is only a reflection of the well-known economics principle: It is impossible for a small, open economy to have free capital flow, a fixed exchange rate, and independent monetary policy. The usual theoretical answer to this impossibility problem is to float the exchange rate. A more heterodox answer is to adopt some mild forms of capital controls on short-term inflows, such as raising the reserve requirements on bank deposits by nonresidents or imposing withholding taxes on short-term instruments held by nonresidents. Many emerging markets did in fact adopt market-based capital controls (see IMF 1995).

There is an important footnote to the impossibility principle. Reducing fiscal deficits (or increasing fiscal surpluses) will ease the overheating pressure brought about by capital inflows. A contractionary impact of fiscal surpluses, such as tax increases or expenditure cuts, is mitigated by the monetary stimulus of unsterilized intervention. In fact, several Asian countries, such as Thailand, adopted this option in the beginning of the 1990s. Many Asian countries did run fiscal surpluses.

The lessons on the danger of too much capital inflow seem to have been learned from the Mexican peso crisis of 1994–95. The governments of many emerging markets have been vigilant about monitoring capital flows. The Asian countries, however, did run into a problem in 1997. The next section analyzes what happened to capital flows in the midst of the currency crisis in Asia.

8.3 The Currency Crisis of 1997

8.3.1 Overview

The Asian currency crisis has been analyzed in several papers and books (see Goldstein 1998; Krugman 1998; Montes 1998; Radelet and Sachs 1998, 2000). Various reasons for the currency crisis were suggested, with three factors identified as the major causes. First, the de facto dollar peg as the currency regime contributed to generating the crisis. China and Hong Kong have maintained the nominal fixed exchange rate to the U.S. dollar. Before the crisis, Thailand, Singapore, Malaysia, and Korea all adopted a currency basket system. However, they in fact had a high weight on the U.S. dollar in the basket (see Frankel and Wei 1994), so the exchange rate regime was de facto dollar pegged. In the period of yen appreciation, Asian exporters enjoy high growth contributing to an overall high economic growth, while in the period of yen depreciation, Asian economies' performance becomes less impressive. In fact, the yen depreciation from 1995 to 1997 was partly the reason for the lower growth of Asian economies (except the Philippines) in 1996–97. Moreover, the dollar peg with high interest rates invited in short-term portfolio investment. Investors and borrowers mistook the stability of the exchange rate for the absence of exchange rate risk.

Second, a weak bank and nonbank sector complicated the currency crisis. Key industries of many Asian countries relied on bank lending for their fund needs. Banks in Korea were lending to industries that were deemed to be important from the point of view of industrial policy. Many Indonesian banks, including one or two state banks, had been seriously burdened by nonperforming loans. Thai finance companies (nonbanks) had large nonperforming loans from an asset inflation (1992–93) and deflation (1996–97). A weak banking system becomes a signal to foreign speculators to attack the currency. When attacked, the central bank could employ a high interest rate policy to encourage capital to stay (or come in). But weak banks would make this policy counterproductive for the domestic banking policy. Knowing this, speculators are more willing to attack a country with a weak banking system. The banking crisis thus causes the currency crisis. Also, many bank liabilities and corporate debts were denominated in U.S. dollars. This was a reflection of the dollar peg. However, when the currency is devalued, dollar-denominated liabilities would become much larger in terms of the local currency. The currency crisis thus often causes the banking crisis. In this sense, the currency crisis and banking crisis are "twin crises" (Kaminsky and Reinhart 1996).

Third, short-term liabilities were mounting in some of the Asian economies, most notably in Thailand, Indonesia, and Korea (recall tables 8.6 and 8.7). This short-term capital can be withdrawn quickly to put pressure on the exchange rate. Withdrawal of funds started slowly in Thailand in 1996. Once the Thai baht was floated, neighboring countries were on the alert list of investors. Withdrawal of short-term funds intensified after September. The refusal to roll over bank loans particularly put pressure on the Korean won.

In addition to these common factors, there are idiosyncratic factors for individual countries. Speculative attack by hedge funds was a trigger for the Thai de facto devaluation, while Indonesia did not intervene so that foreign reserves were ample when it asked for a "precautionary" IMF program. The burst bubble was the major cause for weak financial systems in Bangkok, while reasons other than bubbles explain the weak banking system in Seoul and Jakarta. Controls on capital accounts had been eliminated for a long time in Indonesia, while there were significant capital controls in Korea. Thailand went through financial liberalization several years prior to the currency crisis. Political conflicts were a major problem in Indonesia, while Thailand and Korea had a solid political foundation.

More detailed analysis of mine can be found elsewhere (Ito 1998a, 1998b, 1998c). The rest of this paper is devoted to a concise summary of the observations, emphasizing the role of capital flows and offering some new perspectives. What is new in this paper is to emphasize the common factors and idiosyncratic factors of Asian currency crisis. But, first, background of the crisis must be described.

8.3.2 Shift of the Wind in 1995–96

Several changes in the Asian economic performance occurred in 1996. First, exports precipitously declined in most Asian countries. Export growth rates in 1994 and 1995 had reached 20 to 30 percent in China, Korea, Singapore, Thailand, Malaysia, and Philippines. Then, in 1996, exports of all countries went down sharply. Thai export growth, for example, slowed from more than 20 percent to virtually zero within a year. Korea and Taiwan suffered from a recession in the semiconductor industries. Figures 8.4 and 8.5 show the remarkable decline in exports of NIEs and ASEAN-4 in 1996–97. (More detailed analysis of export deceleration is found in Ito 1998b.) Second, because the region depended heavily on exports, the decline in exports substantially brought down economic growth.

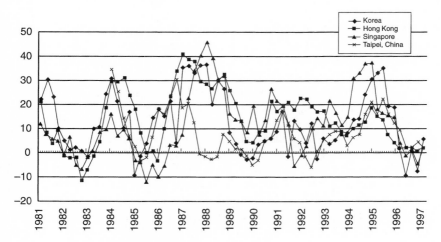

Fig. 8.4   Export ($value) growth rates 1981:1–97:2, NIEs
Source: IFS.

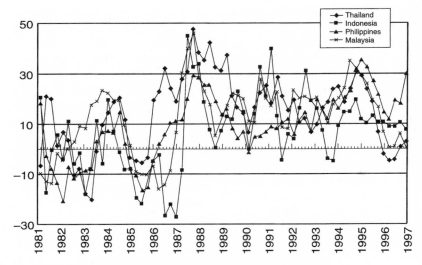

Fig. 8.5   Export ($value) growth rates: 1981:1–97:2, ASEAN-4
Source: IFS.

Third, in some countries, such as Thailand, stock prices started to decline. All of these changes were signaling the end of a long boom. Capital flows, which are sensitive to yields, started to reverse direction.

As exports declined and economic growth slowed, a virtuous cycle turned into a vicious cycle (recall fig. 8.2).

8.3.3   Thailand

The crisis first hit Thailand, which seemed most vulnerable by traditional measures. In 1996, the current account deficit of Thailand had reached 8 percent of GDP, the same level that brought Mexico into a currency crisis in 1994. The export growth rate plummeted from 20 percent per year to virtually zero, although a decline in the economic growth rate was only modest, from about 9 percent to 7 percent. In retrospect, it can be seen that Thailand had experienced a bubble economy from 1993 to 1995. The economy was overheated and stock prices had soared in 1993, as capital flows increased, especially in the form of portfolio flows. (See Ito 1998c and Nukul Commission 1998.)

Note that a major slow down in exports had also occurred back in 1984–85. Recall that the dollar appreciated. This supports the working hypothesis described in the previous sections that dollar appreciation (yen depreciation) is bad for Asian exports and growth.

After the asset bubble burst, banks in Thailand had nonperforming loan problems. In particular, finance companies faced serious problems and borrowed from domestic and foreign banks to finance their property loans. The weakness in the financial system, along with large current account deficits, invited speculative attacks on the baht.

The speculative attack came in several waves, between December 1996 and the spring of 1997, before the massive speculative attack in May 1997. For one week in May, some investors sold the baht in the spot market and others in the futures (or swap) market. The central bank intervened to defend the dollar peg regime, which had been in place since 1984. The dollar peg was considered to be instrumental to winning the confidence of foreign investors. The net result for the central bank position was to lose the foreign reserves in forward position. Although the announced, on-balance figure of the foreign reserve was close to $30 billion, it would be revealed later that the amount of off-balance dollar selling futures contracts exceeded $20 billion. Although the market knew that there were central bank interventions in the futures (swap) market, as a result of defending the baht from speculators, the precise number had not been known. When the central bank decided to float the currency on 2 July, the market was surprised only by the timing.

In the case of the Mexican crisis, the Mexican government did not announce the decline in foreign reserves for almost ten months. This nontransparent practice was criticized because market discipline could not work. This was one of the major reasons that the IMF introduced the Special Data Dissemination Standard (SDDS). In the Thai crisis, the foreign reserves figures were correctly disclosed every month with a one-month lag for statistics collection in compliance with SDDS. However, it was off-balance liability that was not disclosed to the market and that finally brought down the fixed exchange rate peg.

After the baht was floated, it immediately depreciated by 15 percent. Within a few weeks, Malaysia, the Philippines, and Indonesia either floated or significantly widened the band. Central banks of these countries intervened occasionally, but the amount of intervention was limited.

Although the rate was floated, the baht problem was not over. The Bank of Thailand was carrying large forward positions, and commercial banks had large short-term liabilities that could not be rolled over in the following months. The market knew that the Bank of Thailand was carrying forward contracts, but the amount was not accurately known. Thailand sought liquidity assistance from Japan and the United States in vain. In May the Bank of Thailand introduced capital controls that prohibited residents from lending money to nonresidents in offshore markets. The offshore rate deviated from onshore rates in May and June, but deviations became very small after the rate was floated. By the end of July, Thailand decided to ask for assistance from the IMF.

There were two kinds of problems in putting together an IMF program for Thailand. First, the amount of a support package would have to be large, and the limits on standby loans might not be enough. Second, it was not clear what kind of conditionality should be mandated. After intense negotiations, Thailand agreed to IMF conditions that included tightened monetary and fiscal policy, as well as concrete action programs for finance companies. The assistance program also included contributions from Japan and other Asian countries. The IMF's portion was $4 billion (close to 500 percent of quota for Thailand), while the other Asian countries, including Japan, pledged an additional $13.2 billion.[9] It was a quite unusual arrangement in that the Japanese Export-Import Bank provided a parallel loan of $4 billion with the IMF. The agreement was signed on 20 August 1997.

As mentioned above, one of the problems that Thailand experienced during the crisis was the fragile financial system, in particular nonperforming loan problems in the finance companies. In June, the worst sixteen finance companies were suspended. An additional forty-two finance companies were suspended before the IMF agreement was signed in August.

The IMF program did not put an end to the depreciation of the baht. As a result, other currencies in the region became further affected.

The loss of foreign reserves was a major concern in Thailand. The termination of foreign bank lending was also a cause and effect of depreciation. Capital flows out of Thailand were acute (recall fig. 8.1), and they took place mostly in terms of bank lending withdrawal (recall table 8.6).

8.3.4 Indonesia

Indonesia was thought to be doing well with macroeconomic management. The exchange rate had flexibility (slow depreciation vis-à-vis the U.S. dollar on the slide schedule with a band around it) and intervention was restrained to conserve foreign reserves. Indonesia's fundamentals were better than those of neighboring countries. Toward the end of September, however, the Indonesian rupiah depreciated suddenly, and it was decided in Jakarta to seek IMF assistance. This decision was a little surprising in that there was little evidence that the central bank needed to build up foreign reserves at that point. Also, problems in the Indonesian economy lie in the real sector, namely, inefficient big national projects and nontransparent family businesses of the president. The IMF conditions would look quite different from those of other plans.

On 5 November, the IMF program was agreed upon. At the same time, coordinated intervention by other Asian central banks was carried out to help prop up the value of the rupiah. A most remarkable aspect of the IMF program for Indonesia was to close down (not just suspend) sixteen banks with questionable assets. One bank was owned by President Suharto's son. Depositors were paid off only up to a certain amount. There

---

9. The IMF's contribution of $4 billion, or 500 percent of the quota allowed to Thailand, was considered to be the limit at that time, set by the precedent of the Mexican package.

was also no announcement about the health of the remaining banks. This caused a run on some of weaker banks.

One area of uncertainty that was not completely resolved was the size of corporate debts to foreigners. Many firms borrowed from foreign banks (in foreign currency denomination), but the total amount was not known at the time. The IMF, the World Bank, and the Asian Development Bank (ADB) decided to extend $23 billion to Indonesia. The United States, Japan, Singapore, and Asian countries pledged a "secondary line" of support.

Having an IMF program, however, did not stop the depreciation of the rupiah. Ironically, a real currency crisis came after the IMF program was signed. In mid-December, a rumor of President Suharto's poor health, based on his canceling an appearance at an international conference, pushed down the rupiah. Also, whether structural reforms would be carried out was questioned, especially after a bank that had been closed was replaced by a new bank managed by the same person at the same site. After President Suharto announced a new fiscal year budget on 6 January, which was more than 40 percent larger than the previous year's budget, the rupiah was sold heavily. The rate broke the level of 10,000 rupiahs to the dollar and went down to the point where its value was just one-sixth of what it was a year earlier. The rupiah's movement was much more influenced by political news. In the process of rupiah depreciation, foreign investors' role was not as heavy as capital flight.

8.3.5 Korea

Korea was initially thought to be remote from a crisis. Its fundamentals had turned around for better earlier in 1997. The exchange controls were reasonably stringent, so that it would be difficult to speculate against the won. Nonresidents cannot borrow the won. The Korean won did not depreciate more than 20 percent until the end of October. However, suddenly in November, the currency came under heavy pressure. Foreign banks that had lent to Korean banks decided to withdraw funds by not rolling over their lending. The Korean central bank reportedly lent foreign reserves, as foreign currency deposits, to commercial banks, which could not raise funds without paying prohibitively high risk premiums (Korean premium).

Korea decided to ask for IMF assistance toward the end of November, and obtained it on 4 December. Negotiation was carried out in an unusually fast manner. The amount of assistance was also unusually large. The IMF would provide $21 billion, supplemented by $10 billion from the World Bank and $4 billion from ADB. The United States, Japan, and other countries would provide additional $36 billion, bringing the total to $57 billion.

One of the most critical elements in the Korean crisis was how much foreign banks would roll over their lending to Korean banks. It was estimated that short-term liabilities would be close to $100 billion, if guarantees provided by the Korean corporations to their subsidiaries abroad are counted. Table 8.8 summarizes how Korea's external liabilities have changed.

Pressure on the won did not stop with the IMF program of 4 December. Acute problems in liquidity developed for Korean banks. It was not until 24 December, when administrative pressure from monetary authorities of G7 was applied on commercial banks to maintain lending to Korean banks, that the crisis was contained.

Recall that the short-term bank liability to foreign reserve ratio was highest in Korea (table 8.7). The Korean currency crisis, unlike that in Thailand or Indonesia, can be understood in terms of a "bank run" (Radelet and Sachs 1998, 2000).

8.3.6   Contagion

The experience of the Asian currency crises in 1997 certainly exemplifies the process of contagion. In the case of the Mexican peso crisis, the "tequila effect" did not succeed in changing the exchange rate regime, despite pressures on Argentina and Asian countries. In the case of Asian currency crises, however, depreciation spread to a large number of countries.

An interesting question for further research is whether a contagion model, such as that by Eichengreen and Rose (1996), would have predicted such spillovers at the point that Thailand decided to float. How much increase in probability of devaluation of the rupiah, the ringgit, and the Philippine peso would the Thai devaluation of 2 July have indicated? When investigated closely, a contagion process was more complicated than just spillovers from Thailand. Through the summer and up to September, the Thai baht was the currency most depreciated, followed by the rupiah, the peso, and the ringgit. From October to November, however, the degrees of depreciation for the baht and the ringgit were about the same, nearly 40 percent. Up to November, the Korean won depreciated only about 15 to 20 percent. As the crisis in Seoul deepened, the won depreciated further. This process indicates that the direction of spillovers changes over time. This was not the case in a simple devaluation-led crisis like Mexico's in 1994.

Figure 8.6 shows the changes in the currencies of the NIEs and ASEAN-4. From July to October, the baht was the most depreciated currency. Other ASEAN currencies were following the movement of the baht. The magnitude of the peso, ringgit, and rupiah depreciation was about one-half that of the baht depreciation until September 1997. Then the rupiah suddenly depreciated at the end of September. From September to November, the rupiah movement seemed to influence other currencies. The Korean won depreciated sharply in December, reflecting the liquidity problem mentioned above. The Indonesian rupiah depreciated further in January 1998. Therefore, sources of contagion seem to shift from one country to another, as political and economic shocks occur in various countries.

Table 8.8   Korea's External Liabilities

A. Residents' External Liabilities

	Short-Term Liabilities				Long-Term Liabilities					Grand Total
	Korean Banks	Foreign Bank Branches	Korean Corporations	Total	Korean Banks	Foreign Bank Branches	Korean Corporations	Public Sector	Total	
December 1996	65.2	12.8	22.0	100.0	41.5	3.2	13.6	2.4	60.7	160.7
December 1997	37.4	17.2	25.6	80.2	40.4	3.8	17.6	11.0	72.8	153.0

B. External Liabilities to International Banks (by length of maturities)

	Total	Maturities up to and Equal to One Year	Maturities over One Year and up to Two Years	Maturities over Two Years
June 1996	88,027	62,332	3,438	13,434
December 1996	99,953	67,506	4,107	15,884
June 1997	103,432	70,182	4,139	16,366

C. External Liabilities to International Banks (by lending bank nationalities)

	Total	Japan	United States	Germany	France	United Kingdom	Belgium	Netherlands
June 1996	88,027	22,512	9,582	8,529	6,994	4,140	2,312	1,651
December 1996	99,953	24,324	9,355	9,977	8,887	5,643	3,731	1,926
June 1997	103,432	23,732	9,964	10,794	10,070	6,064	3,899	1,736

Source: Panel A: Bank of Korea (quote from Nikkei, 29 January 1998). Panels B and C: Bank for International Settlements, *The Maturity, Sectoral, and Nationality Distribution of International Bank Lending*, Basle, January 1998.

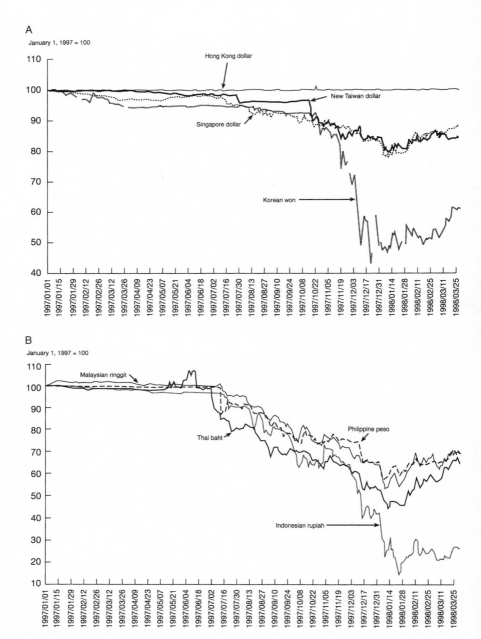

Fig. 8.6 *A*, Changes in the NIE currencies; *B*, Changes in the ASEAN-4 currencies

8.4   Lessons: Capital Flows and Reversal

Many reasons for capital inflows and their subsequent reversal have been suggested. Depending on which reason is accepted, the prescription to prevent a future crisis will be different. In this section, I review some of the current thinking on the issue.[10]

8.4.1   Moral Hazard

A first hypothesis is that capital flows to Asia can be characterized as the result of moral hazard. Some observers have pointed out that the implicit guarantee of deposits and financial institutions by emerging markets invites too much capital flows (Goldstein 1997, 1998; Krugman 1998; McKinnon and Pill 1996). Deposits that pay higher interest rates than the advanced countries are attractive to investors, especially when the economy is growing fast and the exchange rate stability appears to be secured. Mexico before 1994 and Thailand before 1997 are prime examples. The host countries received capital that could not be put into productive use with long-run returns exceeding the interest rates paid to creditors. In Mexico this resulted in a consumption boom and in Thailand a real estate boom. Investors remained complacent just before the crises because they felt their investments were protected by the government guarantee. In the case of Mexico, a large part of capital inflows were explicitly guaranteed because they were government securities (tesobonos). In the case of Thailand, capital flows that rapidly rose in 1994 to 1997 were through its offshore banking facility (BIBF). Investors must have felt that deposits were implicitly guaranteed because the government would bail out banks, as in advanced countries.

Moreover, investors may be reassured by the IMF's handling of Mexico in 1995, because investors were not asked to involuntarily roll over their investment. Borrowers were also mistaken. They might not have invested prudently. They tend to go for a high-risk, high-return project. If the project fails, the government would bail out the bank, and if the project succeeds, the bank benefits. The situation is well known in the deposit insurance literature. Explicit and implicit guarantees caused the moral hazard among investors and borrowers.

If moral hazard is the problem, there are two general solutions. First, prudential regulation on borrowers to avoid building the dangerous positions is important. Second, burden sharing on lenders, once a problem develops, would deter future irresponsible lenders.

One problem with this argument, however, is the timing of the crisis. Why the capital inflows reversed in 1997 so dramatically cannot be ex-

---

10. I owe thanks to Dani Rodrik for suggesting to me some of the policy implications included in this section.

plained adequately from moral hazard. If the blanket guarantee was to be believed, there was no reason for investors to flee so quickly.

Another problem with the moral hazard explanation is the cross-sectional differences. Why were Indonesia and Korea affected most severely, while the Philippines and Malaysia seem to have escaped the worst of the crisis? The blanket guarantees were the same for Asia, and other macroeconomic fundamentals were similar. The moral hazard argument alone would not explain the cross-sectional differences.

One way to combat the moral hazard problem is to ask the involved parties to take losses from easy lending and borrowing. Many observers point out the problem of moral hazard on the part of borrowers. However, overborrowing is overlending. How could the IMF ask "lenders," for example, those who held tesebonos in the Mexican crisis or who invested in fifty-eight companies in Thailand, to take losses? In fact, the IMF packages are usually strict enough that countries do not accept them willingly; the penalty of mismanagement has been severe, negative economic growth for Mexico and Thailand after the crisis. There is little scope for moral hazard on the part of a country to mess up the economy (at least for a decade or two after one crisis). The IMF did not "bail out the country" in Mexico's case because the money was repaid, as it will be in the Asian cases. What IMF packages bail out in Mexican-type crises is actually a group of lenders to the countries, by recovering the asset values (currency, stock, tesobonos, Brady bond, and other bond prices). If Mexican tesobonos holders had been asked to take some losses in the Mexican peso crisis, they might not have extended so much credit to some of the Asian countries that got into trouble in 1997. It would be difficult to devise a program to ask for a fair share of burdens on lenders without causing an international systemic risk, unless the IMF intervenes swiftly.

Another solution is to strengthen prudential regulations. Thailand relaxed banking regulations and capital controls without strengthening bank supervision. Finance companies were outside of the more strict bank regulation. A lack of policy contributed to easy lending. Korean merchant banks were outside the bank regulation that restricted large lending to a single customer. A lesson here is that financial deregulation has to be accompanied by strengthening bank and nonbank supervision.

8.4.2 Bank Run

Radelet and Sachs (1998, 2000) argue that the Asian currency crises were caused by sudden shifts in investors' behavior. Those countries that relied on short-term capital inflows were caught in the liquidity crisis when investors refused to roll over lending. In the case of the Mexican crisis of 1994–95, it was the short-term government securities (tesobonos) that became a focus of the rollover problem. In Thailand and Korea, domestic banks could not obtain enough dollars to repay short-term borrowings when rollovers were refused. Banks were not insolvent by any standard. It was a liquidity problem, or a problem of bank run (Diamond and Dybvig 1983).

When the currency crisis of a country is analyzed as a bank run, investors' behavior of withdrawing funds from the country does not have to be irrational. Given that other creditors are withdrawing funds, it is rational for an investor to withdraw funds. In fact, it is rational to be first in line.

The situation in Korea in November and December 1997 fits the bank run model best. Korean banks faced an acute liquidity shortage in U.S. dollars and the monetary authorities helped them by providing the foreign reserves (as deposits to commercial banks). When foreign reserves were exhausted, there was no choice but to ask for the IMF's assistance.

If the bank run is the sole reason for the crisis, establishing the international lender of last resort would be a good solution. Suppose that the IMF was the international lender of last resort. The IMF would inject foreign reserves, and the central bank would help commercial banks unwind the liability positions, when rollovers are refused. In fact, having the lender of last resort would convince lenders not to refuse to roll over. This is a straightforward application of the role of domestic central banks in international circumstances. If this analogy to the domestic central bank is applicable, the IMF lending to help prevent a bank run should not be tied to stringent conditionality, and disbursement must be quick and front loaded.

The reservation about such an international lender of last resort also comes from the analogy to the domestic central bank. In order to provide liquidity in a massive amount, the monetary authorities regularly conduct strict examinations. Weak institutions are closed or at least restricted in their activities. When a liquidity crisis occurs, the monetary authorities must have confidence that financial institutions are essentially sound before they inject liquidity to help financial institutions. Similarly, the monetary authorities of the emerging markets have to demonstrate that the liquidity support from the international lender of last resort does not go into insolvent institutions. Therefore any recommendation for establishing the international lender of last resort should be accompanied by the proposal to strengthen the banking system and its supervision. Moreover, in practice, it is often very difficult to distinguish the liquidity problem from the insolvency problem.

The best solution to an international bank run is to make the IMF the international lender of last resort. Funding has to be increased and conditionality has to be relaxed. If necessary, a regional fund, comprising the neighboring countries that may be affected by contagion, should be created to supplement the IMF coffer.

8.4.3   Herd Behavior

Similar to the idea of the bank run, the model of herd behavior has been developed in the finance literature. In relation to stock market crashes, Scharfstein and Stein (1990) and Banerjee (1992) developed the so-called herd behavior model. Investors behave as in a herd because it maximizes profits to behave as others do. When others are investing, it is more likely that prices will go up and the currencies will appreciate, so that it makes sense to invest. When others are withdrawing, it is rational to go along because prices and currencies will go down. The self-fulfilling prophecy works.

One might question this simple model by arguing that markets have a self-regulating mechanism that would bring the economy back to equilibrium. A currency depreciation shock by capital flows should promote exports and thus in the long run increase pressure to appreciate the currency. For example, depreciation would hurt the balance sheet of banks and corporations that borrowed in foreign currencies. Thus, lending from banks would be limited and the interest rate would rise. Business activities would be depressed and would struggle to obtain working capital. Depressed domestic demand, consumption, and investment would further depress business activities.

In the meantime, if the inflation rate increases due to the depreciated currencies, the real exchange rate does not warrant much increase in exports. Foreign debts (denominated in nominal terms in foreign currencies) are mushroomed in local currencies.

The fate of Indonesia seems to fit this description of herd behavior and multiple equilibria well. How else could we explain the still-suffering economy (at -15 percent growth rate) at the exchange rate level that is one-sixth of the precrisis level? Other countries, such as Thailand and Korea, also have negative growth, even though their currencies have depreciated by 30 to 40 percent.

Herd behavior can be dealt with by capital controls or a stand-still agreement imposed by the IMF. Temporary capital controls on outflows may calm the market. A stand-still agreement would be an effective tool to start the negotiation process of corporate debts or sovereign bonds. This would eliminate the incentive to withdraw funds first.

8.4.4   Irrational Exuberance and a Bubble

The last model is more ad hoc. Excessive capital inflows can be characterized by irrational "exuberance" (a famous word of Alan Greenspan's on U.S. stock prices) that sooner or later results in an eventual crash. The stock prices and real estate prices of some Asian cities—for example, in Thailand, Hong Kong, and Malaysia—increased so much because of the capital inflows, which were prompted by high economic growth. However, at least in the end, the level of stock prices could not be rationalized by fundamentals. The stories of real estate bubbles in some Asian cities were similar to Japan's bubble and burst cycle from 1985 to 1998. Ito and Iwaisako (1996) explain the stock price movements by applying the stochastic bubble model, à la Blanchard and Watson (1982). A similar methodology can be applied to the Asian crisis.

8.4.5 Early Warning Signal

It has become a popular exercise to look for variables that help predict a future crisis. Frankel and Rose (1996), Eichengreen and Rose (1996), Goldstein (1996), and Kaminsky, Lizondo, and Reinhart (1998) have contributed to the literature of early warning signals. Frankel and Rose (1996) identify, for example, the size of current account deficits and the composition of bank borrowing (short-term and foreign-currency-denominated loans) as factors that increase the probability of a future crisis (large devaluation). Goldstein (1996) lists seven factors as presumptive indicators of vulnerability to a financial crisis: an upturn in international interest rates; a mismatch between the government's/banking system's short-term liabilities and its liquid assets; a large current account deficit; an overvalued exchange rate; a weak banking system and large fiscal deficits that put constraints on the authorities' willingness to increase interest rates; a boom in bank lending followed by a fall in asset prices; and high susceptibility to contagion due to similarities to a financial crisis elsewhere (more likely if the crisis is close by). Eichengreen and Rose also confirm a contagion effect, namely that probability of a crisis increases if a neighboring country experiences a crisis. Kaminsky, Lizondo, and Reinhart (1997) attempt to calculate appropriate widths of thresholds of various macro variables. When an indicator moves beyond certain threshold levels, it is treated as a signal. In any given month, the system would estimate the probability of a crisis within the following twenty-four months conditional on the indicators issuing signals at that moment. The variables are chosen on the basis of indicating correct signals (while minimizing false signals) for a crisis. Although the results are encouraging, there are as many false signals as correct signals even for variables that are less noisy.

8.5   Concluding Remarks

In this paper, characteristics of capital flows in Asia before and after the crisis of 1997 were summarized. Although some common factors are available, each crisis has its own idiosyncratic factors. In fact, Thailand, Indonesia, and Korea present much different kinds of "food for thought," just as their ethnic foods are different. Thailand is much like a classic attack on the reserve for a country with large current account deficits, while Korea seems to be an international bank run. Indonesian problems cannot be understood without investigating political and social shocks. These differences reflect underlying bank and corporate liability structures, which is a result of their policies during the capital inflow phase. The capital outflow crisis investigation must begin with research on capital inflows. For this reason, the detailed data analyses and the description of idiosyncratic factors in this paper may be useful for further research.

References

Banerjee, Abhijit. 1992. A simple model of herd behavior. *Quarterly Journal of Economics* 107:797–817.

Belderbos, René, Giovanni Capannelli, and Kyoji Fukao. 2000. The local content of Japanese electronics manufacturing operations in Asia. In *The role of foreign direct investment in East Asian economic development,* ed. T. Ito and A. O. Krueger. Chicago: University of Chicago Press.

Blanchard, Olivier, and Mark W. Watson. 1982. Bubbles, rational expectations, and financial markets. In *Crisis in the economic and financial structure,* ed. P. Wachtel. Reading, Mass.: Lexington Books.

Diamond, D., and P. Dybvig. 1983. Bank runs, deposit insurance and liquidity. *Journal of Political Economy* 91:401–19.

Economic Planning Agency. 1998. Assessment of trade/investment liberalization and environmental policy using an applied general equilibruim model. *Economic Analysis,* no. 156 (in Japanese). Tokyo: Economic Planning Agency, Economic Research Institute.

Eichengreen, Barry, and Andrew Rose. 1996. Contagious currency crises: Channels of transmission. In *Changes in exchange rates in rapidly developing countries: Theory, practice, and policy issues,* ed. T. Ito and A. O. Krueger. Chicago: University of Chicago Press.

Frankel, Jeffrey A., and Andrew K. Rose. 1996. Currency crashes in emerging markets: Empirical indicators. NBER Working Paper no. 5437. Cambridge, Mass.: National Bureau of Economic Research, January.

Frankel, Jeffrey A., and Shang-Jin Wei. 1994. Yen bloc or dollar bloc? Exchange rate policies of the East Asian economies. In *Macroeconomic linkage: Savings, exchange rates, and capital flows,* ed. T. Ito and A. O. Krueger. Chicago: University of Chicago Press.

Goldstein, Morris. 1996. Presumptive indicators/early warning signals of vulnerability to financial crises in emerging-market economies. Washington, D.C.: Institute for International Economics, January. Photocopy.

———. 1997. *The case for an international banking standard.* Washington, D.C.: Institute for International Economics.

———. 1998. *The Asian financial crisis: Causes, cures, and systemic implications.* Washington, D.C.: Institute for International Economics.

Graham, Edward M., and Paul R. Krugman. 1991. *Foreign direct investment in the United States.* 2d ed. Washington, D.C.: Institute for International Economics.

———. 1993. The surge in foreign direct investment in the 1980s. In *Foreign direct investment,* ed. Kenneth A. Froot. Chicago: University of Chicago Press.

IMF. 1995. *International capital markets: Developments, prospects, and policy issues.* Washington, D.C.: International Monetary Fund.

———. 1996. *International capital markets: Developments, prospects, and policy issues.* Washington, D.C.: International Monetary Fund.

Ito, Takatoshi. 1998a. Bail-out, moral hazard, and credibility: IMF and World Bank policies in crises of the 21st century type. Paper presented at the Wharton Conference on Asian Twin Financial Crises, Tokyo, 10 March.

———. 1998b. Asian exports: Principal causes of deceleration. Asian Development Bank. Mimeo.

———. 1998c. The development of the Thailand currency crisis: A chronological review. *Japan Export-Import Bank, RIID Review* 24 (September): 66–93.

Ito, Takatoshi, and Tokuo Iwaisako. 1996. Explaining asset bubbles in Japan. *Monetary and Economic Studies, Bank of Japan* 14 (July): 143–93.

Kaminsky, Graciela L., Saul Lizondo, and Carmen M. Reinhart. 1998. Leading indicators of currency crises. *IMF Staff Papers* 45, no. 1 (March): 1–48.

Kaminsky, Graciela L., and Carmen M. Reinhart. 1996. The twin crises: The causes of banking and balance-of-payments problems. Washington, D.C.: Board of Governors of the Federal Reserve System, February. Photocopy.

Khan, Mohsin S., and Carmen M. Reinhart. 1995. Macroeconomic management in APEC economies: The response to capital inflows. In *Capital flows in the APEC region,* ed. M. Khan and C. Reinhart, 15–30. IMF Occasional Paper no. 122. Washington, D.C.: International Monetary Fund.

Kojima, Kiyoshi. 1978. *Direct foreign investment.* London: Croom Helm.

Krugman, Paul. 1994. The myth of Asia's miracle. *Foreign Affairs* 73, no. 6 (November/December): 62–78.

———. 1998. What happened to Asia? Unpublished paper, Massachusetts Institute of Technology. Available at http://web.mit.edu/krugman/www/disinter.html.

McKinnon, Ronald, and Huw Pill. 1996. Credible liberalizations and international capital flows: The overborrowing syndrome. In *Financial deregulation and integration in East Asia,* ed. T. Ito and A. O. Krueger. Chicago: University of Chicago Press.

Montes, Manuel F. 1998. *The currency crisis in Southeast Asia.* Updated ed. Singapore: Institute of Southeast Asian Studies.

Nukul Commission. 1998. The Nukul Commission report: Analysis and evaluation on facts behind Thailand's economic crisis. Bangkok: Nation Multimedia Group.

Radelet, Steven, and Jeffrey Sachs. 1998. The East Asian financial crisis: Diagnosis, remedies, prospects. Paper presented at Brookings Panel, Washington, D.C., 26–27 March.

———. 2000. The onset of the East Asian financial crisis. In *Currency crises,* ed. Paul Krugman. Chicago: University of Chicago Press. Forthcoming.

Scharfstein, David, and Jeremy Stein. 1990. Herd behavior and investment. *American Economic Review* 80 (June): 465–79.

Urata, Shujiro, and Hiroki Kawai. 2000. Intrafirm technology transfer by Japanese manufacturing firms in Asia. In *The role of foreign direct investment in East Asian economic development,* ed. T. Ito and A. O. Krueger. Chicago: University of Chicago Press.

World Bank. 1993. *The East Asian miracle: Public policy and economic growth.* Washington, D.C.: World Bank.

Young, Alwyn. 1992. A tale of two cities: Factor accumulation and technical change in Hong Kong and Singapore. *NBER macroeconomics annual,* ed. Olivier Blanchard and Stanley Fischer, 13–54. Cambridge, Mass.: MIT Press.

————. 1994. Lessons from the East Asian NICS: A contrarian view. *European Economic Review* 38:964–73.

Comment   Dani Rodrik

Takatoshi Ito suggests in his conclusions that the crises in Thailand, Indonesia, and Korea offer different types of "food for thought," just as the region's ethnic foods differ. While the spices may have been different in each case, it seems to me that these were just condiments on the same old dish that international capital markets have been serving with regularity over the last twenty years.

Whether driven by moral hazard, financial panic, herd behavior, or irrational exuberance, the boom-and-bust pattern of international lending appears to be integral to the operation of international financial markets. When the crisis strikes, it is always easy to find weaknesses in the borrowing economies to justify ex post the reversal of flows: crony capitalism, industrial policies, exchange rates pegged too rigidly to the dollar, weak financial sectors, implicit insurance, and so on. No one can doubt that these were problems of varying degrees of seriousness in the East Asian economies most severely affected. But it takes a large buildup of short-term external liabilities—denominated in a currency other than your own—to metamorphose these weaknesses into the financial and real meltdowns that Thailand, Indonesia, and South Korea have experienced. Figure 8C.1 shows the close correlation between exposure to short-term debt and currency collapse in East Asia.

Asian-style capitalism—with different ethnic spices in each case—did not evolve in the last five years. Furthermore, this is not the first time that many of these countries have experienced external imbalances. South Korea had a mini debt crisis in 1980 that cost it 5 percentage points of gross domestic product (GDP) in one year. But as Ito emphasizes, large capital inflows, particularly of a short-term kind, are a relatively recent phenomenon. We get the real fireworks only when domestic problems meet international financial markets.

There is much useful information in Ito's paper on the patterns of capital inflows to the region. I must say I am less convinced than he is by the evidence on spillovers from direct foreign investment (DFI). Regressions of output growth on lagged DFI do not provide particularly meaningful evidence, in part because investors are forward looking and in part be-

Dani Rodrik is professor of international political economy at the John F. Kennedy School of Government, Harvard University, and a research associate of the National Bureau of Economic Research.

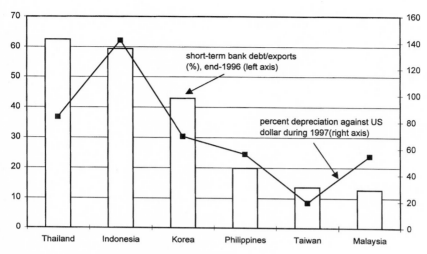

Fig. 8C.1   Short-term debt and currency collapse

cause reverse causality cannot be ruled out when there is persistence in the time series. The more deserved compliment is that DFI moves in rather than out when the short-term investors have bailed out.

It would have been nice if Ito's paper had ended on a more conclusive tone, instead of yielding ground to all the contending theories of the crisis. Nevertheless, it is useful to have a balanced account that does all of them justice.

9

Capital Flows to Central and Eastern Europe and the Former Soviet Union

Stijn Claessens, Daniel Oks, and Rossana Polastri

9.1 Introduction and Background

Capital flows to Central and Eastern Europe (CEE) and the former Soviet Union (FSU) represent a relatively small, albeit growing, share of capital flows to developing countries. Taking all flows together, total net flows to these twenty-five countries were about $44 billion in 1996 (and a preliminary figure of $57 billion for 1997),[1] or about one-eighth of aggregate net flows to all developing countries. These countries accounted, however, for about 20 and 22 percent, respectively, of all developing countries' gross domestic product (GDP) and exports in 1996. As a fraction of their GDP, total inflows were consequently smaller than for many other developing countries, and averaged about 5.4 percent over the 1990–96 period. Taking debt service and capital flight into account, resource inflows were much lower and even negative to some countries (capital flight from Russia alone has been estimated at some $50 billion for 1992–96).

The lower level of capital flows to these countries occurred during a period when global capital flows were very buoyant. Private capital flows to developing countries increased dramatically during the 1990s, especially foreign direct investment (FDI) and portfolio equity investment.

Stijn Claessens is a lead economist in the Financial Sector Strategy and Policy Group at the World Bank. Daniel Oks is manager of the economic analysis department of the Central Bank of Argentina. Rossana Polastri is an economist in the Europe and Central Asia Region at the World Bank.

The authors thank their discussant, Michael Dooley, other participants in the preconference and conference, Ricardo Martin, Frank Lysy, Marcelo Selowsky, and participants in a World Bank workshop for useful comments. The views expressed in this paper are those of the authors and do not necessarily represent those of the World Bank.

1. Excluding grants, the total amount of net flows amounted to US$41 billion in 1996.

While flows to CEE and FSU have also been growing fast—for example, portfolio and FDI flows increased from $1.4 billion in 1990 to $23.5 billion in 1996—between them they still attracted only about 15 percent of total private capital flows to all developing countries in 1996.[2] In 1996, FDI to CEE and FSU, for example, was only $14 billion, equivalent to the total amount received by Malaysia and Mexico in that year. The distribution of FDI flows has also been highly uneven. Over the 1992–96 period, Russia and the Visegrad countries (the Czech Republic, the Slovak Republic, Poland, and Hungary) received the bulk of FDI flows, while many other countries in the region are still all but untouched by FDI.

The still relatively low level of capital flows, especially of private capital, reflects the special nature of the economic development processes in these countries. Several factors are important. First, CEE and FSU are all transition economies. This means, for one thing, that market reforms did not get underway until the end of the 1980s for most of CEE—with the notable exceptions of Hungary and Poland—and until 1991 for the FSU. The transition process also influenced the nature and composition of the capital flows. In particular, early on in the transition the capital flows were mainly fiscally driven and often from official sources. Annual net flows of official development finance—including official development assistance (grants and official concessional loans) and official nonconcessional loans—represented about 40 percent of total net flows in 1990–96 and over 100 percent in 1990–91 (as private net flows were negative in those years). This reflected the sharp deterioration of fiscal revenues at the onset of the transition process and the lack of credit worthiness of some countries. Associated with this process were low private capital inflows, and, as mentioned, for some countries substantial amounts of capital flight. The low level of private inflows was due to a variety of factors, including partial and incomplete reforms or an uncertain commitment to reform in most countries, high political and social costs of the transition process itself, and high levels of corruption and political instability (several countries in the FSU have been affected by civil wars). Many countries in CEE also lost financing and aid from the Soviet Union—they had received a large amount of aid, including above-market export prices and below-market import (especially energy) prices, from the Soviet Union (World Bank 1992), but these flows essentially ceased in 1989—implying a larger financing need for their governments.

In more recent years, there has been a more rapid inflow of private capital, as reform efforts have consolidated and economic prospects improved and, for some countries, as European Union (EU) integration became a possibility for the near future. For some countries, short-term capital has recently become an important source of external financing. Since

---

2. Portfolio and FDI flows to all developing countries in 1996 were $155 billion.

most countries have been "latecomers" to the phenomenon of large private capital inflows, they have not experienced much of the overheating phenomena that have affected other developing countries in the past (Latin America) and recently (East Asia). The main exceptions, indeed, were precisely some of the earlier and faster reformers like Hungary, Poland, the Czech Republic, and Estonia.

At the same time, the transition to a market economy is far from complete for most of the economies in the region. Distortions in factor markets are still prevalent and the institutional development in areas crucial to beneficial financial integration—particularly the legal system and financial sector—is still limited, especially in many of countries of the FSU. Deficiencies, which in other developing countries have been associated with subsequent problems, including poor resource allocation and financial crises, are thus still prevalent in many transition economies. By tackling these issues now, these countries could presumably stand to gain more of the benefits and to run less of the risks associated with more financial integration and large private capital flows.

This paper investigates the amounts, types and sources of capital flows to these countries. It tries to determine the motivation of the various sources of capital flows, distinguishing global and country-specific factors. The paper provides estimates of the (econometric) relationships between, on one hand, the different kinds of capital flows and, on the other hand, the reform process, macroeconomic fundamentals and performance, and external factors. Because the history of capital flows to CEE and FSU is short, historical analysis has significant limitations and econometric estimation is difficult. Lessons from experiences of other countries with private capital flows may, however, be applied to these countries, when taking into account their special characteristics.

The paper is organized as follows. Section 9.2 briefly describes the facts about capital flows to these countries. Section 9.3 discusses important links and relationships between macroeconomic variables and the capital flows, including some of the basic motivations and causes for capital flows. Section 9.4 describes and analyzes the policy framework and policy responses in those countries that received the bulk of capital flows. Econometric tests are presented in section 9.5, while section 9.6 discusses the issues surrounding capital flows that may in the future arise in these countries, and provides some conclusions.

9.2   Facts about Capital Flows to Central and Eastern Europe and the Former Soviet Union

We start by providing some simple raw statistics for the various capital flows. In principle, one can distinguish capital flows by destination (e.g., public versus private); by type (e.g., long-term and short-term debt, FDI, bonds and equity portfolios); and by origin (e.g., commercial, that is private, versus official creditors). One can also combine the three distinctions, for example, by splitting debt-type flows into public and private debt, with the latter further into long and short, and by origin, for example, commercial versus official. For our purposes, and given the data we have at hand and the patterns in capital flows we observe, we create five categories of capital flows: public debt (official) flows; commercial long-term (LT) debt flows; commercial short-term (ST) debt flows; FDI flows; and portfolio (bond and equity) flows. For some purposes, it would be useful to further split commercial debt flows into those going to the banking system and those going to other sectors of the economy, but it turns out that this cannot be done for most of the countries given the data available. Our focus is on net flows; however, while we occasionally also discuss "capital flight" (other than that captured through short-term flows), we do not net out capital flight from our net flow measures. We group countries in two regions: (1) Central Europe and the Baltics, and (2) the rest of Eastern Europe, the Caucasus, and Central Asia.[3] The group of countries in Central Europe is relatively homogeneous. The countries in the second regional group have more diverse economic characteristics.[4]

Descriptive statistics for the different types of flows for all countries (means, medians, standard deviations of flows) are provided in table 9.1. Table 9.2 describes the composition of capital flows by source (private and official) and by type (long-term, short-term, portfolio, and FDI). Total capital flows rose from around $1 billion in 1990 to $57 billion in 1997. Pooling together all observations (by country and by year) and measuring them as a share of GDP, the largest types of flows during the 1992–96 period were official debt flows and FDI (on average, respectively, 2.7 percent and 2 percent of GDP), followed by portfolio flows (0.4 percent of GDP). Of all these flows, the highest standard deviation was for official flows (standard deviation of 3.6 percent of GDP). The following other stylized facts can be observed.[5]

First, the share of official flows has declined sharply over the period (fig. 9.1). At the beginning of the transition, official flows increased sharply, with bilateral and multilateral sources accounting for most of the flows. In 1992, as some of the transition economies regained access to international credit markets, private flows began to exceed official flows and by 1997

3. The CEE and Baltics country group includes Albania, Bulgaria, Croatia, the Czech Republic, Estonia, Latvia, Lithuania, FYR Macedonia, Hungary, Poland, Romania, Slovakia, and Slovenia. The FSU country group includes Armenia, Azerbaijan, Belarus, Georgia, Kazakhstan, the Kyrgyz Republic, Moldova, Russia, Tajikistan, Turkmenistan, and Ukraine.
4. We had to be careful for the exchange rate used in calculating dollar GDP given the large changes in real exchange rate for this period. Some smoothing was necessary, which was done using the World Bank Atlas $-GDP figures.
5. Sobol (1996) also highlights the rapid surge in private capital flows to CEE.

Table 9.1   Capital Flows to CEE and FSU Countries: Descriptive Statistics (percentage of GDP per year)

	Total Capital	Private Capital	Official Capital	FDI	Portfolio	Commercial Debt	Short-Term Debt
Mean	5.92	3.22	2.70	1.98	0.41	0.85	0.56
Median	4.89	2.11	1.78	1.03	0.00	0.18	0.12
Maximum	21.02	17.48	15.04	17.48	10.15	10.92	13.10
Minimum	−3.12	−1.95	−2.98	0.00	−3.33	−2.98	−10.67
Standard deviation	4.84	3.73	3.57	2.61	1.66	1.89	2.49

Table 9.2   Size and Composition of Net Capital Flows (US$ millions)

	1990	1991	1992	1993	1994	1995	1996	1997
	Central Europe, Baltics, and FSU							
By source								
Private flows	-4,047	4,700	13,231	18,939	14,693	31,231	32,930	41,748
Official flows	4,946	13,237	10,423	10,001	10,914	12,578	11,440	15,587
Grants (excluding technical cooperation)	640	3,924	4,718	3,683	4,895	5,217	2,479	4,269
IMF	328	3,641	1,836	2,045	2,352	4,745	3,325	3,400
By type[a]								
Long-term debt flows	10,011	6,863	12,932	11,528	5,481	9,269	12,351	20,030
Short-term debt flows	-11,181	-262	-104	-107	2,720	3,106	2,522	3,480
Foreign direct investment	300	2,246	3,237	5,696	6,406	16,116	14,440	14,939
Portfolio	1,071	1,422	1,047	6,194	3,756	5,177	9,144	8,890
	Central Europe and Baltics							
By source								
Private flows	749	4,179	2,538	16,018	12,448	28,072	21,111	
Official flows	585	5,259	4,191	3,181	4,223	4,665	2,600	
Grants (excluding technical cooperation)	40	3,380	2,116	1,477	2,386	3,749	1,404	
IMF	328	3,641	823	206	107	-2,723	-795	

By type[a]	1,893	9,291	5,448	18,026	14,393	26,085	21,513
Long-term debt flows	974.1	2,541	1,215.6	6,027	3,588	8,131	6,909
Short-term debt flows	−780.5	−761.9	−1,144.2	379	2,201	3,483	2,272
Foreign direct investment	300	2,449	3,507	5,220	4,978	11,874	9,370
Portfolio	1,071	1,422	1,047	6,194	3,519	5,321	3,757
Former Soviet Union							
By source							
Private flows	−4,796	521	10,693	2,921	2,245	3,159	11,818
Official flows	4,361	7,978	6,232	6,820	6,691	7,913	8,840
Grants (excluding technical cooperation)	600	544	2,602	2,206	2,509	1,468	1,075
IMF	0	0	1,013	1,839	2,245	7,468	4,120
By type[a]	−1,363	4,619	13,500	7,329	6,321	12,328	20,269
Long-term debt flows	9,037	4,322	11,716	5,501	1,893	1,138	5,442
Short-term debt flows	−10,400	500	1,040	−486	518	−377	250
Foreign direct investment	0	−203	−269	475	1,428	4,242	5,070
Portfolio	0	0	0	0	237	−143	5,387

Source: Global Financial Development, World Bank 1998. Data for 1997 are preliminary and are only available for the whole region.

[a] Excluding IMF, grants, and technical cooperation.

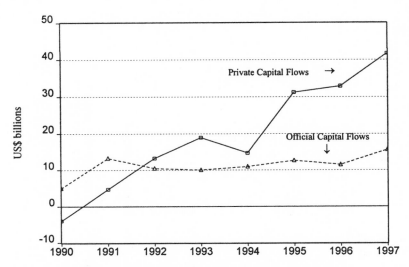

Fig. 9.1   Official versus private capital flows, CEE and FSU countries

they accounted for 73 percent of total flows. This development is not different from what has been observed in other developing countries, but in these transition economies the change in composition appears to have occurred more swiftly. The reduced reliance on official flows has been more marked in Central Europe and the Baltics than in the FSU. While FDI and portfolio flows were already large in Central Europe and the Baltics in 1991–92, they only acquired significance in the FSU after 1994. This is consistent with the onset of earlier reforms and improved access to international capital markets of Central Europe and the Baltics.

Second, there has been a rapid surge of short-term capital flows (short-term debt plus portfolio flows) from about $1 billion in 1991–92 to $20 billion in 1996–97—with the share in total flows increasing from 5 percent to about one-quarter (fig. 9.2). The surge in short-term flows could be a source of concern for policy makers, as short-term flows could be associated with higher volatility. This may be especially so for those countries that received the bulk of short-term flows: During 1993–96, the largest recipients were Hungary, the Czech Republic, Russia, Slovakia, Ukraine, and Slovenia, with these countries in total receiving over 90 percent of all short-term flows.

Third, the destination of private capital flows has been heavily concentrated.[6] A few countries—Russia, Hungary, Poland, and the Czech Re-

---

6. Defined as the sum of FDI, portfolio flows, commercial debt flows, and short-term flows.

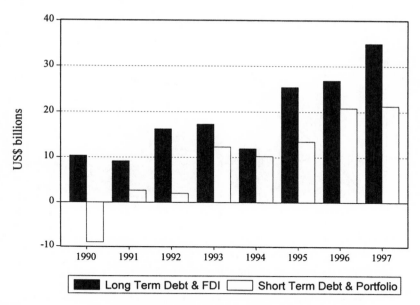

Fig. 9.2   Long-term and short-term capital flows, CEE and FSU countries

public—together accounted for about 80 percent of private capital flows to the region (fig. 9.3). The above four countries, along with a second group of countries—Romania, Kazakhstan, Ukraine, Slovenia, Slovakia, Lithuania, Estonia, and Croatia—accounted for about 98 percent of all private capital flows to the region. The concentration for FDI was even higher. Two countries, Poland and Hungary, for example, received over 50 percent of the 1992–96 cumulative FDI to the region ($46 billion).

Fourth, official capital flows—excluding flows from the International Monetary Fund (IMF)—have also been heavily concentrated, although mostly in a different set of countries than private flows. On a cumulative basis during 1992–96, five countries (Romania, Russia, Kazakhstan, Ukraine, and Bulgaria) received over 75 percent of all official flows (fig. 9.4). Some of the earlier recipients of official flows subsequently repaid large amounts of official debt and, thus, on a net cumulative basis, the significance of official financing for these countries is somewhat understated. Russia and Poland, for example, received around $2.4 billion in official financing in 1993–94 and repaid over $3 billion in 1996.

9.3   Linkages between Macroeconomic Variables and Capital Flows

We start with a description of some of the initial conditions that played an important role in determining the nature and type of capital inflows.

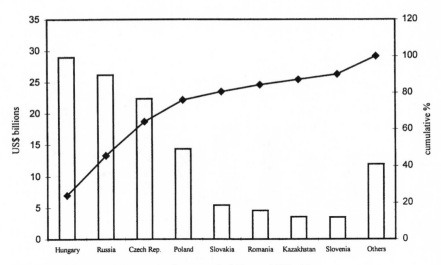

Fig. 9.3   Major recipients of private capital flows, 1990–96

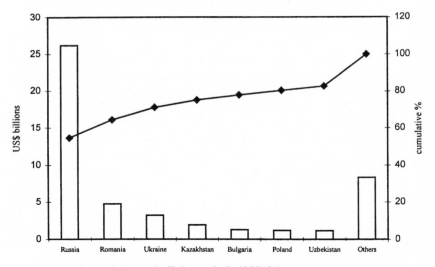

Fig. 9.4   Major recipients of official capital, 1990–96

The underlying factors behind private flows are quite different from those underlying official flows. In the case of private flows, credit worthiness—as a result of structural reforms and strong macroeconomic fundamentals—and economic and financial opportunities—such as high interest rate differentials—tend to drive flows. In the case of official flows, political considerations (including geopolitical or social stability), commitment to reforms (usually reflected in the conditions applied to official financing), and the fiscal deficit tend to be important determinants. We therefore discuss private and official flows separately.

9.3.1   Private Flows

Private capital flows depend on domestic factors and international factors, such as foreign interest rates or demand conditions abroad (see Calvo, Leiderman, and Reinhart 1993). In turn, domestic factors can be broadly classified into structural reforms (e.g., openness, privatization, financial sector deepening, banking sector stability), credit worthiness and macroeconomic fundamentals (e.g., fiscal deficit, debt to GDP ratio, ratio of short-term debt or monetary base to foreign reserves), private sector behavior (e.g., propensity to save), economic performance indicators (e.g., GDP growth), and arbitrage opportunities (e.g., domestic-foreign interest rate differentials adjusted for expected devaluation). As we discuss below, different types of private flows are likely to depend differently on specific subsets of these explanatory variables.

The importance of credit worthiness is well illustrated by the experiences of Poland and Hungary. Poland started the transition period with a large commercial debt stock, the result of heavy borrowing during the early 1980s in an attempt to maintain domestic consumption and government expenditures. As this borrowing occurred under the "umbrella" of the then Soviet Union, Poland's individual credit worthiness mattered less. The subsequent political transition and loss of the umbrella resulted, however, in a rapid loss of credit worthiness in the late 1980s. Poland subsequently had to go through first a Paris and then a Brady plan debt reduction and debt relief program to bring its debt back to sustainable levels. It took until October 1994 before the Brady debt reduction plan was completed and only afterward did private capital flows take off.

Bulgaria also had to go through a debt reduction and rescheduling operation after it incurred large amounts of hard currency debt in the late 1980s when aid from the Soviet Union was sharply reduced. Following Bulgaria's Brady debt agreement, private capital flows became positive for the first time since the onset of transition, and particularly after the country adopted a currency board in mid-1997. It appears that the currency board provided an implicit exchange rate insurance that, combined with a high interest rate differential and increased credit worthiness (through both debt reduction and lengthening of the maturities of external debt), attracted private capital flows.

In the case of Hungary, the initial debt stock was also high, but Hungary did not resort to debt rescheduling or reduction. This signaled Hungary's commitment to servicing its international obligations in full and on time; that, in turn, may have bolstered other kinds of private inflows. Until 1995, Hungary was the largest recipient of private capital flows in the region. However, Hungary relied mostly on FDI and portfolio flows for its financing needs as commercial lenders were reluctant to extend large amounts of new financing (in part this was also due to problems with the provision of accurate balance-of-payment information during the 1980s).

Initially, Russia was in a somewhat better position than most countries as its outstanding debt obligations were relatively low. But large borrowings during the late 1980s, much of it from official sources, led to subsequent debt servicing problems, which were partly resolved through repeated reschedulings. Nevertheless, debt stocks and debt service remained and remain high relative to exports and GDP (it should be noted, however, that Russia has run consistently large trade surpluses). In the case of Russia, what led to large private inflows was probably not so much (the perception of) improved credit worthiness, but rather the very high interest rates on government bonds. In 1996, Russia received $7.3 billion in portfolio flows, most of it to finance the government deficit.

For the rest of the FSU, inherited debt stocks were zero as they all reached agreement in the early 1990s for Russia to assume all debts and assets of the FSU (as the states of the FSU had each signed a joint and several liability agreement for the external debt, assumption of claims was necessary and the only practical solution). This "zero debt" initial condition was a factor in why early reformers—like most of the Baltics—were able to attract substantial private flows from the outset, almost $3 billion over the 1992–96 period.

Non-debt-creating private flows to the region, including FDI, were low until 1990 (less than half a billion dollars annually) with, as noted, most of it going to Hungary. The transition to market economies created opportunities for foreigners to engage in long-term risk investments in the region. But even though FDI grew, from $2.2 billion in 1991 to $6.4 billion in 1994, it remained small relative to other regions. In 1994, for example, it was less than FDI to Mexico in that year. As reform in these countries further progressed, FDI rose significantly, reaching $16.1 billion in 1995— although this figure is somewhat distorted by record-high privatization-related FDI in Hungary ($4.5 billion in 1995).[7] This reflected in part a general increase in FDI to developing countries. But there also appears to have been a threshold effect such that, once reform passed a certain level, a takeoff of private capital flows in general occurred (fig. 9.5).

Domestic reforms aimed at liberalizing prices, trade, and private sector activities have been very important for motivating the inflow of private capital. Countries did pursue many policies to attract capital flows, in particular they quite rapidly liberalized their current and capital accounts. In addition, some provided official guarantees for flows to private borrowers, while others provided special tariff or tax regimes to attract FDI flows. Compared to the impact of general reform, however, specific policies appear to have played a limited role in explaining capital flows.

7. FDI averaged $14.7 billion in 1996–97.

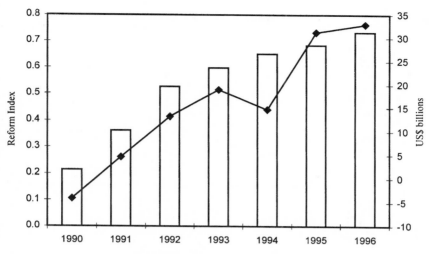

Fig. 9.5   Net private capital flows (*line*) and reform efforts (*columns*)

Some countries experienced large private capital inflows to private companies and state enterprises early on, even prior to the transition, but this most often reflected special circumstances. Several countries are well endowed with natural resources and were as a result able to attract FDI in these sectors, even when overall market reforms were still at an early stage. About half of total net inflows for Azerbaijan and Kazakhstan in 1995 and 1996, for example, were in the form of FDI, even though they scored low on policy reform. In other countries, the privatization strategy that was pursued greatly influenced capital flows (fig. 9.6). For example, since the onset of transition, Estonia, and Hungary even earlier, pursued a policy of actively selling firms on a case-by-case basis to strategic investors, including foreign investors. As a result, FDI inflows dominate private inflows for both countries (FDI inflows to Hungary actually exceeded in 1996 total net flows). And in the case of Russia in recent years, FDI flows have increased significantly as a result of the privatization of a few large resource-based state enterprises.

Capital flows have also been influenced by the behavior of domestic savings. Theoretically, foreign savings can be a complement to or a substitute for private domestic savings. The type of relationship between capital flows and domestic savings can have a bearing on the sustainability of capital flows. Hernandez and Rudolph (1995) found for economies in other regions that capital flows tend to be more sustainable when foreign and domestic savings are complementary. Figure 9.7 suggests a complementarity between aggregate domestic savings and total private flows. Based on this complementarity alone, capital flows are likely to be sustainable.

A few countries have had (temporary) situations of "overheating" associated with large private capital inflows (excluding FDI). For example,

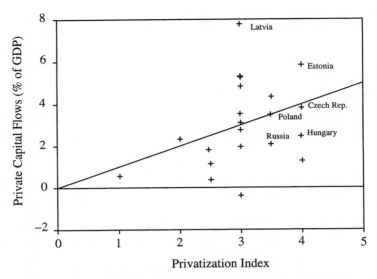

Fig. 9.6   Net private capital flows versus privatization progress, 1992–96
Note: Privatization index is obtained from EBRD Transition Report.

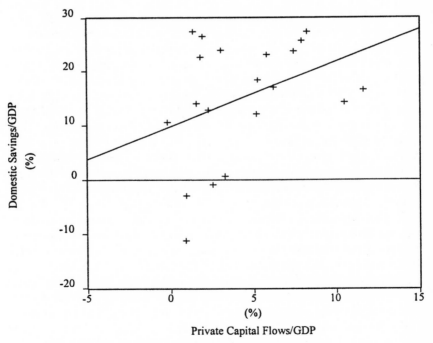

Fig. 9.7   Domestic savings and net private capital flows

private debt flows were large in the Czech Republic and Slovakia during 1995; and portfolio flows were large in Poland and Hungary during 1995, in Russia during 1996, and in Poland during 1997. For the region as a whole, however, short-term private flows (excluding FDI) were insignificant before 1993 and were less than one-third of all flows thereafter. More importantly, with a few exceptions, the share of capital flows relative to GDP remained small. Relative to GDP, only the Czech Republic and Hungary received in 1995 large amounts of private capital flows—10.9 percent and 8.2 percent, respectively. So did some of the smaller FSU countries in some specific years, but this mainly reflected the lumpy nature of private capital flows (e.g., FDI in a gold mine in the Kyrgyz Republic in 1995–96) or, in the case of some Baltics, heavy intermediation of foreign funds by local banks. Even these relatively high levels of capital inflows were well below the sustained high levels of capital inflows seen in recent years for some East Asian and Latin American countries, for those countries had several years of current account deficits up to 8 to 9 percent that were largely privately financed and, unlike in transition economies, often associated with strong declines in domestic saving (see Alba et al. 1999).

Though not for the region as a whole, there are several cases where financial arbitrage likely played a major role in motivating capital flows. For example, in recent years, there has been substantial foreign investment in portfolio flows in the form of purchases of local currency fixed-income instruments, such as Russian, Polish, Hungarian, and Czech treasury bills and treasury bonds. Table 9.3 suggests a positive link between high interest rate differentials (domestic interest rates corrected for the ex post exchange rate devaluation minus the U.S.-dollar London Inter-Bank Offering Rate [LIBOR]) and private capital inflows in these countries. For some countries, bond inflows have coincided with large and rapid equity portfolio inflows, much of it through American depositary receipts (ADRs)/ global depositary receipts (GDRs) and country funds. In the Czech Republic, for example, there were large equity inflows in 1995 when the equity market increased by 150 percent.[8] Similarly, Estonian banks relied heavily on foreign issues of Eurobonds to lower their funding costs during 1996–97. As demand for paper of emerging economies in CEE grew, domestic interest rates declined. The eruption of financial turbulence in Asia led to substantial outflows and a steep rise in spreads of Eurobonds issued by these countries over comparable U.S. treasuries (as well as declines in stock markets). This was especially the case for Russia, Estonia, Poland, and the Czech Republic, but affected more or less all countries in the region. Since then, spreads have declined to close to pre–Asian crisis levels.

Figure 9.8 shows that there has been a positive association between

8. Foreign purchases of equity securities increased from $497 million in 1994 to $1,236 million in 1995.

Table 9.3   **Nonequity Portfolio Flows and Interest Rate Differential**

	Poland			Czech Republic			Slovak Republic			Hungary			Russia		
	1995	1996	1997[a]	1994	1995	1996	1994	1995	1996	1994	1995	1996	1994	1995	1996
Nonequity portfolio (in US$ millions)	250	−531	2,200	733	1,288	562	218	210	−264	2,124	1,729	−1,873	−184	−1,576	−2,320
Interest rate differential (%)	14.4	7.6	0.2	8.3	15.6	6.1	5.5	19.4	5.1	6.4	4.7	−2.3	n.a.	22.1	57.5

[a]Breakup in bonds and equity flows is not available for Poland for 1997; figure reflects total portfolio investment.

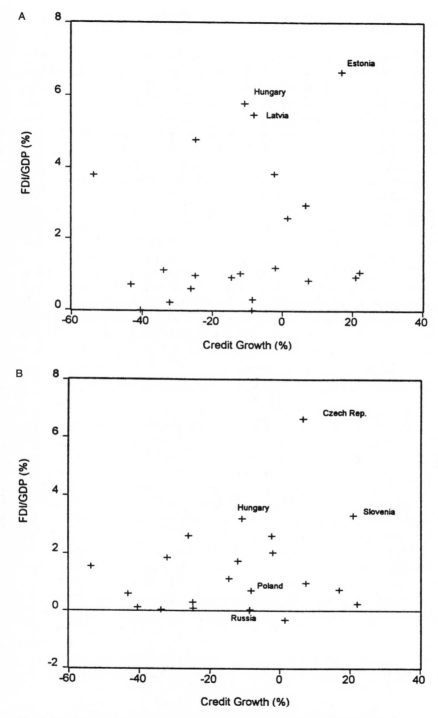

Fig. 9.8   *A*, FDI versus real credit growth; *B*, Private debt flows versus real credit growth

domestic credit growth and private capital inflows for only a few countries. The association for these countries stems both from general equilibrium effects and from banks directly intermediating capital flows. The large credit growth often seen in other developing countries has thus been much less observed for these countries. This may be due to the early phase of the expansionary cycle for most countries or to the poor state of institutional development of the banking systems in these countries, where foreign lenders are reluctant to lend large amounts to still weak banks. Direct intermediation of foreign savings through domestic banks has, for most countries, been limited. An exception has been Estonia, where in 1997 the banking sector relied heavily on foreign issues of Eurobonds to finance their domestic lending. Because of the general equilibrium effects of capital inflows, however, there were a few other countries where high credit growth and large capital inflows coincided (e.g., the Czech Republic).

Finally, while policy variables are what matter most from the point of view of policy makers, there is evidence that capital inflows have been often associated with improvements in key macroeconomic performance indicators such as GDP growth. As figure 9.9 illustrates, private capital flows exhibit a positive relationship with GDP growth. This highly observable performance indicator may serve as a proxy, to private investors, for effective reforms.

9.3.2 Official Flows

In the early stages of reform in CEE and FSU, a major share of official assistance took the form of balance of payments and budgetary support, including official debt relief. This was necessary as the transition meant a substantial drop in fiscal revenues, especially for the FSU countries where government revenues essentially collapsed. Receipts from the state enterprise sector fell sharply, partly as a result of privatization, partly as a result of the elimination (or reductions) of price subsidies, and partly as a result of a breakdown of the tax system. Price liberalization brought into the open the extensive systems of cross-subsidies inherent in the planned economy, shifting all or most of the cost onto the budget. Also, the new tax administrations proved unable to tax the emerging sectors. At the same time, there were pressures to maintain expenditures, especially for social purposes.

Fiscal deficits were large in many transition economies during 1990–96, averaging 6 to 7 percent of GDP in Bulgaria, Hungary, and Uzbekistan. They were even higher in Russia—an average of 8.5 percent of GDP during 1992–96—and continued to be high in 1997. In addition, governments often mandated the banking system to undertake quasi-fiscal activities—most often extending (subsidized) credits to state enterprises (Claessens and Peters [1997] analyze the case of Bulgaria; Claessens and Abdelati [1996] the case of Romania). Among slower reformers, credit subsidies from the central bank were on the order of three times the size of the fiscal deficit (De Melo and Denizer 1997). Much of these fiscal and quasi-fiscal

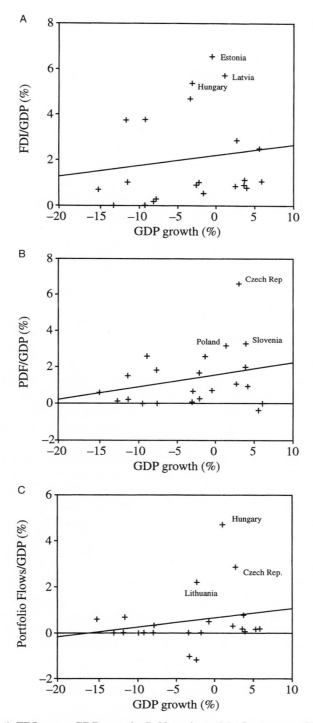

Fig. 9.9   *A*, FDI versus GDP growth; *B*, Net private debt flows versus GDP growth; *C*, Portfolio flows versus GDP growth

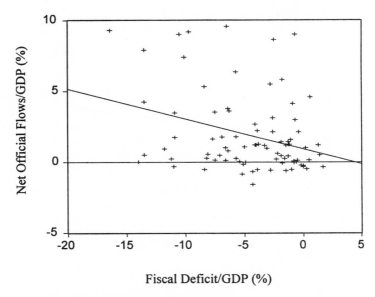

Fig. 9.10   Official capital flows and fiscal deficit

deficits ended up being funded through seignorage and inflation tax. Seignorage averaged more than 16 percent of GDP in Russia during 1992–93, about the same as total central government revenues (Easterly and Viera da Cunha 1994). In CEE, it was more modest, averaging 5 to 6 percent of GDP in Poland and Hungary during 1990–92. As figure 9.10 shows, official flows tend to have a close relationship with the fiscal deficits; the two variables indeed have one of the closest correlation relationships for all types of capital flows and various possible explanatory variables (a correlation coefficient of −0.69, where a fiscal deficit is defined negative).

Official support (from international financial institutions and individual country donors) provided partial financing for these fiscal deficits, thus reducing inflationary pressures. Official support, however, was also conditioned on reform efforts and has typically been larger, relative to population or GDP, for those countries that subsequently advanced further with reforms. For example, the Visegrad countries, the most advanced reformers (along with the Baltics), had received by the end of 1993 more than half of all the disbursements of international financial institutions to the region. Total official disbursements to the CEE, which have generally progressed farthest in their reforms, accounted for an average of about 2.7 percent of their GDP in 1991–93, actually comparable to the Marshall Plan (aid under the Marshall Plan after World War II averaged 2.5 percent of the incomes of recipient countries during the period it was being disbursed). External official finance has thus helped underpin a number of reform and stabilization programs, create confidence (as was true of the Polish stabilization fund), and reduce the need for monetary financing to cover budget deficits. Bilateral and multilateral (mainly the EU) assistance has also had a large component of technical assistance.

But for sustained reformers the period of official flows was short: the Czech Republic, for example, drew on IMF credits and other official loans relatively heavily in 1991 and 1992, but started to repay the IMF earlier than planned—as did Poland and Hungary in 1995. Similarly, Estonia maintains an IMF program but does not draw from it. This may explain why there is a negative correlation between the reform index and official flows for the whole period. A simple regression of a reform index on lagged official flows—see section 9.5—indeed suggests that official flows have exerted a positive impact on subsequent reforms. The results in section 9.5 also suggest that countries that reformed significantly over the period managed to attract higher private flows and may, thus, have experienced less need for official flows.

In 1994, official lending shifted to the FSU, which had previously obtained little official financing, as reforms advanced there. But reform strengths did differ considerably among FSU countries, and so did official flows. Among the FSU, the Baltic states, which had made substantial reforms, received more official assistance in relation to the size of their population as well as to GDP than, for example, did Belarus. Even today, many transition economies in the FSU still depend heavily on external capital flows for the financing for their fiscal deficits, with much of this financing from official sources. This is especially the case in Central Asia and some of the Caucasus countries, where official flows have been more than 5 percent of GDP for several countries. Relatively few countries have been successful in attracting private capital flows to finance their fiscal deficits. Most notable among these countries was Hungary and, in the last two years, Russia, which received some private inflows, mostly in the form of Eurobonds, for fiscal deficit financing.

In summary, official flows have been fiscally driven (for a review of the special fiscal issues experienced by transition economies see Buiter 1996). In conjunction, a *commitment* to subsequent reform appears to have been an important determinant of official flows. The access to capital markets that reforms have facilitated (at least in the most advanced reformers), however, has meant that official financing was quickly substituted by private capital flows (even though successful reformers usually still rely on official flows as contingent support).

9.4 Dealing with Capital Flows: The Policy Framework

As noted, countries improved the framework for capital flows largely through sustained structural reform efforts, involving liberalization, privatization, decentralization, stabilization, and institutional changes. Capital inflows have in general rewarded successful reforms and good policies by helping to finance investment needs and, in the case of FDI, by helping to improve productivity and access to foreign markets—thus helping to foster the further integration of transition economies into the global economy. While the benefits are clear, however, the crises in Mexico and Asia suggest that rapid surges of—particularly short-term—capital flows over a short time span can also pose difficulties to macroeconomic and financial sector management.

In CEE and FSU, only a few countries—and only recently—needed to deal with the potentially adverse effects of large capital inflows. There has consequently, in general, been little need for the responses traditionally employed when countries have faced large capital inflows (i.e., sterilization, exchange rate management, capital controls, prudential measures, capital outflow liberalization, and fiscal restraint; see further Corbo and Hernandez 1996). To illustrate policy responses to recent surges of capital inflows, we focus on the experiences of the Czech Republic, Poland, Estonia, Hungary, and Russia.

9.4.1   The Czech Republic

Following the initial transition years, when capital inflows were largely dominated by official sources, private capital flows became important.[9] After averaging around $2.5 billion annually in 1993–94 (over 80 percent of which was private finance), capital inflows rose in 1995 to $7.7 billion, before declining to about $4 billion in 1996. These large private capital inflows were strongly driven by Czech reforms—including the restructuring needs that followed large-scale privatization, the gradual liberalization of its current and capital accounts starting in 1991, its overall conservative fiscal policy (with on average a fiscal deficit close to zero in 1993–96), and a relatively stable foreign exchange rate combined with a high differential between Czech and foreign interest rates. Expectations of exchange rate appreciation were also an important factor, particularly in motivating portfolio inflows. Strong debt flows occurred in 1995–96, as bank and enterprises borrowed abroad heavily, reflecting the high interest differentials. Also, FDI trebled between 1994 and 1995, to about $2.5 billion, explained largely by the sale of 27 percent of the equity of the Czech telephone company to a Dutch-led consortium (collecting a record $1.45 billion in a single transaction).

As the exchange rate was fixed with respect to the deutsche mark (DM), the Czech Republic's largest trading partner, and inflation remained at around 10 percent the real exchange rate appreciated sharply during the 1994–96 period. Increases in inflation from wage pressures and slow pro-

---

9. This subsection is based in part on Klacek (1997).

ductivity growth led to large increases in relative unit labor costs. A current account surplus in 1993 (equivalent to 2 percent of GDP) turned into a large deficit in 1997 (equivalent to 7 percent of GDP) and a significant export slowdown followed in 1996 and 1997. Since 1996, net capital inflows have declined sharply and the scarcity of foreign financing has been reflected in an increasing interest rate spread between the Prague Inter-Bank Offering Rate (PRIBOR) and LIBOR; the spread rose from around 5 percent in March 1995 to almost 9 percent in early 1997.

The Czech Republic was initially reluctant to interfere with the large capital flows, consistent with its laissez-faire approach to economic management. As capital flows grew in 1995, however, the Czech government started with large sterilized interventions through open market operations, higher reserve requirements on demand and time deposits, and depositing privatization receipts with the central bank. This resulted in a further real appreciation and rise in interest rates. While the adverse monetary impact of reserve growth was partially avoided, high capital inflows continued, motivated increasingly by higher interest rates. The movements in the interest spread followed the capital flow cycle: During the first phase, "exogenous" capital flows driven by sustained reforms lowered the interest differential, but as the current account moved into deficit and the pace of reforms slowed down, higher interest rates were necessary to maintain the "flow of capital."

In March 1996, the government tried to deter speculative capital flows by widening the exchange rate band from 1.5 percent to 15 percent—that is, ±7.5 percent around the central parity. The measure had the desired effect of slowing down and in fact reversing short-term capital inflows. The government did not, however, tighten its fiscal stance or introduce capital controls. Following a banking sector crisis in early 1997 (in which several larger banks were liquidated), and following the growing perception that enterprise and bank restructuring has been advanced less than initially thought, there was a speculative run against the Czech koruna. This led to a sharp downward correction in stock market prices and sizable exchange rate devaluation, followed by significant capital outflows in mid-1997. The government was subsequently forced to tighten fiscal policy and strengthen regulation and supervision of its banking system and capital markets.

9.4.2   Poland

Official inflows played an important role during the first years of the transition, particularly in financing government deficits.[10] During the whole 1990–96 period, however, net flows of long-term official credits were close to zero as Poland repaid significant sums. Private capital flows to

---

10. This subsection is based in part on Durjasz and Kokoszczynski (1997).

Poland initially lagged behind those to the Czech Republic and Hungary; however, a sizable increase occurred following its commercial debt and debt service reduction agreement in October 1994. The bulk of private capital inflows to Poland after 1994 took the form of FDI, which rose from about $1.8 billion annually in 1993–94 to $6.6 billion in 1997. Poland became the largest recipient of FDI in the region on a cumulative basis over 1992–96. Inflows of FDI to Poland were driven by Poland's structural reforms, the de facto zloty convertibility since 1991 (initially for current account transactions and later for most capital account transactions), moderate fiscal deficits, overall good macroeconomic performance (highest cumulative growth of the region over 1992–97), and favorable prospects for EU membership. Privatization of state enterprises can explain about 20 percent of FDI inflows—far less than in Hungary. Most valuable Polish companies have not been privatized yet (copper, telecommunications, energy, insurance, and several of the large banks). Portfolio inflows became significant in 1995, with purchases of treasury bills by foreigners reaching $1 billion that year—encouraged by high yields and expectations of significant nominal zloty appreciation—and in 1997. In 1996–97, several banks and companies issued medium-term paper in the Eurobond market and benefited from low and declining spreads, reaching under one hundred basis points over equivalent U.S. treasuries in 1997.

Capital inflows and a current account surplus in 1995 were associated with strong monetary and credit expansion and with slow disinflation. A 20 percent real exchange rate appreciation in 1995–96 was followed by a deterioration of the current account balance equivalent to almost 8 percentage points of GDP over 1996–97. The government responded to the above concerns with a more flexible exchange rate regime, sterilized interventions, and a tightened monetary and fiscal policy. Poland did not rely on explicit capital controls to manage adverse capital flows. A permission from the central bank for foreign credits and loans with a repayment period of less than twelve months (for services other than commodity circulation and individuals' services) appears to have had no significant effect on the structure of flows. Similar requirements for longer-term loans and credits were lifted as a result of Organization for Economic Cooperation and Development (OECD) membership negotiations.

The greatest concern in the second half of 1994 and 1995 was the impact on inflation of rapid foreign reserve growth. The largest source of foreign reserve accumulation in 1994 and 1995 was "net unclassified transactions" of the current account—$9.6 billion between 1995 and the first quarter of 1996. These refer mostly to flows on account of cross-border trade and tourism, motivated by high price differentials between Poland and Germany, on one hand, and Poland and countries to the east on the other. Other substantial (albeit smaller) sources of reserve growth were portfolio and FDI inflows. The government responded with a combination of sterilized interventions and a more flexible exchange rate policy regime. Open market operations trebled between the first half of 1994 and the second half of 1995. The widely spread perception that the exchange rate was undervalued led to the creation of a wide exchange rate band of ±7 percent around the central parity in May 1995. The exchange rate quickly appreciated to the top of the band and by years end the band itself was appreciated. Following a slowdown in foreign exchange reserve accumulation since the second quarter of 1996—also facilitated by the liberalization of purchases of foreign assets such as real estate and portfolio investments by residents (an OECD membership requirement)—the central bank was able to reduce its sterilization activities and maintain the exchange rate policy adopted during 1995. The above policies were also supported by a deliberate commitment to lower interest rates as a means to discourage portfolio flows driven by high interest rate differentials. The period did see, though, a rapid surge in domestic credit associated with a hike in domestic aggregate demand and a turnaround of the current account from a 4.6 percent of GDP surplus in 1995 to a deficit of 1 percent of GDP in 1996.

The biggest concern in 1997 was the further deterioration of the external current account. Monetary policy was sharply tightened starting early in 1997, with real interest rates in treasury bills and bonds rising from around 0 percent in previous years to about 10 percent during the year. To enhance the effectiveness of the monetary policy transmission mechanism, the central bank accepted deposits directly from the public—thus inducing some large state-owned banks to raise their deposit rates. With high domestic interest rates, there was a new surge of portfolio flows. To reduce these inflows, the government responded by eliminating altogether intraband exchange rate interventions, thus effectively raising the exchange rate uncertainty faced by short-term speculative capital flows, renewing sterilization activity, and imposing a tighter than anticipated fiscal policy. By October, there was a deceleration of credit growth and the current account balance ended the year with a 3.2 percent of GDP deficit, substantially less than had earlier been anticipated.

9.4.3   Estonia

Capital inflows to Estonia were dominated by domestic factors, including the introduction of domestic currency linked through a currency board system to the DM, attractive interest rate differentials, structural reforms (especially trade and banking sector reform), and an active privatization program. Capital inflows (beginning in 1993) preceded the economic recovery—following four years of rapid contraction, output growth only resumed in 1995. Capital inflows were initially dominated by FDI inflows. Since mid-1995, however, there has been a relative decline of FDI in overall capital flows and a surge in domestic banks' access to international capital markets. The counterpart of the latter development was a rapid surge in private domestic credit. Driven by private aggregate demand (fiscal deficits averaged 0.5 percent of GDP during the 1993–96 period), the current account balance declined from a surplus in 1993 to a deficit of over 10 percent of GDP in 1996 and 13 percent in 1997. Under the currency board regime, the central bank's monetary interventions have been limited to buying and selling foreign exchange to preserve the parity with the DM. Since there has been no intervention through open market operations, base money growth has been driven by the demand for domestic assets. Strong demand for domestic assets led to high growth of monetary base, broad money (including foreign exchange deposits), as well as credit between 1992 and 1997. Estonia did not resort to capital controls or to sterilization.

The rapid growth of domestic credit, the declining share of FDI in capital inflows, the high current account deficit, and the turmoil in Asia since mid-1997, however, prompted the government to tighten banking sector prudential regulations and supervision in late 1997. The latter was aimed at curbing fast credit growth and, only indirectly, at curbing portfolio inflows (since banks were funding domestic credit with Eurobond issues). The creation of a stabilization fund—whereby budget surpluses and public sector deposits were invested in foreign assets abroad—and a number of other measures aimed at tightening monetary policy and regulations were announced in early October 1997. These other measures included raising the capital adequacy ratio from 8 percent to 10 percent, curbing local government's borrowing, extending reserve requirements for the banks to include net borrowing from abroad, and increasing the daily liquidity requirement for banks.

The announcement of these measures, combined with some indications from the government that it would remove public sector deposits from commercial banks to create the stabilization fund, and previously unanticipated delays in the funding abroad of several domestic banks, led to a liquidity crisis in the banking sector on 20 October 1997. Interest rates jumped over three hundred basis points and between 20 October and the end of November the stock market price index lost over 60 percent of its value. To restore confidence, the central bank decided to bring forward the implementation of the previously announced measures and announced new measures to tighten banking regulations, including a further increase in capital adequacy requirements to 12 percent—to be implemented at a later (unspecified) stage—and increases in the liquidity ratios of banks. The firm stance of banking regulators and the tightening of fiscal policy were conducive to a significant slowdown of credit growth and to improved liquidity in financial markets.

9.4.4 Hungary

As a reward for its early reform efforts and continuous servicing of its foreign debt, Hungary received large capital inflows (including FDI) from the early 1990s on.[11] Lack of fiscal discipline in 1993–94, however, led to a large surge in its current account deficit, reaching almost 10 percent of GDP in 1994, and created an unsustainable situation. The foreign exchange crisis in 1994 led to an economic downturn, and large debt financing to the public sector was necessary. Following fiscal adjustment and a devaluation in early 1995, there was a new surge in FDI closely linked to an ambitious privatization program (including the privatization of banks and some utilities). A sharp fiscal adjustment along with an intensification of structural reforms led to a rapid contraction in the current account deficit. Capital inflows declined as the path of fast privatization could not be sustained after 1995.

Sterilized intervention was extensively pursued during the periods in which capital inflows threatened the monetary program. To a lesser extent, capital account liberalization also helped as it led to capital outflows. Exchange rate flexibility—that is, a devaluation—was used when capital outflow pressures dominated (1994–95). The sharp fiscal adjustment and monetary tightening subsequently helped to keep the current account deficit under control. Strong productivity growth (supported by structural reforms)—unit labor costs declined sharply—has been another key factor keeping the current account to manageable proportions.

9.4.5 Russia

Capital flows to and from Russia were characterized by large official inflows (on average $3.5 billion during 1993–96), very large capital outflows or "capital flight" (errors and omissions in the balance of payments averaged $8 billion in 1995–96), and since 1996 a surge in portfolio inflows, mostly in the form of purchases of treasury bills (GKO). The surge in both official and portfolio flows was closely linked with the large financing requirements of the budget—8.1 percent of GDP on average during 1993–97—and since 1996 with the government's strategy to increase the share of foreign financing of fiscal deficits as a way of reducing domestic financial and inflationary pressures. While the conditions attached to official flows has been supportive of ongoing reform efforts in the country, legal uncertainties, weak institutions, criminality, and limited opportunities for foreigners to participate in privatizations may explain why FDI has been relatively (to GDP) low. FDI averaged $600 million in 1993–94 and $1.9 billion in 1995–96. However, further increases are anticipated over the coming years as a result of reforms conducive to improving the

---

11. This subsection is based in part on Oblath (1997).

business environment for foreign investors (e.g., faster privatization, improvements to the collateral system, land and tax reform, changes to the bankruptcy law, improved transparency in the accounts of state enterprises, and national treatment for foreign investors).

The scale of capital outflows (to the extent that they result from tax avoidance or evasion) in part explains the difficulties that the government faces in reducing its deficit. Capital outflows may also help explain why the sharp tightening of monetary policy in 1996 induced a strong rise in portfolio inflows (as Russians reinvested their money back into the country). Inflation has fallen substantially from 131 percent in 1995 to 21.8 percent in 1996 and to 11 percent in 1997. Interest rate declines lagged behind, however, with the average treasury bill rate falling from 176 percent in 1995 to 102 percent in 1996 and 33 percent in 1997. The resulting high real interest rates, combined with the sharp real appreciation of the currency in 1995 and 1996, have been key motives behind the surge in portfolio flows targeting fixed income instruments. Portfolio investors, mostly over two hundred foreign investment funds, primarily purchased treasury bills, with purchases in April 1997 peaking at $2 billion. As real interest rates declined in 1997, investors have been increasingly targeting traded shares of Russian enterprises: In early 1997, they owned about one-third of such shares, or about $3 billion. Unlike other large capital-importing countries in the region, Russia did not pursue deliberate policies to slow down capital inflows. However, the exchange rate flexibility conferred by its wide exchange rate band has presumably been some deterrent against short-term portfolio flows.

9.5 Econometric Tests and Evaluation

The above sections suggest that the reasons for the capital flows are largely the pursuit of economic reform. They also make clear that the factors influencing capital flows have differed by the types of capital flow. Furthermore, policy responses (e.g., degree of sterilization, liberalization, or imposition of capital controls) have also differed by the degree and type of capital flows. To make these relationships more precise and to study the separate effects of some of these factors we provide some regression results in this section.

The main aim of the regressions is to try to explain the magnitude of the various types of capital flows for individual countries. Common with the existing literature (e.g., Calvo, Leiderman, and Reinhart 1993; Chuhan, Claessens, and Mamingi 1998; Hernandez and Rudolph 1995; Taylor and Sarnio 1997; see Montiel and Reinhart 1997 for a review of this literature), we distinguish two groups of explanatory variables: international factors ("push factors") and domestic factors ("pull factors"). Push factors are conditions in global capital markets that influence the supply of capital and are outside the control of a particular recipient country. Pull factors are country-specific factors and conditions influencing the interest of foreign capital of investing in that particular country. Some of these factors are under the control of the country, some are initial conditions, and others are outcomes which are in part influenced by capital flows themselves.

For the group of pull factors, we use the U.S.-dollar, six-month LIBOR interest rate and the economic growth in OECD countries. We expect that declines in world interest rates will have a positive effect on capital flows to CEE and FSU, as that will make the rate of return on investing in these countries higher relative to other alternatives. The effect of an increase in OECD growth rate is less obvious. On one hand, it will likely be associated with a rise in the rate of return on investment in OECD countries, thus reducing the attractiveness of investing in transition economies. On the other hand, higher growth may raise the supply of savings in OECD countries, thus stimulating capital flows.

The group of pull factors is divided into policy factors: "reform efforts," initial conditions, and "outcomes." Obviously, it is difficult to quantify the degree of policy reform a country has undertaken in absolute terms. The very similar starting position of most of the transition economies—controlled prices, little private sector activity, limited institutional development, and so forth—makes it somewhat easier to quantify at least the relative degree of policy reform in CEE and FSU. We use the liberalization index from De Melo, Gelb, and Denizer (1996) to rank countries in their relative reform efforts. This index, an indicator between 0 and 1, is available for each country and for each year and aims to measure how far the country has progressed in liberalizing prices, trade, and private sector activities, including privatization. The initial conditions and outcomes variables are more difficult to separate, as capital flows are likely to interact with and affect current outcomes, which then become initial conditions for subsequent capital flows. We use the country's GDP growth rate, inflation, fiscal balance, private saving, and, as a credit worthiness indicator, the change in the country's reserves. We lag the change in the country's reserves and the two saving variables by one period to avoid possible simultaneity (as the sum of private, public, and foreign saving adds up to the change in reserves). In addition, we also use a dummy for the ten CEE countries likely to become EU members.[12]

We focus separately on factors that have likely influenced short-term private capital flows ("arbitrage factors"). In particular, we use the ex-

---

12. We use the following ten countries that have been identified by the EU as candidates: the Czech Republic, Poland, Hungary, Slovenia, Estonia, Romania, Bulgaria, the Slovak Republic, Lithuania, and Latvia. The first five have recently started negotiations with the EU; we set the dummy equal to 2 for these countries. The dummy is set to 1 for the other five countries, and to 0 for all other countries.

change rate adjusted rate of return on holding domestic assets (i.e., the nominal domestic interest rates[13] minus the rate of change in the local currency/dollar exchange rate) minus the U.S.-dollar interest rate. We also investigate the relationship between different types of capital flows and domestic credit growth, as important reinforcing effects for other developing countries have been found between private capital flows and the rate of domestic credit expansion. Depending on the quality of financial intermediation, these reinforcing effects can lead to subsequent problems, as has been found for East Asian countries (see Alba et al. 1999).

We perform regressions for seven different classifications of capital flows, focusing mainly on the source of capital: total capital flows, official flows, all private flows, FDI, commercial debt flows, portfolio flows (bonds and equity), and short-term flows. We study both total flows as well as categories within these flows because there might be substitution between the various flows,[14] both in a narrow sense (e.g., portfolio flows and FDI can be substituted in a particular transaction) as well as in a broader macroeconomic sense (e.g., large inflows of one kind can encourage or deter flows of another kind).

We run our regressions in an unbalanced panel setup using a sample of twenty-one countries for the years 1992–96. The panel is unbalanced as we do not have data for our independent variables for each year for each country and have private capital outflows figures for only a few countries. We also had to eliminate three countries (Azerbaijan, Turkmenistan, and Tajikistan) for lack of reliable data. All our dependent variables, U.S.-dollar capital flows, are scaled by U.S.-dollar GNP based on the Atlas method of the World Bank—which uses the moving average of the exchange rate over three years—to convert local currency GNP to U.S.-dollar GNP. This way we smooth out the effect of large real exchange rate movements.

We have the option of estimating the regression model with individual effects or with a common constant term. The first, the fixed effects model, assumes that differences across the countries can be captured in differences in the constant term. The other option is to use ordinary least squares and estimate the regression model assuming that the constant term is the same across countries. To determine which type of estimation was most appropriate, we conducted F-tests for each regression, testing the hypothesis that the constant terms are all equal. The results suggested that for total, official, private, FDI, and commercial debt flows an estimation using a common constant, in addition to the EU-accession dummy

---

13. We use as much as possible the local treasury bill rate. For those countries where treasury bill rates were not available, we use the interbank interest rate or the bank lending rate.
14. We would like to thank Michael Dooley for reminding us of this possibility.

variable, will provide the most consistent and efficient estimators. For the remaining types of flows, portfolio flows and short-term debt flows, the fixed effects model was more appropriate.

We correct for heteroskedasticity in the error terms of the regressions. In particular, the size of the country has an effect on the relationships. We expect that this effect arises for several reasons. First, because of fixed costs of acquiring information, we expect that small countries exhibit a less clear relationship between explanatory variables and capital flows, as investors will expend fewer resources in analyzing small country characteristics. Second, the lumpiness of some of the flows, particularly FDI but also of official flows, may make for more noisy relationships of flows (when scaled by GDP) for smaller countries. Third, we expect smaller countries to be less economically diversified and more affected by external and internal shocks, thus again creating more noisy relationships. Fourth, available data are likely more problematic for small countries as their statistical systems are less well developed. Plotting the error terms against the size of the country confirms this type of heteroskedasticity. For these reasons we use the estimated cross-section residual variances as weights in the regressions.

In light of the discussion from the previous sections, we start with a benchmark regression for all seven categories of capital flows with the following explanatory variables: reform index, a dummy for EU accession (which takes the value of 2 for those five countries currently in negotiations, 1 for the other five countries, and 0 for all other countries), and the change in the level of foreign exchange reserves (with declines in reserves having a positive sign). As a second step we add single additional explanatory variables, thus keeping the total number of variables to four. Results for these seven regressions are presented in table 9.4.

We find that the reform and reserves variables are significant explanatory variables of all categories of flows; the EU dummy is significant for two of the seven categories. Not surprisingly, we find that the effort in undertaking reform in a particular country is positively associated with all types of flows, except for official and portfolio flows. This suggests that reforms were important motivating factors for private capital flows. Reform effort also matters in determining official flows, but with a negative coefficient. This would suggest that official financing went to those countries that have reformed less. The correct interpretation, however, might be that official financing went to those countries that had achieved less reform initially, but that some conditionality was being applied in official financing. Reform efforts may then have increased following large official flows, and over time the official flows to those countries that had achieved more reform declined. This overall negative relationship for official flows thus reflects that they preceded reform efforts and fell off as reforms

Table 9.4   **Regressions Results—Benchmark Model**

	Total Flows	Total Private Flows	Official Flows	FDI	Portfolio	Short-Term Debt	Commercial Debt
				Dependent Variable			
Reform index$_t$	2.5945	4.0827	-4.2019	0.8901	0.0146	0.5362	1.1191
	(2.19)	(16.94)	(-5.53)	(3.07)	(18.39)	(10.91)	(5.51)
EU accession	0.9688	2.3376		1.5104	1.4364		
	(1.68)	(3.06)		(6.99)	(2.43)		
Reserves$_{t-1}$	-0.1434	-0.0516	0.0572	-0.0359	-0.0023		-0.0261
	(-3.59)	(-2.25)	(3.77)	(-3.70)	(-10.84)		(-3.23)
Adjusted R^2	0.44	0.33	0.50	0.25	0.00	0.01	0.07
Number of observations	77	77	77	77	77	104	77
Pull factors							
Fiscal balance$_{t-1}$	+	ns	±[a]	-	-	+	+
Fiscal balance$_t$	+	ns	±[a]	ns	-	+	+
Private savings$_{t-1}$	-	-	-	-	-	-	+
Domestic credit$_t$	ns	ns	ns	ns	ns	-	-
Official flows$_{t-1}$	+	+		+	ns	ns	-
Interest rate differential	ns	ns	ns	ns	+	-	ns
Push factors							
LIBOR	ns	+	+	+	+	ns	ns
OECD growth rate	ns	+	+	+	ns	+	+

Notes: The estimation procedure is generalized least squares with cross section residual variances as weights. ns = no significant; + = positive significant; − = negative significant. t-statistics are in parentheses.

[a]Due to a high correlation between reform index and fiscal balance (0.83), the sign of the coefficient for fiscal balance becomes negative when reform index is dropped from the regression.

progressed.[15] This result suggests that a dynamic model of official capital flows and progress in liberalization is required. The negative sign for the reform variable in the case of portfolio flows likely reflects that a significant part of portfolio flows was directed toward the financing of fiscal deficits, which may have been larger in countries that reformed less.

For FDI, the dummy for EU accession is positively significant. It is likely that EU accession is most important for FDI as the prospects of increased integration with Western Europe has meant that both opportunities for favorable investments and overall credit worthiness increase in these countries more than in others.

The negative sign for the lagged change in reserves variable for most flows reflects the fact that increased credit worthiness of countries, that is, as they increased reserves, motivated further capital flows. The positive sign for the lagged changes in reserves variable for official flows reflects that, at least initially, official financing was made available on a financing needs basis: As reserves declined, more official financing was made available. Similarly for portfolio flows, much of which was directed to financing of fiscal deficits, financing need was an important determinant.

As mentioned, we added to this basic regression a number of additional variables, including each separately. Specifically, we included public sector balance, current as well as lagged one period (to avoid simultaneity between foreign and domestic savings), private savings (lagged one period), domestic credit growth, lagged official flows, and the interest differential. We also include the two push variables, LIBOR and OECD growth rates. Rather than presenting all the detailed regressions results, we simply present whether the particular additional variable was significant, and if so, with what sign (see table 9.4).

We find that fiscal surpluses, both contemporaneous and lagged, are positively related with about half of the different types of flows. This suggests that increased fiscal surpluses stimulate foreign savings through a credit worthiness effect. The negative coefficients for official flows show that official flows to the public sector have been associated with larger fiscal deficits (see also fig. 9.10 in section 9.3). The coefficient is also negative for portfolio flows, likely because countries with larger fiscal deficits receive more portfolio flows through foreign purchases of government bonds (particularly Russia). Lagged private saving has a negative coefficient for all flows except commercial debt flows. This suggests that there is some substitution between foreign and private saving, a general finding for developing countries (see Cohen 1993). The coefficients are small, however, so concerns about the sustainability of foreign flows, as they end up

---

15. A regression of reform on lagged official flows indeed confirms this relationship. Using a fixed-effect estimator, we find that the coefficient for lagged official flows is significantly positive and has a t-statistic of 2.74.

financing some share of consumption, may not be too serious. The positive sign for private saving in the commercial debt flows regression may reflect a credit worthiness effect.

Domestic credit growth is significantly negative in the case of total private flows, short-term flows, and commercial debt flows. This suggests that the typical reinforcing effect of capital flows on domestic credit growth is not prevalent in these countries. This may be because of the poor institutional development of the domestic financial sector. The negative sign may also reflect that the enterprise restructuring required in these countries was often achieved through tight (hard) budget constraints. Countries with less growth in domestic credit may have been more successful with enterprise restructuring; they thus were more likely candidates for private capital flows because their credit worthiness in general increased and because a greater fraction of domestic firms were restructured and thus of interest to foreign investors.

Lagged official flows have a positive effect on almost all types of capital flows. Since the regression already controls for the reform effort of the particular country, which thus captures the degree to which official lenders may have been successful in their reform conditionality, there is an independent effect of past official lending on private capital flows. This may be because official lending acted as an important signal to private creditors regarding the commitment of the country to undertake further reforms.

The interest differential variable is significant for only two of the types of capital flows: portfolio flows and short-term flows. Only for portfolio flows does it have the expected positive sign, while for short-term flows the sign is negative. This suggests that, once one controls for a few basic variables, capital flows at large have not been motivated by arbitrage conditions.

Push factors appear to play a role in motivating capital flows, but with the opposite sign from what is commonly found. Specifically, increases in international interest rates are associated with increased capital flows. And higher OECD growth rates also increase capital flows. This contradictory finding raises some questions of its own, but at least it does not suggest that capital flows to these countries are at risk for increases in international interest rates and OECD growth. It may rather be that increases in OECD growth enhance the supply of foreign savings available for these countries.

Table 9.5 provides the regression results for the specification chosen for each type of capital flow. The explanatory variables were chosen after some experimentation to achieve a reasonable overall fit for the regression, within constraints of data availability.

In the case of total flows, reform efforts, EU accession, and changes in reserves have the same sign as before. Additional significant explanatory variables are the lagged fiscal balance and lagged official capital flows, both with a positive coefficient.

Table 9.5   Panel Data Regression—Extended Model

	Dependent Variable						
	Total Flows	Total Private Flows	Official Flows	FDI	Portfolio[a]	Short-Term Debt[a]	Commercial Debt[a]
Reform index$_t$	2.797 (3.67)**	4.506 (9.82)**	−0.638 (−0.90)	1.472 (6.47)**		−3.286 (−2.91)**	1.665 (1.74)**
EU accession	0.643 (1.87)**	2.521 (3.43)**	−2.408 (28.59)**	1.896 (10.93)**			
Reserves$_{t-1}$	−0.0754 (1.70)*	−0.1185 (−6.72)**	0.0441 (3.02)**	−0.0394 (−5.05)**		−0.0307 (−1.24)	−0.0541 (−2.07)**
Fiscal balance$_{t-1}$	0.0478 (2.11)**	0.0843 (2.98)**	0.0394 (2.70)**	−0.0125 (−1.19)	0.0976 (2.00)**		
Private savings$_{t-1}$						−0.0243 (−2.14)**	−0.0161 (1.81)**
Domestic credit$_t$		−0.0267 (−13.76)**					
Official flows$_{t-1}$	0.7074 (9.23)**	0.2143 (5.26)**		0.2027 (10.41)**	0.0760 (1.43)*		
LIBOR$_t$					−0.3029 (−1.24)		
OECD growth rate$_t$			0.0912 (2.09)**			0.3496 (2.51)**	
Adjusted R^2	0.49	0.80	0.75	0.46	0.34	0.36	0.92
Number of observations	74	72	74	74	78	76	76
F-value	0.24	1.41	0.73	0.67	3.11	3.00	4.2

[a]Fixed effects model estimation was used for these types of flows, given that the hypothesis that the country effects are the same was rejected (see F-values).
*Significant at the 10 percent level.
**Significant at the 5 percent level.

Total private capital flows depend strongly on reform efforts. We again find a positive coefficient for those countries with possible accession to the EU and a negative relationship with the lagged change in foreign exchange reserves, which suggests that credit worthiness is an important factor. Higher (lagged) fiscal savings tends to raise private flows, suggesting that credit worthiness and reform perceptions are influenced positively by reduced fiscal deficits. More generally, the positive relationship between private capital flows and fiscal saving suggests a complementarity between public and foreign saving. We also find a positive coefficient for lagged official flows, a possible confirmation of the signal from past official lending on future reforms and credit worthiness. Private capital flows are negatively related to domestic credit growth, suggesting that contractions in credit growth may have served as a signal of reform.

In the case of official flows, the results show that reform efforts again enter with a negative (but insignificant) coefficient. Countries that are candidates to become members of the EU have received less official financing, suggesting that, because they received more private financing and progressed further in reforms, they were in less need of official financing. This need for financing is again confirmed in the positive coefficient for the reserve variable, indicating that declines in foreign exchange reserves are associated with more official financing. Lagged fiscal surpluses have a positive relationship with official flows, suggesting official flows were made conditional on past fiscal efforts. The high correlation between fiscal surpluses and reform efforts, however, implies that when the reform variable is removed, the sign of the fiscal surplus variable becomes negative, that is, there is collinearity between regressors. The interpretation in this latter case is more straightforward: Lower fiscal surpluses (higher deficits) are associated with larger official flows. The coefficient for OECD growth rate is significantly positive, suggesting that the supply of official saving may have been a positive function of the business cycle in industrial countries.

As we showed above, FDI is the most important private capital flow for most countries. In this specification, FDI is dependent as before on the three major independent variables: reform efforts, EU accession, and reserve changes. Not surprisingly, as for all private capital flows, FDI is greatly influenced by reform efforts, as the t-statistic for the reform index is large. Lankes and Stern (1999) and Martin and Selowsky (1997) had already noted this. Lagged official flows are positively significant, suggesting again a signaling function of official flows.

Portfolio flows appear to be driven by a number of factors, some of which are collinear, thus leading to mostly insignificant coefficients when many variables are included. The best regression result is then also not very informative. Fiscal balance (lagged one period) now appears to increase portfolio flows, a finding different from the earlier regression where the opposite coefficient was found. Interestingly, the interest rates differential variable is not significant. As noted, not all of these relationships are robust to inclusion of other independent variables, in part likely because of the collinearity of the independent variables, but also because portfolio flows are relatively small and have occurred only in more recent years, thus leading to weaker relationships.

Lastly, we regressed the flow of short-term debt flows and commercial debt flows. As noted, short-term debt has become a large share of private capital flows in recent years for a number of countries. Private debt flows and short-term debt flows appear to be driven by the same factors, except for reform efforts. The degree of reform matters in a positive way for commercial debt flows and negatively for short-term debt flows. The negative sign for short-term flows, which differs from the results in table 9.4, could reflect that lenders were less willing to extend long-term funds, and relatively more willing to extend short-term funds, to countries that had undertaken less reform. Increases in reserves lead to larger commercial debt and short-term flows (the latter is insignificant, however). This suggests that credit worthiness also matters for these flows. Private debt flows appear to be substitutes for domestic private saving as the coefficients are negative. Finally, OECD growth rates matter for short-term flows. We find no evidence of a push effect, as the coefficient for the LIBOR interest rates is insignificant; in other words, the decline in international interest rates has not stimulated commercial debt or short-term flows. Arbitrage factors, that is, the interest differential, do not appear to have a significant effect on short-term flows, which is somewhat surprising.

In short, the overall results indicate that flows are driven for most countries by fundamental reforms and credit worthiness. The possibility of EU accession has been an important determinant of private flows, especially FDI. For official flows, EU accession seems to have lowered the need for official flows. Increased fiscal saving has led to higher volumes for most flows while increased private saving has been associated with lower capital flows, suggesting some degree of substitutability between private and foreign saving. Official flows appear to have had an important signaling value for private capital flows. For no flows did high interest rate differentials (adjusted for exchange rate movements) appear to have mattered. Push effects are only found for commercial debt and short-term debt flows, with growth in OECD countries encouraging flows to the region.

9.6 Conclusions and Forward-Looking Issues

Capital flows to CEE and FSU have been increasing rapidly in recent years—a growth rate of 34 percent per year during 1991–97 but are still a small fraction of global capital flows to developing countries (about 18 percent in 1997). As structural reforms have progressed, the composition of flows has changed: Official flows have declined, and private capital flows have increased to account by 1997 for about 73 percent of total flows. Within private capital flows, FDI was the most important followed by portfolio flows. As the direct and spillover effects of FDI on human, technological, and physical capital accumulation are crucial for the rapid and effective integration of the transition economies to the world economy, this bodes well for these countries.

Perhaps more than in other developing countries, reform efforts have been the most important determinant of private flows, particularly of FDI. Other consistent determinants of private flows have been prospective EU membership—the ten countries that applied for EU membership attracted more private flows (and relied less on official flows)—and credit worthiness. Credit worthiness proxies such as increases in reserves, lower fiscal deficits, and greater past official flows were mostly positively correlated with greater private flows. The association between declines in private saving and higher private debt flows, however, causes some concern.

One key policy implication is that the sustainability of capital flows is associated with the sustainability of reform efforts. The consistency and continuity of structural reforms—particularly those that are conducive to EU integration and improved credit worthiness—can influence the source (official versus private) as well as the type of private capital flow (e.g., the reform's impact on FDI flows is positive while the impact on short-term debt flows is negative). This, in turn, implies that reform efforts matter not just for the level of capital flows, but also for the maturity and potential volatility of flows.

The shift from debt-creating flows to the public sector in the 1980s to non-debt-creating flows to the private sector in the 1990s also has implications for the efficiency of resource and risk allocation. For one, private recipients of capital have better incentives to allocate capital into higher return projects. The shift to non-debt-creating flows, in turn, implies a better risk-sharing arrangement (of fixed-term foreign currency obligations) vis-à-vis foreign investors.

Another feature of capital flows to the region has been the increase in the share of short-term debt and portfolio flows since 1993. The concentration of these potentially more volatile short-term flows in 1993–96 in a few countries raises questions about sustainability of capital flows and vulnerability to international shocks in these economies. For the majority of countries in the region, however, the absolute and relative level of short-term foreign obligations is small compared to the size of their economies as well as compared to the high levels of their foreign exchange reserves.

So far, only a few countries have had to deal with episodes of overheating. Looking forward, it is likely that more countries will have to deal with the constraints that the level and structure of external liabilities may pose on macroeconomic and financial policy. The experiences in the region confirm global lessons: Dealing with overheating requires determined, countercyclical fiscal policies (to counter the potential overheating caused by large capital inflows) and better supervision and tighter prudential regulations on the financial sector (such as raising reserve requirements on foreign borrowings). Sterilization of inflows and exchange rate flexibility can be effective in the short run to reduce large capital inflows and their impact, but are usually constrained by quasi-fiscal implications (in the case of sterilization) and by competitive pressures (in the case of exchange rate flexibility), for example, from exporters.

Looking forward, our analysis raises two other issues of potential concern: fiscal sustainability and the quality of domestic financial intermediation. As already pointed out by Buiter (1996), some countries appear to face fiscal sustainability issues, especially when including public off-balance-sheet activities. Buiter highlights the combination of high domestic real interest rates and the rapid buildup of domestic liabilities, both explicit and implicit through the banking systems. We find evidence here of potential problems with fiscal sustainability from an external perspective as capital flows are sometimes associated with larger fiscal deficits and high interest rates, a combination that is seldom sustainable. For transition economies, potential or hidden liabilities in state-owned enterprises (e.g., resulting from poor governance), in weak financial institutions, and in insolvent social security and health systems thus need to be carefully monitored. The risk otherwise may be a sudden decline in perceived credit worthiness, leading to a sharp contraction or reversal of private flows.

A second concern relates to the quality of domestic intermediation of (external and domestic) funds. The quality of the financial sectors in transition economies is still weak. Cross-country indicators of quality of domestic intermediation (such as those in the annual reports of the European Bank for Reconstruction and Development [EBRD]) suggest for some countries a limited institutional development and a weak financial condition, including large amounts of nonperforming loans. While we did not find that the quality of financial intermediation itself was an important explanatory factor of capital flows, it would be useful to further analyze the issue of banking fragility, also as that has been an issue in other emerging markets and likely a key policy area. A particularly useful area of research could be to investigate the interactions between high domestic credit growth, weak domestic financial intermediation, and the type of capital flows.

References

Alba, Pedro, Amar Bhattacharya, Stijn Claessens, Swati Ghosh, and Leonardo Hernandez. 1999. The role of macro-economic and financial sector linkages in

East Asia's financial crisis. In *The Asian financial crisis: Cause, contagion, and consequences,* ed. P. Agenor, M. Miller, D. Vines, and A. Weber. Cambridge: Cambridge University Press.

Buiter, Willem H. 1996. Aspects of fiscal performance in some transition economies under fund-supported programmes. CEPR Working Paper no. 1535. London: Centre for Economic Policy Research, December.

Calvo, Guillermo, Leonardo Leiderman, and Carmen Reinhart. 1993. Capital inflows and the real exchange rate appreciation in Latin America: The role of external factors. *IMF Staff Papers* 40, no. 1 (March): 108–51.

Chuhan, Punam, Stijn Claessens, and Nlandu Mamingi. 1998. Equity and bond flows to Latin America and Asia: The role of global and country factors. *Journal of Development Economics* 55:439–63.

Claessens, Stijn, and Wafa Abdelati. 1996. Enterprise performance and adjustment in Romania. Washington, D.C.: World Bank, May. Mimeo.

Claessens, Stijn, and R. Kyle Peters Jr. 1997. State enterprise performance and soft budget constraints: The case of Bulgaria. *Economics of Transition* 5 (2): 302–22.

Cohen, Daniel. 1993. Low investment and large LDC debt in the 1980s. *American Economic Review* 83 (June): 437–49.

Corbo, Vittorio, and Leonardo Hernandez. 1996. Macroeconomic adjustment to capital flows: Lessons from recent Latin America and East Asian experiences. *World Bank Research Observer* 11, no. 1 (February): 61–84.

De Melo, Martha, and Cevdet Denizer. 1997. Monetary policy during transition: An overview. World Bank Working Paper no. 1706. Washington, D.C.: World Bank, January.

De Melo, Martha, Alan Gelb, and Cevdet Denizer. 1996. Patterns of transition from plan to market. *World Bank Economic Review* 10, no. 3 (September): 397–424.

Durjasz, Pawel, and Ryszard Kokoszczynski. 1997. Financial inflows to Poland. Paper presented at the workshop Financial Inflows to Transition Economies, organized by the International Institute for Applied Systems Analysis, Laxenburg, Austria, 9–10 May.

Easterly, William, and Paulo Viera da Cunha. 1994. Financing the storm: Macroeconomic crisis in Russia. *Economics of Transition* 2 (December): 443–65.

Hernandez, Leonardo, and Heinz Rudolph. 1995. Sustainability of private capital flows to developing countries: Is general reversal likely? Policy Research and External Affairs Working Paper no. 1518. Washington, D.C.: World Bank, October.

Klacek, Jan. 1997. From attracting foreign capital to managing capital flows: The Czech case. Paper presented at the workshop Financial Inflows to Transition Economies, organized by the International Institute for Applied Systems Analysis, Laxenburg, Austria, 9–10 May.

Lankes, Hans Peter, and Nicholas Stern. 1999. Capital flows to Eastern Europe and the former Soviet Union. In *International capital flows,* ed. Martin Feldstein, 57–97. Chicago: University of Chicago Press.

Martin, Ricardo, and Marcelo Selowsky. 1997. Policy performance and output growth in the transition economies. *American Economic Review Papers and Proceedings* 87, no. 2 (May): 349–53.

Montiel, Peter, and Carmen Reinhart. 1997. The dynamics of capital movements to emerging economies during the 1990s. Williams College and University of Maryland, July, prepared for the UNU/WIDER project Short-Term Capital Movements and Balance of Payments Crises. Mimeo.

Oblath, Gabor. 1997. Recent capital inflows to Hungary and policy responses. Paper presented at the workshop Financial Inflows to Transition Economies, organized by the International Institute for Applied Systems Analysis, Laxenburg, Austria, 9–10 May.

Sobol, Dorothy M. 1996. Central and Eastern Europe: Financial markets and private capital flows. Working Paper no. 9626. New York: Federal Reserve Bank of New York, August.

Taylor, Mark P., and Lucio Sarnio. 1997. Capital flows to developing countries: Long- and short-term determinants. *World Bank Economic Review* 11, no. 3 (September): 451–70.

World Bank. 1992. *World debt tables, 1991/2.* Washington, D.C.: World Bank.

———. 1998. *Global development finance.* Washington, D.C.: World Bank, March.

Comment   Michael P. Dooley

This paper provides a valuable review and evaluation of private capital flows into formerly planned economies. It is particularly useful because it provides a factual basis for comparing these countries' experiences with those of other emerging markets. The paper was completed before the crisis in Russia but cautions readers that Russia and the other formerly planned economies are vulnerable to a reversal of capital inflows.

Perhaps the most striking aspect of this paper is the recognition that recorded private capital inflows to Russia and some of the other countries studied were completely and simultaneously matched by unrecorded private capital outflows. A simple comparison of current account balances, official lending, and reserve accumulation leads to this conclusion.

This, in turn, poses a difficult problem for the econometric work reported and its interpretation. The main result is that reform and reserve accumulation seem to predict recorded capital inflows. But why would these same factors tend to generate unrecorded private capital outflows? The answer probably lies in a more structural story about the incentives faced by residents and nonresidents and governments that lead to cross-hauling of financial claims and liabilities.

In a relatively simple model with a representative private sector investor and a government, we can see how official capital outflows in the form of reserve accumulation might be systematically matched by private capital inflows. The familiar story is that sterilized exchange market intervention designed to resist currency appreciation generates a pattern of interest rate differentials and exchange rate expectations that induce private investors to arbitrage excess returns in the home markets. As the authors point out, this seems to play some role in the pattern of capital inflows observed in several of the countries studied.

But on top of this model we must also consider at least two sets of

Michael P. Dooley is professor of economics at the University of California, Santa Cruz, and a research associate of the National Bureau of Economic Research.

private investors that have different incentives or constraints in allocating their financial portfolios. One possibility is that an extreme case of home bias was being reversed as these markets opened to international capital flows. Residents of Russia and the other countries studied were not permitted to hold foreign assets in the old regime and may have been willing to accept relatively low expected returns on foreign assets. At the same time, nonresidents may have seen Russian assets as a valuable addition to their portfolio since these returns may have been independent of their existing portfolios. This is a welfare improving story that is certainly consistent with the observation that reform seems to have been an important determinant of private capital inflows *and* outflows.

The problem with this interpretation is in understanding why the inflows should be so easily observed in balance of payments data while the outflows are entirely absent from the data. While many interpretations are possible, a plausible answer is that some residents had good reasons to want their wealth in a form that the government could not tax. This can lead to a volatile situation. In this case there are two types of private investors because recorded capital inflows are insured by the government, usually through the banking system, while unrecorded capital outflows cannot be taxed by the government. In this case private capital inflows and outflows generate private gains from trade but the welfare implications are quite different. In general such a pattern of capital flows will generate costly crises when governments' capacity to insure is exhausted, outcomes now clear with the benefit of hindsight.

Contributors

Philippe Bacchetta
Studienzentrum Gerzensee
Dorfstr. 2
3115 Gerzensee, Switzerland

Geert Bekaert
Graduate School of Business
Stanford University
Stanford, CA 94305

Guillermo A. Calvo
Department of Economics
University of Maryland
College Park, MD 20742

Stijn Claessens
The World Bank
Rm. MC 9-627
1818 H Street NW
Washington, DC 20433

José De Gregorio
Center for Applied Economics
Department of Industrial Engineering
Universidad de Chile
Republica 701, Santiago, Chile

Michael P. Dooley
Department of Economics
Social Science I
University of California, Santa Cruz
Santa Cruz, CA 95064

Rudiger Dornbusch
Department of Economics, E52-357
Massachusetts Institute of Technology
Cambridge, MA 02139

Sebastian Edwards
Anderson Graduate School of
  Business
University of California, Los Angeles
110 Westwood Plaza, Suite C508
Box 951481
Los Angeles, CA 90095

Barry Eichengreen
Department of Economics
University of California
549 Evans Hall 3880
Berkeley, CA 94720

Swati Ghosh
The World Bank
1818 H Street, NW
Washington, DC 20431

Campbell R. Harvey
Fuqua School of Business
Duke University
Durham, NC 27708

Takatoshi Ito
Institute of Economic Research
Hitotsubashi University
Naka 2-1, Kunitachi
Tokyo 186-8603 Japan

Paul Krugman
Department of Economics, E52-383a
Massachusetts Institute of Technology
Cambridge, MA 02139

Sylvia Maxfield
Government Department
Harvard University
Cambridge, MA 02139

Enrique G. Mendoza
Department of Economics
Room 305, Social Science Building
Box 90097
Duke University
Durham, NC 27708

Ashoka Mody
The World Bank
1818 H Street, NW
Washington, DC 20431

Daniel Oks
Central Bank of Argentina
Reconquista 266
Edif. Central Office 506
Buenos Aires, 1003 Argentina

Rossana Polastri
The World Bank
1818 H Street, NW
Washington, DC 20431

Carmen M. Reinhart
University of Maryland
School of Public Affairs
4113D Van Munching Hall
College Park, MD 20742

Dani Rodrik
John F. Kennedy School of
   Government
Harvard University
79 JFK Street
Cambridge, MA 02138

Miguel A. Savastano
Research Department, Room 9-718
International Monetary Fund
700 19th Street, NW
Washington, DC 20431

Aaron Tornell
Department of Economics
Harvard University
Cambridge, MA 02138

Eric van Wincoop
Federal Reserve Bank of New York
33 Liberty Street
New York, NY 10045

Holger Wolf
Center for German and European
   Studies and Department of
   Economics
ICC 558
Georgetown University
Washington, DC 20057

Author Index

Subject Index